Struggle, Defeat or Rebirth:
Eugene O'Neill's Vision of Humanity

Struggle, Defeat or Rebirth
Eugene O'Neill's Vision of Humanity

by THIERRY DUBOST

McFarland & Company, Inc., Publishers
Jefferson, North Carolina, and London

Quotations from *Selected Plays of Eugene O'Neill*—*The Hairy Ape* ©1922 and renewed 1950 by Eugene O'Neill; *Desire Under the Elms* ©1924 and renewed 1952 by Eugene O'Neill; *Strange Interlude* ©1928 and renewed 1956 by Carlotta Monterey O'Neill; *Mourning Becomes Electra* ©1931 and renewed 1959 by Carlotta Monterey O'Neill; *The Iceman Cometh* ©1946 by Eugene O'Neill— are reprinted by permission of Random House, Inc., and Jonathan Cape, Ltd. Quotations from *More Stately Mansions* ©1964 by Carlotta Monterey O'Neill, are reprinted by permission of Yale University (courtesy of the Beinecke Library and the Yale Collection of American Literature). Quotations from *Long Day's Journey into Night* ©1955 by Carlotta Monterey O'Neill, are reprinted by permission of Yale University Press and Jonathan Cape, Ltd.

Translated from the French by Rosalind Dilys, Christine McGarry, and Thierry Dubost.

The present work is a reprint of the library bound edition of Sturggle, Defeat or Rebirth: Eugene O'Neill's Vision of Humanity, *first published in 1997 by McFarland.*

LIBRARY OF CONGRESS CATALOGUING-IN-PUBLICATION DATA

Dubost, Thierry, 1958– .
    Struggle, defeat or rebirth : Eugene O'Neill's vision of humanity / by Thierry Dubost.
        p. cm.
    Includes bibliographical references and index.

    ISBN 0-7864-2419-2 (softcover : 50# alkaline paper) ∞

    1. O'Neill, Eugene, 1888–1953—Characters.   2. Characters and characteristics in literature.   I. Title.
PS3529.N5Z6285   2005
812'.52—dc20   96-32268

British Library cataloguing data are available

©1997 Thierry Dubost. All rights reserved.

No part of this book may be reproduced or transmitted in any form or by any means, electronic or mechanical, including photocopying or recording, or by any information storage and retrieval system, without permission in writing from the publisher.

Cover image: Eugene O'Neill *(Theatre Arts Monthly)*

Manufactured in the United States of America

McFarland & Company, Inc., Publishers
  Box 611, Jefferson, North Carolina 28640
    www.mcfarlandpub.com

To my children,
Clarissa and Valentin.

Table of Contents.

Acknowledgments.   xi
List of Abbreviations.   xiii
Introduction.   1

PART I: THE FAMILY.

1. The Family and Its Environment.   7
   Preliminary remarks.   7
   A restricted universe.   8
   Dead parents' society.   9
   The façade.   13
   The enclosure mechanisms.   15

2. The Imprisoned Person.   19
   Heredity.   19
   Visions of space and time.   23
      Time.   23
      Theatrical space.   24
   Flight, an alternative to liberation.   26
   The ultimate flight (dreams, whiskey and firearms).   29
   The ghost of freedom.   31

3. Relations Between the Characters.   33
   The comforts of home.   33
   Father images.   34
   Son images.   37
   Father-son relationships.   38
      Disclosures.   38
      Rejection.   39
   Son-father relationships.   42
   Daughter images.   46
   Father-daughter relationships.   46
   Daughter-father relationships.   50

Mother images. 52
Mother-son relationships. 55
Son-mother relationships. 57
Mother-daughter relationships. 60
Daughter-mother relationships. 61
Brother relationships. 62
Brothers and sisters. 64

4. From the Microcosm to the Macrocosm. 66
The author's approach. 66
The echoes. 67

5. The Image of the Family. 72
A redeeming vision, in a comedy. 72

6. Conclusion. 76

PART II: HUMANITY AND WORLDS.

7. Worlds and the Representation of Them. 81
Humanity in which world? 81
Anchorage in reality. 83
The social perspective. 85

8. The Place of the Human Being in the World. 93
Love's ransoms. 93
Friendship. 104

9. Belonging. 110
Groups. 110
Membership as salvation? 114

10. Non-Belonging. 117
Masks. 117
The dream. 121
Escape. 131

11. Conclusion. 135

PART III: HUMANS FACED WITH THEMSELVES AND INNER WORLDS.

12. The Discovery of Human Beings. 139
A theatre of the soul. 139
Flight strategies. 141

13. Revelation of an Existential Condition. 152
    The roads to discovery. 152
    Nothingness versus pain. 156

14. The Acknowledgment of the Individual. 162
    From the monologue to the confession. 162
    Death. 168
    Suicide. 172
    Time. 174
    The weight of destiny. 183
    The divine. 186
    The end of egocentric blindness and the discovery of the self. 195

15. Nature. 199
    Fog. 199
    The moon. 203
       Loneliness. 204
       Lovers. 205
       Belonging and oneness. 206
    The sun. 207
    The sea. 210
    The natural world. 214

16. Conclusion. 221
    Rebirth, and union with the Whole. 221

17. Beyond the Conclusions. 226

Notes and References. 231
Chronological List of the Plays. 259
List of "Family Plays." 261
Bibliography. 263
Index. 271

Acknowledgments.

This book is a modified translation of my dissertation entitled "L'Homme et le monde dans le théâtre de Eugene O'Neill," which was presented at the University of Paris–Sorbonne. At the very beginning, my mentor, Professor Jean Rouberol, warned me that the task would be as hard as rowing across the Atlantic on one's own. Since my subject was O'Neill's theatre, such a prospect sounded both challenging and promising.

My sailing in O'Neill's waters has certainly been rewarding. There have been hard times but added to the pleasure derived from working on the plays there have also been meetings with people who at one stage or another were a great help for my study.

My first thanks go to all the people who will remain anonymous, but who should know that they are not forgotten. As for Professor Rouberol, who helped me find my wind through this research, his support is gratefully acknowledged.

I am also grateful to the librarians of the universities of Caen, Paris–Sorbonne and Yale, who knew how difficult it was to find articles on O'Neill in France and were always very willing to cooperate. I should like to thank Yale University Press and Random House for allowing me to quote from their editions. In my nautical journey, I should like to mention two lighthouses: *The Eugene O'Neill Newsletter* and *The Eugene O'Neill Review*. As I was a foreigner, cut off from the O'Neillians, their rather regular publication was all the more welcome as it made me feel that my work did not belong to another age. In this respect, I should also like to thank Professor Travis Bogard, who was kind enough to answer my questions.

Thanks are also due to Father Aoun, with whom I discussed what I felt were obscure points of Catholic doctrine. Three professors who teach at the University of Caen, Jean-Louis Chevalier, René Gallet, and Jean-Pierre Fichou, have, each in his own way, helped me with their advice. I am grateful to them for keeping an interest in my work through all these years. I am especially grateful for the helpful criticism I received from Marc Maufort who also made me feel that O'Neill was definitely a contemporary writer, and not a figure from the literary past.

I wish to thank all my friends and relatives for their constant support. My parents deserve a special mention for reading the book before publication, and I should like to acknowledge my gratitude to my two translators, Rosalind Dilys and Christine McGarry.

My greatest thanks go to my wife, who during all these years has accepted life with the ghostly but daily presence of Eugene O'Neill, and cannot be thanked too much for her support.

List of Abbreviations.

Ab	Abortion	*LL*	Lazarus Laughed
AC	Anna Christie	*LVH*	The Long Voyage Home
AGCGW	All God's Chillun Got Wings	*MBE*	Mourning Becomes Electra
AhW	Ah, Wilderness!	*MCa*	The Moon of the Caribbees
B&B	Bread and Butter		
BB	Before Breakfast	*MM*	Marco Millions
BEC	Bound East for Cardiff	*MMis*	A Moon for the Misbegotten
BH	Beyond the Horizon		
DE	Desire Under the Elms	*MSM*	More Stately Mansions
Dif	Diff'rent	*MvM*	The Movie Man
DK	The Dreamy Kid	*NIAY*	Now I Ask You
DWE	Days Without End	*PE*	The Personal Equation
DY	Dynamo	*Reck*	Recklessness
EJ	The Emperor Jones	*Rope*	The Rope
FM	The First Man	*Ser*	Servitude
Fog	Fog	*SI*	Strange Interlude
Fou	The Fountain	*Sn*	The Sniper
GGB	The Great God Brown	*SS*	Shell Shock
Gold	Gold	*Straw*	The Straw
HA	The Hairy Ape	*Thi*	Thirst
Hu	Hughie	*TP*	A Touch of the Poet
IC	The Iceman Cometh	*Wa*	Warnings
Ile	Ile	*WCIM*	Where the Cross Is Made
IZo	In the Zone	*Web*	The Web
LDJN	Long Day's Journey into Night	*Wel*	Welded
		WfL	A Wife for a Life

Introduction.

It seems only fair to start this study acknowledging a general debt to the scholars who devoted much of their time to the transcription and the publication of O'Neill's lost or unfinished plays as well as his correspondence and diaries. When one reads a page of his manuscripts, one understands how difficult it must have been. I wish, therefore, to express my gratitude to the people who completed such a heavy task since these books proved a great help when I was working on my subject.

Forty-nine plays will be analyzed at different stages of this book. I decided not to include *The Calms of Capricorn*, because the author himself did not finish it.[1*] On the other hand, in spite of its being only a "final draft," since O'Neill would probably have cut many lines, I thought that *More Stately Mansions* had to be included in the corpus. Despite its clumsiness, this work deserves to be studied; it was to have been part of a vast cycle, *A Tale of Possessors Self-Dispossessed*, which, unfortunately, could not be completed.

Everybody agrees that the plays he wrote were of uneven value, so it might be tempting not to refer, for instance, to the book entitled *Ten Lost Plays by Eugene O'Neill*. I would probably hold that view if I were a stage director, but in the circumstances, my task was of a different nature. I had no intention of making a hit parade; all the author's works which could be performed on a stage were taken into account. Of course, I realize that some fields are left unexplored. Still I do not regret having retained all his dramatic writings, despite the difficulty it involved, in order to be able to apply my hypotheses to the entire O'Neill canon.

Playing an important part in my choice was the fact that one constantly meets with recurrent themes or actions, which are sometimes viewed in a different light but which in the end make it possible to see links between what at first seemed to belong to completely different worlds. I am well aware that *Desire Under the Elms* and *The Web*, for instance, cannot be treated on equal terms. Still, I hope that this study will show that the decision I made in the beginning was the right one, since I feel that continuity prevails over differences, and this could only be proven by taking all of the works into

*Notes and references begin on page 231.

consideration. One could object and retort that even if links can be found among the forty-nine plays, it would be wrong to state that comedies and tragedies are made of the same stuff. I would agree with such a remark, and I am conscious of the heterogeneity of the corpus. Trying to give a comprehensive interpretation of the canon, I attempted to see how various examples fitted, in their own way, into a more general design.

As for the subject itself, which might be stated as humanity confronted with the world in the theatre of Eugene O'Neill, there is no doubt that the existing links between human beings and the world mattered a great deal to the dramatist, since he kept staging people who were confronted with existential problems. In his theatre, he tried to show the inner truth of characters, and the question of their relationship to the world is one of the most important issues raised in his plays. Men's and women's involvement in their environment varies and gender is no trivial matter in their lives; but what interested me most were human beings who live in a community or more generally, on earth.

In the subject as stated above, *world* is in the singular: I suppose that an explanation is necessary. I feel that, potentially, there is a kind of ideal world which is seen as a whole, even if, in general, fragmentation prevails. It does not mean that it is unique; on the contrary, the whole is not one single reality, but is made of many parts, which intervene at specific levels in the lives of the protagonists. Because of the complexity of the subject and the variety of ways in which it is dealt with, I divided my study into three parts, corresponding to three aspects of the relationship between humanity and the world. Part I deals with the family and the situation of the individual in a family structure. Part II is about the links binding people to others and to society in general. Part III is devoted to the analysis of the inner world of the characters and to their connection with the natural world.

I shall relate this attempt at interpretation of the works of O'Neill to contemporary criticism in the last part of this introduction, but since I mentioned family structure, I feel I have to say a word now about biography. Two excellent biographies, one written by Arthur and Barbara Gelb, and another in two volumes by Louis Sheaffer, have become general references in the world of O'Neill studies. Reading them is very rewarding, and the connections made between the life of the author and his plays is most interesting. Many other critics allude to O'Neill's life in ways that enable their readers to understand passages that otherwise might have remained obscure. I do not object to biography, and I have the greatest respect for the aforementioned authors. I, however, intend to examine O'Neill's theatre from a different angle, without referring to his life.[2]

The first panel of the triptych depicts the relations that exist among the members of the families represented on the stage. I studied the parts given to the protagonists, analyzing how the universe of the family influences the behavior of people and focusing my attention on their responses to the forces acting upon them. Is family structure a help or a hindrance to the fulfillment of the individual? Even at that early stage of my research, I met with a question central to the two other parts, namely, that of individual freedom, an echo of which is to be found in the conflict between the fight or flight impulse.

I then focused my attention on couples, and more generally on characters who were not considered members of a family. The task consisted of analyzing the impact of the social body on the individual, before studying the way he tries to become a member of the community. Some succeed while others fail in their attempt at joining a group, so I examined the behavior of individuals faced with the beliefs and moral values representative of the society they live in. The rites of passage which decide whether they belong to a community had to be taken into account as well. Indeed a sense of belonging becomes the goal in their pursuit of happiness, but this implies that people will only be fulfilled if they can give an appropriate answer to a challenge. A fight is always looming in the background—while some try to escape, others seek renewal in another way which might lead to happiness.

In the third panel of the triptych, one meets again with the tension between a need to find oneself and a wish to escape. Individual freedom is central in this battle, and investigations of it result in a new reading of the plays, knowing that this last part of the study brings the subjects discussed in the first two parts to a logical conclusion. Every character has a specific approach to life—many aspects and influences are explored, from Buddhism to Catholicism, not forgetting, of course, the Nietzschean view of the world. In the end, all these elements lead to a coherent vision of people's relationships with themselves and the natural world in the plays of Eugene O'Neill. What I tried to show was that the vital concept which, in my opinion, gives a cohesion to the whole canon was that of rebirth.

I feel I have to give an overall view of what I intended to demonstrate, even if this introduction will give the reader only a general idea of what is at stake. This personal vision of the plays calls into question a number of ideas about O'Neill's theatre which need to be stated.

I agree that there are some postmodern aspects in some plays, but the lack of true limit between illusion and reality does not mean that the characters are caught in a huge trap that is the world, which is devoid of meaning. My study tries to illustrate, on the contrary, that classifying O'Neill's plays as absurd drama is irrelevant.

Another point I should like to raise, but with less vehemence, is that of the classification of the plays. I can understand critcs' referring to them as "the late plays" or "the early plays" so as to explain briefly which works they have in mind. Still, I cannot agree with the idea of periods, and changes which would have taken place in the author's vision of the world. I am aware that this point of view is unorthodox, but in spite of all the admiration I have for the works of Travis Bogard, I am afraid I have to disagree with him on that point.

According to Professor Bogard,

> In his early conception, man's fate is ironic in direct proportion to its incomprehensibility. Although men seek happiness and try to alter the miserable condition of their lives, their struggles only weave the strands of their webs more tightly about them. Will, therefore, leads to a kind of suicide, and hope is self-delusion. Such shallow and unformed pessimism does not approximate a world view, for O'Neill has neither philosophy nor theology to support his intuitions. In consequence, at the beginning there is nothing to lend explanation to the destruction. There are only victims in a spiderless web.[3]

My hypothesis consists in showing that, contrary to what Travis Bogard says, there are things which "lend explanation to the destruction." Perhaps I should add that, for me, there is a direct continuity between *Abortion* and *The Iceman Cometh*. I am well aware that from a literary point of view, there is a considerable difference between them, but I think that both plays can be understood if one reads them with the idea of rebirth in mind, as I shall try to show in the course of my study. This is but one example, but even apparently antagonistic visions, like Buddhism and Catholicism, will have common points with a pantheistic vision which is central in O'Neill's view. Fate *does* play an important part in the lives of some characters, so does guilt, or the death wish, but it seems to me that a new reading of the plays can be made in the light of the concept which I used. Fortunately, there were crossroads, and even though I sometimes stepped on a few leaves which had not yet been trodden black, I was pleased to share the point of view of critics who sometimes came to similar conclusions, having taken another road.

From what I have said, I suppose it has become obvious that I am a member of the community of critics who find that O'Neill should not be seen as a pessimistic author, because I feel that even tragedy enables him to give a fresh breath to life. To conclude this introductory chapter, I should like to quote another great dramatist, Wole Soyinka, or rather one of his characters, who expresses what I hope to demonstrate in the following pages devoted to the theatre of Eugene O'Neill.

> OLUNDE. I don't find it morbid at all. I find it rather inspiring. It is an affirmative commentary on life.[4]

Part I.
The Family.

MURRAY. A family wouldn't have changed things. From what I've seen that blood-thicker-than-water stuff dope is all wrong. It's thinner than table-d'hôte soup [*Straw* 359].

1. The Family and Its Environment.

Preliminary remarks.

Reading O'Neill's works, I felt that if one were to enter into the analysis of the relations which humanity entertains with the world, it was possible to divide this study into three parts, which often coincide, sometimes merely overlap a bit, but which might be, on the whole, considered independent from each other.[1]

In the course of the first phase of my analysis, I shall attempt to get an insight into the way in which people are defined, looking, at the same time, at the nature of the links which appear in the more restricted frame of the family community.

The definition of the family varies with different periods and places; in this book there will be no attempt to compare that which appears in the plays to preconstructed patterns, but rather to bring to light the image which O'Neill presents to his spectator, and what follows from it. To sum up, and to define more precisely the frame of this research, I shall direct my attention to the links between people bound by blood-ties, and to the existential implications resulting from the place they occupy within this community. An additional question arises as to the way in which this structure appears, and as to the status ascribed to it.

The outline of an answer is given in this comment about *Ah, Wilderness!*:

> Rather than an anomaly among his works, the comedy is based on his obsession with family life and his own past, the twin foundation stones of his finest writings.[2]

This remark lays emphasis on the importance of the family in O'Neill's theatre. One may add that family ties play variable roles in thirty plays; this high figure bears out Louis Sheaffer when he emphasizes their thematic importance.

A restricted universe.

I shall now try to define the profile of the family as it appears in the corpus, through an attempt to discern the limits that are set for this community.

In order to do this, I shall first look at the presence of three generations on the stage, then at the positions occupied by the extended family. These elements, although peripheral in relation to the nucleus constituted by the parent-children relationship, occupy a most revealing place, and these two aspects, which may seem marginal, will provide us with the means of drawing a quick outline of the way in which the family is described.

If one goes to examine the relations between grandchildren and grandparents, one notices that they are very restricted. The relationship is staged in only four plays. In *The Dreamy Kid*, the meeting takes place as the grandmother is on her deathbed, and her grandson is probably about to be killed by the police. In *Beyond the Horizon*, another grandmother, this time with her granddaughter, live together on Robert Mayo's farm, but news is brought of the child's death in the next act. In *More Stately Mansions*, the situation is somewhat different: the grandmother is shown to be the rival of the mother, whose place she attempts to take, in the minds of the boys entrusted to her.

In this quick survey of the links excluding direct lineage, it emerges that grandmothers have, to various degrees, a maternal status; this is why no specific image is bestowed upon them, their particular position in the family tree being implicitly refuted.[3] The predominant impression produced by these few examples is that death incessantly occurs to obstruct the establishment of links between relatives who should otherwise be fairly close. The situation is summed up in *Strange Interlude*, which is an indirect manifestation of the impossibility of seeing children and old people living together. This aspect comes to light when Mrs. Evans announces to Nina that she must have an abortion, even if the motives brought up are the result of other causes.[4] If one wishes to be exhaustive, one should also mention *Desire Under the Elms*; here again, in spite of an indisputable ascendancy, one notes a refusal to consider family relationships from that angle.

> CABOT. He's dead, sart'n. I felt his heart. Pore little critter! (*He blinks back one tear, wiping his sleeve across his nose*) [*DE* 264].

Cabot is moved when he talks about the dead baby, but when he returns to himself, as in classical tragedy, he does not consider him as a grandson, but as the son of Eben, which is why he declares: "If he was Eben's, I be glad he air gone!" (*DE* 264).

The extended temporal dimension of the family resulting from the presence of a third generation is almost nonexistent, or denied. This may seem surprising when one is aware of the importance of the notions which emerge in the plays of heredity and of destiny linked to ancestors, but the destiny of the protagonists is not embodied in actual human beings. Ancestors are often mentioned, sometimes they bear a curse, but the only instance in which they appear on stage to forebode this disastrous fate, is in the form of portraits.[5]

If one now looks at the place bestowed upon the collaterals, one notes that their presence is also very limited.[6] The first figure to whom we shall direct our attention is that of the uncle, a character who appears four times on stage. They are always at some distance from the nucleus of the family,[7] both in time and in space. In *Beyond the Horizon* and *Diff'rent*, they are sailors, and the ephemeral nature of their visit is underlined in *Beyond the Horizon* and *The Rope*.[8]

Caleb and Father Baird have a different status, insofar as they are substitute father-figures for Benny and John; the antagonism which opposes Benny and Caleb has the effect of placing their relationship in the perspective of a late adolescence parental conflict. Father Baird (*Days Without End*) is also an emblematic figure, although in a more complex way, as his image as a guardian combines with that of a spiritual father, against which John has struggled for years as he strove to find his way into life. The image of the father, of the brother or of the son overrides that of the uncle, giving a minor place to this family tie.

Among the women this place is even smaller: Aunts are staged on only two occasions. The first to appear is Mildred, in *The Hairy Ape*, and her role as a chaperon implicitly vests her with a maternal function. The second appearance is in *Diff'rent*, and Benny, who is after her money, leads Emma to believe he wants to marry her. In fact, the title of "Aunt Emmer" given to her by Benny ("EMMA. Why, you know well enough I ain't your aunt anyway" [*Dif* 521]) only serves to bring out the grotesqueness of his matrimonial intentions.

After this brief outline of the various collateral relatives present in the plays, one notes that the author has a very restricted view of the family structure, which could even be termed restrictive. With a few grandchildren, grandparents, uncles and aunts with semiparental status, and no cousins at all, the O'Neillian family, which occupies a considerable place in his work,[9] is above all a nuclear structure, in which the relationship established between parents and children excludes, almost systematically, other members descended from the same stock.

Dead parents' society.

Families admittedly do live together, but mathematical unity is rarely attained, and if one were to account for all the absent members, the list would certainly be very long. The "family plays," as I term those (which are listed in an appendix) in which at least two generations appear on the stage,[10] show us that even if this community is presented as a nuclear cell, composed of a father, a mother, and one or more children, it is also very often marked by the absence of one of its members. Out of the thirty-one plays upon which this analysis is based, we note that sixteen are characterized by the absence of a mother. Eleven plays portray the death of the father, or deal with the absence of the father figure, and in two others dead children are mentioned. These observations pointing to the breaking-up of the family unit would hardly be complete without emphasizing the influence which this incompleteness exerts on the characters.

First and foremost, the one upon whom the place of honor is bestowed: the mother. In this case, her death may become the central theme of the play; in *Dynamo*, Reuben enters into contact with her through communion with the dynamo, which embodies for him both a new God and the absent mother figure.[11] His inability to accept his mother's death leads him to madness and murder, legitimized by an imaginary communication.

> REUBEN. (*Thinking torturedly*) Mother!... I've betrayed you... you will never bless me with the miracle now! [*Dy* 487].

The emotional void can never be breached; the characters do not succeed in erasing the image of the absent one, whose latent presence reveals their inability to free themselves. Confronted with the absence of the mother figure, the only ones to escape the plague of inhibiting uncertainties are the elder sisters, who assume the role of protective mothers[12]; they thus break off from their situation as abandoned children who have to face the world alone.

Her considerable importance is clearly shown when, in *Gold* and *Where the Cross Is Made*, the illness which hits Sarah Bartlett, and then her death, symbolize the downfall of a community which has broken adrift; in the ensuing time-lapse, her nonexistence indicates that the family is heading inexorably towards a downfall. The women who have children fulfill a double role: first, a classical position is attributed to them in the relation between forebears and descendants and, second, they have a symbolic status in that they are in some way the cornerstone of the family structure, which in turn is projected onto the surrounding world. When they fail to fulfill their function in a satisfactory way, the entire edifice runs the risk of collapsing.

The destructive effects of this absence are felt with full force in *Long Day's Journey into Night*, a work in which the protagonists are wounded by a mother figure, who continually attempts to escape from her duty.

> EDMUND. ...I've got consumption!
> MARY. *For a second he seems to have broken through to her. She trembles and her expression becomes terrified. She calls distractedly, as if giving a command to herself.*

> No!
> *And instantly she is far away again. She murmurs gently but impersonally.*
> You must not try to hold me. It isn't right when I am hoping to be a nun [*LDJN* 174].

Beneath appearances, this is not simply a return to the past brought on by drugs. There is an actual loss of contact between Mary and her family circle. She is marking her distances and expressing a desire for virginity which in itself precludes her existence as a mother. This reiterated denial has effects similar to the swallowing of a deadly potion, which slowly kills those whose access to their filial or marital condition is denied.

Although we cannot place them on the same plane, for the father image has a lesser influence than that of the mother, we must allow that the male branch also adds a large number of members to the dead parents' society. Their absence is lamented by certain characters ("BENNY. Gosh, I wish Pa'd lived" [*Dif* 523]), as it only serves to heighten their existential uncertainties. They lack a guide and, consequently, are incapable of finding their real place in the world.

An illustration of the need for a mentor is given in *The Iceman Cometh* which finds its place paradoxically in the present corpus. Although Parritt never knew his immediate ancestor, he undertook the search for Larry, seeking to find in him the moral support and affection which Rosa, whose prime concern was the furthering of revolutionary interests, never gave him. When Parritt talks about the way Larry cared for him when he was younger, he evokes what, in his eyes, are the real attributes of fatherhood, and thus justifies his nomination to the rank of imaginary father.

> PARRITT. And I had no Old Man. You used to take me on your knee and tell me stories and crack jokes and make me laugh. You'd ask me questions and take what I said seriously. I guess I got to feel in the years you lived with us that you'd taken the place of my Old Man [*IC* 588].

His search can be compared to that of Reuben, who tries to enter into contact with his mother after her death. In both cases, the filial characteristic is doubt: all the protagonists attempt to resume links within the frame of a family, in order to obtain answers to questions which they deem themselves incapable of providing. Larry Slade has a double status; he is considered not only as a father, but also as the one who will be able to absolve Parritt at the end of his confession.

The theological dimension is very strong: he stands for a priest when he liberates Parritt from the weight of his guilt and when he supports his suicide, is endowed with a God-like importance as a master of life. This dimension is not a fortuitous addition; it is the sign of a continuity, for Parritt is striving to deny the passage of time, and to bring back and carry to its extreme limit a "family" relationship of the past, no longer valid at the time of the action.

The younger generation is not spared by the tragic destiny and, indirectly, the dead play a leading role in two plays. Indeed, in spite of their premature and remote death, the dead never relinquish their hold on the living; they haunt their speeches, thereby ensuring themselves an eternal presence. In *The First Man*, the couple has turned in upon itself and begun a long latency period, with the intention of honoring the memory of their two little girls, carried off by pneumonia. This is why Curtis reacts violently when Martha announces that she is expecting a child:

> CURTIS. You have broken the promise we made when they died. We were to keep their memories inviolate [*FM* 583].

We shall come back to the temporal aspects in the course of this study; for the present, it is important to note that the family is considered as immutable by Curtis (and also, until very recently, by Martha). Any mutation takes an appearance of sacrilege, as it implies that those whose parents venerated their memory every day are losing their leading role, which is tantamount to a second death. This example is not the only one of its kind; in *Long Day's Journey into Night*, Eugene, the dead child, Edmund's brother (with a symbolic inversion of the names, the author presenting himself as deceased), comes back to haunt the Tyrone household through Mary's speech. The impossible oblivion revives the wounds, and, in the works, many protagonists are condemned to live with omnipresent ghosts.

This inability to carry out the bereavement process, such as it is defined by Freud—an "intrapsychic process, following the loss of an object of attachment, by which the subject gradually succeeds in detaching himself from it"[13]— is a destructive force among the characters. For each of them the absence of one parent obstructs correct integration into the world, for an imaginary family structure is being upheld which is both a source of comfort (respect for the memory of the deceased), and a cause of frustration generated by the absence of any possible evolution of the individual within these kinship structures. The break, even if it is very remote in time, leaves an indelible mark, and causes intense suffering.

The lack of a mother, which is the most frequent cause of O'Neillian bereavement, constituting the most terrible of deprivations for the protagonists, seems to make them lose the meaning of life. When the ideal family structure, composed of father, mother and children, posed explicitly or implicitly as a reference in the plays, is broken (we have established the frequency of this situation), the result for those affected by it is an inability to live, and a marked difficulty in asserting themselves as people, within this very circle, and *a fortiori* in the world.

1. The Family and Its Environment. 13

The façade.

Very strong emotional ties unite the members of the families who appear on stage: the image of the deceased parent sometimes acts as a sort of magnetic pole, drawing to itself the remaining members. The loss can be a source of tension, but it does not lead to a split-up, which would disperse forebears and descendants and thereby be a destruction factor. Rather than a series of sections of people's lives, with characters ignoring the world around them, the spectator is a witness to the recurrent stages of a sentimental *huis-clos* from which the protagonists do not succeed in freeing themselves.

Before studying how the actors live within the family communities, I feel it is necessary to define the relations they entertain with the outside world. To briefly qualify the structure which is formed when two generations live together, such as it appears in the works, one could appropriately refer to a clan element. At the outset, clans may seem alien to the O'Neillian world, but two external sources allow us, at this stage, to take this communal model as a reference. We are familiar with O'Neill's claim to being a descendant of an Irish king, and the pride he derived from it. More prosaically, I quote a letter to his son Eugene, in which he draws a clear distinction between the outside world and the O'Neill household:

> To the outer world we maintained an indomitably united front and lied and lied and lied for each other. A typical pure Irish family.[14]

The monolithic family is exhibited as a rampart of protection to ward off prying into the secrets each member wishes to conceal. We find the illustration of this in *Mourning Becomes Electra*, a major work, in which the author takes up the theme of the Oresteia. This theme indeed held great interest for him as a means of analyzing family relationships.[15] In the opening scene, one is taken through the social ascent of the Mannons and the setting up of the dynasty, with particular emphasis being laid on the palpable difference between this caste and the society in which it lives. This discrepancy is conveyed through the author's use of the Chorus, which is made up of the friends Seth brings onto the property. This group of intruders provides him with a most effective means of displaying the opposition between those who belong and those who do not. This motif, which recurs throughout the triptych, appears for the first time in the stage directions which serve as an introduction:

> These last three are types of townsfolk rather than individuals, a chorus representing the town come to look and listen and spy on the rich and exclusive Mannons [*MBE, Homecoming* 7].

It is all the more difficult to become initiated to the mysteries of the Mannon clan as its members wear the mask of cohesion, in spite of the internal struggles which spring from the hate the protagonists feel for their closest relatives. Indeed, however violent the conflicts which tear the family asunder, they always put on a united front.

The very small number of "family" plays (*Long Day's Journey into Night, The Rope*) in which the action takes place in *huis clos*, with no external elements, does not mean that elsewhere there is any osmosis between the family and its surroundings: Quite the opposite is true. Cabot gives proof of this when, in the course of the celebration he holds of the birth of the child he thinks is his son, he addresses the guests who are under his roof. Their very presence is *a priori* the sign of shared membership of a group, but in his speech he shows them the limits of their short-lived fellowship.

> CABOT. But ye needn't laugh at Eben, none o' ye! He's my blood, if he be a dumb fool. He's better nor any o' yew! He kin do a day's work a'most up t' what I kin—an' that'd put any o' yew pore critters t'shame! [*DE* 249].

Ephraim, a patriarchal figure, who takes on changed features in other dramas, asserts here that the members of his family are different. To those who think they see a flaw in the cohesion, he recalls that blood-ties prevail over antagonisms, and that consequently the unity of his household remains intact.

Sometimes unconsciously, the characters make a show of the differences which distinguish them from the individuals of the surrounding world. An outward appearance of otherness, common to a few characters, symbolizes their common membership in a particular social structure from which outsiders are excluded. These peculiarities are sometimes claimed by the protagonists themselves, but their specificity is often revealed to the spectators by physical characteristics (the use of masks), or by the comments of other actors.

If the members of the group themselves bear a peculiarity which distinguishes them from the rest of society, this mark is even impressed upon the servants who, in spite of their role as mediators with the outside world, also reflect this opposition. Thus, what is said about Seth, who is the guardian of the family's secrets—

> AMES. That's the Mannon look. They grow it on their wives. Seth's growed it on, too, didn't you notice—from bein' with 'em all his life [*MBE, Homecoming* 9].

—reappears in a different form in *Long Day's Journey into Night*:

> CATHLEEN. "It's none of your damned business, but if you must know, it's for the lady I work for, Mrs. Tyrone, who's sitting out in the automobile." That shut him up quick [*LDJN* 103].

Each of the two communities has its own territory. On one hand the family cell, on the other outsiders kept at bay but who nevertheless manage to catch an occasional glimpse of what goes on in an area which is usually inaccessible. An immaterial rampart thwarts the development of links between the two areas, and the explicit banishment of the outsider is distinctly felt by those who attempt to approach. We may note that the mask, an element of prime importance in O'Neill's works, appears here as instrumental in group characterization.

The enclosure mechanisms.

We have, in a preliminary stage, directed our attention to the way in which the family community is perceived by the world which surrounds it. I now propose to look at the relationship which establishes itself in the opposite direction, i.e., the perception which the family has of its relation with the outside world.

We could quote for instance four dramas (*Beyond the Horizon, Desire Under the Elms, A Moon for the Misbegotten,* and *The Rope*) in which the action takes place on a farm. In these plays the geographical isolation echoes the separation between the clan and its environment. Beyond the details of the anecdote, an episode from *A Moon for the Misbegotten* gives a symbolic insight into how these men of the earth conceive of their social relations. In a comic scene, Hogan, a peasant of Irish origin, engaged in a feud with his neighbor Harder, the billionaire, shows him in no uncertain terms where his power falls short:

> HOGAN. I draw the line somewhere, and I'll be damned if I stand for a Standard Oil man trespassing! So will you kindly get the hell out of here before I plant a kick on your backside that'll land you in the Atlantic Ocean [*MMis* 41].

Keeping the world at bay is a deliberate choice. We shall not come back to *Mourning Becomes Electra* or the other rural plays, in which the world is kept at a distance under similar principles. In these the patriarchs—essential figures in the O'Neillian theatre—keep their distances from the rest of society and take an active part in maintaining the gap between two parties whom they do not wish to see reconciled. (Robert Mayo stands as an exception in the lack of respect he arouses: "RUTH. He wouldn't dare act that way with anyone else!" [*BH* 125].)

Choosing to be different is not the privilege of a few atrabilious individuals—it is widespread among the other heroes, who frequently attempt to shut themselves out from a world in which they feel they have no place. Thus, in *The First Man*, Martha and Curtis live in another age. Although they do not integrate into a microcosm, they fully assume the lifestyle they have chosen, for they are naturally set aside by their archeological research expeditions, which mean long periods of exile far from civilization. In yet another context, we find this motif taken up again in *Diff'rent*. O'Neill, in a variation on the theme "I am Emma," emphasizes the deliberate nature of the desire for difference and estrangement among the principal actors:

> It is merely the tale of the eternal romantic idealist who is in all of us—the eternally defeated one—In our innermost hearts we all wish ourselves and others to be "Diff'rent." We are all more or less "Emmas."[16]

An illustration of this romantic aspect is given in *A Touch of the Poet*, in which Cornelius Melody often stands in front of a mirror and declaims lines of Byron. This pathetic character enables us to measure the importance of social barriers, for he bases the meaning of his life on the distance he establishes between himself and the patrons of his tavern. After losing his last fight, which was hardly more than a common brawl, he changes his attitude towards them, and this is a sign that he has given up the struggle for a "real" life.

All these characters consider themselves members of a separate class, which is sometimes a mere figment of their imagination but which more often has distant roots in reality. Withdrawal into oneself is a choice which leads to a certain solitude, but this is generally accepted as the price that must be paid to attain the life-style which the person feels he deserves.

Displaying differences is not the only factor responsible for the breach which appears between the clans and society. Some are actually considered as damned and, as such, are ostracized by society. The absence of links between a particular family group and the surrounding world is not a characteristic proper to landowners unwilling to make friends, or to individuals driven by some ideal. In many of the plays they are ostracized for a variety of reasons that we shall now examine.

In *Gold* and *Where the Cross Is Made*, the family is banished from society by the father's madness. Elsewhere, the question of race relations is used to illustrate this phenomenon. The question having been raised through the mixed marriage of Ella and Jim in *All God's Chillun Got Wings*, we are shown how the transgression outlaws them—the causes may vary, but being different is always a factor of exclusion. Not all of them have the same moral force, or the same vanity as Cornelius Melody. This is why Mary, for example, in *Long Day's Journey into Night*, bitterly denounces the cataloguing of families which has projected the Tyrones into a separate world.

> MARY.—*Then with an undercurrent of lonely yearning.*
> They have friends who entertain them and whom they entertain.
> They're not cut off from everyone [*LDJN* 44].

The rejection to which they fall victim only heightens the impression the characters have of being judged not for what they are but as members of a clan. The protagonists are pariahs, and whatever exchange they may desire, they are forever deprived of it because of the stigma they bear. Mary, who longs for contacts with the other inhabitants in New London, forgets for a few moments that it is her drug-taking which prevents them from leading a normal life.[17]

We may well imagine that these fellow creatures of misfortune might be, in the eyes of society, branded with scarlet letters: an M for madness, a double M for mixed marriage and a D for drugs. In just the same way as their individual peculiarities—of which some are proud—their features of social abnormality are immediately detected by those from whom they vainly try to conceal them. The result is inevitable: Their difference imprisons them in a cage, sometimes golden, but from which there is no escape.

Among the links that have a particularly strong hold over people, we may note the union between them and their land. They are attached to their homeland, and even if their love is not always disinterested—land being a symbol of wealth—the relationship that binds them together cannot be reduced to a mere question of money. Several different readings can be made of the attachment felt by some of the characters for the place they live in, for in similar situations contradictory feelings may sometimes be aroused. Thus, the Mayo family's farmhouse and fields, duly admired by their seafaring uncle, become for Robert a prison from which he longs to escape. Indeed, the immutability resulting from his condition as a farmer means that he will not be able to develop his full potential as an individual. His role as head of the family, which he attempts to assume after his father's death, forces him to take charge of the farm, which gradually destroys him because by doing so he goes against his vital interests.

Desire Under the Elms provides yet another picture of this relationship. In his study of Eben, Roger Asselineau reveals how the land and the farmhouse are interrelated with the family component:

> He is indeed trapped by circumstances—tied up to that bleak New England farm which he somehow considers part of his mother.[18]

This explains why Eben does not follow suit when his brothers leave the farm after Cabot comes home with a new wife, putting an end to all their hopes of an inheritance. Although Eben knows where Ephraim has hidden his savings, he does not take advantage of this knowledge to venture out into the world.

Belonging to the land or to the sea,[19] is often linked to a family relationship, with a motherly, feminine image lingering in the background; a sort of pact has been sealed over the years, even before the character arrives, and when one of the descendants tries to extricate himself, he realizes that this is almost impossible, for he cannot bring himself to forsake his natural element to go and start a fresh life under new skies.

It emerges that the outside world's perception of the family component was accurate. This component can be characterized both by its cohesion and by its rejection of all that is alien. The consciousness it has of itself and of its otherness is sometimes heightened by the rejection it provokes in the surrounding world. The estrangement has manifold origins: It is perceived either as a status-enhancing element by the characters, who consider themselves members of a self-defined aristocracy, or as the consequence of an offense, which prevents them from adhering to social conventions, thereby leading to suffering caused by their exclusion.

2. The Imprisoned Person.

Heredity.

The rooted attachment to the earth we have just described in its mother-son aspect is expressed in a different way in *Beyond the Horizon*, in which James Mayo establishes a direct correlation between the name, hence the ancestors, and the personality of the individual.

> MAYO. Andy's a Mayo bred in the bone, and he's a born farmer, and a damn good one, too. He'll live and die right here on this farm, like I expect to [*BH* 97].

This somewhat abrupt statement contains a terse summary of laws to which all are supposed to submit. According to the father, who by reason of his position at the center of the family is perceived as the possessor of truth, men carry within themselves a family heritage from which they cannot withdraw, and if they choose to take a different path, it will be unnatural. These presuppositions are borne out by the judgment Robert passes against his brother Andrew at the end of the play, when Andrew understands that he went astray when he left the path set out for him.

We note, on the grammatical level, how surnames bear the mark of destiny: Used with the indefinite article they are reduced to the status of common nouns and are used to refer to people as members of a race. (Proper nouns are sometimes used as adjectives, to the same effect: "MRS. BORDEN. She's too Mannon to let anyone see what she feels" [*MBE, The Hunted* 68].) If each clan has its own history, we may not be mistaken in advancing that each one also contains its own future. This is why changes affecting surnames are more revealing than may appear. The branches of the family tree have intricate ramifications, and when conflicts arise the characters' origins are frequently brought to the fore. Heredity is a recurrent theme, both in O'Neill's own correspondence and in his plays.[1]

What he wrote to Harry Weinberger about his children, to be able to disown them with a clear conscience, reveals how he apprehended the notion of genetic heredity; in this light, the sometimes simplistic arguments of certain characters is not surprising:

> I feel my dear little ones are nothing to be proud of, or take pleasure in—
> unlike Eugene—and unless they change drastically, I am off them for life.
> There is too much greedy parasitic Boulton in their blood—I am afraid—
> not to add Boulton stupidity in their brains![2]

Each one has two direct ancestral components, but a Manichean vision of Darwinism and of the code of genetics leads to a view in which the individual descends from a single lineage. The approach which the author adopted with regard to his own descendants is observable in the plays, where the protagonists have a partly erased genealogy.

Few give up the search for a scapegoat, which provides them with the means of exonerating themselves with a clear conscience and throwing the blame on somebody else. This is why, in private, many husbands blame their wives for the misfortunes that befall their children. This strategy is adopted to show that the victims are, admittedly, legitimate members of the family, but their failings are due to a hereditary trait for which the speaker is not responsible. Thus Tyrone, reflecting on the genetic predisposition to which his son owes his tuberculosis, does not fail to attribute its origin to his wife:

> TYRONE. I never thought a child of mine—It doesn't come from my side of the family. There wasn't one of us that didn't have lungs as strong as an ox [*LDJN* 79].

Beyond the puerile character of this denial, we must note that by virtually accusing Mary's forebears, he emphasizes the hereditary aspect of the illness. Here again, we must not underestimate the importance of what remains unsaid. Jamie shows remarkable perspicacity when he stands up against such reasoning, for it implies that one cannot fight against tuberculosis, and that the die is cast.

In the course of a conversation, some characters pride themselves on the blood that flows in their veins; in other cases, this very blood is perceived as indisputable proof of the transmission of family defects, with, obviously, quite opposite consequences. A work which has been the subject of many critical controversies is *Strange Interlude*, in which the discussion of heredity reaches a climax. Mrs. Evans tells Nina that she must bear a child with a man who is not her husband, in order to put an end to the madness that is passed down from one generation to the next. In this case, intuitions and presuppositions give way to certainties. It is not enough to simply express regret about ancestral influence on an individual: a lesson must now be drawn from the past and a family line must be sacrificed. Even when someone's life is placed under an ominous influence, the family circle is, however, unable to predict the future of the person who is to be the victim of a tragic fate. Thus, in the example we have just cited, regardless of all the warnings about madness, Sam is never affected by the dementia feared by his mother. When he dies, in Act Eight, he has become not a raving tragic hero but a lucid plutocrat, like Marco in *Marco Millions*, whose money is a substitute for conscience.

Sam had no knowledge of his misfortune; other characters have a premonition of theirs, and establish a correlation between their destiny and their ascendancy ("BRANT. I have my father's rotten coward blood in me, I think! Aye!" [*MBE, The Hunted* 110]). These incriminations are sparked off in critical situations; the characters thereby become aware of the interior forces which dominate them, and attribute their origin to their genetic heritage.

> REUBEN. But you're yellow, too. And I'm yellow—How could I help being? It's in my blood. (*Hastily*) But I'll get it out of my blood, by God! [*Dy* 449].

They all have to act so as to assert themselves as specific people and not as members of a lineage. The ensuing struggle no longer takes place between family and society but within the minds of the individuals, who must contrive to liberate themselves. Between the expression of a desire for freedom and the actual enjoyment of this freedom, there is a wall which many attempt to overcome, but few ultimately succeed.

Some will put up a fight to free themselves from the grip of the family, but others will later realize that what they believed to be a liberation is nothing but a reincarnation. The attempt to break off from the clan in order to achieve an autonomous existence finds its expression in *Mourning Becomes Electra*. In this play, the author develops a theory that seems strange at first glance, according to which a person's death brings about a metamorphosis in his direct descendant. Lavinia hates her mother, and does her best to differentiate herself, but after the death of her mother she becomes the double of the very one for whose death she was partly responsible; as for Orin, who joined forces with Christine before Ezra's death, he too becomes the double of his father.[3]

Whatever the means deployed to escape from their destiny, the characters never ultimately succeed, for their lives appear as nothing more than the re-enactment of a past they cannot forget. This is why the conclusion of *Mourning Becomes Electra* is that the Mannons are victims of a curse resulting from their offenses, and that atonement can only come about with the extinction of the dynasty.

The strategy in two movements—estrangement followed by merging—finds its illustration in a play written by O'Neill at the end of his career, which shows that over the years this aspect held special importance for him. A reformulation of the theme of the double appears in *More Stately Mansions*, in which Simon retires Thoreau-fashion from the world to live in harmony with nature. After his marriage with Sara, he goes into business and rapidly becomes the spitting image of his father, although his exile had been expressly a rejection of his father and the values he embodied ("DEBORAH. ... You are so like him now, in many ways, it's astonishing" [*MSM* 69]).

After this first approach to hereditary phenomena it would be tempting to see in each individual an embodiment of his ancestor figures. We have already alluded to this, and said the actual facts are more complex. Thus, in *Desire Under the Elms*, Cabot's personality is at the opposite pole to that of Eben's mother, while Eben is considered to be the reincarnation of the images of both his mother and his father, and almost the same words are used to express this likeness ("SIMEON. Like his Paw. PETER. Dead spit an' image!" [*DE* 211]; "CABOT. Soft-headed. Like his Maw. Dead spit 'n' image" [*DE* 246]). The contrast which emerges in the speeches shows how blind the protagonists are, but it also re-examines the implications of this mechanical and simplistic vision of genetic heritage.

In a different context Mildred naively mentions an immunity which she supposes to be innate, but when she is confronted with reality in a human form—Yank in front of his boiler—the dramatic irony of her words takes on its full dimension ("MILDRED. Grandfather started as a puddler. I should have inherited an immunity to heat that would make a salamander shiver" [*HA* 220]).

We shall see, in the course of this study, that other factors are added to the influence of heredity. For the present, we shall simply note two essential facts: The characters cannot claim any power over it, and the course of their destiny is not automatically predetermined.

The theme of the continuity of generations is strongly underlined, and within the frame of the family the notion of the double, which is partly an echo of this theme, deserves our attention. We shall look more particularly at the fathers who, under the impulse of some personal dissatisfaction, frequently seek, through their sons, to attain a certain level in society or exercise some profession that has always been their dream.[4] Confronted with the demands of their elders, the sons' reactions vary from acceptance to revolt. The choice settled on is often an answer to the parent's wish and as such shows how difficult it is to differentiate oneself from this ancestral figure. Such scenes occur in eight plays, when the sons reach an age at which they must decide on their future. There is nothing original about these episodes from everyday life, which are based on the patriarchal image of the family.

The commonplace aspect of these remarks about doubles should not let us lose sight of the ontological consequences of such reasoning, as this is an essential element in the perspective we have chosen. Orin is well aware of the implications when he says to Lavinia: "Can't you see I'm now in Father's place and you're Mother?" (*MBE, The Haunted* 155). He knows that death is the only way out, that the way in which he is to be destroyed is of no importance, but that he is condemned by his blood. When he compares himself to his father, and when he tells Lavinia that he will do his best to disappear, he relinquishes all claim to existence in his own right and becomes a mere puppet in the hands of forces he feels unable to fight. Lavinia rises up against this point of view, for she abhors such a dismissive attitude. She decides to live her life and flout her ancestors, but just as she hopes to bury the past with its evil influences by becoming Peter's wife, a slip of the tongue occurs, revealing to her the extent of her illusions.

What are the consequences of these genetic heritages? If the person is no more than a reincarnation of his ancestors, with a predetermined fate, any choice of existence becomes impossible, and heredity then forms a prison from which there is no escape. It would be premature to draw conclusions at this stage of our study. We shall be content to note that this yoke is not always predominant, even if its influence is considerable. The way in which time is apprehended also has its importance, for it serves as an indicator to discern whether human beings are total prisoners or whether freedom is accessible to them in their lifespan.

Visions of space and time.

Time.

The notion of time has a variable status in the plays and, as they live out various situations, the characters reflect on its meaning and its bearing upon their own lives. Some reminisce nostalgically about bygone days, or confidently evoke a promising future with shining prospects; others, more philosophically, simply refer to its elusive character. This twofold reasoning corresponds to two approaches to time which are as yet unexplored, but to which we shall now direct our attention.

We look first at a vision of temporality which is immediately accessible to perception, for it is explicit in the characters' speech. Their somber words, filled with despair, intensify the ineluctable nature of their fate, the compulsive reiteration of events rendering them incapable of mastering it. This all-victorious time is tragic time—that which, apparently, breaks Orin:

> ORIN. I thought if I could see it clearly in the past, I might be able to foretell what fate is in store for us [*MBE, The Haunted* 153].

Secondly, a structural analysis shows how the cyclic movement of the flow of time is woven into the fabric of a work. Certain tableaux are mere variations of situations that have already been staged or related by the characters, and the recurrence takes on a specific meaning within each play. *The Great God Brown*, whose opening and closing scenes are in many respects identical, is the model to which I am referring—the author's insistence on these repetitive episodes indicates that life is a perpetual rebirth, spring heralding a new generation ("CYBEL. Always spring comes again bearing life! Always, always forever again! Spring again!" [*GGB* 322]).

This vision of an eternal return excludes any possibility for the individuals of a tragic perception of time, for this regular rotation is also a sign of permanence. Cabot gives an example of this in *Desire Under the Elms*. He perceives his immortality to be within nature, and by marrying for the third time, attempts to ensure his reincarnation:

> CABOT. A son is me—my blood—mine. Mine ought t'git mine. An' then it's still mine—even though I be six foot under [*DE* 234].

On the other hand, the circular structure and the repetitive tableaux of *Mourning Becomes Electra* strengthen the idea of an ineluctable destiny. Time is that of the tragedy, in which the hero moves towards an end he knows to be inevitable.

We note that the value of these repetitions is variable. No ready-made interpretations are possible, as context prevails in the presence of conflicting meanings. Nevertheless, these two aspects deserve our attention because they are included among the enclosure mechanisms, which as we have seen are components of the family structure.

Theatrical space.

O'Neill's legendary dissatisfaction over the way his plays were produced, or the way the cast acted, is well known. He claimed to have already seen the plays as he wrote them, and that the actual production was almost always disappointing. This stage whisper about the theatrical world is an indirect reminder to us that his works are made to be put into space. The lengthy stage directions, if they inhibit the imaginations of producers and actors, have at least one advantage in that they indicate the author's wishes in this field. His lively reaction when critics accused him of disregarding the basic rules for theatrical construction, when *Beyond the Horizon* was produced,[5] cannot fail to be an incentive to analyze the way in which he contemplated the production of the "family" works.

The introduction of outdoor scenes marks a break from the rigid set of theatrical codes that O'Neill rejected. He exploited his scenic innovation to the full, and we have just seen that his choice was not capricious. *Desire Under the Elms*, in which outdoor tableaux alternate with indoor ones, shows that even when the characters are out of doors, they cannot shake off the hold the family has over them. The stage directions, which serve as an introduction, indicate that the elms are both a reminder of the unity of the family, here symbolized by the maternal component, and a prison that prevents the characters from developing their full potential.

They appear to protect and at the same time subdue. There is a sinister maternity in their aspect, a crushing, jealous absorption. They have developed from their intimate contact with the life of man in the house an appalling humaneness. They brood oppressively over the house. They are like exhausted women resting their sagging breasts and hair on its roof ... [*DE* 203].

The indoor scenes, which constitute the majority of the tableaux (sixteen plays are set indoors), sometimes reproduce the architectural model of the New London house, or describe confined spaces in which the protagonists are shut up.[6] The scenery sometimes includes a few windows, but these have no direct application as openings onto the world. In a way, they are reminiscent of the description of Professor Leeds' bookshelves ("The books in the cases have never been touched, their austere array shows no gap, but the glass separating them from the world is gray with dust, giving them a blurred ghostly quality" [*SI* 66]).

Conversely, in the plays, we may imagine the characters inside the rooms taking the place of the books and having a very blurred vision of the outside world, with which they have very little in common. The only reminder of its existence is a medley of sounds coming in from outside: music, firecrackers or a foghorn. This acoustic landscape, in the form of an echo, does not act as a bridge linking two worlds—on the contrary it heightens the impression of the group's isolation.

The use of space is an essential element in the interpretation of the works, inasmuch as this aspect throws light on the relations existing between a community and its immediate environment; it is therefore of utmost importance in each case to examine the way in which it is defined by the author. We must take into account the dimension of on-stage space and examine both what is shown and what it means, bearing in mind that for the spectator, if one thinks of what is said in the stage directions, the perception of it will be twofold. As concerns what is shown, it appears in twin forms: We have seen that it is sometimes an open space and, more frequently, a closed area in which the main actors reside.

On the level of what is meant, we have noted that one of the two visions of the outdoors engenders a false impression of openness. In fact, it masks a monastic environment and symbolically represents a family structure from which the characters cannot escape. As concerns the image of the indoors, the drawing-rooms and bedrooms evoke a prison from which the occupants attempt to break out; in spite of all their efforts, they do not succeed in ridding themselves of the bonds that attach them to the place.

On-stage space is manifold. It is possible to draw up classifications, but the reader or spectator should beware of a simplistic categorization in which the duality opposing outdoors and indoors can be seen as corresponding to that of emprisonment and liberty. This first approach shows that a single interpretation of what is meant is impossible; it would be by definition restrictive, and we shall see below that the approach to the outdoors allows several different readings. For the present we shall limit our observations to a single point: in the same way as in the case of time, as we noted above, it emerges that the spatial representation of the environment in which the individuals live contributes very often to intensifying the impression of enclosure which they feel.

Flight, an alternative to liberation.

We have noted that the clan, in its variable forms, with its spatial and hereditary components, encloses the characters within circles from which they cannot escape. If they wish to exist, they must rid themselves of their bonds, sever the umbilical cord, cut the Gordian knot of their existence.

In *Mourning Becomes Electra*, Christine Mannon wishes to elope with Adam Brant so as to leave her past behind and make a fresh start under new skies. After the murder of her husband, which was to have set her free, her chains still remain, symbolized by Lavinia's glances and the oppressive atmosphere in the house.[7] This is why she looks to her departure as a liberation, and aspires to a rebirth when she leaves this accursed family temple.

Mannon, Brant and Orin wish to remove Christine from New England, and from a residence that is a breeding ground of hatred. They all imagine that the Pacific Islands will be the ideal place to live, for their exoticism marks a complete contrast with American society as exemplified by the Mannon family, because it is both stifled by Puritanism and ravaged by civil war.

> BRANT. And they live in as near the Garden of Paradise before sin was discovered as you'll find on this earth! [*MBE*, *Homecoming* 24].

Elsewhere is a place where each one hopes to be able to start a new life and find new virginity. In their ingenuous dreamers' fashion they fail to see that the difficulties arise from their own family ties, and blame the misfortunes that befall them on their geographical position.

The first proof of the protagonists' blindness is given by Orin, who makes a journey to the paradisical islands, but does not manage to rid himself of his undermining feeling of guilt. To Peter's disappointment, travelling does not prove to be a cure with miraculous effects. This outcome is hardly surprising, for the characters had a remedy to suggest, but were incapable of examining the causes of the illness. We find an illustration of this phenomenon in *Strange Interlude*, in which Darrell and Marsden set off for Europe.[8] Both attempt to redress their lives as they travel away, one from his mother's ghost, the other from his mistress. But here again, distance does nothing to improve things, and Marsden's account of the misunderstanding could be applied to Orin.

MARSDEN. My running away was about as successful as his... as if one could leave one's memory behind [*SI* 112].[9]

Flight is seen by many as a chance of salvation. In actual fact, when the links are not completely severed, departure merely presages a return.

Lavinia, who comes back transformed after her stay in the Pacific, could lead one to believe that running away enables one to cast out one's demons. The end of the play shows that this is not so at all, for she cannot escape the damnation that strikes all the descendants of the accursed lineage of the Mannon clan. Her departure from the ancestral home, followed by her reappearance, once she feels she has broken free, indicate that she tried to forget the fate linked to her blood, and that she imagined she was able to master it.

In his study of the motives justifying her self-imposed confinement in the last act, Robert Feldman writes:

> by literally *shutting herself in the house*, Lavinia does not experience the joy of courageously confronting her conflicts in a constructive manner, but only indulges herself in masochistic delight in having a neurotic pseudo solution to the problem of guilt.[10]

This reasoning is, to my mind, doubly misplaced. First, tragedy is not a handbook on the art of living, and second, it is contrary to fact to apply the term masochistic pleasure to Lavinia. This implies that one should disregard the hereditary dimension, in the sense of her being condemned by her blood, and that one should consider her as existing as a person responsible for the working out of her destiny; responsible she may well be, but Feldman's arguments have the further implication that one also supposes her capable of overcoming the forces that are contriving to bring about her downfall. This is in fact what she does hope, for a moment, before she realizes that she has been mistaken and that the joys of wedlock are not for her. In spite of what the critic proposes, with admirable optimism, the choice of marriage would in no way solve a superhuman struggle whose dimensions are beyond her. In fact the tragic conflict is in itself the opposite to what Feldman supposes. The proof is given by Patrice Parvis, who defines it in these terms:

> The tragic is produced by an inevitable and insoluble conflict, not by a series of catastrophes or horrible natural phenomena, but because of a fatality that harries human existence. Tragic agony is irremediable.[11]

Lavinia's attempt to flee is a proclamation of her desire to live. She lays down arms once she understands that she is fighting a lost cause, for she cannot deny her origins. Her attitude is reminiscent of that which characterizes Chris in *Anna Christie*, when he tries to elude the call of the sea but eventually gives up the struggle and signs up to embark on what he foresees will be his last voyage.

Some long for reconciliation, not only with themselves or with the family structure they belong to, but also with the surrounding community. Some would lead us to believe that deliverance is possible, but only the outside world can absolve the guilty parties and release them from the prison of family bonds in which they are cloistered. Orin, conscious of the impossibility of any self-liberation, entreats Lavinia to allow him to confess their crimes, so that they might be judged by society ("ORIN. Let's go now and confess and pay the penalty for Mother's murder, and find peace together!" [*MBE, The Haunted* 165]). A public confession followed by a punishment corresponding to the misdeeds would allow them to free themselves from the weight of the guilt, and be reconciled with the community. Lavinia, unwilling to disown her ancestors, refuses, and her refusal, with the tradition of silence that characterizes the clan, prevents the social body from accomplishing its role of salvation.

Other characters wish to break their chains, and attempt to integrate into a different world, hoping for forgiveness. In *The Web*, the prostitute retraces the steps of her failure; she explains how she tried to break free from her condition but was rejected because she had not managed to conceal her past. The title of this, one of the playwright's earlier works, indicates that a person is always a prisoner of his background, and that the obstacles barring the way to freedom are often on the family level. Thus in the present case the mother is unwilling to separate herself from her child, although she knows that by declining this offer ("ROSE. He said the only hope fur me was to git out in the country, sleep in the open air, and eat a lot of good food. He might jest as well 'uv told me to go to Heaven and I told him so" [*Web* 46]), she foregoes all hope of survival.

The harmful ascendancy of the family, or of fate, correlated with ancestral legacies, could sometimes be avoided if the individual received the help of society in his quest for freedom. Such is not the case, and when society is thus appealed to it only drives the characters back into the very spheres from which they hope to escape, thereby perpetuating situations that will not be amenable to change because of the rigid structure of the clan systems described above.

Faced with the immutability of these structures, some of the characters venture to react. They often meet with failure, but some nurture the hope of finding their salvation and freedom through departure. Imprisoned within their own minds, bound to a particular place, or lacking the necessary willpower ("BESSIE. Listen, why don't you come with us? JOHN. No, it would only add one more failure to the list" [*B&B* 81]), the characters have a difficult struggle for emancipation, which is only complete if they leave without any idea of return. Taking up the role of a mother for the last time, Josie Hogan seals the breach between her brother and the farm. She has more influence than Bessie. Thanks to her, Mike will be able to leave the family farm and start a new life, to emerge at last from his insignificance.

JOSIE. I'm sorry to see you go, but it's the best thing for you. That's why I'm helping you, the same as I helped Thomas and John. You can't stand up to the old man any more than Thomas or John could, and the old devil would always keep you a slave [*MMis* 4].

The emancipation of Simeon and Peter, in *Desire Under the Elms*, is somewhat more spectacular, but they share the same purpose.[12] They all leave the farm to go and seek their fortunes in the world and create a new identity for themselves. Exile means deliberate self-exclusion from an accursed dynasty, for they have understood that blood ties are in their very essence a hindrance to their development as individuals.

The ultimate flight (dreams, whiskey and firearms).

DEBORAH. As for my excursions into Oriental wisdom, I see it now as the flight of one who bored at home, blames the surroundings and sails for far lands, only to find a welcoming figure waiting there to greet one— oneself! [*MSM* 62].

Desire Under the Elms, A Moon for the Misbegotten and *The Rope* are the only plays which stage an estrangement between one member of a family and the rest of the group.[13] However, this aspiration is shared by other protagonists. Several characters in fact have a very strong desire for freedom, but as they are aware of the impossibility of breaking off relations in such a way, they act under deadly escape impulses. The first instance of this occurs in individuals who take refuge in dreams of being in a different place, or leading a different life, for their position within the family community does not match their needs. Thus, in *More Stately Mansions*, Deborah imagines she is the king's mistress, in Louis XIV's court. Her contact with reality takes the form of a twice-daily event when she meets with her family at mealtimes. This event is nothing more than a formal episode, and she is alien to the environment in which her son and her husband move.

In *Strange Interlude*, Nina attempts to find inner freedom outside of the family circle, then reconstructs a new circle around herself. After experiencing a succession of joys and pains, her only wish is to disappear. This is why we may propose that her marriage with Charlie is a reversion to childhood and even a preparation for eternal rest. The absence of a real personal relationship becomes apparent in the fact that marriage, for her, is not so much a question of loving one's partner as enjoying the peace he may bring to a tortured soul. Confronted with such preconceptions, son, husband and lovers necessarily find themselves pushed into the background. In this case, life is a long preparation for death; to exist means renouncing desire and waiting for death, which is perceived as a deliverance. This does not entail a pessimistic reading of *Strange Interlude*; renouncing one's desires is a kind of rebirth.[14]

> NINA. It will be a comfort to get home—to be old and to be home together—to love each other's peace—to sleep with peace together—to die in peace! I'm so contentedly weary with life! [*SI* 200].

To die, perchance to dream. One of the ways in which these ill-fated men and women attempt to brighten the nightmarish vision that hovers before their eyes is to avail themselves of alcohol. The second advantage of this practice is that by resorting unreservedly to whiskey, those who are tormented by despair hasten their end. The prototype character symbolizing this plight is James Tyrone in A *Moon for the Misbegotten*. The sense of guilt which he feels towards his dead mother is his destruction. Indeed, he believes he has been deprived of his filial rights, and this very condemnation, which he has pronounced against himself, has destroyed his desire to live.

In a different context, Con Melody also capitulates, when he admits that he is only a poor innkeeper[15] and not the descendant of an illustrious family. All his *raison d'être* deserts him with the loss of his partly imaginary family background, which had helped him to consider himself as somebody respectable. He refuses to play his role as father and husband; to accept would imply that he also accepts his function as innkeeper. When he faces the facts, and accepts his parental and marital status, his acquiescence, in its full implication, is tantamount to giving up life, for he has lost all reason to fight.

Some say they drink to forget, but their ominous words betray a deeper desire. They are in fact methodically destroying themselves in a purification ritual whereby the curse that binds them is washed away by drinking whiskey, which bestows death and forgiveness upon them. Paradoxically, for these drinkers with Irish names, this resort to alcohol by way of extreme unction (a ritual often accompanied by a confession), is the ultimate sign of belonging, as though they wanted to return to a mythical Ireland, to the mother country where they might find a last resting place.

Alcohol has destructive effects, but it does not find grace in the eyes of all, and some choose more expeditious solutions. In *Now I Ask You*, the heroine plays cat and mouse with her situation as a married woman. She imagines she is Hedda Gabler, and attempts to end her life with a pistol, but the report that follows turns out to be a tire bursting. If one excepts this comic episode, one notes that the other suicides have devastating effects on the characters' health. In *Bread and Butter*, a very strong family ascendancy leads the hero to deny his identity. There are several decisive factors: a very strong patriarchal figure is combined with material considerations which, intensified with emotional blackmail, compel John to give up his vocation as an artist. His first capitulation marks for him an irrevocable defeat; he sinks into alcoholism before deciding to blow his brains out, for he senses that he will not be able to free himself otherwise.

In *Abortion*, the anticipated reaction of his family circle plays a considerable part in Jack's decision to likewise commit suicide. His responsibility for the death of a young woman, following a clandestine abortion, becomes too heavy a burden to bear when her brother declares that he is going to expose him. As a supreme punishment, the hero of the day, whom the crowd adores, is to lose his mask and be obliged to show his real face to his fellow creatures. The prospect of disapproval by his mother, who, he thinks, will not overcome the grief caused by the relinquishing of this idealized image, deals a fatal blow to her son, who would not be able to survive his mother's predictable repudiation.

> JACK. My Mother and Father, my sister, Ev—(*Bites back the name*) This would kill my mother if she knew [*Ab* 163].

Deaths abound in the plays, as each individual ends his life for specific reasons. Without attempting to draw up a typology of the various deadly escape impulses, we shall mention two for the present: an attempt by the character to free himself from the ascendancy of the family circle, and an act which must be correlated with each character's hereditary components. These lethal flights cannot, however, be blamed entirely on the family, and it will be necessary to take into consideration other factors, which will be discussed in further detail.

At this stage of the study, one may note that the characters are marked by the relationship that binds them to their origins or to their family background. The ascendancy of their family environment is such that it is sometimes imperative for them to flee in order to assert themselves as people. This necessary departure often turns out to be impossible, or fruitless in those cases when the characters run away. Escape takes on the appearance of a second birth, but some are content with a partial liberation; this then takes the form of dreams, or of continual drunkenness, each drinker drowning his daily problems in alcohol as he waits for death. Others, unable to bear a superhuman burden, abridge their existential sufferings by taking their lives.

The ghost of freedom.

We noted above how society and the family projected images to each other of two separate worlds, between which any communication was virtually impossible. In a less direct way, we have been able to see in this part how heredity staked its claim to the lives of the protagonists, making them prisoners of their blood. This mixture of scientism and Darwinism shows that the enclosures are not only external, but are also a reflection of the heroes' inner nature. The cyclic time-pattern and the deceptively open space-element can also contribute to the feeling of alienation experienced by the character. How can freedom be achieved? Some resort to dreams or alcohol, while others prefer suicide. The dark picture which seems to emerge when one studies family relationships must be brought into correct perspective, insofar as we are often shown incomplete families which do not constitute the unique vision the author wished to convey. (I shall, however, come to a more optimistic vision in the study of *Ah, Wilderness!*)

Moreover, despite the importance of the family component, this is only one of the factors influencing the destiny of each individual. Not all of those who have formidable ancestors are condemned from birth to insignificant existence, but it cannot be denied that their lives will be difficult to live. At the end of the road leading to freedom, they will often find a room whose walls are covered with mirrors, in which they will see their own faces merging with those of their ancestors. Confronted with a discovery such as this, the temptation to flee will be great, for they sense that the fight they are to lead against the specters of their doubles will be their undoing.

3. Relations Between the Characters.

The comforts of home.

We shall now direct our attention to the links between the characters, as they appear in the plays—between the different members of the family. Until this point the family has been considered as a circle which formed a unit, and confined men and women inside a prison from which they had no means of escape. The unitarian impression previously brought to light was obtained by looking through the eyes of outsiders who were incapable of discerning the composite aspects internal to the clan. Moreover, in spite of the conflicts, which took place privately within the families, and whose violence could have caused the microcosm to shatter, the enclosure mechanisms described above lose nothing of their force.

Within the community in which they live, the relations of people to the world are formed by person-to-person links. I shall first attempt to understand how the link between parents and children is established, before looking at relations between brothers and sisters.

We have noted that there are several factors preventing characters from leaving home; nevertheless, home has nothing of the ideal, where each one could find peace. The houses often reflect the atmosphere that reigns within them, and the inhabitants sometimes complain about the poor quality of their living-space (for instance, *Strange Interlude* or *Beyond the Horizon*, in which the scenery symbolizes decline—temporary in one case, permanent in the other), or associate it with an indefinable but very real feeling of uneasiness (for instance, *Mourning Becomes Electra* and *Desire Under the Elms*). Home is presented as far from an idyllic place,[1] and if they are not all as harsh as Yank, few of them live in it with any serenity:

> YANK. What d'yuh want wit home! (*proudly*) I runned away from mine when I was a kid. On'y too glad to beat it, dat was me. Home was lickings for me, dat's all [*HA* 211].

Yank appears as a hero figure, with superhuman strength; his relations with others have always been rough, and in this extract he indicates that his entry into life was the result of flight from his parents' home, where the treatment he was subjected to left little place for affection. This quotation serves as a good introduction to the relationships that are established between the principal actors, for although actual blows are no longer dealt, they are replaced by verbal aggressions, which in turn generate moral suffering that is at times hard to bear.

This rather dark picture of the family group may not have corresponded completely to the playwright's own; one must, however, note in his writings that when he was in a position of ascendancy, the feelings he claimed to feel towards his offspring were hardly a sign of great enthusiasm.[2]

Father images.

NINA. ... because he is my father... father? ... What is father? [*SI* 15].

It is difficult to answer the questions Nina puts to herself; for other characters the queries would be differently formulated, as in their case the parental figure is associated with absence. This aspect has already been dealt with in our presentation of the family, but the number of plays in which the father is absent, dead, or not mentioned is significant.

We shall begin this study with a work that gives an extreme picture of the relations existing between two generations, but one that reflects, indirectly, a tendency common to many parents. In *The First Man*, the estrangement is established right from the very first scenes, since Curtis rejects the idea of fathering another child, and shows that his interest in mankind is limited to searching for, and examining, its bones. At the birth of his son, whom he refuses to acknowledge at first, because his wife died during childbirth, he decides to leave and devote his time to carrying out excavations aimed at unearthing the traces of the first human beings. His fatherly duty seems of little importance to him; it entails no more than the choice of a nurse, and before his departure he entrusts the baby to his aunt, whom he considers trustworthy, as she has not been corrupted by society. Some time elapses before he recognizes the child, which he only does out of respect for the memory of his late wife.

The child's entry into the world is symbolically accompanied by a denial of his existence on the part of his father. This attitude marks the climax of the generation conflict, since the repudiation of the other person begins with his entry into the world. Confronted with such devastating behavior, the descendants strive to show that they exist. In order to do this, they have to fight with a rival who, if he does not refute their actual presence, never allows them access to adulthood, imprisoning them in a never-ending initiation period, the purpose of which is not to teach them how to live but to confine them to eternal adolescence. (See *Desire Under the Elms, Gold, Long Day's Journey into Night*, and *Where the Cross Is Made*.)

The only answer Curtis is capable of providing is flight; another example in which tragic escape is associated with the idea of fatherhood occurs in *Mourning Becomes Electra*, the son now old enough to play the role of an accuser ("BRANT. He grew ashamed of my mother and me. He sank down and down and my mother worked and supported him" [*MBE, Homecoming* 25]). This inability to assume parental functions, which leads Brant to suicide, is not the rule, but is a sort of variation on a theme that is to become recurrent: the fact of being a father is, in itself, destructive. In this instance his downfall is caused by his inability to mentally erase either the fruit of his guilty love or the woman with whom he committed the sin.

The causes of death are manifold, and not all the deceased have taken their lives in an attempt to escape from their responsibilities. We have already glimpsed how escape involved resorting to dreams, alcohol and sometimes death; it must, however, be noted that the vision of the head of the family resigning his responsibilities is infrequent.

At the opposite extreme to these attitudes of refusal, we meet patriarchs who rule their sons' lives with a strictness that some find difficult to accept. The image of the patriarch comes out in a large number of plays; these characters seem to be eternal, and enjoy an authority that remains intact, in spite of the conflicts which punctuate their daily lives. In *Bread and Butter*, one of the playwright's earlier works, John, who cannot muster enough strength to free himself from his father's domination, and from his family background, defines the characteristics of his forebear, characteristics that reappear under different features in several works.[3]

> JOHN. You consider your children to be your possession, your property, to belong to you. You don't think of them as individuals with ideas and desires of their own [*B&B* 37].

The head of the family is, by his very status, the person who makes the decisions, denying, if not the right to expression, at least indirectly the right to existence; indeed, the character's attempts to assert himself are repressed by the one who knows and chooses because he is the father, and legitimizes himself by invoking his creator ("CABOT. God's hard, not easy!" [*DE* 237]).

The patriarchs described are marked by puritanism and by the intemperance of the New England climate; their speech and their behavior are proof of this, and refer more or less explicitly to the Bible.[4] Without imagining themselves to be divine incarnations, they think that people should take vital inspiration from Biblical models, forsaking pleasures to do all such good works as the Lord has prepared for them. They impose upon their family circle rules of conduct which they feel to be dictated by God, and are the first to carry them out. If on the emotional level the mother-figure enjoyed indisputable supremacy, in the area of the regulation of the family community, her husband wields the powers of a dictator. In this capacity he becomes, on his own level, an image of the supreme Being, who serves as a guide to those who are under his charge, and who is able to take a firm stand when he feels chastisement to be deserved.

Opposed to this image of an intractable forebear, almost inhuman in his hardness, one finds another aspect of the *pater familias* whose predominant quality is goodness—the word may seem Manichean or condescending but this is by no means true. By "goodness" one must understand a certain awareness of his duty and a desire to bring happiness to his family. This role of the understanding protector appears in *Marco Millions* in which Nicolo, with his brother, accompanies Marco on his initiation voyage, meant to make a perfect tradesman of him.

The model father, as an epitome of self-denial, is staged in *Warnings*; here he is locked in a dilemma resulting from the conflicting interests of his close family and of the company employing him.[5] The fact of being the head of the family divests him of his power to choose, and although he is not presented as a martyr figure, his status as a father becomes a form of destiny against which he cannot fight. Whatever decision he takes will lead to disaster. He is aware of this, and when he measures the consequences of his acts he takes full responsibility for them, committing suicide to atone for his wrongdoing when the boat begins to sink.

In another of O'Neill's earlier plays, *Abortion*, one finds a traditional image of the parental relationship, but one particular aspect deserves our attention. Jack asks for financial help to pay for an abortion, and receives thanks for his frankness.

> TOWNSEND. It shows you regard me not only as a father but as a friend; and that is the way I would have it [*Ab* 156].

A speech like this contrasts sharply with the attitudes of Mannon and others like Light, who are unable to show any indulgence towards their sons. In this extract one notes that Townsend makes an abstraction of his right to judge, and wishes to present himself as a friend; his benevolence is accompanied by a desire for mutual recognition, on an equal basis, which seems to be in total contradiction of the menacing father image which appears in the other works.

In fact, we must avoid being too Manichean in our perception, for these petty dictators are themselves prisoners, be it of their puritanism or of their inability to express feelings. O'Neill often protested against a restrictive reading of his characters, that is, giving to the father, in his partriarchal form, the role of the "villain." *The Rope* is the illustration of this misunderstanding.[6] Bentley tries to express his pleasure, but his efforts are somewhat inconclusive.

> LUKE. On the level, I b'lieve the old boy's glad to see me at that. He looks like he was tryin' to grin; and I never seen him grin in my life, I c'n remember [*Rope* 595].

The moral bonds resulting from puritanical ethics have such strength that it is difficult for Bentley to give vent to his joy, and to express it in a comprehensible way. He is situated halfway between the partriarchs, in whose case the language of the heart has become mummified, or is assigned to codes which make it almost unintelligible,[7] and the fathers, who lend a human dimension to parental relationships.

These men take upon themselves the impossible task of helping their descendants by initiating them to the mysteries of life, but both approaches prove to be equally ineffectual in that ultimately the heirs must run the race alone.

Son images.

> MARY. (*Without conviction*) He'll turn out all right in the end, you wait and see.
> TYRONE. He'd better start soon, then. He's nearly thirty-four [*LDJN* 18].

The son-figures, in the plays, are sometimes adolescents, although this category is not limited to characters in the prime of youth: the deciding factor is their position in the family tree, regardless of age, since some grown men are also defined by their status as sons. Thus, in *Desire Under the Elms*, Simeon, a widower, aged 37, does not introduce himself as an adult person, but as the descendant of Ephraim Cabot.[8] Other protagonists of similar age live under the same roof as their parents; this prolonged cohabitation is a source of conflicts, but on another level it is the sign of their subjection.

The financial dependence which characterizes James Tyrone's children is a sign of their enslavement, and even their ability to make merry is subject to his pleasure. Opulence then becomes a mark of power; the younger generation is always bordering on poverty, begging for a few dollars to gain access to the pleasures of the senses, mainly drunkenness. This poverty emphasizes, if need be, the inferiority of the young. The fact that money is one of the attributes of power is illustrated by the attitude of those characters who look on the inheritance to come, or the stolen savings, as emblematic of their liberation.[9]

Living together is difficult, as regardless of their age the heirs are confined to a role that inhibits their personal development. However, even after the death of their forebears, they do not always find in this event the liberating potential necessary for their development. Indeed, one notes that a single cause can give rise to a variety of consequences. Sometimes the absence of a father is experienced as a lack, thereby symbolizing the impossibility of emancipation; at other times it becomes an obsession, emphasizing the difficulty of this emancipation; in favorable circumstances, by contrast, it can come to the aid of the characters in their search for self-definition.

Father-son relationships.

Disclosures.

> The blind selfishness of parents is appalling, the more appalling because it is prompted by love and excites our sympathy for that reason—thus weaving another of the ties that bind.[10]

One notes, about this tension between affection and selfishness, that the affectionate dimension sometimes yields to the sense of parental duty, which in turn takes a stand against more humane considerations, which would enable them to take the personality of their children into consideration. The desire to act for their good is probably what prompts certain types of behavior; however, this fatherly love, which as has been noted seldom comes to the fore, is far from being the rule and is not evenly distributed.

We have mentioned the sons of Ephraim Cabot who, in spite of their age, were chained to a status that prevented them from dealing with their father on a basis of equality. Their situation is by no means an exception; the struggle in which the descendants are engaged thus proves to be a fight to gain power, financial or moral, or at least to obtain the disclosing of a secret that would place them on an equal footing with their father.

Standing out as a kind of counter-example, the only work in which equality is eventually established between members of the two generations is *Where the Cross Is Made*.[11] Nat is aware of his father's flights of imagination, since he wishes to place him in medical care, but he falls victim to his own weakness, which reveals itself in his readiness to believe in the possibility of making a miraculous fortune. Suddenly his superficial composure disappears, he begins to believe in the existence of the treasure, and in turn sinks into madness. The explanation of this delirium, and of his sudden metamorphosis, lies in the disclosing of a cursed piece of knowledge, occurring on completion of an initiation period, when the right to know is bestowed upon him ("NAT. One day my father sent for me and in the presence of the others told me the dream. I was to be heir to the secret" [*WCIM* 560]).

Nat describes an enrollment ritual which marks his change; when Bartlett judges him to be trustworthy, Nat puts an end to his childhood and attains an adulthood characterized by the discovery of what had been concealed. This discovery is all the more atypical, as in the other cases the family structure opposes itself to such internal evolutions. Becoming heir to the mystery, he becomes a reprobate, which condition he will not manage to escape, and when the two characters appear in the last scene, their former differences fade away, their common points prevail and they become equals in madness.[12]

The role of the protective father holding an undisclosable secret has induced a reign of silence which has proved destructive for the protagonists; ultimately it emerges that for the common good the whole truth must be disclosed, without any concealment.[13] Bartlett's trust, when he admits to having lied ("BARTLETT. And I lied to ye, boy" [*Gold* 691]), shows that an exchange is possible between the two men, and the ensuing communion symbolizes a return to peace.

The motif of malefic riches and cursed secrets is reminiscent of an episode described in *Long Day's Journey into Night*, in which Edmund learns that his mother is a drug-addict; in each case, the importance of the discovery is such that the generation conflict, which had hitherto been a focal point, is thrown into the background.

> EDMUND. It was right after that... Papa and Jamie decided they couldn't hide it from me any more. Jamie told me. I called him a liar! I tried to punch him in the nose. But I knew he wasn't lying. (*His voice trembles, his eyes begin to fill with tears.*) God, it made everything in life seem rotten! [*LDJN* 118].

His brother, a substitute father-figure, reveals to him the extent of their mother's guilt; but to know means to die, and they are all too weak to fight, which is why they turn into ghosts (the four haunted Tyrones). From this point of view, the father or his substitute-figure are perceived as destructive elements, with an unnatural role, for the initiation rites they institute are in fact killings.

The revelation of these mysteries to the sons can be compared to a vampire's kiss; they are permanently branded as members of a group from which they never manage to escape. The disclosure utterly destroys them; they are broken forever, and are reincarnated into a world of damned creatures, in which the family hierarchy is perpetuated, although the conflict of generations no longer matters.

Rejection.

If signs of confidence give rise to fresh wounds, what attitude should the elders adopt towards their heirs? Some characters choose indifference, which is the least brutal form taken by the absence of fatherly love, and some, imprisoned in doubts about their existence, or in suffering, rule out the parental status which they are unable to assume. The explanation of their behavior is given in *The Great God Brown,* in which Dion Anthony can only show his real face to Cybel, a prostitute. She discovers a human being where others saw only a mask and denied it or him any specific existence. This lack of recognition leads him to flee from a world which grants him no more than a semblance of life. This is why he pays no attention to his sons ("MARGARET. I wish you'd try to take more interest in the children, Dion" [*GGB* 270]); his situation as a father covers a social reality which means nothing to him since it corresponds in no way to his real personality. By his lack of interest, and by refusing a role that society imposes upon him, Dion becomes a figure of absence: By this token he would deserve to be mentioned on the list of dead parents.

A more common form of rejection is that due to selfishness on the part of the father, which becomes manifest when money matters are at stake. In *Long Day's Journey into Night,* for example, James Tyrone refuses to pay the price for Edmund's recovery and to send him to a renowned sanatorium[14]; he justifies his stinginess in two ways. He has a fear of ending his life in a poorhouse and, without saying so, he is convinced that tuberculosis is an incurable disease and therefore does not wish to spend money unnecessarily. His miserliness is all the more vehemently condemned by Edmund and Jamie for not being motivated by any lack of money. It is the indisputable proof of his selfishness, since he spends identical amounts on buying land.[15]

These marks of egocentricity, or of indifference, are hurtful for those who suffer from them. They generally give rise to violent differences of opinion, for this type of behavior indirectly ties in with what we noted in connection with the denial of existence, the son's death appearing unimportant compared to the parents' comfort.

Generational conflicts are not an inherent part of the characters' destinies. In *Beyond the Horizon* harmony reigns at the beginning of the play, for Andrew is designated as his father's successor. Nothing comes to mar the family unity, for the characters are bound to the earth, and this tie is the sign of a certain sense of belonging which gives meaning to their lives. After an emotional disappointment, Andrew claims to have lost all taste for farming and then announces his departure. James Mayo cannot bear this lie, for it reveals Andrew's inability to control his feelings, which leads Andrew to break away from his true nature: This is why Mayo disowns him.

> MAYO. Yes,—go!—go!—You're no son o' mine—no son o' mine! You can go to hell if you want to! [*BH* 108].

Mayo finds it unacceptable that a member of the clan should allow himself to be led by his feelings, for they break the tie between man and nature.

To his mind, affirming one's existence as a sufferer is nonsensical since it implies denying one's true character. The denial of one's roots contravenes the latent puritanical doctrine whereby man should offer himself wholly to nature. The gift of oneself thus guarantees one's belonging, which gives meaning to life ("CABOT. When ye kin make corn sprout out o' stones, God's livin' in yew!" [*DE* 236]). Mayo's reaction is all the more violent as Andrew embodied both his double and an ideal man, whose transgression endangers a world in which harmony once reigned.

Andrew's denial and departure are unique acts; fury is only let loose *once*, unlike the other plays, in which verbal aggressions are repetitive. We observe a reverse movement to that which we mentioned above, i.e., a "good" father turns into an intractable patriarch and disowns and banishes his son.[16] Indifference sometimes, disappointment or selfishness more often—the motives which prompt the parents' acts are variable, but the antagonism is such that in most cases hate ultimately prevails.

> CABOT. I lived with the boys. They hated me 'cause I was hard. I hated them 'cause they was soft [*DE* 238].

In the course of this study we have noted that the possibilities of escape were very limited; the family space is therefore frequently transformed into a closed battlefield, where the two generations are engaged in a duel whose aim is the "death" of the other. The arms used are generally words; they wound, but are not deadly, and the conflicts draw painfully on, as none of the parties can escape.

An episode in *Desire Under the Elms* symbolizes this relentless combat, when Cabot strangles Eben, before Abbie asks for his mercy. For each party, the struggles are an attempt at self-assertion. They generally achieve nothing more than the upholding of the *status quo* and confirm filial enslavement. Furthermore, the omnipotent *pater familias* refuses to accept that his children should be less resistant and less powerful than himself, for their weakness is a sign that they have lost the deep awareness of the harmony binding them to a very harsh natural element, from which they were to take example.[17] On the strength of these austere principles, the fathers experience their sons' weakness as a betrayal. These strong men condemn all those who fall, and are implacable towards their heirs, whom they treat as slaves.

The violence of the antagonism reveals the fierceness of an instinct whose existence the characters themselves had not suspected. *A priori*, the young male is an object of dread, for there is a risk that he may steal the wife from her husband; this latent threat is not a mere figment of the imagination, it becomes reality when the woman dies giving birth to a son (in, for instance, *A Moon for the Misbegotten* and *The First Man*). This case is an extreme example, but a revealing one, for it partly explains the anguish felt by the patriarch, and the resentment he shows towards his descendants.

In the triangular relationship that is set up, the mother is a source of conflict, and the father's aggressive behavior can be explained in terms of the attention the children receive. They are perceived as direct rivals, the difference between love within the married couple and parental love being of little importance, for the husband claims all the mother's attention, if not all her love.[18] Jealousy gives rise to a deadly struggle in which the fathers show their basest qualities and try to reduce the younger generation to silence in order to secure their wives' exclusive affection.

> LIGHT. When I read them, I realized that Amelia had been thinking of you all the time. And I felt betrayed! I hated her and you! I was insane with hatred! God forgive me! [*Dy* 465].

As in many other cases in which the protagonists are jealous of one other, one notes here that when conflicts break out, a constant back-and-forth movement is set up between verbal violence and begging for pardon, as though the fathers were unable to live to the full their roles as killers. In Light's case it is in some way the voice of God which imposes self-restraint upon him; as for Tyrone, his fatherly instinct repeatedly surfaces, and makes him take back the hurtful remarks he makes to Jamie and Edmund whom, in spite of everything, he cannot help loving ("TYRONE. ... You're no great shakes as a son. It's a case of 'A poor thing but mine own'" [*LDJN* 143]).

The plays we have studied give an archetypal image of the father-son relationships, in which relations between the dominated and the dominator are considered immutable within a family structure which confines the younger generation to infantilism. The "good" father rapidly disappears, leaving the inflexible patriarch, who appears as a powerful, dominating person, visiting destruction upon his descendants, whom he considers as rivals. However, even in the most violent conflicts, the characters are held back by an instinct which prevents them from carrying their acts to fulfillment. Indeed, the father's role does not consist in killing the son but in reducing him to silence, and then in ensuring that he does not develop as a human being, so as to keep him in the limbo of existence.

Son-father relationships.

Confronted with a type of behavior characterized by permanent aggressiveness, the younger generation's reactions are often very violent. If they were able, the young would put up a merciless struggle.[19]

> SIMEON. Ye'd oughtn't t' said that, Eben.
> PETER. 'T wa'n't righteous.
> EBEN. What?

3. *Relations Between the Characters.*   43

SIMEON. Ye prayed he'd died.
EBEN. Waal—don't yew pray it? (*a pause.*)
PETER. He's our Paw [*DE* 206].

This exchange between Eben and his brothers illustrates the two ways in which the sons appear in the works. Firstly, Eben considers that Ephraim is responsible for his mother's death and, more generally, for the sufferings of those around him, which explains why his resentment is so strong; secondly, Simeon and Peter feel that a more moderate judgment should be passed on the head of the family, for he adheres faithfully to principles whose validity they do not question. These positions are in fact gradable: Some abhor their forebears, while others cannot bring themselves to hate them.[20]

In the preceding part, we emphasized the violence of the feelings of hatred felt by the patriarchs towards their male descendants. The first example, in time, is provided by Mannon who, right from the birth of Orin, admits having to make an effort not to hate him. Conversely, the children adopt a type of behavior which will be a response to the father's attitude, for they assert themselves as victims of destructive oppression. They execrate their parent and justify themselves through reference to the way in which they have been mistreated.

One of the ways of avoiding lethal confrontations is to develop dodging strategies. Some understand that their elders wish to confine them to inferior roles which inhibit their development, and therefore react accordingly. One of the ways to find freedom, as noted above, was exile. In *Where the Cross Is Made*, the situation is distinctive: Nat tries to step into ownership of the property by having Bartlett interned, so as to be permanently rid of a parental figure who stifles and destroys him. This is a variation of the usual procedure, in which the son's escape leaves the partriarch master of the land.

If in some cases flight momentarily marks the end of a deadly struggle, some protagonists refuse to surrender, and opt for insubordination. Before launching into battle, some express a desire for freedom, which often turns out to be a declaration of hate toward the father. Commenting on Nat's words, in *Where the Cross Is Made*, Gabriela Szigeti says:

> "NAT. I do hate him!" This is the cry of expressionism, the cry of revolt against parental authority—against all authority. It expresses the will to break free, and the desire to be oneself.[21]

One cannot but concur with the idea of rebellion, but the "revolt against all authority" is less obvious. Thus, in the words qualified by James Tyrone as "anarchist" ("TYRONE. Keep your damned anarchists remarks to yourself. I won't have them in my house" [*LDJN* 24]), one should read, I feel, more of a denial of parental values than a real challenge leveled against institutions.[22] Moreover, one must not lose sight of the fact that the struggle takes place within the family, in a closed space, and that the perception the protagonists have of the outside world is of less importance than the cherished victory, upon which hang their very lives. The sons attack what they feel symbolizes their parent's beliefs, hoping in this way to wound him. It will later be shown that these attacks are mainly symbolic, and they are all too elated by their duels to take any real interest in the various forms of institutional oppression or in social evolution.

By leading this struggle against an emasculating authority, the descendants hope to rid themselves of an inhibiting ancestor. The total war waged between the two sides leaves little room for chivalrous speeches, and both parties express their feelings in a very crude way.

> TYRONE. You ought to be glad you've got him for a father. Mine was an old bastard.
> JOSIE. He wasn't! He was one of the finest, kindest gentlemen ever lived.
> TYRONE. (*Sneeringly*) Outside the family, sure. Inside, he was a lousy tightwad bastard.
> JOSIE. (*Repelled*) You ought to be ashamed!
> TYRONE. To speak ill of the dead? Nuts! He can't hear, and he knows I hated him, anyway—as much as he hated me [*MMis* 83].

One response to aggression is bitterness: This defense strategy is adopted by the heirs who wish to assert themselves. By taking the offensive, they abandon their defensive position and strive to render eye for eye and tooth for tooth. The causes of the fathers' rejection have already been expounded, and we shall not come back to this point, but we must note that they give rise to various strategies of resistance which in turn spark hostility. The characters have no illusions as to their antagonists' feelings; nothing remains unsaid, even if hurtful words are often followed by begging forgiveness, which may mark a truce but very often does little more than prepare the next onslaught.

The conflict between the two generations ends in the stripping away of false pretenses; each party knows when the other is lying or deluding himself, and these confrontations lead to the lowering of the protective masks. The family circle becomes the stage of sordid revelations, where clashes bring to light intolerable truths. A cascade of verbal violence ensues, the ignobility of the fathers towards their sons is unmasked, and the strategies employed leave no place for pity, for each one hopes to be able to deal the final blow.

Eben (*Desire Under the Elms*) and Luke (*The Rope*) stand as exceptions, for we noted that they were prepared to fight the battle to its bitter end, coldly contemplating their father's death. As concerns the other characters, we observe, as in the case of the patriarchs, that the sons are unable to carry the struggle to its end. In the part dealing with the imprisoned person, we showed how the sons became the doubles of their fathers: they try vainly to free themselves from the image of the patriarch, which projects back to them a slightly deformed portrait of themselves, which they find difficult to assume; when the father leaves, they undergo a change and, as there is no longer any need for distances to be kept, they draw closer to the deceased.

The most outstanding phenomenon is in *Mourning Becomes Electra*, in which O'Neill insists in the stage directions that the resemblance between Mannon and Orin should be even more marked after the former's death.[23] As they are aware of this shared identity, even if almost unconsciously, the descendants are never able to fulfill their desire for death.[24] A reflection of themselves prevents them from appeasing their thirst for vengeance, for they sense that, in a certain way, they would be killing themselves.[25] Even though they refuse to acquit him, they nevertheless consider that their father is no more than a man, unable to control himself or to change his true nature, and therefore cannot be held completely responsible for his behavior. In spite of the many grudges he holds against James Tyrone, Edmund is the one who proves to be the most lenient ("EDMUND. I'm like Mama, I can't help liking you in spite of everything" [*LDJN* 142]). He stands at the opposite pole from Eben, who epitomizes filial hatred, and shows here the limits that are set to the affection which can bind together members of these two *a priori* antagonistic groups.

Granting forgiveness demands of those concerned such moral force and magnanimity as very few find within themselves. Indeed, what is challenged, for the heirs, is their very existence; faced with such stakes, one may appreciate their reluctance to show any leniency.

> MARSDEN. ... his voice had withdrawn so far away... I couldn't understand him... what son can ever understand? ...always too near, too soon, too distant or too late! [*SI* 4].

Reconciliation is all the more difficult to achieve as forgiveness presupposes an understanding of the other person's attitude, and the principles which led him to act in such a way. Although these are not necessarily different from the rules chosen by the younger generation, its members are imprisoned within their struggle, and seldom find points of convergence. One fact emerges clearly: the filial status immures them as individuals and prevents them from asserting themselves as people. In order to fight against this confinement of their existence, the sons are obliged to enter into conflict with their fathers, who try to keep them in their inferior roles, using various coercive methods; this is why the sons define themselves in terms of retaliation to the fathers' aggressions. Their feelings oscillate between aversion and compassion; the characters strive to find some common meeting-ground, but the inexpressible quality of their emotions, and their tactlessness, pave the way for a fresh onslaught of hatred. Genuine exchanges, which lead to family harmony, prove to be impossible, for nobody succeeds in finding the right distance to observe. The main obstacle is the pulling down of the masks, for the conflicts reveal the true face of each person, and this laying bare is in itself too destructive for the person who brought it about to be forgiven.

Daughter images.

Apart from the child who appears in *Beyond the Horizon*, the daughters in the plays are in their late adolescence, or are already young women. Unlike what we described in the case of the sons, they are not exclusively defined by their status as daughters. They are undoubtedly considered the offspring of their fathers, but their situation is particular because of their belonging to the second sex, which excludes them from the line of inheritance and also from the conflicts which permanently oppose the patriarchs to their male heirs, the origin of which can be traced to a desire for possession, which is an obstacle to the males' harmonious relations. Moreover, in many of O'Neill's works, the daughter could legitimately claim to belong to both generations, since she replaces the absent mother and thus becomes the mistress of the household (See *Gold*, *A Moon for the Misbegotten*, *The Rope*, *Strange Interlude*, *The Straw*, and *Where the Cross Is Made*.)

The place ascribed to them cannot be defined well; nevertheless, the simple fact that they are able to stand in as substitute mother figures indicates that their presence is not negligible.

The importance of O'Neill's female characters vary but they are not relegated to minor roles; thus, in *Mourning Becomes Electra*, *Anna Christie*, *A Moon for the Misbegotten*, and *Strange Interlude*, the heroines play leading roles.

Father-daughter relationships.

We shall not come back to the image of the father, insofar as what was said in the first part is still applicable; the difference, when it appears, will be felt in the extent to which it affects the relationships the fathers entertain with their female descendants, which have but few points in common with what we have described up to this point.

The only instance in which one might believe that the relation which springs up between the two generations could follow the pattern described between father and son is in *The Rope*. Annie has doubts about Bentley's understanding, and when she introduces herself to him, he rejects her and denies her the status of a daughter, for he judges her unworthy of him.

ANNIE. This is Annie—your Annie, Paw.
BENTLEY. (*Bursting into a senile rage*) None o' mine! [*Rope* 580].

The only heir he recognizes is Luke, who has left the farm after having stolen part of his father's savings. In spite of this misdeed, which ought to disqualify him in Bentley's eyes, the father persists in his love; as for Annie, she is cast aside from the beginning, and will never be able to claim her share of the estate. One finds, here, indirectly, an echo of one of the rules laid down by Cabot, when his new wife expresses the hope of owning the farm after his death: This unwritten rule requires that the estate should pass into the hands of a member of the clan, who must be a male. Annie's words are part of a whole, and one notes the appearance of signs of misogyny in the plays, consisting in ascribing a particular status, often inferior, to members of the female sex.[26] However, these material considerations should not allow us to forget that on other levels, that of emotions for example, women are given a first-rate position, and hence become superior to men.

When conflicts do arise, they take a different form from that described until this point. We noted, in the father-son relationships, how both parties were caught up in a chain of conflict generated by the inability of the patriarchs and their descendants to find a *modus vivendi* that would allow each person to live without attacking the other. The father-daughter relationships also give rise to conflicts, but the elders then find themselves in a defensive situation.[27] In these confrontations, contrary to what the preceding remarks may lead one to believe, the daughters take the upper hand; they are bearers of truth, and they sometimes speak out the unacceptable, whether they be Anna, Nina, or even Sara, who, in *A Touch of the Poet,* brings to light realities which are denied because they are too disconcerting. In each case, the fathers try to avoid a devastating confrontation, for this pulls down the masks.

There is a striking contrast between the powerlessness of the fathers when they are confronted by their daughters and the implacable hardness they show towards their sons. This ability to bring to light the innermost shortcomings of each of these victims, thus bringing about their downfall, characterizes the women. Assailed by their speech, the man becomes a defenseless creature, and shows his inmost self with all the consequences this entails. Unlike the aggressions of the male heirs, which were destructive but were part of an unending struggle, the words uttered by the women have such power that some characters,[28] like Melody, beg for mercy so as to avert the total collapse of their world.

> MELODY. (*Has been visibly crumbling as he listens until he appears to have no character left in which to hide and defend himself. He cries wildly and despairingly, as if he saw his last hope of escape suddenly cut off*) Sara! For the love of God, stop—let me go! [*TP* 178].

If one wishes to discover a global view of this particular aspect of the relationships between the generations, a study covering only the subjects of discord would hardly suffice; while in the father-son exchanges these were the dominant feature, this is not at all the case in the father-daughter relationships. A significant example is staged in *Beyond the Horizon*, in which the links which unite Robert and Mary symbolize ideal communion between two beings, a rarity in the works of O'Neill. Even if it is not always in the forefront (compare *Where the Cross Is Made* and *Gold*), parental affection seems to be inherent to fatherhood; thus, when Chris and Anna meet, in *Anna Christie*, Chris is moved and his attitude suggests that there is a sort of innate attachment of the father for his daughter—"CHRIS. (*Grasps her arms and looks into her face—then overcome by a wave of fierce tenderness*) Anna Lilla! Anna Lilla! (*Takes her in his arms.*)" (*AC* 20)—although he has hardly ever seen her. One notes furthermore that the paternal strain is strong enough to override the revelation of the misfortune which befalls Anna, and her past life as a prostitute does not lead him to disown her; quite to the contrary.

In *A Moon for the Misbegotten*, Hogan gives another example of this, for he does all he can to promote the union of Josie and James Tyrone and their future happiness; the strength of his feelings and his self-denial can be appreciated when, bringing up the subject of Josie's departure, which she had brandished as a threat after his fruitless manœuvres, he says:

> HOGAN. (*His face lights up joyfully. He is almost himself again—ruefully*) You had me punished, that's sure. I was thinking after you'd gone I'd drown myself in Harder's ice pond [*MMis* 114].

Josie is very dear to him, and his undertakings, which were to lead to her marriage with James Tyrone, are all the more praiseworthy as he dreads being left alone when she is gone. Indeed, all these patriarchs, presented as pillars of strength, are balanced by the presence of their women descendants, to whom they have left the leading role, that of the mother, thus giving to them the status of mistresses of the household.

Without questioning the authenticity of paternal love, one cannot but note that it is not exclusively governed by altruistic motives. As the fathers grow old, they fear solitude, and are all the more appreciative of this feminine attendance by their sides, as it will be a support to them in the days of their old age. (Carmody's chief worry, in *The Straw*, is not Eileen's illness, but his uncertainty as to who is to keep house for him, as he is a widower.) Even those who seem strongest need this womanly presence, with which they can be in harmony, and which can break the solitude that sometimes seems like a God-sent punishment.

The other person's understanding is what the fathers long for, and they find it quite naturally among the women members of the clan. This is why some grasp desperately at what seems to be their last chance of happiness. Thus, in *Strange Interlude*, Professor Leeds admits having selfishly prevented Nina from having a liaison with Gordon Shaw.[29] A similar speech can be heard in *Anna Christie* ("CHRIS. Ay'm gatting ole. Ay gat no one in vold but you" [*AC* 22]); in each case the fear of growing old alone emerges. As for the relationship they anticipate, it is primarily a protective one, for the fathers are in quest of a form of protection which brings back the image of the mother.

The absence of a companion creates an agonizing emptiness for the husband (see *Anna Christie, Gold, A Moon for the Misbegotten, The Rope, Strange Interlude, The Straw*, and *Where the Cross Is Made*). This probably contributes to confirming the idea that the women descendants do not replace the wife but become substitute mother figures. According to Judith Barlow, this paradoxical view of the links which develop between the two generations can be explained in terms of a sort of projection of the playwright himself onto the characters he creates.

> For the most part, O'Neill's female characters are perceived from outside, from a masculine perspective that wishfully invests them with powerful maternal desires or condemns them for the lack of such feelings.[30]

In fact, this point of view reveals the limits of the playwright's supposed misogyny, for the women (in this case, the daughters) are strong characters, supporting weakened partriarchs.

Some parents content themselves with this *modus vivendi*. If they lay down arms, they benefit, in return, from the services of a protective spirit who establishes a barrier between themselves and the world, and places them, or has the power to do so, in a cocoon from which they do not wish to emerge. Mannon, who has experienced beforehand what the others are to go through at a later stage, has no illusions about his situation as a husband. In the affection shown by Lavinia he sees no more than an incomplete substitute for what a marital relationship should be ("MANNON. I turned to Vinnie, but a daughter's not a wife" [*MBE, Homecoming* 55]). However, this companionship is not negligible, because it enables him to break the unbearable solitude of his life.

The fathers are generally on good terms with their daughters, and willingly grant them a special status. They recognize their difference, and seek their presence, hoping to find in their company a form of moral support which resembles the lost love of a mother. We observed that the patriarchs relegated their male heirs to positions of infantilism, but here we witness quite the reverse phenomenon. The men appear as fragile beings, anxious at all costs to avoid clashes, for they sense beforehand that they will not emerge victorious. However, even if they prove to be incapable of confronting these young women,[31] it is not solely through cowardice that they try to live on good terms with them; it is also because they are very attached to them.

Daughter-father relationships.

The feelings which the women descendants have for their fathers vary greatly and cannot be studied within a single frame. In *Mourning Becomes Electra,* for example, Lavinia embodies the character of Electra; her admiration for Mannon is boundless, and her devotion confines her to her role as a daughter, preventing her from defining herself in her own right. When Peter returns from the war and asks for her hand, her refusal is irrevocable; her answer implies that her status as a daughter has priority over her womanhood, which is tantamount to denying her very existence.

> LAVINIA. I can't marry anyone, Peter. I've got to stay home. Father needs me.
> PETER. He's got your mother.
> LAVINIA. (*Sharply*). He needs me more! [*MBE, Homecoming* 14].

Lavinia defines her position in terms of duty; from an emotional point of view, which is in fact the essential one, their relations are governed by different laws, which are not entirely of the playwright's creation. Indeed, this trilogy shows signs of the influence of Freud, of whom O'Neill had read a few works[32]; as for the relation presented between Lavinia and her father, it describes an Electra complex, which here follows the same pattern as the Oedipus complex.[33]

We have mentioned above the very strong links which bound Robert Mayo to his child. The affection they felt for each other was mutual. This is why, when he mentions the possibility of going away, Mary begs him to stay. Needing the other person is not a one-way notion; if the women descendants find themselves in a position to lend support to their elders, the reverse can also occur. The case just quoted is not an isolated one, and one observes, in another play, that this absence sometimes has dramatic consequences ("ANNA. If you'd even had been a regular father and had me with you—maybe things would be different" [*AC* 58]).

Anna, in *Anna Christie*, explains how she was quite alone in the world and, without throwing all the blame on the parents' absence, she intimates that the parental support she so keenly missed might have saved her from becoming a prostitute. These three protagonists associated with childhood[34] illustrate the importance of the father figure to them, for it means protection, which they feel, or have once felt, to be vitally necessary.

Between the daughters who express their need for security, and those who are called upon to act as mothers towards their fathers, one finds characters who are in conflict with their fathers. For various reasons, this parent obstructs their emancipation, and prevents them from living their lives as they see fit.

3. Relations Between the Characters. 51

> NINA. (*Her voice becoming a bit uncanny, her thoughts breaking through*) No, I'm not myself yet. That's just it. Not all myself. But I've been becoming myself. And I must finish [*SI* 18].

Nina expresses here what Ada (in *Dynamo*) could claim about her romantic preferences, or Lucy (in *Now I Ask You*) concerning her social views. Unlike the situation we observed in studying the male branch, the patriarchs are here considered harmless opponents, with little inclination for battle. With few exceptions, the conflicts never reach violent proportions; the characters are shown growing up, and the periods of conflict, during which they clash with their parents, are shown to be a necessary stage of their inner transformation.

The only daughter in whom hate prevails is Sara, who, even after Con Melody's death, keeps within herself an image from which she never manages to get free.[35] Here one observes a relationship equivalent to that which opposed the patriarchs to their sons. In fact, the liberating process is relatively easy for these young women, who do not find any real opposition to their asserting themselves as people.

We have already noted the importance of the departed mothers; their absence is not without consequence for the daughters' status. In many works, young women are required to replace their mothers, and they are consequently ascribed a special place within the family structure.[36] In six plays (*A Moon for the Misbegotten, Gold, Strange Interlude, The Rope, The Straw* and *Where the Cross Is Made*), they are called upon to preside over the destinies of their homes, and in three of these plays, the head of the family appears to have lost his reason (*Gold, The Rope,* and *Where the Cross Is Made*). They apply themselves to their task with devotion, and become the uncontested mistresses of the homes under their charge.[37] An indisputable proof of this is given by Hogan, the patriarch who is hated by his sons, dreaded by his neighbors, but unable to dominate Josie.

The study of the daughter-father relationships leads us to put forward a few remarks. They are, on the whole, characterized by strong affection, which is not monolithic and which alternates between companionship and compassion. When the father stands in the way of his daughter's inner liberation or the development of her personality, he is destroyed; whatever the case, his presence seldom endangers the well-being of the cherished daughter.

When childhood is over, the daughters accept the new role which is thrust upon them by circumstances, and find themselves with family responsibilities without having procreated, as though for young women the maternal instinct prevailed over any other feeling. This presupposition is of prime importance in the works, where the mother's place erases the woman's, and where, as we noted for the grandmothers, the appending of a maternal dimension to the daughters denies them a status of their own.

Mother images.

To give an image of the mother in O'Neill's plays is to attempt the impossible. Her influence surpasses the frame of her function, which itself imperfectly accounts for the radiance that characterizes her and that stretches far beyond the limits imposed on her in the normal family edifice. The family, such as we have defined it up to this point, consists of three poles, a patriarch, the descendants, and the mother, whose presence is indispensable for the harmony of the groups who appear on stage. With her husband, she belongs to, and sides with, the elder generation, emphasizing the time gap which separates them from their descendants; it is hardly possible, however to infer from this that she should be identified with her husband, who, as has been noted, is characterized by a number of quite distinctive features having no bearing upon those of his wife. We shall see at a later stage that, although she occupies a fairly well-defined place in the communal hierarchy, any attempt to limit her importance to her visible power would be to underestimate her real strength.

Her position is an essential one since, in the O'Neillian vision, she has the monopoly of fertility, the male branch being almost totally absent from the vital process. (If one excepts the bawdy jokes of *Desire Under the Elms* and *Strange Interlude*, no allusion is made to it.) Her first mission, far surpassing her duties as a wife or her right to life as a woman, making the essential choices of existence herself, consists in ensuring the continuity of generations by giving birth to a son, who will be able to take over the name, the farm, or the other parts of the estate which are his rightful possessions.[38] Without dwelling, at this stage, on the links which develop between the different members of the community and the all-important figure who stands at its center, we must note that the mother is presented primarily as she who has actually given birth to descendants, or who has the power to do so.

> ABBIE. I want a son now.
> CABOT. (*Excitedly clutching both of her hands in his*) It'd be the blessin' o' God, Abbie—the blessin' o' God A'mighty on me—in my old age—in my lonesomeness! They ain't nothin' I wouldn't do fur ye then, Abbie. Ye'd hev on'y t'ask it—anythn' ye'd a mind t'! [*DE* 235].

Cabot, whom many associate with the image of an intractable patriarch, is prepared to submit to all of Abbie's desires, on condition that she give him a son. In the course of the play, we learn that he has not always shown such tenderness towards his wives, once they had given him heirs. However, in spite of the occasional hardness of some husbands, one notes that through motherhood a special place is granted to those who give birth: they acquire a sort of divine aura, in the sense that they are likened to the earth, whose produce provides men with a livelihood. (It is probably not by chance that Cabot makes comparisons which stress this aspect: "CABOT. Yer belly be like a heap o' wheat" [*DE* 232].)

This particular point of view, in which joy is associated with motherhood, is not the exclusive privilege of outside characters, who would not be capable of evaluating the person's reactions, and would simply apply a series of presuppositions to women of an age to have children. In *The First Man*, Martha presents her desire to procreate as a vital necessity. When they return from abroad, her life seems devoid of any real interest. The fact of not having any descendants goes against a deep inner need and therefore constitutes a denial of her personality. This is why she breaks the pact she made with her husband after the death of their two little girls, and decides to have a child. Between the time when she makes her decision and its materialization, she undergoes a change; the unsatisfied longing disappears, leaving her with the certainty of having achieved a purpose, and this generates a feeling of elation, which she had hardly suspected before, springing up in the desire to become a mother.

In *Strange Interlude*, a pregnant Nina shares her thoughts with the audience; these tie in with what we noted about the divine character of conception, and with the sense of fulfillment associated with the fact of giving life.

> NINA. (*She settles back and stares dreamily before her—a pause*) There... again... his child!... my child moving in my life... my life moving in my child... ... suspended in the movement of the tide, I feel life move in me, suspended in me... no whys matter... there is no why... I am a mother... God is a Mother [*SI* 92].

Any addition to this seems superfluous, after declaring such access to the divine through motherhood. In fact, reality is more complex than it would seem from Nina's thoughts, for after childbirth the women return to a more direct contact with society. This does not necessarily mean a break in the state of grace, but its continuation is not automatic. This is why I propose to study the image of mothers after they have given birth to heirs, and not during the preparatory phases described up to this point.

In general, the mothers are wives (their status can undergo change, but what we postulate is true, from the first scene, except in *All God's Chillun Got Wings*, *Diff'rent*, and *The Iceman Cometh*) and they are not necessarily crushed by the strength of the patriarchs,[39] although this does sometimes occur. If their place is indisputably with the older generation, this in no way implies that they should be replicas or extensions of their husbands. In the absolute, they ought to be complementary counterparts of their spouses; some of them do achieve this, thereby guaranteeing the family's harmony, alleviating differences of opinion, and temporarily hushing the conflicts which spring up between other members of the clan, thus bringing about short but redeeming spells of serenity within relationships which are sometimes problematic.[40]

One is aware of the strength of money and its importance in the plays, for it is associated with both power and corruption. One observes that the women are excluded from this aspect, and do not have this asset at their disposal in their relations with those around them. (When women are associated with money, it is generally linked with an inheritance of which they have been bereft—in *Desire Under the Elms* and *The Rope*—or they are practically penniless—*Fog, Recklessness, A Wife for a Life*.) Sara is the only woman who escapes this rule, forsaking her role as a mother to take over the management of Simon's financial empire, but this example is an exception: in the last act, Sara understands how wrong she has been, and resumes the role she had abandoned.

It would be a mistake to construe, in this part of O'Neill's work, an avant-garde view of the feminine condition. The women's place is in the home, and the dissimilarity between them and the patriarchs is both recognized and stressed. Although they do not wield the arms that contribute to the reinforcement of the patriarchs' authority, they are endowed with a special aura, which is not of the same nature as their husbands' but which is of much greater importance.

We shall at a later stage study the hold O'Neill's women have over those around them, and the potential influence they exert on the various characters, according to the position of each one in the hierarchy. At this stage, we shall simply note that they stand for a kind of moral authority, which serves as a foundation for the whole community. Metaphor always provides restrictive views, but if we choose the image of a building, we can advance the thought that the mother is one of the principal pillars of the family structure, although her function is not limited to this; she is also the mortar which cements the whole, allowing those who belong to it to spread out within its walls.

If in a previous section we mentioned the absence of the mother, and the disastrous consequences this had on the other members of the clan, we must also mention those mothers who, although present, cannot serve as reliable references for those around them. The downfall of the mother, and her inability to fulfill her role towards her children in a satisfactory manner, has dire consequences. One calls to mind plays like *Long Day's Journey into Night, The Iceman Cometh*, or *Mourning Becomes Electra*, for example, which show how the smooth running of the family depends on the qualities of the mothers. On the other hand, one could cite a large number of mother figures who, from *Now I Ask You* to *A Touch of the Poet*, by their devotion and their understanding, lessen the impact of the aggressions to which the members of the group are exposed. This aspect is generally overlooked by critics, and I feel there are two reasons for this: The commonplace aspect of their status as wives and model mothers provides little ground for comments, and their influence is only truly felt once they are affected by some existential disorder. Indeed, their great numbers and the positive power they hold are pushed into the background, and one does not fully realize what strength they wield in everyday life, until it deviates and they become destructive elements.

Mother-son relationships.

We briefly mentioned these relationships at the beginning of our study of the family, and at this point we shall simply retain the essential factors that enable us to show the nature of the links existing between the two generations. Without trying to minimize the eschatological dimension of O'Neill's writing—one indeed recalls that he claimed to be chiefly interested in man's relation to God—one cannot but recognize that the link which binds sons to their mothers, or to substitute mother figures, is of capital importance in his work. The place occupied by maternal love in the plays is far from negligible. It is staged with varying degrees of intensity, but from the situations presented on stage one cannot infer that mothers always love their sons. The grading of the strength of this attachment is decisive, not only within the frame of the exchanges between the two characters in question, but also for the way in which they conduct their lives.

> CHRISTINE. I feel you are really—my flesh and blood! She isn't. She is your father's! You're part of me! [*MBE, The Hunted* 85].

Christine Mannon declares how dear Orin is to her; this is a common phenomenon ("MRS. MAYO. You've never had any children. You don't know what it means to be parted from them" [*BH* 96]), and these characters weave protective cocoons around their sons; this reminds one of the fathers' domination because it is another way of confining them to a filial status. They do not all, however, nurture the same feelings towards their offspring, and Christine's words should not be taken as indisputable proof of what is actually true. Her speech stands against a background of struggle between two conflicting interests, her own and those of Lavinia, who has taken up her father's colors. In fact, Christine's words go amiss, for they correspond to a bygone sentimental situation, valid before Orin left for the war, but obsolete since her passion for Adam Brant. She involuntarily explicates the discrepancy between her words and her real thoughts, thus showing how much precaution should be taken concerning the treatment of her message. (In *Strange Interlude* the discrepancy between what is said and what is thought will emerge even more clearly.)

One also observes how the roles evolve according to the ages of the heirs, who are not obliged to engage a merciless struggle to obtain their freedom.

The affection remains, but the mothers are aware that they must inevitably drift away—this is the price exacted by the passage of time (compare the epilogue to *The Great God Brown*).

> NINA. He's not my son now, nor Gordon's, nor Sam's, nor Ned's... He has become that stranger, another woman's lover [*SI* 190].

In fact, even if Nina seems to accept this verdict with stoicism, she only manages to make this point of view her own after having fought with all her might to maintain sentimental supremacy. The reaction of possessive mothers therefore proves to be more complex than it appears, and time undoubtedly has a great influence on the way their relations develop, but it is not the only factor which should be retained.

Before accepting the loss of sovereignty over Gordon's heart, Nina fought a hard battle to keep him to herself. The filial dimension was still important, but in the case we have just quoted, one notes that what emerges and prevails at a certain time is her reaction as a woman, refusing to relinquish her central position. At the beginning, in their selfishness, they wish to organize their children's happiness around themselves, which is why they are prepared to go to any lengths to eliminate their rivals (for instance: "MRS. LIGHT. I'd like to see her try to catch my Reuben" [*Dy* 427]).

It would be a mistake to see in the mothers' love of their male offspring a model of abnegation and self-effacement.[41] The stifling affection which is projected onto them inhibits their development as individuals; it has an explanation, however, for a mother's attachment for her sons is what gives meaning to her life and, if they show jealousy towards those who claim their succession, this can be explained by their fear of the loneliness which would ensue after the departure of those whom they brought into the world.[42]

> ELSA. It's simply that I've grown... sick of marriage and motherhood. And I'm tired of... pretending to myself I have to go on for the children's sakes, and that they make up to me for everything, which they don't at all [*DWE* 519].

In appearance, and paradoxically when one remembers the views he had of women, O'Neill could have anticipated a certain form of feminist reasoning aimed at liberating women from a stereotyped image in which she is the central pillar of the family structure, a role which might not justify the sacrifices exacted. This is another manifestation, I feel, of a disguised form of the refusal of motherhood, which has already been mentioned (in the *Dead parents' society* section above), and which finds its expression both in the imaginary wall separating Ella from Jamie and Edmund, in *Long Day's Journey into Night*, and in the absent mothers, whose importance in numbers we have noted.

Maternal love is therefore not innate; the examples given are proof of this.

Contrary to the common view, the birth of the child can have dramatic consequences for the mother, who avenges herself by rejecting the one who, symbolically, she refuses to recognize. (The refusal is not only symbolic: One recalls the infanticide in *Desire Under the Elms*, in which the child's birth obstructs Eben's love for Abbie.) Giving life: This creative act gives to those who have procreated a special place, whatever their feelings may be towards their offspring. Long after their childbirth, they remain all-powerful over children to whom they may only grant a semblance of existence.

> DEBORAH. I remember how tender he became in the garden—how loving—how much he needed me—my beloved son! never to be taken from me again—every evening in the garden I will encourage him to live with me in the past before he knew her—before he ever thought of women—to be my little boy again—I will bind him to me so he can never reject me and escape again [*MSM* 201].

Deborah is sure of her power; act by act, Simon can be seen going down a path which gradually takes him back to childhood to relive an episode that had marked his separation from the woman who was in a position to open the door to an unknown world. This irreparable trauma still haunted him in adulthood. His journey into his past, comparable to a psychoanalysis, leads to regression, accompanied by an inescapable recovery of the absolute power of the mother who will decide on the subject's potential entry into the adult world.

Whether absent or present on stage, the mothers play a predominant part in the construction of the works. From love to indifference, or to rejection, they are essential characters; the extent of their power is not necessarily indicated by their rank in the family hierarchy, but this power comes into its own in the influence which they exert on the protagonists who revolve around them. They generate a relationship with their descendants which is of such importance that it becomes one of the main themes in the plays; the effects, which we shall now study, are almost unrequited, as instances of sons' expressing any desire to enter into fusion with the mothers will hardly ever be acknowledged by their elders.[43]

Son-mother relationships.

A good starting point for our analysis is provided by O'Neill's own remarks about *Dynamo*, whose central theme, according to the author, was the relationship between Reuben and Mrs. Light.

> No one seems to have gotten the real human relationship story, what his mother does to the boy and what that leads to in his sacrifice of the girl to a maternal deity in the end—the girl his mother hated and was jealous

of—that all that was the boy's real God struggle, or prompted it. This all fits in with the general theme of American life in back of the play, America being the land of the mother complex.[44]

We shall now try to define the characteristics of the mother-son relationships beyond the scope of *Dynamo*, basing our study on the whole of the present corpus, bearing in mind the fact that the playwright himself stressed in many instances the importance of this subject in his works. We have observed, in the course of this study, how the patriarchs maintained their heirs in their filial roles, and how the sons suffered from their fathers' attitudes. The relationship between the two generations is seen to change radically when the focus is placed on the links which bind the mothers to their sons. Indeed, while we noted that the mothers proved to be alternatively possessive or indifferent, the desires of the sons, on the contrary, are convergent, for they all wish to maintain their special status. Whether prompted by hatred or by exacerbated filial love—in the form of an unresolved Oedipus complex—and regardless of their age, they take their stand as the children of a beloved mother, from whom they refuse to be separated.

There is no denying it: Even if some imagine that they have freed themselves of their bonds, an analysis of their behavior shows that this is not true. At the beginning of *More Stately Mansions*, Simon seems to escape this rule, and his proclamation of indifference, and the refusal of what he perceives to be nothing but an unfounded social convention, merely serve to heighten the dramatic irony of the closing situation, which shows how he has been blinded.

> SIMON. But what's the use of pretending we have anything in common anymore, when we haven't. Just because she happened to bear me in the world! This absurd sentimental sense of obligation between parents and children! Obligation for what? Almost any fool of a woman can have a son, and every fool of a man has had a mother! It's no great achievement on either side, and the hypocritical values we set on the relationship are stupidity [*MSM* 144].

These words which, at the beginning, the spectator considers to be an assertion, are in fact the expression of an unconscious wish to emancipate himself from the indisputable sovereignty of his mother. This speech is all the more interesting as it is unique; Simon is the only son who attempts to deny the force of this attachment, although the other characters are not unaware of the importance of this fundamental link. The unfolding of the play shows how immensely he deludes himself; he regresses down to the last stages of infancy, then proceeds unconsciously towards an ideal phase, which he perceives as the fœtal stage. For him, this relation carries more weight than anything else which has ever counted. If one trusts the author's declarations, the son-mother relationship is described against the background of a common theme in American literature; there is no doubt that its importance is also justified by difficulties of a personal nature, which go beyond the frame of this study.

For the O'Neillian characters, the son-mother ties take on a special value, for in the beginning, filial love is what gives the characters their very existence, as the mother serves as a first reference point for self-definition. Unlike what we observed in the confrontation between the patriarchs and their heirs, when the descendants' attempt to emancipate themselves led to a period in which they denied their sonhood within a fixed family hierarchy, here they claim it as their right. They refuse to lose the link, which they consider vital to their well-being, for the loss of the mother, in whatever form this may occur, makes their world collapse.

> REUBEN. She cheated me! ... when I trusted her! ... when I loved her better than anyone in the world! [*Dy* 448].

Whether this occurs through a straightforward betrayal, as in Reuben's case, or through death, the separation inflicts incurable pain, and all those who fall victim to it inevitably lapse into decline. Their lives are transformed into a long period of expectancy of the time when they will at last return to their lost paradise, which consisted in a harmonious relationship with the woman who had brought them into the world.[45] The sons stand in so great a need of their mothers that love sometimes turns into hatred, when a breach appears between the two generations. The characters cannot bear the separation, for this means a denial of their very existence. They feel that the parental care they received is not enough, and that it is a lack of protection that causes the suffering which incapacitates them in their normal dealings with society.

One recalls Parritt's long confession in *The Iceman Cometh*: "PARRITT. I may as well confess, Larry. There's no use lying any more. You know anyway. I didn't give a damn about the money. It was because I hated her" (*IC* 207); it is not an isolated case. Edmund and Jamie's feelings in *Long Day's Journey* oscillate between opposite poles: sometimes the brothers show understanding, and sometimes a desire for revenge flares up. As for Tiberius, his act of reprisal is astonishingly close to what Parritt describes.[46] This behavior can be compared to the suicidal impulses studied above, and which, in *The Iceman Cometh*, are carried out. More generally, one senses a scuppering process; the protagonists, feeling that they are lost, long to share their scanty existence with others.

As the mother's death is not automatically followed by her son's, some find themselves alone to confront a hostile world, and feel like orphans, whatever their age (for instance, Marsden in *Strange Interlude* or James Tyrone in *Moon for the Misbegotten*). How are they to survive the loss of a mother? We have measured how difficult this was, but this situation sometimes triggers a revelation; thus, Reuben and Eben are once more able to experience the symbiotic union with their mother by speaking to her "presence."

EBEN. (*To the presence he feels in the room.*) Maw! Maw! What d'ye want? What air ye tellin' me? [*DE* 263].

Through this invocation, one sees that the characters invest this relationship with a strength which might defy the power of death. The world of the living and that of the dead are no longer separated by an insurmountable wall, and the union between the characters transcends the barriers of reality. Out of context, one is struck by the naïveté of Eben's evocation; however, by stretching the spectator's potential investment to its extreme limit,[47] O'Neill was trying to put across his vision of a link which bare facts would not be able to convey, and the nature of his words perhaps justified his recourse to a form of communication that goes beyond commonly accepted limits.

As the critic becomes familiar with O'Neill's plays, he meets with mother figures who are omnipresent and all-powerful, or considered as such by their offspring.

When quoting the playwright's point of view about *Dynamo*, I wished to point out the eschatological dimension of the work, and connect it with the mother-son relationships, in order to stress the importance of these links. Over and above their respective thematic importance, what deserves our attention is the convergence of the two themes, of divinity and motherhood. In a certain way, the mother is a divine incarnation, because she is a creator and, having given life, she retains her qualities as a genitrix long after the birth of her descendants. The loss of fœtal serenity is the misfortune which befalls the male characters, and the importance of this event can be explained by the fact that, for the sons, their mother is the world.

For them, to be born does not mean to enter the human community but to live in exile; paradise vanishes the day that contact is broken between the mother-goddess and the child, and their existence will henceforth consist in trying to find the way back to Eden, from which they have been banished. Viewing the situation solely from the son's angle, one might say, in short, that from an ontological point of view, it is a chronicle of accepted faint existence, for the characters seek above all to define themselves as sons, without attempting to exist as individuals, and are faced with a universe reduced to a single dimension—that of the mother.[48]

Mother-daughter relationships.

In most of the situations in which a mother and a daughter are staged together, harmony prevails, for both generations are credited with the same characteristics, principally motherly solicitude, and an ability to understand the other person, which are the basic elements of the family's stability.

> BENTLEY. As is the mother, so is her daughter! (*He cackles to himself*) So is her daughter!
> ANNIE. (*Her face flushing with anger*) And if I am, I'm glad I take after her and not you, y'old wizard! [*Rope* 580].

As concerns the idea of doubles, and of reincarnation, Bentley seems here to voice a truth which will not be contradicted, even by Lavinia.[49]

From *Dynamo* to *Now I Ask You,* the mothers' kindness is depicted, and they skillfully defuse the conflicts which arise between the fathers and their daughters. They place human relationships on the plane of love, which gives a meaning to what may seem meaningless, and discreetly support their daughters, when they claim to be struggling to assert themselves as people.

Opposed to the ideal mother figure, represented in some plays, one meets with a shrewish specimen, staged in *Beyond the Horizon*.[50] Even if one excepts this marginal example, another conflictual relationship is staged between two women, showing that serenity does not always reign among the female characters.

> CHRISTINE. (*Shaken—defensively*) I tried to love you. I told myself it wasn't human not to love my own child, born of my body. [*MBE, Homecoming* 31].

When she recognizes that maternal love is not innate, Christine feels guilty, but she cannot take back her confession which, for Lavinia, is only half a surprise. The voicing of this taboo marks a turning point from drama to tragedy, for there is no longer any reason to show leniency, since natural affection is nonexistent; this is why the struggle which ensues must be carried through to the end, and to the death of one of the opponents.

The sons' hate for their fathers was proclaimed, but always in an indirect way; in the presence of third parties. The heirs confessed their hatred for their parents, and the patriarchs admitted having similar feelings for their sons, but the truth was never voiced in such a direct way. The clash here is all the more violent as Christine's aim is not to confine Lavinia to a filial role, but to deny her all right to existence, in the same way as she had tried to eliminate her husband from her living space, before resorting to poison. After the fight, which Christine loses, one is able to measure the limits of the mother's power, and when she refuses Lavinia her affection, this does not lead her daughter to suicide, but on the contrary encourages her to take up arms.

Daughter-mother relationships.

The maternal aspect, which characterizes many of the female characters in O'Neill's plays, prevents any direct antagonism between the two generations.

The mothers are not considered obstacles to the development of the personalities of their daughters, who in return lavish all their affection on them. The absence of opposition materializes in two plays (*All God's Chillun Got Wings* and *Gold*) in which, in spite of their mothers' presence, the daughters take charge of the household. (This is not without recalling the relationships between daughters and fathers, in which the elder generation were in quest of a mother's protection.)

These relations are reversed in *Mourning Becomes Electra*, giving an image which is very close to what we observed in our study of the son-patriarch relationship.[51] However, unlike the effects produced on the sons when deprived of a mother's love, this denial does not break Lavinia; it relieves her from her feelings of guilt,[52] and prompts her to launch into a merciless battle. The mother figure proves to be no more than a goddess with feet of clay, and her daughter's hatred—which can be explained at once by the desire to supplant her[53] and by the suffering inflicted by her lack of affection—serves as a catalyst to reveal her opponent's strength.

Whether one adopts the elder or the younger generation's point of view is of little importance, for they are identical; this observation brings to light the insignificance of this aspect of family life. Lavinia and Christine are exceptions, in the sense that the women protagonists are generally characterized by their maternal facet; the daughters are mothers before they are women (in Part II of this work we shall come back to *All God's Chillun Got Wings*, and Hattie) and this, in the O'Neillian perspective, implies deletion of personality,[54] or at least self-sacrifice.

Brother relationships.

Before studying doubles—enemies or companions—we shall dwell on two groups of brothers presented in the plays, one of which provides an insight into O'Neill's conception of brotherhood. In *The Great God Brown*, Margaret's sons are defined as such, and they embody the successive stages of development of the same person; in fact, they are walk-ons, whose individual differences are deleted, for they are presented primarily as perfect children, true to the American ideal.[55] In *More Stately Mansions*, the four sons are given a certain importance, and their personalities are revealed through the plans they make for the future.

>DEBORAH. You will grow up to be a philosopher, I think.
>WOLFE. (*Distrustfully*) What's a philosopher? (*Then with a quick indifference*) I don't care what I grow up to be.
>JONATHAN. I'm going to own a railroad. Father wants me to.
>HONEY. I'm going to be a gentleman and 'lected President of America, like Mother wants me.

3. Relations Between the Characters.

> DEBORAH. (*Smiling*) I'm afraid you can't be both nowadays, Honey [*MSM* 169].

A breach is established between the materialists and those who have other ambitions—the fourth son, Ethan, being driven by a combined love for the sea and for the poetry of Lord Byron. The way in which the roles are cast in the family follows the same pattern as appeared in the preceding works: The brothers can be divided into two categories, which then constitute the two opposite poles of certain individuals' personalities; the spectator then distinguishes those who have a poetic profile, "a touch of the poet," from the others, who are more rustic, for whom materialism serves as a religion. This dichotomy established between the materialists and the poets is not simply anecdotal, for it reappears many times in the works. The character who is endowed with poetic sensitivity has the matching physical characteristics,[56] and one notes how these descriptions are repeated each time a "poet" appears on stage.

Antagonism is not inevitable, although it is frequent, according to James Mayo, but the acceptance of each other's differences contributes to the development of the family's harmony.

> MAYO. They ain't like most brothers. They've been thick as thieves all their lives, with nary a quarrel I kin remember [*BH* 97].

Robert and Andrew are both in love with Ruth, but the passion they share does not divide them; the fraternal link is rather strengthened by this trial, for it finally triumphs over the pressure brought to bear upon it. In *Bread and Butter*, similar rivalry over a love relationship impairs Edmund and John's good relations. However, although jealousy is one component of the brothers' dissension, what emerges most clearly from it is the clash between two conceptions of the world, one materialistic—echoing the title of the play, which proclaims that one must work hard to earn a living—and the other individualistic, in which a youth tries to find his own way and challenges the established order.

Between the two above-mentioned characters, O'Neill's choice is obvious, and the artist—behind whom lurks a thinly-disguised self-portrait—has his preferences.[57] The brother not only stands for a form of opposition, similar to the patriarch figure, he is also the one who mirrors the image of one's double. Thus, in *Beyond the Horizon*, where love has caused their destinies to interchange, Robert measures the failure of his life when Andrew returns, and Andrew in turn is able to appreciate how wrong he has been in his choice of a road.

Not all the characters are as serene as James Mayo's descendants; the reasons for the opposition between Jamie and Edmund in *Long Day's Journey into*

Night are given, and the spectator knows why Jamie "hates" his younger brother ("JAMIE. And it was your being born that started Mama on dope" [*LDJN* 166]). This example shows how strong the desire for vengeance can become, and retraces it to its origins; however, one should not deduce from this that the antagonisms have expressible and rational justifications, clearly defined in the minds of the protagonists. In fact, the ebb and flow of feelings can also be explained by the fact that these exchanges, which take the form of mutual appraisal, project back upon the character who looks and judges an image of himself which is difficult to accept.

> JAMIE. You're a damned fine kid. Ought to be. I made you [*LDJN* 167].

In this extract, Jamie is shown as an initiator, and his claim to the authorship of this act of creation conveys an implicit message of love, for in spite of the animus he nurtures for his brother ("JAMIE. But don't get the wrong idea, Kid. I love you more than I hate you" [*LDJN* 166]), he insists on their common identity. The brother is another self, and rejection, in its fratricidal and liberating aspect, is ultimately an attempt to flee from the unacceptable image of one's own identity.[58] In these rewritings of what one could perceive as a re-enactment of Cain and Abel's combat, one discerns the outline of every human being, condemned as he is to reconcile within himself two conflicting but inseparable facets.

The brother relationships oscillate between benevolent companionship and fratricidal impulses; as is the case in other relationships within the family, there often coexist both contradictory feelings and a latent sameness, and both are at the root of the impossible desire to sever the links. These fraternal relationships forebode the presence of duality, which causes contradictory desires to appear in certain characters, who have difficulty in coming to terms with them[59]; one realizes, when one observes the way each character defines himself, that the particularity of the brother's role is that he represents another part of the person facing him, who is both complementary and contrary to him.

Brothers and sisters.

> JOSIE. Well, that's the last of you, Mike and good riddance. It was the little boy you used to be that I had to mother, and not you, I stole the money for [*MMis* 7].

Josie is defining the principal characteristics of the brother-sister relationship, where young women are seen as substitute mother figures, providing the boys, who long for affection, with the understanding and care they need.

This definition can be applied to the following plays: *Bread and Butter, Where the Cross Is Made, The Straw, Gold, Diff'rent, Mourning Becomes Electra,* and *A Moon for the Misbegotten*. (In *Warnings* and *The Straw*, the brother-sister relations between the squabbling children are of no interest.)

In *Mourning Becomes Electra,* Orin, in the same way as other heroes with unresolved Oedipus complexes, projects onto Lavinia the love he felt for Christine, which leads him to incestuous desires.[60] He is completely under Lavinia's orders, for she holds the key to his potential deliverance, and when she refuses him any possible way out, he accepts death without any further struggle for freedom. In her role as sister-mother, Lavinia is all-powerful[61] and, aware of her power, she declares:

> LAVINIA. Don't you know I'm your sister, who loves you, who would give her life to bring you peace? [*MBE, The Haunted* 156].

She actually is in a position to bring him peace, and has at her disposal an indisputable supremacy, which shows that she has taken the empty place left by Christine. Her speech is just as deceptive as her mother's, since she has no qualms about letting him commit suicide, for he is an obstacle to the liberation she desires at all costs. The maternal component, to which she refers indirectly, is only a protective mask. It serves as a cover while she does all she can to find happiness.

The relations between brothers and sisters are marked by the shadow of the mothers, for whom the sisters tend to act as substitutes. However, although they are able to afford comfort to those under their charge, their influence is much less, and the brothers, with the exception of Orin, have no difficulty in asserting themselves as people, through their opposition to these women who do not wield a mother's sovereignty (see *All God's Chillun Got Wings, Gold,* and *Where the Cross Is Made*).

4. From the Microcosm to the Macrocosm.

The author's approach.

In the first part of the present work I limited the field of my research to the study of family links, and to the ties which bound members of the same family together. Although the worlds that are shown are sometimes places set apart, this does not mean they are cut off from reality, and it is often possible to establish a link between what is shown on the stage and certain aspects of American society.

We shall now direct our attention more particularly to three works emblematic of this desire to proceed from the particular to the general, through the vision of the family, which is an instrument of representation for the world as a whole. We begin with *The First Man*. The playwright here shows his desire to relate what occurs within the community with the surrounding social structure. One of the characters is an archeologist who leaves on an expedition to explore the origins of humanity; the drama which precedes his departure provides an insight into the author's views on the development of people as social beings, the Jayson clan representing society. The second element in our study of the representation of the world through a dynasty consists of the first two parts of what was to be an unprecedented theatrical series. At the end of his life, O'Neill decided to write a cycle of four or five plays,[1] entitled *A Tale of Possessors Self-Dispossessed*, in which he wished to tell the story of a family. Of this project, only *A Touch of the Poet* and *More Stately Mansions* remain, the other works, unfinished, having been destroyed. The third object of our attention is a satirical drama, *Marco Millions*, in which the author discusses the voyage of Marco Polo, while denouncing the failure of Western values.

Without seeking to justify my own approach, I feel it may be of interest to quote O'Neill's point of view concerning the relation between the microcosm and the macrocosm, since our aim is to direct outwardly one's attention to the study of these works, focusing on the reflection they provide of American society, seen strictly through a family perspective.

I'm not giving a damn whether the dramatic event of each play has any significance in the growth of the country or not, as long as it is significant in the spiritual and psychological history of the American family in the plays. The Cycle is primarily just that, the history of a family. What larger significance I can give my people as extraordinary examples and symbols in the drama of American possessiveness and materialism is something else again. But I don't want anyone to get the idea that this Cycle is much concerned with what is usually understood by American history, for it isn't.[2]

The refutation of a potential classification of the cycle as a succession of historical plays can be explained by the fact that *A Touch of the Poet* is situated in the Jacksonian era, early in the Republic, and the last works of the saga were to belong to the present-day period. The implicit warning in the quotation probably finds its explanation in the fear of seeing a restrictive reading imposed on a complex project, generating misunderstanding, which he had often had to face. Without putting forward any of his preconceptions of the nature of the relationships that were to build up between this dynasty and the history of the United States, the playwright does not exclude the fact that the family should be representative of the whole.

The echoes.

We observed that the enclosure mechanisms could take several forms, as the characters were at once prisoners of their ascendancy, of the clan structure, and of the space in which they lived. The family gathering, staged in *The First Man*, provides an insight into the way in which the playwright gives depth to his words. Taking as his target the stifling effect[3] induced by the presence of the whole of the Jayson branch, and the prejudices which they convey, he shows how one proceeds from the microcosm to the macrocosm.

As they have doubts about Martha's conjugal fidelity, and the identity of the child's father, their first worry is to prevent the rumor from spreading— "JAYSON. (*Hastily*) Yes, yes. We must keep up appearances" (*FM* 601). To do this, they put on a united front. The family serves as the first frame in the restrictive process, for it exerts pressure on Martha to make her change her attitude, not only for her own sake, but also for the sake of the Jason clan, which has to live with the constraints imposed by the rest of the community. Lily is sent as an emissary, to specify the rules of behavior in force; she establishes a link between the immediate family, who sermonize to her, and the inhabitants of Bridgetown, who will not tolerate the relaxing of the behavior codes.

> LILY. Oh, I hate their narrow small town ethics as much as you do, Martha. I sympathize with you, indeed I do. But I have to live with them and so, for comfort's sake, I've had to make compromises. And you're going

to live in our midst from now on, aren't you? Well then, you'll have to make compromises, too—if you want any peace [*FM* 560].

"Compromises" is the master word; in fact, they are more aptly termed allegiances, in which each one is obliged to forego a certain measure of freedom in order to be accepted by society. The family, the first link in the social chain, projects the image of a narrow small-town mentality, from which there is no escape. Some refuse to be impressed by this demonstration of moral principles; they place the situations, and the very real power of the prohibitions, in a context of whose narrowness they are aware ("LILY. Martha is properly unimpressed by big frogs in tiny puddles" [*FM* 568]).

The distancing of communal references, the echo of which one also finds in *Long Day's Journey into Night*,[4] indicates her refusal to recognize the social prohibitions conveyed by their immediate family; but the ostracizing of Martha and Curtis, after this declaration of independence, shows that the choice of liberty induces a banishment from social life.[5] Unless one escapes to Africa, like Curtis, or lives in the West, where the social codes have not attained the same degree of rigidity—"MARTHA. We keep open house, you know—Western fashion. (*She accentuates this*)" (*FM* 571)—it is impossible to escape from the constraints imposed by the social body. This point of view is expressed ironically when John, in a fit of jingoistic nationalism, proclaims:

JOHN. It's one of the most prosperous and wealthy towns in the U.S.—and that means in the world, nowadays [*FM* 571].

The enclosure process is carried out on two planes: The family restrains the individual, but is itself a prisoner of the surrounding world, from which it cannot escape, for it represents a miniaturization of a world with all-powerful values. The moral foundations are not respected as such, but are protected by a rampart of hypocrisy, and if they are accepted by common consent, they are applied primarily out of fear of what the neighbors will say. The price to be paid for choosing this as the basis for social relations is a weakening of the structures, both in the community and in the family, both of which find their existence challenged when appearances, which are the mortar of this cohesion, are tested.

Appearances—a word to rally honest citizens—are shown to be limited in their effectiveness. The disunity brought to light by the play is projected onto a world which then judges on false appearances, as its own principles are not supported by deep convictions. This hypocrisy is denounced by Martha, who is aware of the superficiality of the moral anchorage to which everybody refers ("MARTHA. Chinese ancestor worship is far more dignified than ours. After all, you know, theirs is religion, not snobbery" [*FM* 572]). It seems difficult not to establish a link between the title, *The First Man*, and the assessment of human evolution implicitly drawn up in the last act: Human beings are immutable, and their appearance is hardly a cheering one.[6] One remembers *The Great God Brown,* and the finale which exactly reproduced the opening scene with, in the background, the idea of an eternal return. Here, the latent recurrence stresses another aspect: The family guarantees the survival of pseudo-virtues, and represents a world in conflict, resting on a code of primitive and unjust ethics to which the characters cling, ensuring its persistence by their immobility. (*Now I Ask You,* a comedy in which Lucy challenges the deep convictions of her father and family circle, is a demonstration of this. This imitation Hedda Gabler quickly ends her revolutionary career and integrates perfectly into the bourgeois world which is hers.)

Between continuity and metamorphosis, cohesion and estrangement, the tensions between the characters reveal a permanent struggle between antagonistic elements of the microcosm, but these clashes are also the sign of a certain immutability. The incessant oppositions of close members of the family indicate that duality is almost inherent in the family structure. In fact, it is quite common to find a clan divided between the dreamers (assimilated to artists), and the financers, money serving as a revealer for the gap which separates the two worlds. (One remembers the financial clashes in *Bread and Butter, Long Day's Journey into Night, Diff'rent, The Great God Brown,* and *Now I Ask You,* where money is a bone of contention.) In *Gold,* and *Where the Cross Is Made,* the corrupting desire to acquire money brings about the couple's destruction, and causes Mrs. Bartlett's death. The abandonment of the rules which, up to this point, had guided the protagonists, causes their common existence to lose its meaning. We note that money is what causes the characters to reject the values of the clan, and the family's breakup symbolizes a world falling into decadence for want of success in maintaining unifying ethics.

The Personal Equation follows the opposite path. This play stages two generations, with conflicting political conceptions. One is that of a conservative, who thinks that American society is perfect and imagines that its founding principles, which convey an ideal of righteousness, are actually applied; the other, Tom, is a supporter of violent struggle against the system, and is prepared to sabotage the boat upon which his father has embarked. During the fight, in an attempt to protect his engines, the father shoots at his son, who as a result, will suffer from a mental handicap for the rest of his life. This drama reveals the shortcomings of a society which prompts such actions ("THE CROWD, SAYING TO EACH OTHER. He's killed him! Dead as hell! His own son!" [*PE* 60]); the certainties of the past are swept away, leaving place for what is essential, that sense of community which had been erased by ideology. The last scene consecrates the family's reunification, putting the capitalist and anarchist creeds back to back and showing the ineptitude of these concepts, the uselessness of fighting, and how lethal this vain division is on the social level. (We are reminded of Abraham Lincoln's, "A house divided against itself cannot stand.")

Social estrangement, as exemplified in the opposition between the elder and the younger generations, is not the only type to appear in the works. The members of a clan sometimes rally around a belief, but this cultural heritage may clash with the values of another family.

Duality is not a phenomenon inherent exclusively to one particular structure; in *Marco Millions*, O'Neill builds an opposition between East and West, using two lineages as emblems of these estranged worlds. What Maffeo and Nicolo pass on to Marco is, above all, a mercantile adulation for their God: gold. Conversely, Kukachin, who comes from a background where spiritual values are prevalent, is ignorant of material contingencies, and proves capable of feeling the pangs of love, which endows her with a human status.

> KUKACHIN. Marco!
> MARCO. (*His voice thrilling for this second with oblivious passion*) Kukachin!
> MAFFEO. (*Suddenly slapping a stack of coins into the chest with a resounding clank*) One million! [*MM* 415].

Maffeo's interruption is symbolic; it characterizes Marco's inability to free himself from the hold of his mental conditioning, which teaches him that the experience of pleasure is limited to the accumulation of worldly goods. Such a lifelong pursuit leaves no place for love. This attitude is symptomatic of the alienation affecting Western civilization, of which Marco is the symbol. The mercantile instinct dehumanizes people, and financial successes provide concrete expression to their baseness.[7] The scene of the return to Italy draws up an assessment of the Polo expedition; the initiation journey to China is nothing more than a commercial tour, for the Westerners are prisoners of their materialism.[8] The way Marco is represented, as a new Babbitt with the air of a buffoon, shows how Western values, such as are transmitted by the family, which imply that happiness can be measured in terms of dollars, lead to a deadlock when they are respected.[9]

Marco has failed to seize his opportunity; a woman's love has not transformed him. What is left to the characters? In the final cycle, maternal love — the supreme reference in the O'Neillian world — is also demolished, and is shown to mask love of a selfish kind. The family drama which takes place in *More Stately Mansions* can be interpreted on different levels, but one of the keys to the play is the power struggle which develops between Sara, Simon's wife, and Deborah, his mother. When they find themselves together under the same roof, they fight for influence, each hoping to deprive the other of Simon's love. This struggle for his feelings is doubled by another rivalry, one of Deborah's aims being to gain the affection of her grandchildren, so as to take their mother's place (we shall remain within the frame of the triangular relationship between Sara, Simon and Deborah). The two women's antagonism heightens as time passes, and each is prepared to go to any lengths to achieve her purpose. Sara

4. From the Microcosm to the Macrocosm.

forsakes her role as a wife to become Simon's mistress; as for Deborah, she gradually lures him onto the ground of his childhood memories, where she acquires a supremacy that might lead to his destruction. At the end of the play, Sara capitulates, and concedes the victory to Deborah.

> SARA. I will—for the love of him—to save him. You can have him all to yourself again. I know I can trust your love for him, once I'm out of the way, to protect him from himself—and from your own mad dreams. And I know when he has only you to love, he'll forget me and he won't be destroyed and torn between us within himself [*MSM* 292].

She lays down arms, out of love for Simon, for she senses the disastrous consequences their struggle has brought upon him. In fact, their hostility is such that Simon has ceased to exist as a person, which is all the more paradoxical as the two women have been competing to obtain the monopoly of his affection. Love itself is dehumanizing; it turns the other person into an object, without taking into account his existence as a subject. Sara's renunciation, then Deborah's, occurs only at the last moment, when their desire for possession puts the life of their loved one in danger. The disappearance of human relationships between the characters can also be found on the level of the community, when in the struggle for financial supremacy the vampire-like characters are prepared to go to any lengths to achieve undivided domination, even if this means the annihilation of the other person.

The presentation of the exchanges between relatives, within the frame of the family, is probably not primarily aimed at criticizing a world in which people enter into conflict and have to fight to assert themselves as people. However, through the moral yoke which is brought to bear on the protagonists by their closest relatives, one senses the fetters with which society shackles citizens. Between members of a clan the causes for disunity are numerous; they sometimes reflect a social disorder brought about by the putting aside of the founding principles, which causes the community to fall into decadence. People become fragile and, as they give in to their desire for power, they unwittingly lose what gives a meaning to their lives. Without establishing a systematic parallel between family situations and society, one cannot fail to note the ties which link them. The selection of works quoted above shows, to varying degrees, how the tensions between relatives implicitly suggest the presence of collective corruption, and draws up a criticism of a world in search of its values.

5. The Image of the Family.

A redeeming vision, in a comedy.

Against the background of an attempt to critically examine the O'Neillian family, one appreciates the irony of the quotation which opens Part I of this study (page 5), for the immediate circle is an essential component of the characters' lives and, to paraphrase Robert Frost, whose poetry O'Neill appreciated, one might say that this element is what has made all the difference. Between the prison-like image of a rigid system, which thwarts the characters' development as people while leaving no prospect of release but flight, and the weight of heredity in the form of ineluctable fate, the image of the family is far from idyllic.

However, in spite of the unaccommodating aspect of the O'Neillian vision, it would be a mistake to conclude too hastily that the family is, by essence, evil for the individual. For some, the prospect of starting a family brings hope.

> LAVINIA. We'll be married soon, won't we, and settle out in the country away from folks and their evil talk. We'll make an island for ourselves on land, and we'll have children and love them and teach them to love life so that they can never be possessed by hate and death! [*MBE, The Haunted* 147].

The abandonment of past tenses in favor of the future shows how she desires to rid herself of the ghosts of memory, and hopes to make a fresh start elsewhere on a sound basis. This discontinuity in the time element is a sign of the characters' haunting desire for virginity, and their longing to shake off the unbearable weight of their destiny, embodied in a heredity which alienates them. Insularity, with in the background the paradisical image of the Garden of Eden, symbolizes how necessary it is for them, if they wish to establish a new line, for it to be founded on solid ground. This is the lesson which transpires throughout the works: When the foundations of a community are impure, a succession of misfortunes assails the descendants.[1] This is why, in *Mourning Becomes Electra*, Lavinia renounces her forthcoming marriage with Peter after having called him Adam. She understands that their union would only produce a new generation of damned creatures, for their love is already placed under the sign of division, her slip of the tongue revealing the strength of the past, against which she would be powerless to fight.

The need to break away is remarkably expressed in *Strange Interlude*, in which the quest for happiness entails procreation, but on condition that one begins by breaking the spell embodied by the hereditary genetic defects ("MRS. EVANS. Whatever you can do to make him happy is good—is good, Nina! I don't care what! You've got to have a healthy baby—sometime—so's you can both be happy! It's your rightful duty!" [*SI* 64]). To achieve this, anything is permitted; the moral codes (marital fidelity) are rejected, because when a heroine is involved, her right to happiness entails the conception of a child.

> MRS. KEENEY. I sometimes think if we could only have had a child. (*Keeney turns away from her, deeply moved. She grabs his arm and turns him around to face her—intensely*) And I've always been a good wife to you haven't I, David? [*Ile* 549].

Mrs. Keeney is one of the small number of childless women—some of them unmarried—who suffer from this deprivation[2]; this is not the only instance and, as one reads the plays, one becomes increasingly aware that the young women are destined to be mothers. Refusal of motherhood is very rare, and when it does occur, the women come to realize that they have been following the wrong path,[3] by denying what, according to the O'Neillian vision, constitutes a woman's primary *raison d'être*.

Far from campaigning in favor of the extinction of a human race whom he seemed to find somewhat deficient,[4] we note, through the selection of works quoted above, that the playwright believes that one of the ways to achieve fulfillment, if one is a woman, consists in giving birth[5] and founding a home. This structure, whose shortcomings were revealed in the first part of our study, is not judged as intrinsically harmful and irrevocably condemned, but on the contrary finds grace in his eyes, and is the object of a comedy, *Ah, Wilderness!*

O'Neill's momentary setting aside of the tragedy is less surprising than it may seem, first, because he was not without a certain sense of humor, and second, because the subject under discussion is very close to those already staged in different dramatic forms.[6] This comedy, emblematic of an ideal,[7] shows us uncommon scenes of family life, as the action takes place on the Fourth of July. However, the relative banality of the events provides an insight into the atmosphere habitually reigning there. As in many plays, the family as an institution is put to the test—here, by the intractable behavior of Richard. This adolescent occupies the intermediate position between his two brothers, one of whom, a student at Yale, has already stepped out towards adulthood and is preparing to enter into American society, and the other of whom is still a child, whose

Fourth of July celebrations mean little more than a good opportunity to throw firecrackers. Richard is reaching the stage of adolescence during which one gradually take one's place in the adult world, and he challenges all his parents' values. One notes, however, that his libertarian declarations are met by the elder generation with benevolent tolerance, or countered with a touch of humor, without denying him his freedom of expression.

Behind the apparent oppositions is an underlying foundation of love between the protagonists; this affection is revealed in the broad-mindedness which the parents show. Richard meets with neither hurtful opposition nor indifference; he is free to express himself, and gives his family his own definition of what he is, through his words, something that was forbidden the sons in the other plays. Being able to speak and be heard is one of the secrets of the well-being and development of the individual within the frame of the family. What reinforces the positive dimension of this structure is that the acknowledgment of the other person in his specificity is not the result of condescension towards an adolescent attempting to define himself; far from being the exclusive privilege of Richard, it extends to all its members. When Mrs. Miller laments about her brother's behavior, Lily recognizes his right to be himself, although she suffers from it herself: "MRS. MILLER. (*Angrily*) He's a dumb fool—a stupid dumb fool, that's what he is! LILY. (*Quietly*) No. He's just Sid" (*AhW* 212).

Under cover of liberalism, Nat Miller is not, however, prepared to accept anything and everything and, when he begins to wonder whether his son is not actually trying to disturb the innocence of a young lady's thoughts, or perhaps worse still, he brings the threat of a severe punishment to bear upon him.[8] The father's duty is to mete out justice, but his leniency is not a sign of laxity. On the contrary, the regulating principles of the group are known to all, and nobody would think of contravening them. The only infringement to the communal moral code occurs when Mrs. Miller leads her husband to believe that he never eats a certain kind of fish which he claims to be unable to digest, while she regularly serves it to him. This treason is more amusing than scandalizing; it shows, in a comic mode, the limits not to be transgressed in marital disloyalty.

When Muriel's father comes to complain to Nat Miller about his son's attitude, Miller takes up Richard's defense; the two men threaten reprisals against each other, and the conflict takes on a dimension which then goes beyond the frame of the family.

>MILLER. I'll start a campaign to encourage capital to open a dry-goods store in opposition to you that won't be the public swindle I can prove yours is!
>
>MCCOMBER. (*A bit shaken by this threat—but in the same flat tone*) I'll sue you for libel.
>
>MILLER. When I get through, there won't be a person in town will buy a dishrag in your place! [*AhW* 204].

5. The Image of the Family.

After McComber's departure, Nat declares to Sid that, contrary to what he has just said, he will not use his newspaper in his fight against McComber, for his professional ethics forbid him to use his daily paper for personal ends. The social and family tensions staged serve to reveal the solidity of the codes of behavior. They are clearly defined and respected by the members of the family, who do not allow themselves to be guided by events. Far from showing egocentricity, they are able to place the facts in a wider perspective, which differentiates the Miller clan from the Jayson dynasty (*The First Man*), who were characterized by their narrow-mindedness. (Thus, Richard's nocturnal escapade, and the drinking bout which ensues, are not presented as dramatic, but considered as an unpleasant episode in the educational process.)

The subject of this comedy is a rite of passage. Richard has had an experience which has given him an opportunity to reflect on his opinions and measure the uprightness of his acts. The family frame, far from countering this awakening, has helped Richard in his life-learning process. When the curtain drops, and nothing but impressions remain, the dominant one is that the family itself is enhanced by this trial, showing that the cornerstone in the social edifice is sound, resting on principles whose strength is reflected in the nation.

"Men are weak" (*AhW* 212), declares Mrs. Miller, and the introduction of the members of the clan could turn into a catalogue of the defects and shortcomings of each member, beginning with Sid's alcoholism, and continuing with Nat Miller's nostalgic rambling. Each one of them is presented in an unbecoming way, showing the weak points which they try to hide. However, in spite of these weaknesses, the protagonists regain their dignity when they affirm their fundamental beliefs, their principles, and their unshakable confidence in the people around them.

Whether continuity or counterpoint, this work appears to be situated at the antipode of the struggle for identity staged in the other plays. In fact, O'Neill shows his interest in this theme, presented here in a different way, by giving vent to his nostalgia for a golden age, when people were bound together by deep attachment in families like the Millers, and thus lived in an environment favoring their development. By the magnanimity they showed in everyday life, they gave another dimension to a society which is always threatened by the loss of its founding values and, through this play, the playwright glances surreptitiously towards the future, with the hope of seeing a return to the essentials.

6. Conclusion.

This first part of this research has led us to direct our attention to human beings as members of a family. We have discussed the nature of the ties which linked the various protagonists in order to study the way they were influenced by them. In a more general way, we wished to see how the individual situated himself in relation to a social structure, in which he was either included from birth or had created himself by founding a family.

The nuclear family presented in the works proves to be incomplete, and the essential characteristic of many of these families is the absence of one of the parents, in particular the mother. This lack becomes one of the revealing signs of the dysfunction of the family structure, which is rarely a suitable environment within which each person could develop, as it can aptly be described as a set of antagonistic forces ceaselessly questioning the very foundations of the family members' personalities and thwarting their development.

As concerns the space in which the dramas take place, we noted that it was a closed-in area, often cut off from the rest of the world, defining itself more particularly through opposition to its immediate environment. The characters also contribute to heightening the idea of a world apart, for outside agents ascribe to them physical or moral characteristics, true or imaginary, that distinguish them from common mortals. It is not rare for the people concerned to flatter themselves with their otherness; this otherness is only partial, for although the dichotomy between the person and the outside world is not entirely imaginary, it no longer prevails when one considers the group to which the individual is associated. The proof of this is given by the value attached to names. These are sometimes likened to banners, for they are a kind of rallying point, and symbolize the belonging of the individuals to a structure which was qualified as clan-like.

The breach which is displayed or advocated by the principal characters can also mark a form of exclusion, insofar as the estrangement, emphasized by all, may have occurred because the family community has either outlawed itself or has been outlawed by society. The breach between the two worlds is a reality which cannot pass unnoticed; in the face of this situation, made all the more uncomfortable by the incessant clashes which punctuate the characters' everyday lives, some try to escape from an environment which stifles them. Their

6. Conclusion. 77

desire to escape arouses their consciousness; they find themselves confronted with obstacles, hitherto unknown, and they realize how difficult it is for them to free themselves from powers whose force they had not always measured.

Among these discoveries is that of being included in a time cycle which places them, for example, in positions as descendants, their function consisting in replacing their predecessors when they die. Indeed, they tend to reproduce their parents' behavior, and have to contend with the legacies that befall them from the outset, whose force they sometimes underestimate but which end by imposing themselves on them. This idea of a human cycle, possibly stretching into eternity, is not the only one which can be linked to the temporal dimension in these plays, for in a more general way, the notion emerges of a sort of fate linked to the dynasty, against which many fight in vain.

Enclosure is not limited to the passage of time; it also takes on a spatial dimension, for the departures are, in general, followed by a return. This is why, sensing the impossibility of a real escape, some decide to flee without leaving their place of residence. While some escape permanently, never to return to their childhood haunts, others prefer to stay, and choose to live in an elsewhere conjured up by dreams or by recourse to whiskey. When the perception of their everyday fate becomes too nightmarish, and they can no longer bear being subjected to permanent denials by a family structure which stifles them, the last door open to them is suicide, and they do not all back away.

Liberation processes are very difficult to carry out; family relations are undoubtedly placed under the sign of conflict, but they are also characterized by almost immutable bonds, in that membership in a clan materializes in hereditary factors which cannot be ignored. It therefore would seem paradoxical to assert the existence of a very strong cohesion, for the incessant clashes could give the impression of a divided world; in fact, such an impression is not true, and the breach with the outside world only heightens the difficulty each character encounters when he tries to break his bonds. Indeed, the feelings alternate between hate and love, but never take the form of mutual indifference, which would allow a living space for each of them, and prevent the continual struggling.

This part of our study, bearing specifically on the relations between members of the clan, has enabled us to appreciate to what extent these relationships appear in terms of antagonism, aimed at nearly destroying the opponent, yet leaving him a breath of life so as not to transgress a latent prohibition. The inconclusiveness which thus characterizes the duels turns the end of each battle into a preparation for the one to come, and explains the permanent character of the conflicts.

In the study of the various functions—parent, son or daughter—we have discovered that these often constituted an extra enclosure mechanism, for the individuals try to free themselves of their sonhood, fatherhood, or motherhood, because it confines them within a predefined role which proves to be detrimental to their development. It cannot be denied that some protagonists find in parenthood a means of achieving happiness; but many characters—of both the older and the younger generation—claim their emancipation, often indirectly, and seek to rid themselves of a burden which prevents them from being themselves.

Before entering into the subject of the place of human beings in the world, we have established a parallel between what occurs on the domestic level, and what emerges on the scale of the social body. Indeed, the disorder proper to each family structure seems to echo an equally deep crisis located at the level of the nation. The family is the first building block leading to the edifice of a society, which is then constituted by the grouping of all such building blocks. This is why, when we pass from the microcosm to the macrocosm, we find in the upper levels of the communal edifice the echo of the dysfunction that appeared on the first level.

In the face of this somewhat tarnished image of the family structure, O'Neill advances a quite different perspective; in *Ah, Wilderness!*, it becomes an ideal place to live. It is within the family that individuals find the most favorable conditions for their development, even if all those who move within it do not correspond to the vision of the perfect citizen such as could be defined by social codes.

The essential difference between these two conflicting views of family structure resides in the manner in which the protagonists situate themselves in relation to the frames defined by the family. Each one is seeking to exist as a person, and strives to rid himself of the chains which thwart the assertion of his personality. The characters refuse the predetermined functions imposed upon them, and display a desire to be considered as individuals. In the course of this quest for freedom, which entails the proclamation of their identity, some of them delude themselves, or take wrong paths, which lead them to dead ends, for they only multiply the number of pitfalls that prevent them from achieving self-definition, which, in other words, could be called rebirth.

There is therefore no condemnation as such of the family structure, but O'Neill draws a somewhat severe picture, in the sense that instead of contributing, in a natural way, to the development of the individual, the family constitutes the first obstacle each member must face in order be able to be reborn and present himself as a human being responsible for what he is.

Part II.
Humanity and Worlds.

LARRY. He's so satisfied with life he's never set foot outside this place since his wife died twenty years ago. He has no need for the outside world at all [*IC* 37].

7. Worlds and the Representation of Them.

Humanity in which world?

Having looked at the way in which characters live within the frame of the family, we are going to broaden the scope of this study, in order to try to highlight the relationships characters have with society. We have noted that the family was often isolated and, before examining the links which are established between the main characters, we shall consider the places chosen for the setting of the plays. Saying that imprisonment is found in all the plays would be a claim refuted by many counter-examples. This theme, in a modified form, will, however, reappear in the presentation of the places where the dramas unfold. These places can be roughly classified in three categories: Some scenes take place in houses or apartments, others on board ships, and others in bars.[1] This triptych, although forming an incomplete typology, allows us to derive an essential element of the choice of place for the plays, that is to say, a kind of spatial autarky.

In fact, these three settings are representative of the vast majority of the plays, and the exceptions do not call into question the idea of a place that is, if not enclosed, at least cut off from the rest of the world,[2] where the characters live in an autonomous space, far removed from the rest of the social body. It would be precipitous to conclude from this that the existence of life round about is denied—its presence is manifested in many different ways which I shall mention—but there is a permanent gap between the outside and the place where the characters live. From *Long Day's Journey into Night* to *Bound East for Cardiff* or *The Iceman Cometh*, situated in the characteristic worlds of house, ship, and bar, the Tyrones, Larry Slade, and friends of Driscoll all remain apart from society.

The absence of contact with the outside world is sometimes symbolized by the presence of fog ("EDMUND. The fog was where I wanted to be. Halfway down the path you can't see the house. You'd never know it was there" [*LDJN* 131]), or by sounds from another place, often nearby, but from which the characters are excluded ("*The Clerk's mind has slipped away to the clanging bounce of garbage in the outer night*" [*Hu* 17]).[3] These elements, directly perceptible, reinforce the idea of isolation inherent in the chosen locations. To clarify our remarks, we will look at *The Iceman Cometh*, which conveys at different levels this very apparent break with the group. The quotation underlined in our second section, where Larry explains that Harry Hope has no need of the outside world, and that he is happy with his lot, is emblematic of the behavior of the drinkers gathered in this bar. They are all seeking a refuge. The first quality of this place is that it looks like a *cimetière marin*, where human wrecks disintegrate in indifference, without the rest of society taking any notice.

There are many reasons for the gathering together of these characters. In the first part of this study, they were united by blood ties. For the sailors, it is their belonging to the same ship that unites them, and for the customers of Harry Hope's low dive, the desire to escape from an unbearable reality. In other plays, the protagonists form a group after a shipwreck (*Fog* and *Thirst*), or following circumstances which bring them together for a short time, cutting them off from the world.[4]

> PARRITT. What kind of joint is it, anyway?
> LARRY. (*With a sardonic grin*) What is it? It's the No Chance Saloon. It's Bedrock Bar, The End of the Line Café, the Bottom of the Sea Rathskeller! Don't you notice the beautiful calm in the atmosphere? That's because it's the last harbour [*IC* 587].

This dialogue reveals that it is not so much an imprisonment (with the negative connotations this carries), the mechanisms of which within the framework of the family we have studied, as it is a distancing from society, interactions between the latter and the characters being fairly limited. The idea of a place apart is concretized in *The Iceman Cometh* where, to open the play, the playwright uses Larry to present the regular patrons of the bar. It is a clever process, and it is evidence of O'Neill's command of dramatic writing, for this presentation makes sense within the play. Larry has the role of initiator, he guides Parritt through strange territory, and his wide knowledge of the lives of the other customers testifies to a common experience, discernible by their connivance, marking the union of a community whose members are linked not simply by whiskey.

Why this apparent break between two worlds which are not conscious of each other? One of the explanations is the difficulty in representing on stage the whole social body,[5] the other is the playwright's choosing to have characters that represent nations. Thus on board ship the sailors form a separate society, defined in part by its opposition with those on land, but the notion of a crew is surpassed by O'Neill's desire to put on stage the whole of the human species in order to reveal the true face of humanity.

> The men themselves should resemble those pictures in which the appearance of Neanderthal Man is guessed at. All are hairy-chested, with long arms of tremendous power, and low, receding brows above their small, fierce, resentful eyes. All the civilized white races are represented, but except for the slight differentiation in color of hair, skin, eyes, all these men are alike [*HA* 207].

No one will interrupt the course of their lives to announce that war has been declared, or that a revolution has begun. Conflicts and revolutions are internal, and will occur before the eyes of the spectator. Contrary to what this impression of the *huis clos* could lead us to believe, the break with the surrounding universe is far from complete, and the action, although it is centered on the relationships between the characters within a community, is often representative of the world in general. We see again here what we have already evoked in the relationship of microcosm to macrocosm. What we see on stage symbolizes the whole.

Anchorage in reality.

The preceding remarks lead us to question the representation of reality in the plays. One of the peculiarities of O'Neill's theater is the abundance of stage directions. We may think, for example, of the six pages preceding the text in *The Iceman Cometh*, the extent of which is surprising at first glance.[6] The playwright's method of working no doubt has much to do with this, for he began by drafting out long scenarios, before writing the dialogues.[7] On the other hand, his distrust of actors is famous, and he felt it necessary to give them indications as to the tone and gesture he wanted, leaving them very little opportunity for initiative. His intention to carry his creation to the point of a sculpting of individuals and his many demands lead to deadlock,[8] with some of his demands being inaccessible. He wished, for example, to have actors who would fit the physical descriptions of the characters ("*A thick neck is jammed like a post into the heavy trunk of his body. His arms with their big, hairy, freckled hands, and his stumpy legs terminating in large flat feet, are awkwardly short and muscular*" [*AC* 5]). Some statements imply that he was not as fastidious as the detail of the stage directions might suggest, but his attitude concerning the choice of Josie, in *A Moon for the Misbegotten*, is evidence to the contrary. We can perceive a constant opposition between an endeavor towards creation and the desire to obtain a representation faithful to reality.

The primary function of stage directions is to describe what is going to appear on stage. Just as was noted in regard to the way the characters interpret the role and their physical appearance, the descriptions of scenery are very detailed, and directly call into question the status of reality, which O'Neill was quite aware posed a problem:

Damn that word "realism." When I first spoke to you of the play as a "last word in realism"; I meant something "really real," in the sense of being spiritually true, not meticulously life-like.[9]

What are the implications of these words, and what significance will objects represented on stage have, in a context which is presumedly realist? During a performance, objects take on the status of signs, and we are going to consider for a moment the meaning they could or should have in the spectator's interpretation. The temper of the playwright can be explained by his annoyance at being taken too literally, without any analysis of the value of what is signified by physical objects. This value is a double one: On the one hand, by placing tables, chairs,[10] and bookshelves in his scenery, the author is seeking, on the level of what is signified, to create an *effet de réél* which will sweep away the artifice inherent in any theatrical performance. On the other hand, in other plays, the signified takes on a symbolic value—the elms in *Desire Under the Elms*, the hum of the turbine in *Dynamo*, both incarnating in their own way a maternal element.

What makes analysis a little more complex is the fact that we can find elements within a play that contribute to an effect of realism while the work as a whole invites an expressionist reading. In *The Hairy Ape*, the language of the sailors is aimed at reproducing the way in which members of a crew might express themselves. This linguistic naturalism could lead to a reading wherein only the important social dimension would be taken into account. Aware of the risk of interpretative error, O'Neill adds:

> *The treatment of this scene, or of any other scene in the play, should by no means be naturalistic* [*HA* 207].

This remark is not contradictory to the linguistic naturalism previously evoked, but we can understand why some spectators have not grasped the expressionist dimension of the play.[11] Other examples show that the playwright did not have much confidence in the analytical capacity of his audiences.[12] His desire to show reality goes as far as tautology,[13] although whether the plays lean towards expressionism or realism, they are anchored in reality through characteristic signs or through scenes of everyday life, from which the author can put across his message.

Between effects of realism and symbolic content, the playwright situates the action of his plays in concrete spaces; "the willing suspension of disbelief," so dear to Coleridge, is not deemed essential by O'Neill in his approach to theatrical production. The worlds which the spectator discovers are not ethereal. They recall concretely, or symbolically, the one in which he is living and, even if they are far removed from his immediate experience, for example in the plays which have a marked historical content, they never take him to magical places. (It would be difficult to find an equivalent of *A Midsummer Night's Dream* in the plays, for even in *The Emperor Jones* there is a direct, almost concrete, relation between Jones' visions and his own experience.)

The social perspective.

O'Neill always asserted the need for a reasonable distance between his everyday life and what was represented in his plays, invoking a period of maturing necessary for the elaboration of a more conceptual vision by which he could express himself.[14] We can understand his rejection of a militant theater, knowing how harmful such a choice of writing could be to the quality of theatrical production. O'Neill however, did not live on Mars, and his opposition to a direct involvement in history cannot be taken for indifference.[15] His opinions evolved over time, and he acknowledged this,[16] but the essential element does not stem so much from one or another position, held at a given moment in his life, as from the formulation of social discontent found in many of his plays.

On the whole he paints a dark picture of American society, sometimes quoting, often deriding the pseudo-veneration of fundamental principles which are belied by sordid reality.

> LONG. We wasn't born this rotten way. All men is born free and ekal. That's in the bleedin' Bible, maties. But what d'they care for the Bible— [*HA* 211].[17]

A humorous dig aimed at comparing some principles around which the community has been formed and the evolution of those principles; the playwright knows that the character's mistake in identifying the origins of the quotation underlines the loss of collective memory. Without launching into an anticapitalist diatribe—his vision of the opposing ideology is hardly more flattering—the playwright denounces the alienation and loss of identity of these boiler men, whom one might believe to be the incarnation of chthonian forces, but who in fact are merely puppets whose lives are devoid of meaning. For a few moments, the sailors realize that they are the victims of oppression, and rise up against the injustice they have endured, but their revolt will be short-lived. The shared joke around the philosophizing of Yank foreshadows this. Awareness, a prelude to reflection, is fleeting, and will quickly turn to anger which will soon be overcome by alcohol.

The equality of birth invoked by Long, and the possibility of flourishing in a free world were called into question in *All God's Chillun Got Wings*, a play which caused a scandal and which had to go before the censor because in it an African American marries a white woman. O'Neill claimed that the problem of mixed marriages was not his main concern, for he was more interested in the relationship between two people, within a couple. However, the racial aspect cannot be ignored. It reveals a break with society, mixed marriages being perceived as a transgression. The African and white Americans live side by side, and the coming together imposed by the marriage of Jim and Ella leads to a rejection by the two families, who see this union as a provocation.

> O'Neill was exceptional among white Americans in that he understood racial as well as class oppression. He broke ground in the American theatre by making clear that the problems of Black Americans were caused by whites and by portraying blacks as real men, not unlike white men, rather than in the type of traditional stereotypes.[18]

I do not subscribe to all of Jane Torrey's analysis, for American blacks are or were victims of a double ostracism, imposed by both black and white communities, who interpret this union as a disavowal that could lead to a loss of identity. This is not an ordinary marriage, and society brings to bear upon it the full weight of its disapproval, putting the strength of Ella's and Jim's feelings to the test. Their union is made impossible not only by those around them,[19] by the world in which they live, but also by the memory, inscribed in them by the social body, depriving them of a virgin consciousness. In *The Hairy Ape*, Long conveyed the loss of a collective memory; here, in spite of themselves, the characters cannot make a clean sweep of their past. In *The Emperor Jones*, the historical flashback highlights archetypal images, which constitute the personality of Edmund Jones. *All God's Chillun Got Wings*, with a different construction, takes up this same theme. A dominant force is expressed in spite of the individual's desire to repress it, as if the thoughts of the characters were almost genetically implanted. (The following dialogue shows how difficult it is to reduce this perspective to the notion of the collective subconscious without incorporating the idea of genetic heritage, which is referred to when Hattie talks of race.)

> HATTIE. And then, she suddenly called me a dirty nigger.
> JIM. (*Torturedly*) She doesn't mean it! She isn't responsible for what she's saying!
> HATTIE. I know she isn't—yet she is just the same. It's deep down in her or it wouldn't come out.
> JIM. Deep down in her people—not deep down in her.
> HATTIE. I can't make such distinctions. The race in me, deep in me, can't stand it [*AGCGW* 334].

Not all members of the human community are easily integrated into the melting pot, and not all wounds of history heal.

There are other social rejects, not for racial reasons (and one does not forget the sick in *The Straw*, and Mary in *Long Day's Journey into Night*). There are, for example, families whom poverty has enslaved to the point of forcing them to act against their principles (see *Warnings*). The United States, the land of great promise, where immigrants hope to make their fortune, is only a falsely open country. Anxious to end the myth that success is accessible to all, in one of his early plays, *Fog*, O'Neill is concerned with the fate of those who have chosen exile and whose future is unlikely to be a happy one.[20]

Poverty, like a hereditary disease, is one of the grievances some nurture against an iniquitous system. O'Neill's critique of this, in relation to money, is not limited to the devastating diatribe addressed by Hogan to Harder ("HOGAN. But I couldn't bring myself to set foot on land bought with Standard Oil money that was stolen from the poor it ground in the dust beneath its dirty heel—land that's watered with the tears of starving widows and orphans" [*MMis* 40]). It also includes the denunciation of prejudices that stem from questionable philosophical positions. Castes are established on the basis of fortunes built up by ancestors, which fortunes act as one of the exclusion factors—the breaking down of social barriers, when it happens, being generally presented as a mistake.[21]

Financial heredity is difficult to come to terms with, money or the lack of it boxing the characters into categories difficult for them to get out of. The notion of heritage is therefore brought once again to the forefront, this time perceived in a context outside of the family. Society, through its ideology, incites the characters to make a monetary evaluation of others, the poverty of forebears becoming a burden which is carried throughout one's whole life.[22]

Without presenting a Marxist ideology, O'Neill is concerned with showing that there are social classes which are anxious to maintain their exclusivity, and the protection mechanisms they create are criticized, because they are ossifying and hinder the existential choice of individuals. (The example of Harford, in *A Touch of the Poet*, trying to bribe Con Melody so that his daughter will give up her plan to marry Simon, is characteristic.) Socially, people are not born with clean slates, they carry with them an obvious heritage. And throughout their lives they are subject to intractable judgments against which there is no appeal. Only the strongest survive, and those who cannot resist these judgments do not have a second chance. See Bigelow (*The First Man*); the same can be said of Rose and Tim (*The Web*). Other legacies are less apparent, but will influence people's behavior, even if only in response to the attacks to which they fall victim.

Faced with crushing financial power, or the omnipotence of the castes which exert moral pressure on the citizens they chaperon (see *The First Man* and, in another form, *The Straw*), ought one to aspire to a more democratic world, where the law will be that of the greatest number? The question is posed indirectly in *A Touch of the Poet*, in the electoral battle raging between the supporters of Andrew Jackson and those of John Quincy Adams. The final scenes show the end of Con Melody's dream, which marks both a liberation and a renunciation of his true self. He had built his whole life around an ideal vision of himself, calling himself an aristocrat, in spite of his profession of innkeeper. His surrender, symbolized by his use of popular language, corresponds to his siding with Andrew Jackson, whose supporters, henchmen of Bacchus, are more concerned with whiskey than with the welfare of the nation.

> MELODY. But he will be the next President, I predict, for all we others can do to prevent. There is a cursed destiny in these decadent times. Everywhere the scum rises to the top [*TP* 37].

One could not be more critical of a system and of a man to whom he will give his backing at the end of the play, but his belated support goes hand in hand with the death of a part of himself, which is projected onto society as if the arrival of Jackson corresponded to the loss of the ideal of fundamental values. As a general rule, those who represent the people are not accomplished individuals and they are looked upon fairly critically. The individual is considered superior to the scarcely human mass which surrounds him. From the contempt of Jones for his subjects, to the power of Yank in relation to the other sailors, who hardly ever think, or even the crowd embodied by the choruses (one thinks of the opening of *Mourning Becomes Electra*, or the uncompromising portraits of the entourage of Lazarus in *Lazarus Laughed*), or yet again the weighing scene in *The Straw*, the dominant impression, the message of the playwright, is that humanity is worth nothing when it runs in a pack and that masses, as such, carry no hope.[23]

Is a perfect world possible? Utopia makes its appearance in *A Touch of the Poet*, where Simon Harford retreats to a cabin he has built himself by a lake and begins writing a book on ideal society. His Rousseauistic naïveté is treated with skeptical benevolence by Sara, who is aware of the extent of his illusions.[24] Sara's lack of confidence in her fellow creatures sadly will prove in the future realistic. Simon himself will become a captain of industry, before abandoning everything and returning to meditate by the side of his lake. His case deserves further consideration, for it marks the beginning of a recurrent process that will lead characters to their downfall. (In the continuation of the cycle, some plays which O'Neill was unable to write, but for which the scenarios had already been set out, show how the protagonists follow a disastrous path, based on the same principles.)

> There is reason to believe that his Cycle became, progressively, a vehicle for his denunciation of the selfish materialism of American history and of what he considered the hypocrisy of "The American Dream."[25]

Simon becomes a symbol of the derailment of American ideals, and as the play progresses the idealist dreamer described in *A Touch of the Poet* is transformed into an unscrupulous industrialist. However, like many of O'Neill's heroes he has a dual personality. In the evening, after work, he remains alone in his study to continue reflecting on the constitution of a perfect community. The apparent break between the first play, where the notion of a cooperative community had seemed necessary to the construction of an idyllic world, and the second, where Simon becomes a prominent industrialist, is minimal and the author is careful to underline the points at which they converge. In *More Stately Mansions*, Simon's goal is to own a shipping company, a bank, a railway company, and cotton mills (he achieves this before his fall), and to build a village around his factories in order to increase his profits ("SIMON. Of course, it would be the crowning achievement if I could conceive a scheme by which the public could be compelled to buy your cotton goods and only yours—So you would own your own consumer slaves, too" [*MSM* 250]). Paradoxically, his financial ascendancy brings him back to his initial plan, characterized by the desire for autarky: a self-sufficient microcosm but this time omitting the human element. Utopia, which we know can be so destructive, is not condemned *per se*. What is denounced is the loss of meaning, the realization of a capitalist ideal bringing about a dehumanization of individuals, who become slaves (Simon being the first of these), leading to the opposite of what the characters initially sought.[26]

Who should be held responsible for the harmful attraction pulling people away from their ideals and leading them to their downfall? On the social level, the answer is money. It acts like a drug in that the protagonists are caught in an infernal cycle, which makes them want to get rich at all costs, even if they lose their own identity in the process (we remember that such a connection had already been made for *Gold* and *Where the Cross Is Made*, in a similar context). Not having much sympathy for exchange brokers,[27] O'Neill attacks speculators, considering them collectively as predators and individually as ectoplasms who have deprived themselves of their vital substance.

In *A Touch of the Poet*, Simon's father is ruined after speculating in the Western territories, much to the surprise of his family, for whom his infatuation with speculating is both inexplicable and absurd. Simon also loses everything, with the help of Sara, after having created a system where the acquisition of property implies the need to hoard more and more money. Father and son almost follow the same behavioral pattern, heralding further rises and falls to come (in the unwritten plays that were to continue the cycle). Regarding the final phase of speculative fever, the process invariably follows the same course, and far from being absurd, the form of speculation that marks financial collapse is foreshadowed from the start in the frantic desire to accumulate wealth. The characters make their fortune, then see it slip through their fingers, but this loss is presented as a victory, and their suicidal behavior is the first step in their liberation. An explanation of the paradoxical rules of the who-loses-wins game is provided by Robert, who shows that the accumulation of material wealth is at the expense of what really matters in life and that in seeking to gain the world one loses one's soul:

> ROBERT. You—a farmer—to gamble on a wheat pit with scraps of paper. There's a spiritual significance in that picture, Andy. (*He smiles bitterly*) I'm a failure, and Ruth's another—but we can both justly lay some of the blame for our stumbling on God. But you're the deepest dyed failure of the three, Andy. You've spent eight years away from yourself [*BH* 161].

Society is open to monetary success, which does not mean that social barriers come down, but the price paid for the right to make one's fortune seems excessive, compared with the results, for this pseudosuccess inevitably leads individuals to their downfall.

By attacking what seems to be the national god, the dollar, O'Neill shows in the plays how his characters are tempted with a desire for personal development, which they equate with a quest for prosperity. The dynamic which carries them along creates in them an inability to control their desire. They are tempted by the acquisition of material wealth and, as they progressively reach their goal, sink into moral decline. The parallel between taking drugs and the need to make a fortune is striking—they seem to pay in blood for the gold they accumulate, and disintegrate morally and physically (see Simon, at the end of *More Stately Mansions*: "*He falls back in her arms in a faint*" [296]). The cycle, representative of the evolution of a world, was to be called *A Tale of Possessors Self-Dispossessed*, the responsibility seeming to fall on the protagonists if we limit ourselves to the word "Self." But the representation is more complex. Their autolysis stems both from an innate weakness in humankind, and from a pecuniary snare held out to them by society that they are unable to resist.[28] James Tyrone, in his confession, shows how he has become a prisoner of money, after the experience of life has given him a magical respect for the dollar, a consequence of having spent his childhood in extreme poverty.

> TYRONE. Thirty five to forty thousand dollars net profit a season like snapping your fingers! It was too great a temptation. Yet before I bought the damned thing I was considered one of the three or four young actors with the greatest artistic promise in America [*LDJN* 150].

How can one survive in a world where people have difficulty in finding their way and which, in the guise of an offering, holds out its snares in order to lure them to their downfall? The critique is caustic, and all the more so because the failures are set against founding values, which, although they are not constantly brought to mind, are always there in the background.

Writing is not a gratuitous act. Everyone is free to define or not to define his position. In the case of O'Neill, it cannot be said that his theater demonstrates a vocation of social criticism, but his existence within the world generates meanings, some of which go beyond the context set out by the author.[29] Moreover, the anchorage in reality is too strong for him to declare, for example, as another did, that "the action takes place in Poland, in other words

Nowhere."[30] For a long time O'Neill fled the scrutiny of strangers, allowing only a few of his closest friends to come into his home. In spite of his need for solitude, he did not, however, live cut off from the rest of his contemporaries, ignorant of current affairs. His standpoints, which were very harsh in relation to the United States, reveal the interest he took in them.

> I'm going on the theory that the United States, instead of being the most successful country in the world, is the greatest failure. It's the greatest failure because it was given everything, more than any other country. Through moving as rapidly as it has, it hasn't acquired any real roots. Its main idea is that everlasting game of trying to possess your own soul by the possession of something outside it, thereby losing your own soul and the thing outside of it, too.[31]

The force of such a statement may be surprising, but it takes up elements which we have highlighted in the preceding pages. It will therefore come as no surprise that his plays were given a very cool reception by those who promote the image of an idyllic America. We may remember *All God's Chillun Got Wings*, which was the subject of much controversy before it even appeared on stage. His career was punctuated by disputes with the censor, indicating the gap between harmless light comedies and the immorality which, in the eyes of those censors, characterized some of his plays. Even in 1947, eleven years after receiving the Nobel Prize, at the first performances of *A Moon for the Misbegotten*, he had to face the censor's scissors, as Travis Bogard recalls in his very interesting book.[32]

This is not a unique event. His whole career as a dramatist was punctuated with similar incidents. From the very first, the violence of some of his plays (the force of *Thirst*, when it was first published, must have shocked), and the reactions of critics were likely to send the censors into action.[33] However it would be difficult to present O'Neill as antiestablishment or as a lesson-giver. The purpose of his writing is not to denounce the effects of one or another negative aspect of American society, inequality, corruption, or loss of collective memory, but rather to discover what it is deep within humanity that prevents it from breaking free of its chains. This is where the strength of O'Neill's theater lies. This is what, at the time, and perhaps even today, is felt as a threat by the defenders of a set or fixed society, for the stage becomes a mirror and the deep truths contained within it are destabilizing.

How much distance must be put between the plays and what was going on around him? There are certainly definite points of criticism, but is that what really matters, and can we reproach him for not getting more involved in social affairs? The question does arise, going by some often quite abrupt judgments:

> O'Neill might have grown into a key figure in American literature ... if he could have gone beyond his anticapitalistic attitude and arrived at the

positive perspective of a socialistic future that could have replaced the festering American imperialism.[34]

The "might have grown" is at the very least surprising, and the analysis seems a little perfunctory. Indeed we cannot reduce O'Neill's work to a political tract which does not quite succeed. Confronted with this criticism, we think of Yank's response, when he explains to Long how wrong he is in his simplistic proselytism: "YANK. De Cap'talist class, huh? Aw nix on dat Salvation Army–Socialist bull" (*HA* 212). If it were needed, the infantile protestation of Richard in *Ah, Wilderness!* is another indication of the lack of enthusiasm the author had for any credo, anticapitalist or otherwise.

His skepticism prevails. Evil is neither truly structural, nor does it arise out of certain economic conditions. It stems mainly from the impossibility for humanity to attain the grandeur necessary for the constitution of a world in which it could flourish. As for the possibility of beginning again on a new basis, this seems to be totally excluded.

> NIGHT CLERK. Yes, it's a goddamned racket when you stop to think, isn't it 492? But we might as well make the best of it because—well, you can't burn it all down, can you? There's too much steel and stone. There'd always be something left to start it going again [*Hu* 33].

The night porter is less optimistic than Zarathustra, for the impossible death of the city removes all hope of rebirth.[35] Life in a community is difficult, there are many obstacles, and the environment is scarcely conducive to personal fulfilment.[36] The day-to-day life presented in the plays is in sharp contrast to these idyllic islands which, from time to time, come up in the dialogue of the characters, and are described as places where individuals can directly find harmony. Existential difficulty, partly caused by the social body is, however, a kind of challenge thrown out to each one. If the characters allow themselves to be seduced by alluring escape mechanisms, they are heading for their downfall. Cabot is a typical example: tempted for a moment by the prospect of easy money in the West, he has come back to his own land and has made it prosper. His development as a person has become a fit reward and the sign of his adequacy with regard to the world. Society as such should not be blamed too much for its shortcomings. The ultimate choice comes down to individuals. It is the refusal to flee to some other illusory place, and the constant struggle—a very condition of rebirth—which makes for the grandeur of humankind.

8. The Place of the Human Being in the World.

Love's ransoms.

> Most modern plays are concerned with the relation between man and man, but that does not interest me at all. I am interested only in the relation between man and God.[1]

As is often the case, O'Neill's declarations tend to apply brakes to critical enthusiasm; but it is not possible to confine oneself to one statement, seeking to emphasize an aspect he was afraid would be neglected, at the expense of secondary questions. At first glance, his assertion could leave one confused if it were taken word for word, for it would partly contradict the body of his work as a whole. In fact, this point is more complicated than it seems, for contact between individuals sometimes lies within the relations between man and God, or more precisely, the divinity, the concept of which remains difficult to define insofar as O'Neill did not have a precise intuition of it himself. We have already envisaged the relationship which people have with the world, *via* their familial attachments. We shall now try to discover the links which unite the characters with those around them, concerning ourselves more especially with couples.

We shall see in this part of our study that, far from being insignificant, the relations that are established between two people of the opposite sex, and their temporal transformation, have an important place within O'Neill's work. The plays reveal an evolution of love or its consequences through the passage of time. The term "love" may seem surprising, when we think, for example, of *Before Breakfast*, *Bread and Butter*, or the ending of *Beyond the Horizon*. However, this tragedy is representative of love's metamorphoses, for it illustrates the progression from a hidden sentiment to the enunciation of a declaration of love, which will be transformed into hate, before sinking into a weary indifference.

> LUIS. Love is a flower
> Forever blooming.

> Life is a fountain
> Forever leaping
> Upward to catch the golden sunlight,
> Striving to reach the azure heaven;
> Failing, falling,
> Ever returning
> To kiss the earth that the flower may live [*Fou* 384].

With a prevailing mood of an eternal return, love takes hold of both the characters and their destiny, then has them pass through various stages of the life of lovers. Dream or reality, this condition has consequences for the lives of those whom it inhabits. We may, for instance, remember Richard (*Ah, Wilderness!*), and his behavior which is thought to be extravagant, resulting in his idyll with Muriel. From Richard to Reuben (*Dynamo*), when those in love find themselves forced to explain themselves regarding the nature of their affection towards their lady-love, they declare their intention to marry (*Abortion* could be an exception to this, but we may remember that Jack is already engaged to Evelyn Sands; O'Neill prefers suicide to bigamy, for his hero). The subject, seeking a kindred spirit, moves further away from reality—a force sweeps down on him like a net to ensnare him, which then binds him in an emotional web that is quickly transformed into a series of obligations from which he cannot free himself. Cupid wastes no time in demanding his ransom, which takes the form of an obligatory appearance before a minister or justice of the peace. Couples which are formed in this way appear on stage at different periods of their conjugal life, and the reasons for the marriage are not necessarily romantic.

> ERIE. Then he fell in love—or kidded himself he was—and got married. Met her on a subway train. It stopped sudden and she was jerked into him, and he put his arms around her, and they started talking, and the poor boob never stood a chance [*Hu* 23].

Driven by the desire to establish their own household, or forced to make a proposal,[2] the characters are lead inevitably towards a marriage which they enshroud in the veil of their own illusions. When they can see more clearly, they realize, too late, that the wedding bands on their fingers have been turned into handcuffs. In *Hughie*, Erie evokes the disillusionment of the couple, followed by the resignation of the two parties[3]—which is an exception, for in general disenchantment precedes conflict.

Before concentrating our attention on the matrimonial variants to be encountered in the plays, we will pause to consider an emblematic example of conjugal difficulty, that of Curtis in *The First Man*: "CURTIS. I love you. You are me and I am you! What use is all this vivisecting?" (588). Unable to live without his wife, he presupposes a unity with her, which shows the extent of his blindness. His inability to accept his wife's desire for a child is easily understood: the introduction of a son would put an end to the union of two people which has been built up over the years and within which Martha hides her pain. In fact, their relationship is not based on an absolute love but rather, as far as he is concerned, on a need, and for Martha, on a permanent sacrifice ("CURTIS. I love you so, Martha! You've made yourself part of my life, my work—I need you so! [*FM* 586]). He asks her to prolong their partnership, centered upon his work, which sets them apart from the rest of the world, isolation being the guarantee of happiness. He defines his expectations, and the rupture of the previous harmony is the result of Martha's inability to satisfy his desire. The passage from perfect harmony to discord comes about suddenly, and these differences are facilitated by the innumerable needs each member of the couple has. In the plays the characters are frequently in pursuit of an *alter ego*, able to meet the many demands which the characters feel are necessary for their own fulfillment. In *More Stately Mansions*, Sara points out what is indispensable for the happiness of husbands.

> SARA. He has no life except in my love. And I love him more than ever woman loved a man! I'm mother, wife and mistress in one [*MSM* 264].

This says it all. The model wife devotes herself entirely to her husband, and is able to fulfill her three main roles—we note that the premier position occupied by the maternal component underlines its importance. We can understand the annoyance shown by some feminist critics who find these matrimonial desires a little narrow and difficult to accept in this day and age. We may remember the critique made by J. Barlow, regarding the image of women; however we must not condemn the playwright, for reality is always complex.[4] Two points need to be underlined. First, we cannot reproach too severely the external nature of the O'Neillian vision. He was a man and as such was trying to understand the female character from a perspective which can only be an external one. (I believe that it is in this sense that the reproach is made against him, for otherwise the critique would lose its relevance, as Nina, in *Strange Interlude*, is presented from the inside, through her thoughts.) Second, to declare that his vision is a masculine one seems a little hasty. Indeed, if the ideal female companion, described in the plays, has a threefold mental configuration, one part maternal, the other corresponding to the wife, and the third to the lover, the ideal man, such as he appears in *Strange Interlude* and *Days Without End*,[5] is supposed to comply with the same criteria. It is therefore not a simplistic masculine vision, even if it is shared by certain other men, who are also tortured by their Oedipus complex, but rather an O'Neillian perspective, which we may nonetheless regret is not more subtle and profound. Whatever the reactions of critics and spectators may be, we must point out that this image of woman is particular to the author, and is found, with very slight variations, in a very large number of his plays.

The relationship which is established between the couple turns, if not quite into slavery, at least to self-denial by one of them, who sacrifices himself or herself that the other might enjoy happiness in their daily life. This theme is very apparent; it was the subject of one of the author's first works, *Servitude,* and is developed in his last, *A Touch of the Poet* and *More Stately Mansions* (and, to a certain extent, in *A Moon for the Misbegotten*). Critics could find room for more comment on this aspect of the servant-wife, for some plays are an exhortation to sacrifice and place women in a secondary role which does not allow her to be a partner worthy of her husband.

> MRS. ROYLSTON. Love means servitude, and *my* love is *my* happiness [*Ser* 270].

She sums up in very few words the role of women in the O'Neillian universe, and says that she is prepared to do anything in order that Mr. Roylston, the well-known writer, may be happy ("MRS. ROYLSTON. How many of you would make the sacrifice I will make? How many of you would be willing to give him up to another woman because your love was so great?" [*Ser* 270]). This unrequited love is received by the husbands as being their due, and they avoid questioning themselves about their conjugal life, or else they see the blind admiration of their spouse as proof that, intellectually, their union is morganatic ("ROYLSTON. I have always rejected the temptation to analyze my home relations. They are pleasant enough and that is all I care to know" [*Ser* 249]; "FIFE. I might as well be married to a cow" [*Dy* 429]). Faced with this half-unconsciousness of the devotion of the other partner, the only example where daily crucifixion is recognized as such is given in *The Iceman Cometh*. Here, Hickey is aware of his baseness. The saintliness of Evelyn becomes unbearable to him because it highlights his spinelessness and, no longer able to accept the image of himself that is being reflected, he kills her.

Sacrifice is principally inscribed in the feminine; it constitutes, according to Mrs. Roylston, the road to happiness, but when renunciation is made to appear more masculine, it becomes a catastrophe. In *Bread and Butter*, John abandons his career as an artist at the insistence of Maud, and the loss of his *raison d'être* is the cause of his decline, which he terminates by his suicide. Their marriage had become a kind of hell; by suppressing his vocation, he destroyed what was strongest in him and, even for love, this self-destructive denial can only lead to failure. Another tragic example of masculine self-denial is in *Diff'rent*: Caleb, seeing himself betrayed after thirty years of betrothal, hangs himself after having realized the extent of his baseness and how contemptible were his expectations. Conjugal happiness is possible, in a sacrificial perspective, as long as the women devote themselves entirely to satisfying the desires of their spouses, and the egoism of the latter, or their blindness, is strong enough to allow them to live harmoniously. This emotional latency is partially successful, but where it exists, the awareness of the failure of the marriage engenders conflict between the characters; it is here that the dual influence of Ibsen and Strindberg becomes apparent in the structure of the plays. (In *Before Breakfast*, the husband, plagued by his wife and his own guilt, slits his throat, and the noise of the body overturning a chair as it falls to the floor reminds one of the gunshot of *Hedda Gabler*.) The break-up of the marriage contract could be brought about by divorce, but this solution, which is less radical than the repeated suicides, scarcely has a role in the O'Neillian universe (the option of divorce seen in *Bread and Butter* is immediately rejected: "JOHN. You forget my wife is a good member of the church. She has principles. She remembers the sacred duty of every God-fearing wife toward her husband—to make him as miserable as possible" [*B&B* 78]). We could look for the causes of this in the paralyzing puritanism described by John, but we will see later that the reasons are altogether different. As for puritanism, the main reproach made against this dogma is the danger that individuals, through their sacrifice, will deny themselves which, according to the author, is a fundamental error.

Before beginning the chronicle of lovelessness, and studying the sources of antagonism, we must pause to consider what it is that prevents people from flourishing within the couple and, more generally, what their relationship with love is.

> DION. Why am I afraid to love, I who love? ... Why was I born without a skin, O God, that I must wear armor in order to touch or to be touched? [*GGB* 264].

Love has a destabilizing effect and, from Dion to Caligula (*Lazarus Laughed*), there are many who fear its consequences ("LOVING. He saw that underneath all his hypocritical pretense he really hated love. He wanted to deliver himself from its power and be free again" [*DWE* 538]). Both aware of and suffering from his human fragility, Dion testifies to the need for protection, which will shelter him from external aggression. The refusal or the hatred of love arises from the first condition attached to achieving it: each must take off his mask, and reveal himself as he really is. With a lover's naïveté, Dion, believing he has found the perfect union with Margaret, reveals his true face to her. He is rejected however, and manages to shake off his social image only when he is with Cybel, the prostitute, with whom he finds the motherly concern and understanding he needs. Hating, or not loving, signifies that the character has retreated from the world, sheltered from the wounds to his ego which are as painful as those caused by the refusal of maternal affection. Attachments increase the vulnerability of the characters. Consequently, all unreciprocated declarations of love are unbearable. The protagonists put their very beings on the line, and the refusal of the other person, or their indifference, is as good as a death sentence for him or her who has declared their feelings. *The*

Straw is an example of this. All hopes of a cure for Eileen fade away, for fighting against her illness becomes futile after Murray has confessed that he does not share her feelings. Here, to say "I love you" has two-fold consequences. First, whoever may be on the receiving end, the speaker, at the moment of expressing himself, asserts his existence through the use of the "I," and second, the relationship that he establishes gives the receiver of his declaration of love the power to destroy him, by failing to respond to his expectations, or by removing any hope, however minute, that his love will one day be returned.

To dare to show one's true colors, to externalize one's feelings is a moral *coup de force* which some have the courage to make. However, in spite of these valiant acts—we have seen how vulnerable the characters are—these declarations carry no guarantee of happiness.

> KEENEY. (*In amazed embarrassment at this outburst*) Love you? Why d'you ask me such a question, Annie?
> MRS. KEENEY. (*Shaking him—fiercely*) But you do, don't you, David? Tell me!
> KEENEY. I'm your husband, Annie, and you're my wife. Could there be aught but love between us after all these years?
> MRS. KEENEY. (*Shaking him again—still more fiercely*) Then you do love me. Say it!
> KEENEY. (*Simply*) I do, Annie! [*Ile* 548-9].

The need for moral reassurance, and the impossibility of putting up with the icy environment any longer, have led to this confrontation, during which Mrs. Keeney asks her husband, the captain, to turn the boat around with the hold half empty, he who has always returned to port with it full of oil. She begs him to cast aside his pride, in other words a part of himself, and to turn and go back, for she is afraid she will go mad. He hesitates between his love for her and the damage he dare not inflict on the ideal image of himself which has guided him throughout his whole life. The cries from the crow's nest, signaling the sighting of whales, sound the knell of his hesitation, and everyone springs into action on the bridge while Mrs. Keeney sinks into madness. O'Neill does not condemn the character's selfishness. On the contrary, reinforced by his Nietzschean reading, he presents egoism, in its masculine form and from the point of view of being true to oneself, as a virtue. The picture of this elderly couple presents a union that is paradoxical but very O'Neillian. How can we make sense of the final line, the assurance of affection given to the wife; must we replace the "I do" with "I don't know"? In fact, this play develops an essential idea we find in several works. (We can think of *Diff'rent*, but also of Cabot in *Desire Under the Elms*, who doubts and wonders if he has not been too severe. He is a prisoner of his convictions, of his belief in an inflexible God, and he cannot go back—give up, if we remember the condemnation of the speculators in *Beyond the Horizon*—without life's losing all its meaning for him.) Keeney is a prisoner because he is true to an idea of himself that he cannot give up without destroying himself. If he sails back, the world he has built up bit by bit, the image of himself, which allows him to live, will disappear; the play will then turn towards a new version of *Bread and Butter*, where John renounces through love and condemns himself to death. His choice leads to the mental disintegration of his wife, who made her tragic end inevitable by abandoning her home to follow her husband, leaving a place where she had a role, even if it was an imperfect one. Every renunciation is suicidal, the characters must hold on, fight against adversity, if they have to, suppress their affection, and stay on the course they have decided upon lest they get lost. Destroy or be destroyed, such is the impossible choice each member of the couples must confront.

Running away is a possibility—to find, somewhere else, if not a new kind of stability at least some consolation for these unhappy loves. The fate of former lovers is barely brighter than that of husbands. Whiskey cannot dissolve memories, time does not efface them,[6] and forgetfulness comes only with death.

> PARRITT. It's really Mother you still love—isn't it?—in spite of the dirty deal she gave you [*IC* 157].

However much Larry may feign a pseudophilosophical detachment, he does not succeed in putting his tumultuous liaison with Rosa down to just another lost passion. He remains a prisoner of his regrets, which take the form of the unforgettable portrait of a lady. Lucid, he surrenders his arms. His opposition to change constitutes a long wait for death, while other victims of incurable break-ups have chosen to flee, boarding steamships (*In the Zone* and *The Moon of the Caribees* present characters whose lives have been reduced to the veneration of a memory, and who make up the sad number of those who have led a lost existence, because they could not emulate the strength of the other's love). Some, bruised by their emotional disappointments, have lost their zest for life, but we must avoid easy generalizations. In a world of play-actors, the wounds of love are sometimes simulated, because playing the role of the unhappy lover or husband enables them to mask a reality that is even more sordid: "HICKEY. (*Ignoring this—with a kidding grin*) But I'll bet when you admit the truth to yourself, you'll confess you were pretty sick of her hating you for getting drunk. I'll bet you were really damned relieved when she gave you such a good excuse" (*IC* 657).

Should every attachment be given up? Not everyone loses hope and, conscious of the lack of fulfillment in their union, some tell their partner of the emptiness they feel inside. In two confession scenes, Cabot (*Desire Under the Elms*) and Mannon (*Mourning Becomes Electra*) try to communicate with their wives. To do this they remove their masks and confess how lonely they feel:

> MANNON. But my life as just me ending, that didn't appear worth a thought one way or another. But listen, me as your husband being killed, that seemed queer and wrong—like something dying that had never lived. Then all the years we've been man and woman would rise up in my mind and I would try to look at them. But nothing was clear except that there'd always been some barrier between us—a wall hiding us from each other! [*MBE, Homecoming* 54].

Christine does not have the courage to listen to these words. Abbie's mind is elsewhere, and at the end of their confessions, the two men find themselves just as alone, wounded by the incomprehension of their spouses. Cabot states his loneliness and his quest for someone who could understand him, and his third marriage constitutes the final step of a quest which has lasted his whole life. Fatalistic, he has a feeling that his wishes will never be fulfilled. However he does not give up, as if the possibility of total communion with another soul were being refused him by a merciless God who demands that he never give up hope. Holding on—such is the motto of these two pathetic solitary figures. Orin, explaining to Lavinia the origin of his father's nickname,[7] points out precisely what made him great—Cabot would also be worthy of such a tribute.

With no illusions, Mannon knows that the tasks to which he has devoted himself are only a refuge from the unhappiness which weighs him down. Sounding the retreat is his form of resistance. Contrary to his brother, defeated by alcohol, he never gives up: Bold, his lucidity in the time of trial is the mark of his courage. Contrary to those who want to make their fortune and destroy themselves in the process, his activities do not lead to his downfall, for he knows they are only a way out which allows him to hide the extent of his existential solitude. His community activities are no more than a stop-gap measure. His emotional destitution is painful for him, but he does not deceive himself regarding the futility of his ascent up the social ladder, which he would gladly give up for a fulfilling relationship with his wife.[8]

The discovery of the other person comes down in part to a variation on the misunderstanding theme. Couples are formed in the hope of finding the ideal partner, but time takes its toll, and the blindness of the lovers gives way to the gnawing criticism of spouses. Many of the works are chronicles of lovelessness, and the causes of conjugal misunderstanding are numerous. *Beyond the Horizon* develops the theme of lost illusions, which are one of the main causes of discord. Indeed after the blissful honeymoon period of a relationship, some characters find themselves tied to a partner whom they discover too late to be very different from themselves. Symbolic of disappointed heroines, Mary Tyrone exemplifies the passage from the blindness of love to disillusionment.

> MARY. And he was handsomer than my wildest dream, in his make up and his nobleman's costume that was so becoming to him. He was different from all ordinary men, like someone from another world [*LDJN* 105].

8. The Place of the Human Being in the World.

The actor's make-up and costume are symbolic. They indicate very clearly the error made by Mary, a prisoner of appearances, in not trying to find out who was really behind this mask. This vision inevitably constitutes the prelude to many bitter days in the future and, in her case, contact with reality is a very brutal experience. In other works, the heroes and heroines go through similar episodes.[9]

There is a classic pessimism in this perception of conjugal life. What is distinctive about the O'Neillian vision is a particular relationship which goes beyond the difficulty of two very different people living together. We have already alluded to the impossibility of divorce as a means of separating the characters; what prevents them from having access to this social solution comes from the specific nature of their conjugal ties. Come success or failure, the couples live in an isolated sphere; those around them, even those closest to them are relegated to a distant position, with an often negative, but limited, capacity for action. If conjugal life turns into a hell, the hope of individual freedom from it could justify a separation, but this is shown to be impossible. Social or familial considerations are not taken into account. It is only the existence of alternate feelings which prevents them from splitting up, for separation is as unbearable to them as living together. An archetype of this situation is in *Welded*, a play with an evocative title, where Eleanor and Michael Cape have a passionate love relationship, undermined by jealousy and the need for a total communion every minute of the day, which is at the root of conflicts.[10]

> CAPE. I've grown inward into our life. But you keep trying to escape as if it were a prison. You feel the need of what is outside. I'm not enough for you.
> ELEANOR. Why is it I can never know you? I try to know you and I can't. I desire to take all of you into my heart, but there's a great alien force— I hate that unknown power in you which would destroy me [*Wel* 453].

We cannot state that the desire for separation is always present in the woman, and the wish for relegation belongs to the man. On the other hand, without making any gender classification, we can say that the desire for closeness, suffocating for the partner, and the desire to escape are recurrent themes. For the family, we talked about the kiss of the vampire which marks one as being a definitive member of a community. Here it is more like a praying mantis (women do not have a monopoly on psychological ravaging: see Cape in *Welded*): Marriage is destructive, at least for one of the parties to the contract. Seeing the characters one thinks of the androgynous figure who lives with the mad hope of finding another part of himself, which is a constant in love relationships. In opposition to this desire for symbiosis, there hides a thirst for freedom, a refusal of the union, for it implies a loss of individuality, and this latent rejection slowly undermines all attempts at conjugal understanding. Thus, Jim and Ella (in *All God's Chillun Got Wings*), whose love is continually battered in spite of themselves, present an example of two people each of whom drives the other to madness. They do not manage to find harmony, for psychologically they are not pure. The causes of the failure of their marriage are twofold: For Ella, the weight of the past takes the form of a subconscious racism,[11] and for Jim, an inferiority complex makes him aspire to a metamorphosis, which will be a real denial of his personality.

We find here once again the idea of the loss of one's identity, exposed by O'Neill when he evokes the speculators. The harmony, sought for but impossible to achieve, kills itself because the contradictory demands it makes are insoluble: joining together gives rise to a partial renunciation of who one really is, but when this happens, it makes the union lose its meaning; moreover, to remain oneself destroys the partner. In the majority of plays the conclusion drawn by the spectator is that the fusion of two human beings can only take place in the land of pipe dreams.

O'Neillian drama makes one think of the tales of chivalry, where love is granted only after the knight has overcome all the obstacles. Here the difficulty is greater, for both parties are constantly subjected to initiation tests. Some manage momentarily to avoid the traps, and join together in spite of the hostility of their environment (for instance, Sara and Simon in *More Stately Mansions* and *A Touch of the Poet*, as well as Mrs. Baldwin and Fred in *Recklessness*); declarations follow on, passion isolates the characters, they give absolute priority to their lovers' exaltation without regard to its consequences.

> MRS. BALDWIN. I'd rather die of starvation with you than live the way I'm living now [*Reck* 115].

This fervor has a dual effect: on the one hand, the future lovers create their own universe, without any direct relation with those around them, and on the other hand, they imagine, falsely, as individuals this time, that they are cut off from the rest of the world by the force of their feelings. At the end of *Anna Christie*, the prospect of the heroes' getting married earned O'Neill a few run-ins with the critics, who denounced what they saw as the easy optimism of the final scene; with hindsight, this false interpretation is almost amusing.

Anna Christie and Mat Burke decide to marry: Strengthened by their love, they feel a sense of autonomy; the prospect of establishing a family has them imagine a future whose center is a child still to be born, their view of future times having no concept of the power of fate. Chris' final words are, however, a bad omen. They outline the limits of the characteristic detachment of those who have been touched by Cupid's arrows. Their faith in impunity can perhaps be explained by an imagined generalization of a purification process through love; we note indeed that the flame which inhabits the protagonists has purifying qualities—thus, Anna, the prostitute, claims her metamorphosis and feels that she has regained a state of innocence:

ANNA. (*She pleads passionately*) Will you believe me if I tell you that loving you has made me—clean? [*AC* 59-60].

Shared love is a rebirth, and each offers to his or her partner the possibility of a fresh start. The characters find it difficult to evaluate the consequences of their feelings. It is a revelation, first of all because the individuals find a part of themselves that they did not know existed—exemplified in the confession of Mat Burke, who recognizes his failure for the first time in his life—and second, because it is a delayed love at first sight. The realization of their reciprocal passion, and of its intensity, happens very suddenly: in *Anna Christie*, *Desire Under the Elms*, or *The Straw*, the characters do not at first realize how much the presence of their partner is necessary to them. The revelation is sudden; they experience an indefinable sensation, which turns out to be love.[12] Mat Burke, Eben, and Murray distance themselves from the woman they love, but each knows that escape is impossible. They all realize that their place is at the side of the one they are trying in vain to keep away from, even if it is to take them to the gallows. When they understand this, they find in their union a force which gives them serenity.

Beyond the purifying aspect of love, O'Neill shows the ephemeral, the flame which glows before it dies. The union between two characters becomes timeless; this timelessness is, however, short-lived, for it is impossible to escape from time and from the world. The communion between two people has a mystical aspect; the sexual dimension is not removed but O'Neill refuses to give it a prominent position. He demonstrates that taking into account only the physical aspect of relations between two characters will lead them to their downfall, for putting too much value on it is restrictive and primitive: "REUBEN. You can tell her I've read up on love in biology, and I know what it is now, and I've proved it with more than one female (*Dy* 458). As opposed to Reuben's claims to know everything about love, Mannon takes an entirely different position, in which he undermines the importance of carnal relations that, Christine believes, constitute his brutal and only conception of conjugal bliss:

> MANNON. (*With bitter scorn*) Your body? What are bodies to me? I've seen too many rotting in the sun to make grass greener! Ashes to ashes, dirt to dirt! Is that your notion of love? Do you think I married a body?... You were lying to me tonight as you've always lied! You were only pretending love! You let me take you as if you were a nigger slave I'd bought at auction! You made me appear a lustful beast in my own eyes! [*MBE*, *Homecoming* 60].

One could quite wrongly, it seems to me, deduce that puritanism has entangled the author in a purified vision of love. There is nothing of the sort; the ideas upheld in *The Calms of Capricorn*[13] testify to that. However, whether it be a case of passion or of very strong attachments, the emotions felt allow the characters to forget the past and those around them—the encounter between James Tyrone and Josie illustrates this. She, on the other hand, speaks of the men with whom she has had casual affairs, her solitude, and her disgust as she waited for dawn, for what matters to her, in her relationship with James, is not specifically the absence of sexual intercourse, but what differentiates that particular night from all the others. As the action progresses, we find strong echoes of the Platonic vision of love. Initially, Tyrone evokes the physical beauty of Josie; he then moves on to another dimension, that of the soul, and Josie, perceiving the difference, is ready to respond to his proposal: "JOSIE. But it might be different with you. Love could make it different. And I've been head over heels in love ever since you said you loved my beautiful soul" (*MMis* 81). Everyone is seeking unity with the other person and through their lover's quest we recognize the myth of the androgyne developed by Plato (but which O'Neill may also have found in Chinese or Indian mythology).[14]

The figures of the mother and the child have often been evoked—the pietà in *A Moon for the Misbegotten*—and this evocation is legitimate, but there is in the background a unity which surpasses the relationship of the child to the mother; the androgyne which denies the differences, the individual having found the path to absolute cohesion.[15]

> JOSIE. You'll never see me again now, and I know that's best for us both, but I can't bear to have you ashamed you wanted my love to comfort your sorrow—when I'm so proud I could give it [*MMis* 112].

The grip loosens, and the two protagonists find themselves alone once more to face the world. The only couple who attain perfect union are Eben and Abbie, and time will be unable to separate them for they are going to die. In the two examples quoted, Eben and James Tyrone, the maternal image disappears in favor of that of a complementary character, which allows them to find the much sought-after union. Even if the ecstasy is short-lived, through love and by finding their ideal partner, the characters attain serenity, the total wholeness which, when the harmony is broken, will remain with them as a moment which gave their lives meaning. The return to the original unity is the sign of belonging to the whole, a rebirth which allows one to go beyond reality in a union that is almost divine.

Friendship.

Couples are not necessarily made up of a man and a woman. In the plays it is often two men who form a nucleus within a community. We have already discussed brotherly relationships, which constitute one specific case of the masculine links; we will now turn our attention to the relationships established between two characters who have become inseparable from each other.

8. The Place of the Human Being in the World. 105

> DRISCOLL. Five years and more ut is since first I shipped wid him, and we've stuck together ivir since through good luck and bad. Fights we've had, God help us, but 'twas only when we'd a bit av drink taken, and we always shook hands the nixt mornin' [*BEC* 480].

Sailors, who spend their lives traveling the seas, strike up friendships and, drifting wherever their voyages carry them, for a period of time they share the destiny of other sailors. Not having any real attachments, the rare allusions to their family roots often take the form of an obituary column; it is around these friendships that they build their lives.[16] In the episode quoted, as Yank lay dying, the men find themselves in the crew's quarters awaiting their turn to take the watch. He evaluates the links he has with the rest of the world and, having gone through a few memories, the only name which remains with him is that of Driscoll, his friend. On his death bed, he talks about a plan for the future, for which he knows it is too late, involving a complete change in his life, a change he felt ready to make, provided his companion went with him.[17] Yank's despair is all the more pathetic in that, through fear of being hurt, he had not dared to tell his dream to someone he considered a brother. Duality is found where one would not expect it.

Behind the superman image of the sailor hide characters who are afraid to show who they really are, afraid of being destroyed by the mocking laughter of one of their fellows. Yank is left with only regrets. Between rattling coughs, he bemoans the fact of having made one voyage too many, and deplores not having begun a new life on land. Perhaps his plans should be classed as utopian, for his real place is on board a ship, but even if that were the case, they are part of those delusions which help the characters to live. Driscoll, while being one of those closest to him, fulfilled a role similar to that of the dreams or plans for the future. For Yank he represented a traveling companion whose constant presence gave him the courage to persevere, to accept day after day the thankless tasks he had to undertake, without their lives' appearing meaningless. Cursing the crew members who are disturbing Yank's rest, Driscoll fulfills his duty as a loyal friend by comforting him. When remorse is too much for Yank, his friend helps him to exorcise it and, with clumsy helplessness, stays by his side right up until his last breath.

How can one live on when the other dies? In *Hughie*, a magnificent play in the form of an elegy for a night porter, O'Neill conveys the despair of Erie Smith following the death of Hughie. The context is different but the emptiness is described, the affective void which takes from the characters their desire to live. Every evening, Erie provided Hughie with the chance to escape to a magical world. As for the passive naïveté of the night porter, who listened to him recount unlikely stories, and let him win at dice, it allowed him to build up an image of an invincible player, making him forget how sordid his daily activities as a failed gambler were. In a final friendly gesture, Erie decides to give his sidekick a grandiose funeral, reflecting the scale of his affection for him.

ERIE. That was some display, Pal. It'd knock your eye out! Set me back a hundred bucks, and no kiddin'! A big horseshoe of red roses! I knew Hughie 'd want a horseshoe because that made it look like he'd been a horse player. And around the top printed in forget-me-nots was "Good-by, Old Pal." Hughie liked to kid himself he was my pal.
He adds sadly.
And so he was, at that—even if he was a sucker [*Hu* 31].

Little by little, his long monologue reveals the nature of the feelings he had for Hughie. At first, he shows his grief, but speaks of the night porter with a condescension which gradually disappears, and he ends up by confessing how much he misses his alter ego: "ERIE. I miss Hughie, I guess. I guess I'd got to like him a lot" (*Hu* 18). Between this line and the ones quoted immediately above, Erie has evolved, he has realized how important Hughie was to him. He finally acknowledges it by conferring on him the status of friend. He attributes his lack of luck to the death of Hughie, but the audience can see that his distress goes beyond the preoccupations caused by temporary indigence. The loss of his companion leaves him distraught, alone in a world where he no longer has a place. He no longer has any way of constructing an ideal picture for himself, which used to sustain him in his struggle against his existentialist fear, by providing him with a means to face the world with complete confidence.

Not everyone has the chance to have such friends. The twosomes put on stage are sometimes composed of characters who view each other critically but who have a tacit agreement to avoid caustic remarks. To speak of hypocrisy would be to go too far. At the very most it is fawning, for none really deludes himself as to the gullibility of those around him. Each accepts that the other is presenting a potentially ideal portrait, which he pretends to believe in. In return, the partner is lending himself qualities he does not really believe in himself, but external approbation is necessary to his existence. Hughie allowed Erie Smith to construct a character and conversely, Erie helped the poor night watchman lead a gallant and adventurous life by proxy. Is that the only purpose served by friendship? What is the use of having friends? Upon the death of Con Melody, Cregan questions the justification of his attitude and the role he played.

NORA. You were the one friend he had in the world.
CREGAN.(*Bitterly*) I'm thinkin' now I was maybe only a drunken sponge who helped him kill himself.
NORA. Don't think it. Sure you know as well as me, it was the broken heart of his pride murthered him, not dhrink. Think of what good you did him. It was only wid you he'd forgit once in a while and let himself remember what he used to be. An' wid me [*MSM* 26-7].

Of what good is it to tell the truth, and which truth? From the O'Neillian perspective, traveling companions must support those close to them, helping

8. The Place of the Human Being in the World. 107

them to face up to day to day living, but it is not for them to put aside others' masks. *The Iceman Cometh* presents on stage a group of characters who have been rejected by society and eaten away by alcohol, but who still believe that if they wanted to they could once more fit into the world from which they have been excluded. None is taken in by the words of their neighbor, and the Piet Wetjoen–Cecil Lewis pair is clear proof of this. Everyone agrees with what their sidekick says, until the moment when Hickey calls the alliances into question and the official version of the existential ruination each of them is going through is expounded by the one who had given the impression of believing in them the most. The effects are disastrous and all find themselves alone, faced with an unbearable truth. Unable to accept this destructive vision of themselves, which is the equivalent of a death sentence, they return to the fold with the secret hope of being able to forget everything. In a group therapy session, where they speak one after the other, those who surround the speaker turn into a group of friends, ready to believe any assertion he may make. Each character then recounts how he has overcome the obstacle without deceiving himself and leading Hickey to believe that he was really about to begin a new chapter. Life is reconstructed around lies and half-truths which the bruised characters need to carry on living.

From the examples quoted, one could be led to believe that the only role played by friends is to listen to a truncated speech. This is not the case. They must above all know how to share, and listening is only one particular form of empathy.[18] As such, *The First Man*, is a very enlightening work: Curtis, on bad terms with his wife ever since he found out that she was pregnant, feels the need to confide in someone. He refuses the pseudo–moral support which the members of his family are ready to offer him, and wants more than anything to contact one single friend. By confiding his darkest thoughts to Bigelow, who is horrified by his words, he exorcises that which was preventing him from living normally. He was a prisoner of his morbid desires, which he knew were unacceptable, and was no longer able to be himself. His friendship with Bigelow therefore allows him to break free from the isolation he was suffering.

As is often the case in O'Neill's plays, one feeling gives rise to its opposite. At first glance, it may seem surprising to include *The Great God Brown* in this section devoted to friendship, but the Brown-Anthony twosome functions in a way very similar to that of the couples seen in the other plays. Their relationship is one of both opposition and sacred alliance. Their antagonism goes back to their childhood, when Brown's betrayal united them forever, insofar as this action marked both a division and a link, an original sin, the consequences of which will be felt throughout their whole lives.

> DION. One day when I was four years old, a boy sneaked up behind when I was drawing a picture in the sand he couldn't draw and hit me on the

> head with a stick and kicked out my picture and laughed when I cried. It wasn't what he'd done that made me cry, but him! I had loved and trusted him and suddenly the good God was disproved in his person and the evil and injustice of Man was born! Everyone called me crybaby, so I became silent for life and designed a mask of the Bad Boy Pan in which to live and rebel against that other boy's God and protect myself from His cruelty. And that other boy, secretly he felt ashamed but he couldn't acknowledge it; so from that day he instinctively developed into the good boy, the good friend, the good man, William Brown! [*GGB* 295].

Everything is there in this primitive scene. The guilt of the one and the pathological insecurity of the other will lead to a subconscious pact, from which they will be unable to free themselves. The "good friend" is shown to be of relative benevolence. In spite of himself, he cannot help desiring what the other possesses, and Dion himself is unable to break away from the one with whom a link was made in his early childhood. In their case, harmony is impossible. By contrast, it is symbolically achieved in the architectural projects they conceive together, which allow them to bring out their complementary nature. In fact, they are too different for a symbiosis to be possible. Paradoxically, it is that which separates them—their complementary nature—that prevents them from detaching themselves completely one from the other. It is a phenomenon identical to the one we saw as regards the couples in love. The proof of this impossible fusion is found when William attempts to assume the character of Dion after his death. This ends in failure and his life becomes hell, for in taking on the mask of Dion, he has lost his own identity. Can we call the links which unite them amicable? It seems possible to reply in the affirmative, although they are the opposite of those of Orestes and Pylades. If the wound evoked in the dialogue quoted above has never healed, friendship has always remained in the background. It has been bruised, their feelings are extreme and contradictory, alternating between love and hate, but that corresponds perfectly to the O'Neillian vision of a normal relationship between two people. Following the example of certain characters whom we have seen mutually destroy each other, they cannot break their attachment, and are dependent on their double for survival. They know the real side of their fraternal enemy, and know how to discern what lies behind appearances. Consequently, each knows that with the other he will be able to express himself and be understood, and will even be able to reveal his true nature without fear.

The death of Dion, by William Brown's side, is a prelude to that of William, who dies in Cybel's arms. Each has found a confessor, someone with whom they can stop putting on an act. With Cybel, they have found the maternal solicitude they needed, but apart from this prostitute, only their fraternal enemy knows who they really are. The triangular relationship which builds up between Cybel, William and Dion is such that it may give rise to certain questioning. However, in the play, the sexual dimension between the two men is almost disposed of. We could of course speak of latent homosexuality, which seems to be undeniable, but this time, if the individuals are looking for the androgyne, the masculine component is confined to the symbolic level, and the author seems to have tried to polarize sexuality around Cybel. This is not a sentimental quest. They are looking first and foremost for an alter ego with whom they will be able to put aside their masks, but undoubtedly the most important thing is that the presence of their double, even if he is hated, reassures them about their own existence and, paradoxically, helps them to live.

Friendships are at the root of confidences, which often take the form of a confession, and are an indispensable element of individual well-being. In the dialogues, the contact which is established leads to a to-ing and fro-ing between the "I" and the "you." There is a response from the listener, which is contrary to the social indifference towards the words of the solitary speakers. Indeed the play between the personal pronouns reveals a void between an isolated "I" and a "they" formed by impenetrable worlds, throwing back a sad image of the individuals because they are perceived as object and not as subject, which constitutes a denial of existence. We can therefore say that friendship, even when it has unorthodox aspects, occupies a position of prime importance, for following the example of communion between lovers, which we saw to be exceptional and fragile, friendships provide a support, a necessary moral sustenance, in a world where sources of comfort are thin on the ground.

9. Belonging.

Groups.

Evolving within a family environment, supported by the love or the friendship of another person, the characters manage to survive if they find among those close to them the opportunity to be listened to. One of the other means of escaping the anxiety borne of an existential solitude is to be part of a group.

In the sea plays, O'Neill presents a section of the crew of a cargo ship, which makes up a human mosaic of which each element is necessary to the coherence of the whole. Initially, the individual as such is of little importance. What matters is the internal cohesion which joins the different sailors together, for in spite of their diverse nationalities, they form a closely linked team within which each character can find his place. With Bacchus and Neptune as their only gods, they know how to pay them homage, and their libations seal their membership in the community of sailors. There is no doubt in their minds that they are members of a class apart, one to which they are proud to belong. The relationship they have with the rest of the world is summed up by Yank, in *The Hairy Ape*, who has nothing but contempt for those who do not have the honor of belonging to the caste:

> YANK. Dem boids don't amount to nothin'. Dey're just baggage. Who makes dis old tub run? Ain't it us guys? Well, den, we belong, don't we? We belong and dey don't. Dat's all [*HA* 212].

He is to realize that the postulate of a symbiosis between him and the sea, via his boat, which gave meaning to his life, is not at all obvious. Like his companions, he was deluding himself as to the importance of his position as an element making up part of a whole. His hard labor, consisting in supplying machines with fuel, when it is viewed by a stranger, loses the magical dimension he had attributed to it, and this disillusionment makes him aware of his status as an inferior being. Paddy's speech about the past was not just due to the nostalgia of a drunken old sailor. It rang true, demonstrating the extent to which man had lost his unity with the elements, in abandoning the wind in favor of mechanical propellants: "PADDY. 'Twas them days men belonged to ships, not now. 'Twas them days a ship was part of the sea, and man was part of a ship, and the sea joined all together and made it one" (*HA* 214).

Mildred's arrival will confirm the validity of his diagnosis, and Yank, conscious of this lost harmony, will launch himself in a quest aimed at establishing his identity, and his place in society. However, even if there has been a corruption, to the extent that the pure relationship which existed between man and the sea has been perverted, we must not underestimate the importance for the sailors of the sea and of community life. Kelli Larson[1] declares that they are without ties, and for this reason they do not belong to a group. It seems to me that this point of view is erroneous for several reasons. In fact the sea plays show that the crew constitutes a kind of family, within which the sailors feel at ease (bringing to mind the human mass described in *The Iceman Cometh*), even if their feeling of being linked to a whole is based partly on self-deception, as Paddy's speech proves.[2] Moreover, if, when they are on land, their activities do not provoke admiration, what is described is part of a kind of ritual which each sailor must undergo. The aim of O'Neill in presenting them on stage was undoubtedly not to launch moralizing lectures. Finally they are navigators of the sea; the main error Kelli Larson makes is to believe that a settled way of life is in itself a sign of belonging.[3] The fact of their own belonging is undeniable. Even if the possibility of a symbiosis with the environment is not afforded them every instant, their vocation, their destiny, is inscribed within them. Wanting to escape would be futile, as it would go against what lies in the very depth of their beings. Anna Christie understands this well. After she has spent some time with her father on his barge she declares, "Here's where you belong. (*She makes a sweeping gesture seaward*) But not on a coal barge. You belong on a real ship, sailing all over the world" (*AC* 27). Of course we remember that O'Neill had adapted *The Rime of the Ancient Mariner* for the theater, but in the plays which we are concerned with, wandering is not a punishment, it is part of existence. Their lack of attachment to dry land in no way justifies the supposition that there is no possible relation between them and a higher dimension; quite the contrary. Life on board brings about an effacing of their personalities, which marks adhesion to the world of the sailors. The unity of the team is a first step towards union with the whole. As other men do, they may find inner harmony; it is a difficult path, and they will only reach it by taking to the high seas.[4]

We might think that *All God's Chillun Got Wings* and *The Emperor Jones* are worlds apart from the SS Glencairn cycle. However, we are going to study the notion of belonging to a group, and try to see how this theme allows us to establish a link between these plays.

The plays involving black actors have given rise to a number of controversies and contradictory accusations, some seeing in O'Neill a subconscious racism, and others saying he was too favorable to African Americans. These often aggressive stances, taking the form of accusations made on the basis of supposed intentions, partly result in prefabricated analyzes tacked on to the plays. Without claiming to have found any kind of truth, I shall try to understand the significance of what the characters say, and then I shall try to see how that fits into a broader perspective.

> MICKEY. Coons, why don't yuh say it right! De trouble wit' you is yuh're gittin' stuck up, dat's what! Stay where yeh belong, see! Yer old man made coin at de truckin' game and yuh're tryin' to buy yerself white—[*AGCGW* 309].

Jim's efforts do not go down well with his old friends, for in his solitude, they perceive a desire to efface himself and his past. Mickey's reproach echoes the practice he had resorted to as a child, which consisted in drinking chalk to make his skin turn white. We must analyze what Mickey says in context if we want to extract the meaning of it. When he declares, "Stay where yeh belong," it could in fact be that he holds it against Jim for having pursued an education and that, consequently, he thinks that because he is black the university is not for him. On the other hand, when the curtain falls, this is not the impression one is left with. If his family and friends accuse him of betrayal and of denial, it is not because he pursues his studies but because of the spirit in which he works. For him, having letters after his name is only a pretext. He hopes they will allow him to integrate into white society and to break all ties with the past. This argument could appear specious, if we opt for another interpretation according to which an African American must confine himself to the menial tasks destined for him, knowing that this is probably the meaning behind Mickey's words. However, when we consider the play as a whole, we note that this refutation does not stand up. Hattie, Jim's sister, has achieved college success, but the basis of her desire to study is in harmony with her true personality. It is not a denial, she is not trying to make herself white through the acquisition of diplomas. To the contrary, her intellectual success fixes her all the more firmly in the world that she has come from, and allows her to find inner serenity.

> HATTIE. I've worked so hard. First I went away to college, you know—then I took up post graduate study—when suddenly I decided I'd accomplish more good if I gave up learning and took up teaching [*AGCGW* 327].

From Joe, whose words betray his poor level of education, to Hattie, each can find their place, at different levels, in the black community, and in society as a whole. This integration is easy as long as one is in harmony with oneself and not seeking to deny what is in the very depths of one's being, symbolized here in the first instance by the color of the skin, the blackness of which Jim would like to be able to tone down. Subconsciously, he remains marked by his desire to change his skin, which takes a more subtle form over the passage of time. We find a variation on the theme of denial in *The Emperor Jones*, but the author places more emphasis here on mental legacies. Brutus Jones has built an empire for himself by exploiting the credulity of the black inhabitants of the village in which he set up his business, after having proclaimed himself emperor. He arrives in this foreign land, and does not try to integrate into the group, but puts himself in a dominating position, exploiting the villagers, and counting on making a quick escape before a revolt breaks out. Caught unaware by their uprising, he flees into the forest and tries to leave the country. While he is wandering among the trees, he goes back over his life, and that of the black people. He is taken back in time to the age of slavery, before being confronted with an image of primitive Africa through the encounter with a witch-doctor and the veneration of a crocodile-god. Becoming afraid at the sight of these strange and unreal manifestations, he questions himself and is surprised that he should have been affected in such a way.

> JONES. Ha'nts! You fool nigger, dey ain't no such things! Don't de Baptist parson tell you dat many time? Is you civilized, or is you like dese ign'rent black niggers heah? Sho'! Dat was all in yo' own head. Wasn't nothin' dere [*EJ* 193].

What he saw, or thought he saw, was not in the forest, but within himself. The affirmation of his difference from the others, of his status as emperor, even if he cast a critical eye over a function which placed him de facto above the rest of his blood brothers—all that is denied by the reference to slavery and to their common African roots. Through the revelation of archetypes underlining the links he has with those whom he considered to be his inferiors, the author shows us the extent to which he was on the wrong track. To refuse to belong to a group and to see oneself as a superior being may lead to ruin.

Does salvation lie in a social contract? We could not make this assertion and no one is forced to integrate permanently into a clan. On the other hand, the denial of original ties and strategies for personal enrichment, at the expense of others, inevitably leads to failure or death. Seeking to exploit society for profit constitutes a fault. It leads the characters into a logic of desire over which they no longer have control and which results in madness or death. Whether their name be Jim or Brutus Jones, they condemn themselves by their attempt to run away, to deny that which is at the very heart of their being. In this they join the ranks of many like them in O'Neill's works, who, regardless of their race, are like runners trying to get away from their shadows. Their struggle is futile and, if they manage to make the shadows disappear it means that they themselves have ceased to exist.

This credo, which advocates a high level of integration into the community, may seem surprising, for, in general, the characters tend to claim their individuality, and to reject the masses. However, we could compare the idea of a perfect circle, within which men may find their place, such as we find in *Ah, Wilderness!* and the connection *All God's Chillun Got Wings* has with O'Neill's vision of the family. The way in which the family is presented does not paint a flattering picture of it, whereas in *Ah, Wilderness!* the author describes what he thought to be the perfect family. There is no real equivalent regarding the community, but it would seem a pity to confine oneself to appearances, to pass over the positive aspects, and to condemn without appeal crews and other groupings, on the pretext that these gatherings are composed of uncouth men and their consumption of alcohol is excessive.

> In a sense, and this point carries all through the O'Neill canon, O'Neill is most hopeful when he is not trying especially to be hopeful, as he does not seem to be in the early sea plays. In the SS Glencairn plays, O'Neill is simply describing, not preaching: yet in the dialogue and scenic images of these short plays, he is announcing in basic, uncomplicated fashion the terms in which human existence is viable.[5]

We can only agree with the analysis of Michael Manheim, and if individualism is valued in a great number of plays, we note that in others, integration into a whole is regarded favorably for some for, without really denying their true self (this is true especially for the sailors), it allows them to escape the torments of existential solitude,[6] and thus to be able to cope more easily with life.

Membership as salvation?

Seeking to become a member of a group implies (we have already alluded to this) a fading of individuality, and the reassuring cohesion is exchanged for signs of allegiance. Apart from the sailors—for whom belonging to a group could constitute a first step towards a relationship with a whole, which gives their lives meaning—for the other characters in the plays, the situation is completely different, and membership in a community is like going into limbo, for the chosen ones. There are many different indications of subordination, but when the protagonists enter a new society, they are transformed and thereby abandon a part of themselves. *The Hairy Ape* presents the stages through which Yank must pass, to find out to which camp he should belong, and lists the signals one must project to show the social strata to which one is adhering. At the beginning of the play, he is part of the crew. Looked upon as the leader, he proudly displays the attributes of his class: physical strength, hard drinking, and uncouth language which includes sailors' songs. Realizing that all the signs he had believed to be markers of his freedom convey instead his alienation, he abandons his ship and his companions to find a society within which he can be himself. He is greatly disappointed when, addressing himself to the trade union officials, he is rejected, having imagined that he would be immediately accepted, thanks to his natural abilities:

> YANK. Yuh call me? Well I got noive, too! Here's my hand. Yuh wanter blow tings up, don't yuh? Well, dat's me! I belong!
> SECRETARY. (*With pretended carelessness*) You mean change the unequal conditions of society by legitimate direct action—or with dynamite?
> YANK. Dynamite! [*HA* 248].

The distance is first of all one of language. Yank believes he can be himself, but the answers he receives demonstrate the extent of his delusion. As we have already seen, what matters is to be able to express oneself, to have a common language, whether it be within a group, a friendship or a relationship with a lover. The trade unionists, with whom he had hoped to find refuge, are themselves prisoners of their fossilized phraseology, within which he has no place. His voyage of initiation into the world will have him come up against numerous barriers which he couldn't see at the outset and which he will only gradually become aware of. The only authentic place is the cell in which he finds himself imprisoned. Indeed, the bars he twists constitute a tangible aspect of incarceration, of successive prisons where he would like to shut himself away, symbolizing alienating microcosms in which other characters are confined.[7] On every level, from the words of the union official to those of the senator who denounces the anarchists, not forgetting the inhuman politeness of the strollers who look like puppets, all persons project signs of belonging to communities, the main characteristic of which is the denial of the profound existence of the individuals.

> If man is essentially still an ape, he has become a machine and, in self delusion, thinks that the eternal primitive force which he has retained and converted into steel can be an adequate end in itself. He enjoys a false sense of belonging to something, of being a part of steel and of machinery, whereas he is actually their slave.[8]

Edwin Engel underlines the feeling of well-being which stems from a false impression, for the protagonists deceive themselves as to their place in life, in the universe in which they are evolving. However this semiconscious illusion (pipe dreams) sees them through their daily lives, by providing them with the ration of hope that they need.

Is it necessary or not to join clans, microcosms and other groups? The question is an intense one; joining is an act that binds. Perceiving that any adherence implies a partial surrender of sovereignty, a part of them sometimes hesitates before taking a definitive decision. The period of doubt is usually very short, for the isolated characters, without having the moral strength of Yank, can nonetheless be compared with him. In the last scene of *The Hairy Ape*, he bemoans his existential solitude, which lasts even to his final moments:

> YANK. He got me, aw right. I'm trou. Even him didn't tink I belonged. (*Then, with sudden passionate despair*) Christ, where do I get off at? Where do I fit in? [*HA* 254].

How can he avoid sinking into despair? Rejected by his fellow men, who see in him only the traits of an outsider, he considers how severe his punishment is. Behind these few sentences we sense questions on the meaning of life peeping through, questions others would like to avoid by joining sect-like communities which will bring them through their anxieties.

Not all are condemned to live such a despairing life. One response to this solitude is given in *A Moon for the Misbegotten*, when James Tyrone, in an expression which carries a certain reminder of a wedding ceremony, declares, quite simply, his love for Josie Hogan:

> JOSIE. I must be eaten up with jealousy for them, that's it.
> TYRONE. You needn't be. They don't belong.
> JOSIE. And I do?
> TYRONE. Yes. You do [*MMis* 76].

Between the search for happiness and its conquest there is the discovery of a moment where communion is possible, and in the space of one night, James and Josie will find a satisfaction which will allow them to bear the black nights which lie before them. What does it matter that he must give up part of himself, if it is compensated for by the hope of being able to find his place, if not with a kindred spirit, at least within a group, and thus to avoid having to carry alone the weight of a crushing solitude?

10. Non-Belonging.

Masks.

We noted in the first part of this study that the worlds described projected an image of a falsely open society. Whether it be families like that of the Mannons or other clans which define the criteria which must be satisfied for entry, these worlds are characterized by a strong propensity to close their doors to strangers. If salvation depends on belonging to a group, those who wish to survive must establish strategies aimed at denying the fact that they do not belong.

The assertion of one's difference, of one's own existence, brings about a banishment and one of the means of avoiding this threat involves the wearing of a mask. O'Neill has used this technique in several plays,[1] one of its essential functions being to show someone's face at a precise moment, in the knowledge that we are only seeing one of its many facets. Through this game of distorting mirrors, he was able to develop certain themes. The first of these on which we will concentrate is the images projected on individuals. An episode in *The Great God Brown* illustrates this aspect, testifying to the fact that no one is free to appear as he really is.

> (...*Brown has just time to turn his head and get his mask on.*)
> MAN. (*Briskly*) Ah, good morning! I came right in. Hope I didn't disturb...?
> BROWN. (*The successful architect now—urbanely*) Not at all, sir. How are you? [*GGB* 306].

Brown was in the middle of a dialogue with his double when his client entered the room. His instantaneous metamorphosis is made necessary by the style of life he has adopted. It is not possible for him to present his real face, for his physiognomy would not correspond to the social expectations he must satisfy. We will see the proof of this when, tortured by his change of identity, he will allow his feelings to infiltrate his words. Visitors and employees will quickly deduce from this that he is sinking into alcoholism. The function determines the appearance, and the conditions of his integration are dictated by his professional status. He has had to play a part his whole life, and could only reveal to society what it wanted to see, in order to have a place within it. (When protagonists do not manage to hide their true nature, they are implacably rejected, as in the scene in *In the Zone* where the sailors draw up a list of the indications of the implausibility of Smitty's claims to the title of seaman.) The impossibility Brown confronts, that of appearing as he really is, causes him acute suffering. However, we must note that total opposition between appearance and reality is not inevitable.

A kind of osmosis can arise between the individual and the portrait created by the way other people see him. The case of Lavinia is striking, for to strangers, her demeanor indicates that she belongs to the Mannon dynasty—it is therefore a mask—and, at the same time, she partly exposes her true characteristics, which bear the mark of puritanism, so dear to one branch of the family.

> Lavinia is nothing but a mask, the hideous mask of "Puritanism" of which she is unconsciously the first victim.[2]

Anne-Marie Soulier's interpretation highlights the intrinsic ambiguity of the mask. Lavinia could not be reduced to a fixed figure for, in the next part of the trilogy, we will discover another woman, very different from the one put forward here. Whatever her comportment, her way of thinking, her bearing are not merely veils with which she adorns herself as a means of rejecting the outside world. They constitute a whole which reflects her character. The last stage direction in *Mourning Becomes Electra*, "(…LAVINIA *turns and, stiffly erect, her face stern and mask-like, follows* ORIN *into the house)*" (*Homecoming* 125), describes her when she is alone, and her transfixed personality appears. There is therefore a coherence between appearances, the characteristic impassivity of the Mannon clan, and what she really is deep down inside (bearing in mind that one part of it, opposed to this impassivity, will present itself under a different exterior; here, there is a coherence between the mask and the person, even if the latter is divided).

If some are fortunate enough to be in line with the image their entourage has of them, quite the opposite is true for numerous characters, for whom the split personality, engendered by the necessity to put across an appearance quite different from their true self, has unfortunate consequences. Society offers them a series of functions, predefined according to criteria of race or class, but which can equally be cultural or professional. They must adapt, fit into a mold, suppressing the components of their individuality which do not correspond to the expectations of society. The constraints are numerous and often difficult to live with. We may think of the weariness of Lucy, deceived, accepting to play the role of the tolerant spouse ("LUCY. It's simply that I've grown sick of my life, sick of all the lying and faking of it, sick of marriage and motherhood, sick of myself! … And I'm tired of pretending I don't mind, tired of really minding underneath…" [*DWE* 519]), or of Darrell, having difficulty in hiding his role of lover behind a friendly façade (in *Strange Interlude*). The effects of this continual game of hide-and-seek do not lead merely to a fleeting dissatisfaction in those who are subject to it. This duality sometimes results in madness. Thus, in *Shell Shock*, one of O'Neill's early plays, where the interesting feature is the presence of themes developed in future works, the playwright recounts why a soldier became insane: The authorities rewarded him for a false act of bravery and the burden of the lie, together with the role he must play, have caused him to lose his mind. (The feeling of guilt is unbearable. It will not disappear until the hero confesses. This episode recalls the guilt of James Tyrone, in *A Moon for the Misbegotten*, when he evokes the way he acted at his mother's funeral, and his lack of grief.)

We can see through the examples quoted above that references to the mask go far beyond the concrete object, whose dramatic possibilities O'Neill had wished to exploit in a new approach to the theater. The mask must be understood in its conceptual sense, as an element which allows the characters to escape the scrutiny of others, like a veil covering a reality which they wish to keep private (a theme of all of the playwright's works). In spite of some limited disadvantages inherent in its nature, the mask can have at least two functions, which are sometimes antagonistic but which have potentially beneficial effects. The first one we identified is that of a means of integration. The dissimulation of the self allows one to be welcomed into the circle, access to which would have been impossible had the characters allowed their differences to be perceived. The second function is opposite to the first in the way it is carried out, for the misrepresentation stems from the will of the characters themselves. It helps those who have recourse to it to arm themselves against the curiosity of those around them.

On entering society novices are made aware of the necessity of putting on armor, for the fragility of individuals is such that they could not survive too direct a critical examination by those with whom they come into contact. Judgment can be the result of an analysis of appearances, and the dress becomes a criterion of evaluation[3]—but it is speech that matters most. Words, which tell stories and make others believe that what is being said conforms to reality, are the principal means of dissimulation.

The characters are helped in their endeavor by the frequent inattentiveness of those to whom they speak, but in the longer term individual truths surface. All are betrayed by their verbal incompetence. Incoherences follow clumsy repetitions, then the real version crops up in the course of a sentence, only to be immediately denied, drawing the speakers into an incessant coming and going between confession and dissimulation. Erie, who, in the course of his "funeral oration," says more than he meant to, is a case in point. He remembers how, every evening, in the sordid foyer of a cheap hotel, he managed to look like a winner, thanks to the force of his convictions,[4] and to Hughie's need for escapism.

> ERIE. Don't get the wrong idea, Pal. What I fed Hughie wasn't all lies. The tales about gambling wasn't [*Hu* 29].

Seeing that, in spite of himself, he is presenting the image of an inveterate liar, he stops himself short so as not to lose a game which has begun badly, the stakes of which consist in capturing the attention of someone who, in the future, could become a precious ally. Denials follow flattering statements, the speaker finally battling to paint a credible self-portrait, one which will protect him. Later, possibly, Erie will use the self-portrait to integrate himself into a community, without the risk that its members would harm him by detecting thinly veiled weaknesses.

The anxieties of the narrators are not always justified. Thus, in *The Iceman Cometh*, we see that it matters very little to the patrons of the bar if a customer seeks to have them believe one story rather than another. Each raconteur is free to invent his own scenario. Everyone recognizes the need for this, and generally no one tries to unmask his companions, for fear of falling victim to a similar process. Taking the O'Neillian œuvre as a whole, we note that the obligation to resort to personal protection is a universal theme. It facilitates the establishment of social intercourse between people, which would be difficult if they exposed their true selves.

> DEBORAH. (*Regretfully*) Much as I detest her treachery, I find something in me wishing he had not unmasked her—is there any one of us whose soul, stripped naked, is not ugly with meanness?—Life is at best a polite pretending not to see one another—a game in which we tacitly agree to make believe we are not what we are—a convenant not to watch one's friends too clearly, for the sake of friendship [*MSM* 204].

Deborah's thoughts highlight one tacit component of the social contract, to which each subscribes when he comes into contact with his fellow humans. In some plays, we have seen characters caught between two contradictory desires. On the one hand they claimed their right to belong to a group, and on the other they wished to break a pledge of allegiance, whose nature they perceived to be destructive. What is said of Juan Ponce de Leon sums up many other cases where the characters vacillate between two contradictory components of their personalities: "JUAN. (*Beneath the bitter, mocking mask there is an expression of deep, hidden conflict and suffering on his face as if he were at war with himself*)" (*Fou* 408).

By demanding too great a submission, society denies individuals the right of existence, and the ransom demanded for integration into the community is thus judged to be excessive by the victims of this coercion. Throughout their lives the characters will try to remodel the masks which they wear. They will endeavor to make the appearance attributed to them by the group coincide with the image they want to portray. Their suffering, a sign of isolation, and not of belonging, stems from the impossibility of a fusion between contradictory representations.

Their thirst for complete freedom will rarely be satisfied. Apart from some rare moments of completeness, when it is possible to lower them, masks are a permanent feature. They must not be considered optional. They are necessary for the individual, but not only to integrate into the community or to give protection from the scrutiny of others—they are indispensable because they hide an ugliness and brutality inherent in the human condition.[5]

The dream.

We could place O'Neill under the double patronage of Shakespeare[6] and Calderón, for dreams play an essential role in the destiny of so many of the characters. Their lives, although they cannot be reduced to a simple reverie, are marked by the need they feel to relive their memories, or to construct imaginary worlds in the present and in the future. Without attempting to establish a precise typology of the dream, the number of specific cases prohibiting such an exercise, we will limit ourselves to a classification which allows a division into three categories.

First, the term *dream* covers the usual meaning, a succession of nocturnal images the sense of which is not always clear to the dreamer; this first category has a very minor place in the works.[7] The second is the day-dream. The protagonists abandon their environment for a time and escape into a world which, for them, tends to become more real than reality. The third way in which the dream is manifested is a little ambiguous, to the extent that it could be qualified as a plan, a hope for a future life, different from the present one, and we shall see that these plans are sometimes carried through to completion. However this dreaming also takes another form, that of a day-to-day illusion, a personal utopia, which O'Neill commonly called a "pipe dream." The two latter categories, which we will return to, highlight attitudes which are individual responses, for the characters cannot find their place in impenetrable circles. Their relationship with the dream is like the history of a war. Some are full of hope and prepare to join battle, while others will coil up in a safe place, and take a fallback position, which they may never leave.

Trying to fall into line with the milieu in which they are evolving, some try to hang on using various techniques. We have evoked the dissimulation strategies employed to combat exclusion from the different communities. Another way of integrating consists in believing in collective utopias.[8] As such, they are able to take their place in a society which has its own plan, difficult to define, and which is limited to a materialistic vision of world, where the accumulation of wealth is substituted for all other desires. Those who adhere to it find social recognition, in proportion to the financial realization of their efforts, money giving a symbolic right of passage to the highest echelons of the group. We know to what extent this mercenary perspective was maligned by O'Neill, but the possibility of getting rich, of joining the ranks of the well-to-do—to see their American dream realized—is one of the unifying aspirations around which many gather.

> DEBORAH. After all this is an inevitable step in the corruption of your character that I have had to watch for years, until I could hardly recognize my son in the unscrupulous greedy trader, whose soul was dead, whose one dream was material gain! [*MSM* 176].

This bit of dialogue highlights a dialectic of fusion and exclusion, where the dominant theme is one of metamorphosis: The idealist who has good feelings becomes an unscrupulous captain of industry. This has similarities with the course followed by those who wore a mask with the aim of social integration, and ended up as strangers to themselves. We can discern here the critical view of the playwright for, according to him, material acquisition corrupts the moral integrity of the individual. The hopes some characters have of prospering are crowned with success, but this is subsequently judged according to criteria different from those at the beginning. Simon is proof of this. He will become a great industrialist, feared by all, the constitution of his empire will be in perfect symbiosis with the dominant ideology,[9] but apparently in complete opposition to the image given of himself at the beginning of the play. It is for this reason that when he reaches the top of the ladder, and is able to obtain total success, he subconsciously abdicates.

> SIMON. My goal is to make the Company entirely self-sufficient. It must not be dependent upon anything outside itself for anything. It must need nothing but what it contains within itself. It must attain the all embracing security of complete self-possession—the might which is the sole right not to be a slave [*MSM* 181].

The upper case granted to the word "Company" is symbolic. In this speech we notice that Simon has effected a transfer, which is conveyed by a passage from the individual utopia towards society. There are some points of convergence between the two apparently antagonistic states, as if the industrialist had wanted to develop the utopian idea without recognizing that the means employed held within them the seeds of disaster. Indeed, the priorities have been reversed, the human element has disappeared from the plan of community. Human beings have taken on the status of objects, and the "Company" has become the subject. After the crashing down of his house of cards, he will give up his fortune, for he understands its power of corruption. He will then seek a new source of hope, which will give him fresh reasons to live. In fact, success serves as an enlightener, and allows one to evaluate failure. Paradoxically, the dream, when it is linked to the search for personal prosperity, is the best means to encounter reality: Such is the unexpected lesson from this long maieutics. The characters follow a difficult initiation path but to all appearances the results obtained are opposed to the hope at the root of the original quest (in appearance only, for at the end of their journey they discover that treasures lie not in safes but within the human heart). At the end of this quest, they open their eyes and take stock of the magnitude of their illusions. They can then renounce these idle fancies and set out on another road.[10]

In *More Stately Mansions*, Simon remembers a story his mother told him as a child. It was the story of a king banished from his kingdom, condemned to exile for many years, until the day when he arrived at a particular door. At that moment, a voice gave him a warning.

> SIMON. If you dare to open the door you may discover this is no longer your old happy realm but has been changed by me into a barren desert, where it is always night, haunted by terrible ghosts, and ruled over by a hideous witch, who wishes to destroy your claim to her realm, and the moment you cross the threshold she will tear you to pieces and devour you [*MSM* 192-3].

The long journey of the king is similar to that taken by the characters to reach the end of their quest. However they are not devoured by a wicked witch and, contrary to the king, who does not go beyond the doorway, they see the idyllic world they had dreamed about reduced to dust. Unlike the poor king, they do not risk death. If we had to put a name to them they would deserve that of the phoenix, for although the loss of their illusions is destructive, it is almost always followed by their rebirth. It is indisputable that the fact of having opened the door of the kingdom, realized the extent of their error, and been able to draw conclusions from it, is to the credit of those who have taken the step. We know how much O'Neill was influenced by Nietzsche, but what comes across here even more is a debt to Hegelian dialectic, where each term leads to its opposite, and is indissociable from it. In short, one could say that success is failure and failure is success.

If we follow the fates of Andrew (in *Beyond the Horizon*) and Simon, we see that each is in his own way severely punished for having completely altered his initial plan, but the return to his roots takes the form of a rebirth. The two see that they have been granted the opportunity of starting again, even if their environment is far from being idyllic. Simon returns to his first beliefs, and to poverty—the symbol of another utopia, to a desire to live in an autarky—like Thoreau, who said that wealth could be measured by the number of things one could do without. They begin to live in a different world, following the rhythm of nature, which will help them, for they will have to struggle to regain their lost harmony. Andrew will also have to repent of having denied his roots and chosen the easy road, a prelude to personal downfall.

These disillusions bring about a rejection of the sphere in which the characters had tried to flourish and even more so of the materialist dream characteristic of their desire to occupy a strong position within the system. Following these abortive attempts, the watchword is withdrawal into oneself, and rejection of a community whose fundamental principles are corrupt. The characters prefer to abandon it, and divorce is rendered inevitable by the absence of any real hope for reform (we think of *The Personal Equation*, and the author's caustic vision of the good intentions of the unions). It is worth noting that at the root of the characters' hopes was a desire for integration, the wish to find a place in the group. Once there, those who have opened their eyes look for an isolated spot where they can find their roots again, away from the risk of being corrupted by the group.

Through the failure of individual hopes, we can gauge that of the society which generated them. This vision, both chimerical and materialistic, whose pernicious effects are depicted by the author, will serve to deal a few more strong blows to the real world, weakened by the loss of its values. Indeed, the realization of the failures implies a calling into question of the social structure, in that those who have conformed to its laws have suffered moral bankruptcy. This is why, in some plays—in a symbolic form—O'Neill puts an American dream on the stage. Through the cliché of the man who builds his fortune by the sweat of his brow, he gives a very strong critique of one of the federated myths to which many subscribe.

The consequences of the thirst for utopia, which drives the myth subscribers to the American social contract, are found at several levels. First, we see that it is impossible for people to live in a country which is heading in the wrong direction and which is dragging them down with it. Second, individual awareness projects a less than flattering image of an environment that has been denounced for its corrupting influence. The relationships which characters have with their illusions reflect to some extent those which the community has in turn with its illusions, and the plays highlight the perverse effects that result from this. The questioning of the values governing the world into which each character tries to merge cannot be seen as a central element in the plays, but it is there nonetheless. The insistence on the diversion from the basic principles constitutes a corrosive attack on the American way of life. O'Neill's comments about *Dynamo* help to pinpoint the way he intended to express his point of view.

> It is really the first play of a trilogy that will dig at the roots of the sickness of Today as I feel it—the death of the old God and the failure of Science and Materialism to give any satisfying new one for the surviving primitive religious instinct to find a meaning for life in, and to comfort its fears of death with.[11]

We can see that the aim is not to denounce a social malaise. That is certainly important but it remains contingent in the face of the message the author wishes to put across. Through the actors, he probably hoped to share emotional intimacy with the audience, by drawing attention to the metaphysical aspects revealed by the human dramas rather than the materialistic ones.

The relationships which emerge between the actors and each member of the audience are difficult to analyze exhaustively, but the attitude of the public has been very well defined by Henri Gouhier. He takes further the presuppositions established by Coleridge, and concentrates on the moment when the individual "gives himself over to the performance," putting his finger on what has later been called the work of the spectator.[12] In the plays we are studying, there may be an identification or a sense of communion with the characters, which sometimes takes the form of a catharsis, and everyone can become involved in the plays.

What are the effects of this ephemeral intellectual involvement? No one knows, for the impact of the performance is impossible to measure with any kind of precision. However, the consequences of the playwright's remarks on the subject must not be ignored. The questioning of unifying creeds, of the American dream, constitutes a commitment against the illusions conveyed by the ambient ideology. The potential objective was to bring about an awareness in individuals of their relationship to the world, to combat the collective blindness to which all tend to subscribe. Was O'Neill's aim to kill the dream through theatrical illusion? After the spectator has seen the performance—when, as he leaves the theater and rejoins the real world, he becomes once more a "person before the world," following the example of the characters—he will perhaps gauge the extent to which he has gone astray. However the playwright had not written a new *Werther*, and the influence of the plays on those who have seen them can scarcely be quantified. (O'Neill was aware of this aspect: At the end of *Marco Millions*, Marco exits, and mingles with the audience, carrying on into the real world a story which everyone had beforehand agreed to believe in, but only inside the theater.)

In showing how dreams turn to nightmares, and how the heroes become lost, O'Neill leaves the kingdom of the imaginary and rejoins the destroyers of materialism and its god, the dollar. He shows that humanity is heading for its downfall by involuntarily pledging allegiance to materialistic visions. His comments on the dream thus tie in with the social perspective expressed elsewhere. While questions are asked, no solution will, however, be proposed, as any answer would indicate that the one who is giving the warning is himself prey to the shortcomings he is highlighting, believing that he alone holds the truth. When all is said and done, the playwright seeks less to condemn than to arouse compassion for those who are going astray.[13]

The hope which drives the characters is not necessarily motivated first and foremost by the desire to merge into the surrounding community. The dream is often a plan which allows those who wish to put it into operation to distance themselves from the world, that they might live in harmony with another individual. For Christine,[14] the realization of happiness hangs on the acquisition of a poison which will allow her to kill her husband. Orin, for his part, thinks that a trip to the Pacific islands will necessarily be enchanting, but each time, confrontation with reality is a very harsh experience. In fact, when the characters attain the goal they had set themselves, they realize their error of judgment, as the result obtained cuts a sorry figure in relation to their hopes.[15] All are bruised, but more often than not their despair is fairly short-lived. Some are on the point of death,[16] and no longer have enough time to start again, setting new goals in their search for happiness. On the other hand, for those who have suffered only one failure, the process of illusion and disillusion begins once more its interminable cycle.

> DEBORAH. But evidently he has found a new romantic dream by way of recompense. As I might have known he would. Simon is an inveterate dreamer—a weakness he inherited from me, I'm afraid, although I must admit the Harfords have been great dreamers too, in their way [*TP* 82].

Deborah stresses here the hereditary aspect, but the need to depart from reality, to go to an imaginary other place, goes beyond simple genetic patrimony. Almost all subscribe to the need for illusion in one form or another, and very few protagonists succeed in divesting themselves of it.

Up to this point we have studied two forms of the dream; the identification with the American dream, born of a materialist desire to succeed and a wish for social integration, and a variation on this, when a character wishes to obtain something, not wishing to share the vision of the community. In the examples studied, the characters had a strong attachment to the world, and tried to transform it, to make it conform to their hopes. There was therefore a transformation of reality. Their mental inventions were built around their immediate environment and remained in the realm of possibility, their ideal world taking as its point of reference the community in which they lived and to which they wanted to make some adjustments. In the examples we are going to look at now, we will see a different process. In fact, some will impose their imaginary world on the real one, making it lose its true nature. This is from *Where the Cross Is Made*:

> NAT. Guess what, Doctor?
> HIGGINS. (*With an answering smile*) Treasure, of course.
> NAT. (*Leaning forward and pointing his finger accusingly at the other*) You see! The root of the belief is in you, too! (*Then he leans back with a hollow chuckle*) Why, yes. Treasure, to be sure. What else? They landed it and you can guess the rest, too—diamonds, emeralds, gold ornaments—innumerable of course. Why limit the stuff of dreams? [*WCIM* 560].

Nat highlights a cultural predisposition to believe in the existence of a treasure island. Reality will therefore serve as the basis for an invention, but this will become so important that the characters will be prisoners of their beliefs, to the point of no longer seeing what they want. Nat goes from cynicism to irony when he recounts the fabulous tale of this false treasure, but when Bartlett hails the members of an imaginary crew, in spite of his initial reserve, he finds himself caught in the trap of this paternal fabrication. He cannot help recognizing it as real, although he knows that the material evidence invalidates his father's words. The need to believe in this providential fortune brings about a general metamorphosis. The house is transformed, becoming the crow's nest of the phantom captain, but the changes go even further, to the extent that they affect the perception of daily existence. Even the language signals are scrambled, as is illustrated by the opposite ways of referring to reality depending on whether Nat or Sue are speaking. Indeed, when the latter himself takes up the declarations of their father, saying that he has seen his boat, the doubt is instilled in the spectator, right up until the moment when Sue, herself disturbed and no longer knowing where the truth lies, goes to the window and declares that they are the victims of an hallucination. Two worlds are distinguished, that of illusion or madness, which has ever more hold on reality with the passage of time, because two people are victims of the same hallucinations, and that of the palpable or tangible sphere, which is banished by that of visions. On the other hand sordid, everyday life remains, perceived through the eyes of Sue, but it in turn takes on nightmarish aspects. (We shall encounter a more philosophical vision of a similar idea in *Marco Millions*: "CHU-YIN. Life is perhaps most wisely regarded as a bad dream between two awakenings, and everyday is a life in miniature" [*MM* 402].)

In *Where the Cross Is Made*, the dreams have become so widespread as to form a coherent whole. The dreamers are living on hope in another world, and their time is one of anticipation. Their life now only has meaning in relation to the arrival of a lost boat, but accepting reality would amount to a death sentence, which is precisely what happens at the end of the play,[17] when the illusion is gone: "DOCTOR. That darn dream of his has become his life" (*Gold* 676). The doctor indirectly implies that this situation is vital for Bartlett. The motto of these characters could be summed up as "I dream therefore I am," which would make any reformulation in the negative difficult.

The need for dreams had been developed in the characters following a cultural impregnation. They had within them a propensity to believe in the possibility of a financial miracle, which would have allowed them to leave their immediate environment, to live in a fabulous kingdom. For them, the recourse to the imaginary did not express so much a desire to transform the world, to make it correspond to their wishes, as a need to experience a fairy-tale adventure. The process for them consisted in denying the relevance of reality and recreating another world. The rupture with the immediate environment was so great that it is difficult to say that there was any basis of resistance in their attitude. They were elsewhere, in a fictitious world, which they would not and could no longer leave and which, to others, took the name of madness.

Other characters turn to the dream, in different forms, but at the root of their quest we find a dissatisfaction which is due to the position they have been granted in the community in which they are evolving. Deborah Harford chooses voluntary seclusion. She retreats into her garden and gives herself over to her thoughts, for she does not succeed in finding her place in the society of which she is supposed to be a part ("DEBORAH. No, nothing is there but I. My mind. The past, Dreams. My life, I suppose you might call it, since I have never lived except in mind" [*MSM* 81]). Like Bartlett, her illusions have taken hold of her. When she meets her son, she cannot link up again with reality and imagines herself, in the presence of Simon, to be a courtesan at the court of Louis XIV. Unlike Nat, Simon does not take this act seriously. He breaks her illusions with a burst of laughter, which brings Deborah back to reality. With her pride hurt, she gives up her illusions, and decides that from now on she will be interested only in material things.

> DEBORAH. I have kept the oath I made to myself then. Have not allowed myself to dream. Have not hidden from my life. Have made myself accept it as it is. Made myself a decently resigned old woman, saying to myself: "So is so, and you must not hope it could be more" [*MSM* 82].

This is one stage of her life for after several years she will once again turn to the imaginary world, but the period during which she stopped dreaming is a failure. It has been marked by her physical decline, as if she had condemned herself by no longer escaping to the places where her real self could go. The two snatches of dialogue quoted above highlight a fundamental contradiction. In fact, Deborah describes her life in antagonistic terms, in one line associating it with a long succession of dreams, and in another, placing it in an everyday perspective, stressing her role as wife. As is often the case, certainties are not always where we expect to find them. In ceasing to act out her part, Deborah denies a part of herself. The consequences are all the more disastrous in that when she presents herself as the wife of a rich industrialist, she continues to play a role, this time a prescriptive one, whose narrow codes smother her personality. Her voluntary incarceration, in this mental prison, is at the root of her decline.

The place where she escapes is a private place, to which only those closest to her have access. Conversely, others integrate their imaginary worlds into their everyday lives. Their relationship to them is different in that recourse to the dream is often motivated by nostalgia, the rupture with everyday life consisting in recreating, in embellishing, what the characters considered to be a glorious past. Con Melody, for example, cannot accept his status as innkeeper. It is therefore vital for him, if he wants to change the image people have of him, that he present another picture, conforming to what he used to be, at the peak of his glory. This flattering self-portrait supports him in his continual struggle to build around him (with the aid of his illusions) the conditions he needs to flourish.

> SARA. Poor Father! God forgive him. He never knew what he was himself. He never lived in life, but only in a bad dream [*MSM* 35].

By reciting the verses of Byron in front of his mirror, he gives himself the strength to play his role again, and to show that he is not an innkeeper, as some might think, but Major Melody. He half succeeds in convincing them, for the patrons do not consider him as an ordinary manager, and treat him with deference. At the moment when he recites "The Childe Harold Ballad" in front of his mirror, he escapes, and becomes what he was in the past. However, even when the poetic bewitchment is over, he never completely reintegrates into the world in which he lives. His blindness lasts after he has stopped dreaming. In his everyday life, he likes to think of himself as a gentleman, and is anxious to maintain his imaginary status, by keeping a beautiful mare in the stable. The respect for the fictitious character he gets from customers, in spite of the reticence of some of them, helps him to keep up the myth.[18]

There is a two-way process in operation between the dream of a glorious past, which allows him to break away from the world, and its actualization in the presence of those around him. Although despised, they are in fact necessary to the recreation of this phantasmagoria, in that their approval confirms Melody's role of heroic soldier. By going along with his game, the regulars have an essential function in the smooth running of the mechanism of illusion.

We have seen, in the study of masks, that some characters pretended to believe in appearances, and that in fact, their blindness stemmed from a tacit convention. In the case of Con Melody, the face he wishes to show is more than a mask: It corresponds to what he still would like to be, deep within himself. The objective is no longer to hide his true nature by giving a false picture of himself in order to protect himself from reality, but to make this idyllic self-portrait, in his everyday life, sweep away the image of the low class alcoholic he sometimes sees reflected. When a complete rupture from reality is impossible, and this is most often the case (since a total break, taking the form of a permanent day-dream, leads to madness), the complicity of the entourage becomes necessary to sustain the illusion.

There are many motives behind the indulgence of those close to the protagonists—it can, for example, be due to love or friendship. In other cases, there is a vested interest, and they hope to reap the fruit of their flattery and to be integrated into the illusion in which the character is evolving. Indeed

Larry in *The Iceman Cometh* points out how vital the need to escape is, and that such a need cannot be confined to a few dreamers who have lost their way in life:

> LARRY. To hell with the truth! As the history of the world proves, the truth has no bearing on anything. It's irrelevant and immaterial, as the lawyers say. The lie of a pipe dream is what gives life to the whole misbegotten mad lot of us, drunk or sober [*IC* 578].

The dream is an idol with feet of clay. It needs to be protected from attack. For this reason deference and complicity of language could be thought of as collective gifts, allowing the heroes to continue to escape. The dream constitutes a saving escape mechanism, for those who cannot find their place in the world in which they live. It guarantees their survival in a world in which they feel lost, and where escape offers the only guarantee of well-being.

> In the final tragedies, the veil of Maya seems to be torn aside and all the illusions of human life laid bare. Romantic dreams are exposed as the delusions they are. And yet, unlike O'Neill's earlier dramas and unlike all the romantic literature of the modern Occident, these dreams are no longer seen as beautiful, nor are they seen as evil. Rather, they are recognized as the very substance of human life.[19]

Without being quite as categorical as Frederick Carpenter, we can only be in full agreement with him when he points out the importance of dreams for each individual. There is within humanity an almost innate need for illusion, but systematic recourse to the imaginary world is also a trap, for whatever form it might take, no one is able to master it. The dream may become a nightmare but the characters continue to hope. Their recourse to the dream can be explained by the fact that when life offers them all the satisfactions they have a right to expect, it becomes unreal. This is perhaps why they try to find this sensation again, by escaping into imaginary kingdoms, instead of trying to find it in their everyday world.[20]

The search for happiness is transformed into a quest of fleeting pleasure, the inadequacy of the characters in the world pushing them to seek means of escape which will allow them to free themselves from the hold of society. The effects are certainly pernicious, but they must be considered in relation to the momentary happiness, we could even say intense joy, which overcomes the beneficiaries of it, and whose impressions O'Neill describes, not without humor:

> *The Night Clerk dreams, a rapt hero worship transfiguring his pimply face: "Arnold Rothstein! He must be some guy! I read a story about him. He'll gamble for any limit on anything, and always wins... Beatific vision swoons on the empty pools of the Night Clerk's eyes. He resembles a holy saint, recently elected to Paradise* [*Hu* 32].

Escape.

The night porter had previously declared that it was impossible to destroy the town, therefore the only way to leave his environment is to plunge himself into long periods of dreaming. Some resort to different methods, and try to cut themselves off from the world by seeking elsewhere a place where they will be, if not in harmony, at least shielded from situations which prevent them from continuing to live some kind of life. Thus in *In the Zone*, Smitty runs away so as not to be forced to admit to his woman friend that he has started drinking again. His shipmate gets hold of a letter she sent him:

> DRISCOLL. (*Reads slowly...*) ... "So you have run away to sea loike the coward you are because you knew I had found out the truth—the truth you have covered over with your mean little lies all the time I was away in Berlin and blindly trusted you..." [*IZo* 531–32].

His desire to hide, borne out by his search for anonymity, draws him into a process of exclusion, at the end of which he is laid bare, before all the members of the crew, producing a result opposite to that which he had expected. In any case, this intrusion by his companions in his private life is a kind of prelude to a return, which we may suppose would have happened a little later, and which would have provoked a confrontation. This comment is not aimed at inventing a follow-up to the story. Its purpose is rather to draw attention to the fact that departures[21] are very often followed by an arrival at the very point of departure. This temporal loop shows how impossible it is for the characters to burn the bridges of their past, whether it take the form of a mistress, a mother, or an original environment, to which they are brought back.[22]

The Long Voyage Home, with an ironic title, is seen as an exception, but Olson's inability to make the journey back to his native land reveals the hold that destiny has on the lives of the characters. Indeed, we see here the rupture of what could be qualified as a cycle, a long circular journey, in the form of an eternal return, which appears in other plays. The sailor has the firm intention of returning to his country, but fate decides otherwise, and will not allow him to see his old mother again. Some, like Peter and Simon (*Desire Under the Elms*), manage to break their attachments, but they stand as counter-examples. In many of the plays, going back, or the desire for it, is a path that must be taken,[23] which shows how difficult it is to escape for good.

At the end of their journey they will perhaps not abound in social grace and good reason, but they will, in common with the travelers quoted by Du Bellay, come back to the roots that they had abandoned for a time. However we must note that their absence does not provide any definitive solution to their existential malaise. The origins of this are diverse, going from family conflicts to an inability to reach an understanding with the person one loves or, more generally, to an abortive integration into the community. All these obstacles very quickly rise up when the heroes return to the fold, and produce effects identical to those which made them leave in the first place.

What then, is the good of going away? When exile comes to be synonymous with failure, a paralyzing shell comes down around the characters, who are reduced to finding artificial ways to escape. Sometimes the dream finds favor with them, but it is difficult to reach the perfection of Deborah. For this reason, anxious to break free from a world from which they feel excluded, they try to blot out the problems in their lives by turning to drink or drugs.

> BRANT. He'd taken to drink. He was a coward—like all Mannons—once he felt the world looked down on him [*MBE, Homecoming* 25].

Brant speaks of the fragility of those who have shown themselves to be unable to face up to rejection or, more generally, who cannot live with their exclusion from the group to which they had belonged up until then or that they would like to become part of. The result of their opt-out attitude is that they must run away. They beat a retreat, and the aim of their last battle is not to defeat the enemy but to fight against both time and lucidity, one of their allies being alcohol. Providing a cheap means of losing consciousness, it reigns supreme to the extent that it prevents any analysis of the true relations which exist between the characters and the world. Thanks to alcohol, those who partake of it manage to persuade themselves that their condition is not as debased as they thought. The effect it produces of being out of step with reality gives it a grotesque aspect ("HUGO. It's all great joke, no? So ve get drunk, and ve laugh like hell, and den ve die, and de pipe dream vanish!" [*IC* 635]), but the accompanying laughter is like a death rattle. When this artificial gaiety disappears, it gives way to protests that all their faults are due to unfair circumstances, or the cruelty of others—various causes which have forced them to chose whiskey as a final refuge.

The characters do not find they have in them the will to fight. They let themselves go, reckoning that they have lost the battle and finding in the conditions of their defeat sufficient pretext to justify their surrender.[24] Alcohol and drugs serve only to accelerate their decline, and the means of escape becomes in turn a disgrace, from which they must hide. (A case in point is Con Melody, who is humiliated by his alcoholism, but denies it: "MELODY. Ashamed? I don't understand you. A gentleman drinks as he pleases—provided he can hold his liquor as he should" [*TP* 46].)

> MELODY.
> "I have not loved the World, nor the World me;
> I have not flattered its rank breath, nor bowed
> To its idolatries a patient knee,
> Nor coined my cheek to smiles,—nor cried aloud

10. Non-Belonging.

> In worship of an echo: in the crowd
> They could not deem me one of such—I stood
> Among them, but not of them..." [*TP* 43]

Is it a case of loving the world, or of flattering it? Some, we have seen, have tried different strategies, to conquer it. However at the end of their endeavors, they invariably mark up a failure, which leads them to reject the community into which they had tried to integrate. Melody's assessment testifies to the impossibility of sharing something, of an obvious break between the characters and the rest of the world. Contrary to the heroes of the poem, those who evolve in the plays have difficulty in standing tall and accepting that they are different. The outstretched hand leads only to rejection. As for the perception of idiosyncrasies, and the acceptance of them, they imply that each must analyze his own situation, which they refuse to do. In spite of their desire to close their eyes and forget, they are aware of not being integrated into the group. They feel the lack of belonging, which is constantly refused them and seems to be at the root of their existential instability. The strategies designed to aid a flight from reality, whether they be dreams or other means aimed at reaching an artificial paradise, share the common factor of being written in time. In this connection, we could evoke the principle of entropy, in that the defense systems always end up crumbling. When they disintegrate, their annihilation takes the form of a broken dream, of a sobering up, or of an insufficient quantity of morphine, no longer allowing those who have turned to these artificial aids to prolong their escape into the imaginary world. The temptation to take the next step and use even more draconian methods rests just beneath the surface, for the characters can no longer cope with the difficult times when they find themselves confronted with a reality whose significance they cannot deny, and whose destructive power annihilates them.

> MANNON. All victory ends in the defeat of death. That's sure. But does defeat end in the victory of death? [*MBE, Homecoming* 48].

The question arises for some. Indeed, the passage from life to death would offer them the possibility of putting an end to their existential malaise. In this case, death would mark the end of constant suffering, which many seek to be rid of. All those whose life's journey we have traced cope very badly with their exclusion. Since the remedies they choose are unable to satisfy them, suicide could emerge in response to their quest for a permanent solution. In fact, although we can identify a large number of cases where individual attitudes could be considered as suicidal—dipsomania included in these—actual suicide occurs in only nine plays. It is undeniable that the percentage remains high, but the majority of the protagonists opt to undergo a decline rather than make the brutal decision to end their life. The general attitude seems to be one of passivity, of a waiting game, rather than the final stage of the kind of depression which is resolved in death. Most of the characters skirt around the grave and, not wishing to die for ideas, opt for a slow death.[25]

> Like Christine's faint after poisoning Ezra Mannon, which is both a denial of an appalling reality and orgasmic, James Tyrone sinks into Josie Hogan's arms in *Moon*, Reuben Light fatally embraces the dynamo after shooting Ada Fife, Eben condemns himself to hang in *Desire*, and Hickey both falls into slumber and condemns himself to ultimate electrocution. Death inevitably rivals O'Neill's heroes, enjoying their loved ones at last. And like most suicides, their deaths manifest a surge of self-justifying aggression against others.[26]

It seems awkward to group together under the same name attitudes which, although having a similar outcome, namely death, are often opposed. In fact, when Eben decides to turn himself in to the police, the process leading up to his choice is completely different from that of Reuben. In the one example, Eben demonstrates his grandeur, surpassing his fear of death, which becomes a secondary consideration in relation to his love.[27] In the other example, electrocuting himself allows Reuben to escape, to free himself from his fear of life, that he might find Mrs. Light, and have his sin forgiven[28] for, by joining up with Ada, he has betrayed his mother. The fact of having ruined one's life only rarely justifies resorting to extreme measures. This happens only in *Bread and Butter* and *Diff'rent*. The loss of the loved one explains the one we find in *Recklessness*. Most often, suicide is compensation for an error (see *Abortion, Before Breakfast, Diff'rent, Dynamo, The Iceman Cometh, Mourning Becomes Electra*, and *Warnings*) that has made it impossible for the one who committed it to go on living. The guilt is such that the characters cannot avoid a tragic dénouement, by confessing to others or trying to forget what they are responsible for. The only way out for them, if they want to find peace, consists in definitively breaking free from the world in which they continue to survive, that they might put an end to their suffering and, who knows, go on living in another world ("ORIN. Death is an island of Peace, too. Mother will be waiting for me there" [*MBE, The Haunted* 166].

The point of view of Emil Roy quoted above, which sees aggression towards those who are left behind and self-justification in the suicides, is not really effective in the cases where the step towards suicide is actually taken. In this perspective, the deaths do not call the community or any members of it into question. The characters are worn down by a burden too great to bear; they are destroyed by constant guilt. Consequently, it is no longer a question of justification but rather of expiation of the faults of which they have made themselves guilty. When this stage is achieved, the scrutiny of society matters very little to them. The message they want to leave behind, if there is one, is not important compared to their quest for inner peace, which they find only in death.

11. Conclusion

The relationships interwoven among the protagonists are most often depicted in an isolated space, which reminds one of the enclosure mechanisms described in Part I. Even if the characters are not portrayed amidst crowds, what is presented on stage reflects what is going on in society as a whole. Leaving behind his family group, each character attempts his own social ascension, but the access to a closed world, and effective recognition by its members, is dependent upon a rite of passage, at the end of which some strangers are rewarded by an acknowledgment of their belonging.

Awareness of the difficulties of integration is a slow process. Regardless of the social circle in which they evolve, the characters are never looked at in a neutral way. Indeed, all are marked by their social or racial origins, as well as by a history inscribed in them in the form of archetypes which will always influence their dealings with their friends and acquaintances. The outward signs they display will be the criteria used by their entourage to evaluate who they really are. They know they must be careful, for to display one's difference leads to exclusion. After being judged, they will be confined to pigeonholes from which it will be difficult to escape.

There are numerous reasons behind the desire of O'Neill's characters for fusion with the social body. The first arises from wanting to occupy a prime position in a society which, at first glance, presents itself as an idyllic place, fostering utopian ideas about itself, acting as a kind of lure, drawing in applicants who will not discover the shortcomings of the community until later. The gap that emerges between the noble utopias around which the social structure is formed and reality, which is far from being perfect, stems from manmade corruption.

The characters eventually become aware of the bleak aspects of society, but they think they can overcome its faults and decide to go ahead, hoping to merge into the group, which seems disposed to grant them their chance of happiness. What is at stake through their belonging to a group is their being recognized as individuals. This is why they are prepared to make such heavy sacrifices. However they are themselves the cause of their failures, because the process followed in their pursuit of happiness carries within it the seeds of failure. To attain their ideal, they are prepared to sacrifice everything, but the means used to reach their goal are incompatible with the principles decreed at the beginning. They perceive numerous possibilities. One of them is to make their fortune, the power of money being such that it will procure for them the social situation they dream of, but, on setting off down this road, they hardly consider the foreseeable effects. Another solution is to adopt the uniform of the community they wish to belong to and to hide behind masks, but in doing so the characters deny what they really are. In fact, when they hide behind appearances, or confine themselves to some ready-made way of thinking, their personality is suppressed, and the results are disastrous. Now the characters react and rebel against a world in which it is impossible to be themselves, now they let themselves go, and fall victim to moral inertia, which taints their lives with lethargy.

Rejection of what they perceive as a corrupt society does not always imply a new beginning, for not all have the courage to start again. Some lay down their arms and perfect their defeat by turning to alcohol, drugs or suicide. Others seek a compromise, which would allow them to continue to live in an illusory world of their own, without having to give up their role of active citizen. They must not reject society per se, and must have the strength to begin their lives again on another basis, seeking a new definition of themselves, when the principles they have followed prove to have been wrong. Rejection of community structures is difficult, however, to come to terms with for it casts the characters into existential solitude, which is a crushing burden. They seek out friends or companions with whom they can reveal their true personalities and who can bring them the happiness to which they aspire. Not all are lucky enough to find a kindred spirit. Moreover, their search for an alter ego is made difficult by the need for too great a closeness frequently manifested by one of the characters, for whom the process of unmasking proves both necessary and perilous. Couples show how hard it is to find a balance. The existence of one is necessary for the existence of the other, and the relationship is marked by conflict. Finding a partner is one of the wishes of the protagonists, but harmony continually gives way, and the characters often live in difficult domestic situations.

Their existential quest for belonging outside the family is rewarded when they meet an alter ego or join in a group where they are not considered aliens. When they finally meet the person they have been looking for, even if their relationship is short-lived, the weight of solitude disappears, and they can attain momentary completeness, which they will remember when the skies cloud over. Most experiences will be painful; nonetheless, the few positive ones indicate that the characters can be integrated into society and even find happiness there. Few, however, will remain true to themselves. Many prefer inertia to life. They fall prey to dreams, alcohol or easy excuses, giving up any hope for a rebirth through companionship because they are too weak to take up the challenges inherent in forming a union with another human being.

Part III. Humans Faced with Themselves and Inner Worlds.

JIM.—and then, and that way only, by being brave, we'd free ourselves, and gain confidence, and be really free inside and able then to go anywhere and live in peace and equality with ourselves and the world without any guilty, uncomfortable feeling to rile us [*AGCGW* 326].

12. The Discovery of Human Beings.

A theater of the soul.

In this third section, the first two having shown successively the nature of people's relationship with their families and the way in which they integrated with their social environment, we will now broach an examination of the inner life of human beings. These inner worlds are essential elements which, together with other elements previously discussed—heredity and determinism, for example—are constituent parts of the human personality. In an analysis of the links that exist between the individual and other members of the community, it becomes apparent that there was sometimes a suppression of individuality in favor of the social or familial function. We have stressed this aspect, attempting to evaluate the impact of such an attitude; now attention will be focused on the way in which the personality of each character is revealed despite numerous psychological blocks.

The observation of what unites microcosm and macrocosm will henceforth give way to an examination of the way the characters regard their own existence; in so doing we will be concerning ourselves with what O'Neill called the theater of the soul:

> After all, what I've tried to write is a play where at the end you know the souls of seventeen men and women who appear, and the women who don't appear.[1]

The playwright's desire for metaphysical reflection sometimes led him, if not to didactic discourse, at least to laying too great an emphasis on the themes he wished to develop, to the detriment of the quality of his productions. I must reiterate at this point that classification of the plays according to their literary value is not the purpose of this study; by stressing the perverse effects of his desire to express the state of his own thought through his plays, I simply wish to underline the importance given within them to reflections on humanity. Tragedies, satirical comedies, historical dramas, with, depending on the period, naturalism or expressionism among other esthetic choices—they all, with variations, hesitations and reversals, interpret some aspect of the human condition.

The reasons he turned to writing, if there are any, will necessarily lead to incomplete answers; I have just suggested one, but we must also note that O'Neill often takes the stage in his own plays, and his actual presence is not without significance. It seems that we must see in this a dimension which goes beyond simple narcissism, and that these appearances are both the expression of a need for liberation, and the mark of his continual questioning of what human beings should be. (We must not forget the questioning of destiny and of belonging to a clan. We could perhaps see in Orin's recounting of the Mannon dynasty a kind of self-portrait of the artist, seeking through his writing to answer the questions with which he is assailed.)

It is perhaps not coincidental that his autobiographical masterpiece, *Long Day's Journey into Night*, was written when he had turned sixty years of age. This time it no longer seemed necessary for the author to hide behind more or less crude masks. In spite of all the pain attached to working, during this period of his life he had acquired sufficient strength to retrace his own history and narrate it; it is for this reason that he declares in the dedication addressed to his third wife:

> *I mean it as a tribute to your love and tenderness which gave me the faith in love that enabled me to face my dead at last and write this play—write it with deep pity and understanding and forgiveness for all the four haunted Tyrones* [*LDJN* 7].

We notice that he considers himself to be a ghost of the past because he mentions the four members of the family. Writing, and this example is not unique, allows him to go back to his former life, and in so doing to relive the conflicts of that period in the hope of finding peace when the struggle is over. To bring this autobiographical work to a successful conclusion, he had to distance himself somewhat from what he was; this detachment has been achieved through the course of time, but it remains partial, and we know that writing this play was a painful experience for him. His biographers testify to the difficulty he experienced in the drafting of the play, where he was forced to relive painful episodes of his life. I mention this briefly in order to establish a link between the author and his characters, who in some way devote a large proportion of their time to talking about their life histories.

We notice a convergence between the attitude of the author who, little by little, manages to express what is really important to him, but which he had been incapable of saying before, and that of the principal characters who progressively become aware of the truth about themselves. *Long Day's Journey into Night* is both a reflection on a personal journey, and an evaluation made by four characters of what their existence means; the dialogues reveal their distress and, without taking on an expressionistic dimension, as was the case in *The Hairy Ape*, the play comes across as a reflection on life and on the human condition.

It goes without saying that the division into three categories, family relations, social relations and the inner life, has been established for reasons of convenience. They all coexist, and influence each other, as we shall see later. However, this analysis of a human being face to face with himself is not simply the third wing of a triptych. It has been made necessary by what has become apparent in the course of the preceding stages of this study, namely that family and society serve to reveal the existential solitude of individuals. They offer some means of escape, which allow an avoidance of self-reflection, but the threat of a direct confrontation with the inner self continually weighs on each individual, a confrontation which appears more formidable than conflicts with other people. Whether a relationship is established with the exterior world, or the community rejects the outsider, is of little importance; the two situations have the same consequences. In fact, when there is a confrontation, it brings with it a profound individual questioning; not content with appearances, it reveals what everyone had tried to hide, even from themselves. A similar process takes place when those who have been isolated question their own lives.

The stage becomes a place where each character divulges what he really is, and through this, O'Neill expresses his anxieties and his certainties concerning the ability of human beings to show themselves worthy of the name. The truth comes out progressively, despite the resistance of individuals who try by every possible means to escape from it; this state is transitory and from denial to renunciation all try to mask once more what has been revealed about themselves.

Before looking at the way in which the protagonists understand their existence, we will study the strategies established to avoid analysis. The fear of having to face up to what they really are, of which they are vaguely conscious, leads individuals to resort to many subterfuges so that they might escape all kinds of inquisition, including introspection.

Flight strategies.

In *Marco Millions*, a satirical comedy, O'Neill tried to show the limited nature of the materialist vision characteristic of Occidental society in relation to a more spiritual perspective, corresponding, according to him, to the vision of the Oriental world. Not afraid to overdo the stereotype, the author presents Marco as a man who claims to have a soul but who, in fact, reveals an extreme baseness of character, incapable of any kind of elevation, the financial domain aside. At the end of his voyage, gazing deeply into the eyes of Kukachin, he succumbs for a moment to the love she has for him, but the cry let out by his uncle, who is counting his gold, brings him back to reason; he pulls himself up and does not kiss the princess. This episode illustrates the extent of Marco's blindness. He cannot understand the kinds of feelings that the princess has for him, for they are not manifested in the materialist sphere. His incomprehension symbolizes his incapacity to think, to break away from the down to earth dimension of his daily life, and even more the impossibility for him to construct any kind of existential evaluation. His simple satisfaction, his propensity to deal only with the contingent makes of him someone set apart; the complete absence of any meditation on the meaning of his life is the sign of his abjection. As such he constitutes a perfect counterexample, for the other characters lack this arrogance. In fact they often have to establish a defense strategy that they might escape the risks involved in individual evaluations, which constantly threaten them.

One of the ways to protect oneself against the devastating effects of a personal analysis which goes too deep is to wear a mask. We have already seen how each character presents to the rest of the world a face which often corresponds only partially to reality; the course taken is identical when the discourse takes the form of a monologue. This statement may seem surprising, but in fact, Mary Tyrone herself explains a phenomenon which one finds, in a different form, in other plays:

> MARY. Nothing, I don't blame you. How could you believe me—when I can't believe myself? I've become such a liar. I never lied about anything once upon a time. Now I have to lie, especially to myself [*LDJN* 93].

As regards Mary, her incessant lies and betrayals are explained by her drug addiction. In other cases, the recourse to pretense is shown to be necessary for continued survival, concealing to oneself the sordid nature of existence. We have noted in the study of the relationships between the characters and those around them that the latter were rarely taken in by the explanations invented to justify the situations in which they found themselves. In fact, if these accounts are aimed at spectators, the first of these is the speaker himself, who is seeking to persuade himself by enunciating half-truths. Everyone needs to convince himself of the veracity of his own words, and the audience, sometimes party to it, helps him to create his fiction.

Such is not the case with Mary, who enjoys no family support whatever, when she wants to pretend to those close to her and to herself that morphine has not taken hold of her once more. Driven into this corner by her children, she pretends not to understand the meaning of their words, so as not to be confronted with what she has become. In a more expansive moment she confesses to her son that she is a prisoner of her lies but that they are as necessary to her as the drug itself, for they help to shield her from a reality which has become unbearable. The desire to believe in an image of oneself masking a deep distress allows those who are lost to continue their journey, without thinking they are obliged to make an irreversible decision. When the attempts to flee from oneself end in failure, and the day of reckoning arrives, those who cannot put on an outward show to avoid a confrontation with their inner truth are made to suffer. Before committing suicide, John retraces the path he has taken. As is true in general of the relationships between the protagonists and those around them, he realizes that wearing a mask has proven fatal for him:

> JOHN. Oh, I've lied to you and the rest of the world until I guess no one doubts I'm the happiest married man [in the world] on earth. Why, I've lied even to myself and shut my eyes to the truth. The struggle to appear happy has worn me out [B&B 79].

What is to be done? There seems to be no satisfactory way out for all these souls who have gone adrift. In spite of its many disadvantages, they consider hiding one's face to be such a way out, if only a partial one, because it allows them to buy some time, to give themselves over to the pipe dream that the lives they are living do have their positive aspects, even if waking from this dream is very painful and often leads victims to a sleep from which they will never rise.

Thus Con Melody (in *A Touch of the Poet*), struggling to hide his status of innkeeper behind his claims of being a gentleman, is the incarnation of the necessity each character has to conform to a positive image of himself, the loss of which would be an annihilation. One of the favorite pastimes of the Major is to stand in front of the mirror and recite verses of Byron, with which he identifies because they convey a schism between the self and the world. The interest of these scenes lies in the manifestation of Melody's blindness, for faced with the portrait of an old man, wasted away by alcohol and pushed to the lower end of the social ladder, he sees only what he was in his days of glory, even when he is not wearing his military uniform. His attitude may seem absurd; at some moments he feels his mask slipping and seems on the point of coming apart completely, perceiving how much he is deluding himself. When, after the confrontation with the police, he realizes, however, that the person he believed he was still incarnating is really dead, he gives up the pretense then. After he has shot his mare, he declares that the Major is no longer, and that the innkeeper has just been born. He thus signs his death certificate, for living has lost all interest for him, if he can no longer believe himself to be the valiant officer who had women falling at his feet.

In another situation, Professor Leeds demonstrates the power of words, which allow one momentarily to sidestep a latent truth that individuals refuse to take on board:

> PROFESSOR LEEDS. And she acts towards me exactly as if she thought I had deliberately destroyed her happiness, that I had hoped for Gordon's

death and been secretly overjoyed when the news came! (*His voice shaking with emotion*) And there you have it Charlie—the whole absurd mess! (*Thinking with a strident accusation*) And it's true, you contemptible...! (*Then miserably defending himself*) No!...I acted unselfishly...for her sake! [*SI* 11].

In this episode, he finds himself indirectly faced with his inner self, giving one version of the present situation while taking refuge behind his duty in order to hide what he suspects are the real motivations for his attitude. This scene illustrates a course frequently taken. The characters construct a narrative in the way one might forge an alibi, but the truth never ceases to break through, and they must constantly beat it back, that they might preserve for a little while longer a semblance of inner peace. In the case of Professor Leeds, his fight against the truth will be brief, for Nina will force him to confess the reasons he acted the way he did:

PROFESSOR LEEDS. Yes, I did it for your sake, Nina.
NINA. (*In the same voice as before*) It's too late for lies!
PROFESSOR LEEDS. Let us say then that I *persuaded* myself it was for your sake [*SI* 20].

Having put on stage an ape, one might imagine that O'Neill is turning to ostriches. Indeed, he constantly underlines the extent to which individuals delude themselves or recoil from a merciless self-portrait taking shape before their eyes. Professor Leeds is conscious of what he did not want to see. This is not always the case for others, and there is a gradation in their errors of evaluation. These errors do not result from a single process and despite the vehement denial of any possible Freudian influence in his writing, it does seem that the playwright had assimilated Freud's theory, and that it left its mark in his work. John Alvis stresses this: Not all the errors are deliberate, but they are often subconscious.[2]

When Christine Mannon accuses her daughter Lavinia of being in love with Christine's lover, Lavinia defends herself, declaring that she feels nothing but contempt for this adventurer. At that moment there is nothing to indicate that Lavinia is deliberately deceiving herself; she is driven by the hatred she feels for her mother and the desire to avenge her father's honor. It is only when she finds herself alone with Peter that she becomes aware of the true nature of her feelings towards Adam:

LAVINIA. Want me! Take me, Adam! (*She is brought back to herself with a start by this name escaping her—bewilderedly, laughing idiotically*) Adam? Why did I call you Adam? I never even heard that name before—outside of the Bible! (*Then suddenly with a hopeless, dead finality*) Always the dead between! It's no good trying any more! [*MBE, The Haunted* 177].

12. The Discovery of Human Beings.

She understands that invoking the name of Adam effectively puts an end to all her hopes of happiness, in that his ghost would come between her and Peter were they to marry. The statement is without appeal; it signifies that, contrary to her previous declarations, she will not be able to find happiness with another man, and that the weight of the past, of the fault inherent in being born into the Mannon clan, eternally condemns her.

The distinction between the situation of Lavinia and those we previously evoked lies in the way in which the revelation of these feelings is brought about. Contrary to the previous examples, she is under no constraint whatsoever from her environment and spontaneously names the man she desires. As for Peter, he could not be accused of forcing her to confess an attachment of which he knew nothing.

In *The Iceman Cometh*, the process of awareness is the same, but the way in which Hickey goes back on his confessions runs counter to Lavinia's progression; in so doing he rejoins the ranks of those whose despair we have seen piercing through the mask:

> HICKEY. I remember I heard myself speaking to her, as if it was something I'd always wanted to say: "Well, you know what you can do with your pipe dream now, you damned bitch!" (*He stops with a horrified start, as if shocked out of a nightmare, as if he couldn't believe he heard what he had just said. He stammers*) No! I never!—... (*Bursts into frantic denial*) No! That's a lie! I never said—Good God, I couldn't have said that! If I did, I'd gone insane! Why I loved Evelyn better than anything in life! [*IC* 716].

No one forced him to confess his crime. On the contrary, his drinking cronies often told him to be quiet, but he was no longer capable of keeping to himself something that prevented him from getting on with his life. The interesting aspect of his confession stems from the fact that he is no longer in control of what he is saying and that, carried away with his own enthusiasm in his desire to make a clean sweep, he is overtaken by words that reveal to him a reality which he refuses to believe and from which he will try to escape.[3] In fact, he is prepared to acknowledge his crime, but the motive presents a problem, for he says that he was fully aware of the reasons for what he did, claiming to have wanted his wife to rest in peace at last, when in fact his allegations do not stand up.

When he understands why he acted in the way he did, he hides behind temporary madness. He knows such madness never existed but by putting into play this defense strategy, he creates a new image of himself which allows him to deny the real motives that led him to become a murderer. This process puts him in the category of Professor Leeds, Mary or John, who resorted to the mask so as not to be obliged to acknowledge a truth about themselves, a truth so unbearable that death sometimes seemed the better option.

Perhaps the essence of the theater consists in projecting before our eyes the drama of life in true perspective and restoring to the subconscious—formerly ignored on the stage—its real psychological and dramatic value. O'Neill's merit is having attempted this through many courageous experiments, considering those experiments not as ends in themselves, but as means sometimes awkward, almost always crude, to reach the realization of an ideal dear to him.[4]

The representation of life is manifestly complex; O'Neill has attempted to show the different components by highlighting the aspects thus far ignored, as Maurice Le Breton points out. Through his characters, he stresses the vulnerablility of human beings who find themselves forced to hide behind a shield, not only to protect themselves from the environment, which represents a potential danger for them, but also to avoid having to face an image of themselves which they would be unable to endure. I have said that when the beneficiaries of this protection are not aware of its existence, it is often through them that it is revealed. Whether the mask is worn with a conscious objective, the aim remains the same; one must arm oneself against the effects of a vision of the self, which not everyone may be capable of apprehending satisfactorily.

Putting forward an appearance at the expense of what really is, is not the sign of frivolity, which could be added to the long list of human inadequacies. It is rather due to the feeling of fragility which many have, and in the face of which they have no other choice but to flee. The wearing of a mask is one of the strategies that allow the protagonists to overcome the destructive repulsion taking possession of them, when they are confronted with a picture of themselves.

Not all are capable of expertise in the dissimulation exercises required for their own protection. Some of the protagonists take refuge in a universe of their own creation, in which they are able to invent roles for themselves that are very different from their usual appearance ("SARA. He has queer lonely spells at times when I feel he's in a dream world far away from me" [*MSM* 41]). We may also remember the choice made by Deborah, who had chosen to relive the life of a *demi-mondaine* at the court of Louis XIV; in other cases less exotic "other places" are presented, but at the root of the many individual choices we find the same principles in operation. They are the result of an irresistible desire to escape, engendered by the existential malaise of each individual. The importance bestowed on this escape into the imaginary world varies according to the situations, and some are able to continue living almost normally, considering that the flattering attributes, which they vociferously claim for themselves, are part of the real world ("MRS. FRAZER. ... but in your life you regard yourself as the only individual in the world. You cannot see beyond that. You have reconstructed the world for yourself—well and good" [*Ser* 280]). Others escape temporarily. By putting the real world to one side, they give themselves the strength once more to re-establish contact with their environment, which serves as a mirror and presents an uncompromising portrait of them. I wrote previously of the way in which the characters resorted to dreams to keep control of their relationship with the external world; the process undertaken to avoid having to make an evaluation of their lives is close to that one, with some differences we will now discuss. Given that a permanent questioning of the existence of society itself, of which they are a part, is impossible, the characters sometimes have recourse to another technique. They accept that they are a part of society but denounce the image they have within it as not corresponding to reality.

> ROCKY. (*Winks at Larry*). Aw, Harry, me and Chuck was on'y kiddin'.
> HOPE. (*More drowsily*). I'll fire both of you. Bejees, if you think you can play me for an easy mark, you've come to the wrong house. No one ever played Harry for a sucker!
> ROCKY. (*To Larry*). No one but everybody [*IC* 582].

In this extract, we can see that those around him are not taken in by the flattering self-portrait drawn by Harry. His friends pretend to believe in it, and in so doing, they allow him to take a position in a world the reality of which has not been denied. In the example we have just quoted, the break with reality is the first level, for Harry wishes to refute the evidence and present himself as what he manifestly is not. On the second level, the process is a little different in the sense that when his friends' turns come, they do not fight against the situation as it appears; they admit that their present condition could possibly cause a stranger to draw erroneous conclusions were they to be based on mere appearances. They keep their distance in relation to the person they are supposed to portray for the benefit of others, and accord him only a provisional existence. This strategy does offer some advantages, including access to a greater serenity due to the absence of continual recourse to the imagination through which some construct a fictional environment. All the empires built on imaginary contexts constantly threaten, however, to crumble and their inventors are continually at the edge of the abyss, while the second level makes self-judgment or personal attacks more difficult. The contradiction endures between what they claim to be and what they really are. From this a tension emerges between the here and now, which is automatically associated with the ephemeral, and the "other place," which they are in no doubt will be definitive. As for the departure for this other place, symbol of a rebirth—it is presented as imminent.

We have noted the very strong influence the past has on the present of each character. In *The Iceman Cometh*—in which the phenomenon, while not confined to this play only, is illustrated very clearly: "LARRY. This dump is the Palace of Pipe Dreams!" (*IC* 623)—the past has a very unusual place, in that it is idealized and serves as the basis for a projection into the future. The characters all reconstruct their lives in a flattering way, and this new perspective is in itself a denial of the state in which they find themselves, for the contrast, which one cannot fail to notice, between the two situations, gives a strange, almost unnatural character to their coexistence.

> JIMMY. (*As if reminded of something—with a pathetic attempt at a brisk, no-more-nonsense air*). Tomorrow, yes. It's high time I straightened out and got down to business again. (*He brushes his sleeve fastidiously.*) I must have this suit cleaned and pressed. I can't look like a tramp when I— [*IC* 600].

The bridge between past and future is automatically established. Classing the present as something ephemeral is a denial if not of reality itself at least of its relevance. The whiskey drinkers claim to have lost nothing of the imposing bearing they had in the past and declare that tomorrow or very soon they will regain their former status. This illusion, this pipe dream, is a variation on the mask; they all admit the concrete aspects of the present situation but add that this is only transitory and will not be taken into account in their self-evaluation.[5]

This self-analysis is based on an extreme optimism, for the characters are *de facto* in a condition which is by no means transitory, whether we are speaking of Con Melody or other characters who have gone adrift. Their situation is not simply rooted in the present. It has existed for some time, and the blind discourse of each individual could not be sustained for long if it were not supported by that indispensable ally in the fight against the truth, alcohol (or drugs in the case of Mary Tyrone in *Long Day's Journey into Night*). The creation of a dual personality is made easier by whiskey, which dulls the intellectual capacities of those who drink it to excess, allowing them to believe quite easily that what they profess about their double conforms to reality. The benevolent complicity of those close to them not always being attained, drunkenness permits them to retreat from the world so that they are able even to refute the existence of the present or sometimes take refuge in the past. Thus, after Anna Christie has admitted to them that she was a prostitute, Mat Burke and Chris leave the ship only to seek the comfort of forgetfulness in a whiskey bottle until they cease to be aware of their misfortune:

> ANNA. (*With a harsh laugh*) So I'm driving you to drink, too, eh? I suppose you want to get drunk so's you can forget—like him?
> CHRIS. (*Bursting out angrily*) Yes, Ay vant! You tank Ay like hear dem tangs? [*AC* 61].

Unfortunately for them, they do not succeed in shaking off the images which haunt them, even after consuming vast quantities of alcohol ("BURKE. ...and drinking oceans of booze that'd make me forget. Forget? Divil a word

I'd forget, and your face grinning always in front of my eyes, awake or asleep, 'til I do be thinking a madhouse is the proper place for me" [*AC* 70]). In some plays, a certain rhythm is given to the action in the uninterrupted and apparently perpetual ritual of glasses which are filled and then emptied. Paradoxically, this slow, recurrent, dipsomaniac mechanism is shown to be an attempt at negation of time, which by virtue of the weight of the past or of present misery oppresses the drinkers, who seem desperately to invoke a modern-day Bacchus who could shelter them for a few hours from the scourge of existence.

Drinking to forget, getting drunk so as not to see; the aims are delusory in that they can never be attained, and the path taken by those who choose to flee turns in on them like a trap. Drunkenness brings about a slight loss of control of oneself. The result obtained, contrary to the one sought, is an involuntary liberation. Their attitude amounts to a surrender, and, letting themselves be carried along, they are no longer able to stop themselves from declaring publicly what they wanted to keep within themselves. The process does recall in some ways what we observed when we evoked subconscious masks. The subjects lose control of their language and, overcome with the need to express themselves, betray their true feelings.[6]

Escape through alcohol constitutes a double dead-end, for far from satisfying the obvious needs of the characters, this formula serves only to demean them further. Once embarked on this road, all are caught up in a descending spiral at the end of which they reach the ultimate level of decadence, shown on stage in *The Iceman Cometh*. When this point of individual degeneration has been reached, whatever the reasons for it may have been, the means used to escape reality tend to override the initial motives and to become the primary cause of disgrace, a situation which makes any return to a normal life impossible.

> JOHN. I used to paint a bit, but Maud didn't want me to leave her alone and was bored if she came with me, and I slid deeper into the rut and gave up altogether. (*He sighs*) Just plain degeneration, you see.
> BESSIE. (*Pointing to the bottle on the table with frank disgust*) Don't you think that may be to blame for this degenerating? [*B&B* 80].

What was at first perceived as a means of escape forms the basis of an exclusion which must not be thought of purely in terms of social ostracism. Indeed, inebriation cannot be permanent and therefore all are led to admit that they have become incapable of regaining control of their lives, for they have been overcome by their own desire for an alcoholic escape. John provides the proof of this. Apprehending the extent of his own degradation he will take his own life, this gesture indicating a rejection of his unacceptable metamorphosis.[7] He will realize too late that what he took to be a means of escape was in fact a prison, whose walls he had built himself with empty bottles.

What ultimate lifeline is offered to those who are drowning? When they believe they can see a hand held out to them, it disappears the moment they think they have taken hold of it. They are incessantly pushed back under and find themselves caught up in a current which, seeking to engulf them, will carry them to their death. From one failure to another, in a final effort they try to cling to life, but once again they fail to free themselves from what is oppressing them. Their desire to flee is the proof that this exorcism is impossible.

We could sum up all their struggles by saying that they have attempted to escape by joining a battle (words versus reality) where what they say is opposed to the reality of their situation. Before admitting defeat, they attempt to regain contact with the present; they put forward their own reading of the universe in which they have evolved, making use of all the means I have previously discussed.

The power of words is undeniable. We may remember for example the influence that the legends recounted by the Muslim poet, and then by Nano, had on the destiny of Don Juan (in *The Fountain*). I have also alluded to the story invented by Deborah, which became a *roman familial* for Simon, whose entire life consisted in putting into perspective a narrative the run of which had been broken, in order that he might free himself from its curse:

> DEBORAH. But—it is all so silly and childish—so absurd and perverse—and revolting—for you, a grown man—a great man of the worldly affairs—to remember—to make into a literal fact—an old fairy story—a passing fantasy of my brain—I made up in an idle moment to amuse you and make you laugh [*MSM* 285].

Whatever Deborah's real motives may have been, Simon has obviously been very much affected by this story, a product of the maternal imagination. Through him, we realize that the imaginary, which partly covers the existential reality of individuals, ends up being so important that reality is greatly influenced by it.

Words, the final fortress against the truth, will allow each character to reconstruct the world around himself, taking fragments of his biography. By presenting it in his own way, he will try to take control of his own existence and to give an interpretation of it contrary to the one which seems to be emerging. Thanks to these half-fabrications, he is even able to proceed to a rewriting of his own history, which will allow him, by a projection into the future that we have already evoked, to break free from the pain of confinement. The claim to an otherness, the assertion that the "I" is someone else is all the more plausible in that the individuals, in their social life, cannot appear as themselves. What they say could come across as a revelation of their personality, which they would not have been aware of up to this point.

The tasks associated with this recreation of language, where each character decides what he is, are of varying degrees of difficulty and depend on the individual situations. Indeed, not all have the verve of Erie Smith (in *Hughie*) and there are few who attain Jimmy's level of decadence (in *Iceman*). As far as he is concerned, even his speech on the reconstruction of his environment is marked by doubt:

> JIMMY. I've heard rumors the management were at their wits' end and would be only too glad to have me run it for them again. I think all I'd have to do would be to go and see them and they'd offer me the position [*IC* 604].

However the others inevitably end up by joining him in the proffering of uncertain remarks. When the final stage of narration has been reached, each knows within himself that the truth is going to break through and that a final verbal disguise will not be enough to give him a fresh opportunity for escape.

The characters give the impression of being in the middle of a large room, with mirrors on all the walls. Sometimes they pretend to accept what is real—it is actually a "yes, but"—then surreptitiously try to move away from the center, where the light is, because they are too exposed. They therefore head away from the center, but when they see a glimmer of hope and move towards it, they find themselves faced with themselves. They therefore have to turn round and go back, and lick their wounds, before being bruised again, a process which continues until they give up.

In this respect, *Hughie* is an interesting work for it shows how Erie Smith manages to avoid the fall and to resume his life. The death of his companion has deprived him of a part of himself, and the first meeting with the new night porter is his last chance for survival. He finds himself on the edge of the precipice, and if he does not make a huge leap, he will be annihilated. In fact, the disappearance of his friend must not be considered merely an emotional shock, due to the loss of a loved one; it constitutes a kind of obligatory prelude to a reflection on the meaning of his own existence and foreshadows an acknowledgment of failure which, like many others, he will try very hard to avoid. The harrowing nature of all these confrontations with reality stems from the fact that there is a risk of disastrous consequences for the protagonists. In spite of all the negative aspects of each person's own illusions, they are necessary, almost indispensable to those who have recourse to them:

> HICKEY. Do you suppose I give a damn about life now? Why, you bonehead, I haven't got a single damned lying hope or pipe dream left! [*IC* 719].

Hickey provides the proof of this, as when he has become aware of the truth, he finds himself stripped of every vital instinct. At that moment, he seems no longer to have any hope of survival, for he can no longer delude himself about the meaning of his deed, which would have provided him with a motive for escape, and would have allowed him to avoid destructive introspection.

13. Revelation of an Existential Condition.

The roads to discovery.

In the first part of this study, we noted the often conflicting nature of family relationships; in the second, I asserted that integration into a community is also the source of many clashes. Whatever the origins may be, from all these oppositions flow many instances of self-questioning that are difficult to assume. Choosing exile and leading a monastic life far from the rest of society would reduce to nothing the risks of discord, but the examples of this are rare in O'Neill's work. In *A Touch of the Poet*, Simon goes into retreat at a lakeside, and meditates on what the relationship of human beings to the world ought to be. The consequence, which is both logical and paradoxical, of the elaboration of a social system where he lives outside any human community is that he finds an inner harmony in solitude and is able to construct his idyllic, utopian vision without its being subjected to the scrutiny of those around him, for he has much less intercourse with his fellow men. In this play we do not witness a real reflection on the human condition, with the hazards of reflective thought and the roads that lead nowhere, for Simon's intellectual autarky makes him avoid any confrontation, any putting to the test from which might stem the confusion or at least the doubt as to the validity of his convictions.

In fact we can say that it is not isolation but rather contact with other people which leads to self-reflection, in that relatives and friends present to those close to them an image of themselves to which they cannot remain indifferent. The responses vary but all are based on common principles. Each person finds himself in a position whereby he must make a personal readjustment and it sometimes take on a revelatory aspect. We shall see the effects of this clash in *The Hairy Ape* (but a similar effect is also produced in *Days Without End, Diff'rent, Mourning Becomes Electra* [Lavinia's slip of the tongue], *The Personal Equation,* and *The Straw*):

> MILDRED. Take me away! Oh, the filthy beast! (*She faints. They carry her quickly back, disappearing in the darkness at the left, rear. An iron door*

13. Revelation of an Existential Condition. 153

clangs shut. Rage and bewildered fury rush back on YANK. He feels himself insulted in some unknown fashion in the very heart of his pride.) [*HA* 226].

The reaction can be immediate, spontaneous and brutal. Contrary to his companions, who do not accept any more than he does this violation of their privacy, this exhibition which makes circus animals of them, Yank does not react only to the insult of a stranger entering the boiler room. He is suffering because Mildred's outburst has swept away all his certitudes. The collapse of a universe, within which he had granted himself a central position, has bruised him, for it has caused him to lose his status as an invincible man, by turning him into a wounded animal. A single glance has broken the artificial harmony which, so he thought, allowed him to form a coherent whole with the boat, the steel and the steam, elements symbolizing a power he felt himself to be a part of. Contrary to the other characters whose behavior we have studied, he does not retreat behind prevarications, for he is seeking precisely to discover who he really is. Mildred has laid him bare, but he has not discovered which traits characterize him. He does not know where he fits into a world that has become incomprehensible to him, which is the reason for his wandering, his pathetic quest for a community where he would be accepted and could at last be himself. Beneath his desire to belong, the essential question arises, a question to which he has no reply: Who am I?

Yank will never be in a position to reply to this question, while others will be pushed into a corner by a hostile environment that will force them to face up to their own image. Indeed, the behavior of Yank, trying to define himself, is atypical of the general attitude of the characters, for most of them try to hide behind a feigned ignorance of the truth, afraid that it would expose them in too brutal a way. In the few examples we are now going to consider, I shall attempt to evaluate the impact of the human environment on the revelation of the personality of each individual.

Before Breakfast, one of O'Neill's very early works, is an extreme example, for Mr. Rowland finds himself indicted by his wife, and the charges she lays against him are damning. She presents him as an abject character whose life is a failure; she says that he drags down with him all the women with whom he has had romantic attachments. His wife takes on the role of a public prosecutor; she condemns not only his faults, but his very existence, which is the cause of much subsequent unhappiness ("MRS. ROWLAND. But life with you would soon wear anyone down" [*BB* 632]). Her husband is all the more wounded by her words because he cannot contest the truth of them. He punctuates the accusations against him by crying out when he cuts himself, and then by what the author calls grunts, his final response being conveyed by the sound of drops of blood falling on the floor. His resignation, his silence before his suicide, constitute a symbolic acquiescence to the sentence being pronounced against him.

Other defendants try to put forward arguments which could perhaps help them to plead innocence. In *Abortion*, another early work the theme of which is very similar to the one we have just evoked, Jack calls upon outside forces that would allow him to exculpate himself, by asserting that his attitude is the result of a social environment that led him to behave in the way he does and for which he is being reproached:

> JACK. Some impulses are stronger than we are, have proved themselves so throughout the world's history. Is it not rather our ideals of conduct, Right and Wrong, our ethics, which are unnatural and monstrously distorted? Is society not suffering from a case of the evil eye which sees evil where there is none? Isn't it our moral laws which force me into evasions like the one which you have just found fault with? [*Ab* 155].

By denying his responsibility, Jack wants to shield himself from a condemnation which he deserves. His desire to share the blame is not the fruit of a generous altruism, but is part of an attempt to divert the accusation. The same phenomenon arises in *Long Day's Journey into Night*, when some characters want to protect themselves from the scrutiny they are undergoing. In the Tyrone family, it seems as if the harassment will never end; the assailants reiterate their criticisms until the victims of their attacks acknowledge the partial validity of their assertions. The words of other people represent a permanent danger and the duration of the suffering contrasts with O'Neill's other works, where people choose to put an end to it. Thus, when Jack is finished with his father, Evelyn's brother comes to announce to him that she is dead. This time, every rhetorical way out seems closed to him and he takes his own life, having been forced to confront a disaster for which he was responsible.

When conflicts arise in the relationships between the characters, and this happens frequently, a procedure commonly followed consists in attacking the person whom they want to destroy, by forcing them to see that which they are trying with all their might to mask. The examples chosen are not the only ones to illustrate this technique. One may also think of *A Touch of the Poet*, and Sarah's behavior, trying hard to break down the false image her father wanted to keep of himself. Without trying to draw up an exhaustive list of all the plays where this phenomenon occurs, because it is of varying importance in each, we could say that the second way in which people are forced to become aware of their personality, namely confrontation with those around them, does play a significant role in O'Neill's work.

The third road leading to self-discovery is meditation. In fact, confronted with the existential calling into question of the identity of the character, one finds a graduated response, stemming from a period of reflection at the end of which each person is able to define himself in accordance with the truth whatever it may be, or else he has realized what that truth is. The access to knowledge is not permanent, in that people are constantly evolving, but at some point the veil is drawn back and all are confronted with themselves.

13. Revelation of an Existential Condition.

We have twice seen how this progressive discovery is brought about: in *Desire Under the Elms*, when Eben discovers that he was wrong and that he loves Abbie, and, in a situation where the circumstances are reversed, in the evocation of the attitude of Hickey (in *The Iceman Cometh*), when he realizes that his argument does not stand up and that he did not kill his wife for love but rather out of hate. The characters' errors regarding their attachment for another highlight their emotional blindness and in a more profound way their ignorance of their own identity. The third example is to be found in *The Emperor Jones*. We see Jones, distraught, forced to face up to an inner reality he had previously rejected because he thought it did not apply to him:

> JONES. What—what is I doin'? What is—dis place? Seems like I know dat tree—an' dem stones—an' de river. I remember—seems like I been heah befo'.(*Tremblingly*) Oh, Gorry, I'se skeered in dis place! I'se skeered. Oh, Lawd, pertect dis sinner! [*EJ* 200].

This scene is the prelude to a final revelation, which will put an end to the slow process of awareness of what he is. In fact, while not being taken in by his emperor's role, he grants himself nonetheless a place apart, distancing himself from ordinary mortals. In all his utterances, he declares his superiority, which he believes emanates from the fact that he is different. However, the play demonstrates that in spite of his utterances, he has a common past with those whom he rejected, having judged them to be inferior ("JONES. You didn't s'pose I was holdin' down dis Emperor job for de glory in it, did you? Sho'! De fuss and gloria part of it, dat's only to turn de heads o' de low flung, bush niggers dat's here" [*EJ* 177]).

The previous quotation illustrates the extent to which all genuine self-knowledge brings with it an overturning of certitudes and, when this process begins, the seeds of turmoil are sown in the minds of those who can no longer ignore the nightmarish vision before their eyes. As far as Brutus Jones is concerned, the scenes from the past finally make up a kind of robe which enshrouds him, and presents an image of himself which until that point, he had unconsciously challenged. Contrary to Hickey, Eben or Don Juan, he is not capable of synthesizing the portraits being presented to him, accepting that the person he is seeing is himself and drawing conclusions from that. The scenes which take place in the forest, however, develop what in other plays will play a lesser role, namely the thought processes of the characters; the point of convergence rests in the description of the path which leads towards the revelation of what one is and what one is not.

The game of hide-and-seek with oneself, which numerous characters engage in, leads inevitably to a realization of what they really are, and to a clearer vision of their relations with the world. We will now consider the consequences of this, by trying to find what meaning the discovery of one's own identity has for each character.

Nothingness versus pain.

The progressive divulging of what one is, of which I have described some of the stages, is like giving birth, which involves pain, and they all seem all the more disarmed in that, at each stage, the portraits become more precise. If we retain the idea of a birth, we must say that it is not a deliverance, a state of well-being granted to the characters, but that the torment continues when they are forced to face the truth about themselves.

> If its immediate purpose is not suffering we may say that our life has no reason to be in this world. For it is absurd to contend that the endless suffering born of the inherent woes of life and filling the world should be a mere accident and not the purpose itself.[1]

We know the influence Schopenhauer had on O'Neill, at least in his youth, and we have already noted the extent to which suffering forms an integral part of the characters on stage. Indeed suffering, the origins of which are numerous, arises at every stage of their lives, the responses to it varying according to the people concerned and the situations. The escape routes to which they resort, in order to free themselves, are shown to be futile, in that it is impossible to deny what will eventually be established as the truth. We could not however affirm that the writer adheres completely to the words of the philosopher, for their aim does not correspond completely to the ideas developed in the plays. In the latter, the concern is more with life, which is in essence pain, the idea of goal or purpose, being somewhat misleading.

If we take the body of O'Neill's work as a whole, we notice that comedies and satire have been given a very small place; as for dramas and other tragedies, they illustrate in sometimes very poignant ways the existential problems of each individual. As regards three plays that are of a very distinctive type: Although they are written from a different perspective, they nonetheless present on stage characters on whom pain has left its mark. Kukachin (of *Marco Millions*) and Lucy (of *Now I Ask You*) have experienced the torments of love, one of them hoping in vain that she will finally be valued and loved, the other doubting the sincerity of her husband's feelings. Kukachin renounces life, and dies. Lucy proceeds in a parallel fashion, her clumsy use of a pistol indicating how painful it was for her to live in doubt. In a specific context, within a model family, we may remember the scene (in the third play, *Ah, Wilderness!* 258) during which Sid declares that his life is a total failure, that only suicide could put an end to the nightmare, but that he does not have the strength to do it.

In fact, we should not be surprised at the omnipresence of pain in the lives of the characters, for behind the assertions of Schopenhauer, we can see the Buddhist influence, the four Noble Truths of which we should perhaps remind the reader.[2] Having lost his faith, O'Neill did not give up mystic reflection;

13. Revelation of an Existential Condition. 157

until the end of his life, he took an interest in, among others, Buddhism and Taoism.³ Some studies, among them that of James Robinson,⁴ have shown that it was not just a passing interest, but that he did in fact have considerable knowledge of both belief systems.

We will now try to see where Buddhist influences are manifested in his writing, taking as our reference the sermon of Benarès, during which the Buddha uttered the four Noble Truths (we note the importance of *dukkka* in his discourse, *dukkka*, which for reasons of convenience, I shall call suffering). I have indicated the importance given to pain in O'Neill's work, but the fact that the characters suffer is not enough in itself to justify such a reading. I shall therefore turn my attention to the second and third Noble Truths,⁵ the fourth, leading to the understanding of *Nirvâna*, being of little interest for the purposes of this study.

Desire being considered as the source of all suffering, those who wish to be free must fight against it. This aspect, the attempt to free oneself through renunciation, is developed in several different contexts. We may think of *More Stately Mansions*, and in a less obvious way, in the first part of the cycle, *A Touch of the Poet*.⁶ At the end of *More Stately Mansions*, Sara, realizing that they are thwarting their own happiness, sees to it that they lose the empire that Simon had built, that she might live again fully with him, freed from all desire to accumulate material wealth.⁷ As such, their progression is similar to that of Eben and Abbie (in *Desire Under the Elms*)⁸ who tear each other apart, because each one claims the ownership of the farm. At the end of their struggle they realize the extent of their error, and are liberated only when they become sensitive to the beauty of the land, without their view of it being corrupted by the greed which was the cause of their unhappiness:

> EBEN. (*They go out the door in rear, the men following, and come from the house, walking hand in hand to the gate. Eben stops there and points to the sunrise sky*) Sun's a rizin'. Purty, hain't it?
> ABBIE. Ay-eh. (*They both stand for a moment looking up raptly in attitudes strangely aloof and devout.*)
> SHERIFF. (*Looking around at the farm enviously—to his companions*) It's a jim-dandy farm, no denyin'. Wished I owned it! [*DE* 269].

Throughout this last scene, the contrast is striking between those who have attained a higher reality, by renouncing all desire for possession, and those who are driven by the lure of gain, a sign of blindness which can only lead them to their downfall. The renunciation⁹ and accumulation of material wealth does not imply that one must make a Buddhist reading of the texts cited (and I am not necessarily making one myself, as shall be seen later; I simply wish to point out that it seems difficult to pass by this particular track without comment). Other schools of thought could legitimately assert their own rights of interpretation, by invoking different sources; one should perhaps simply say that there is a compatibility between Buddhism and the ideas developed in the scenes that we have evoked. Moreover, the Buddhist influence comes through elsewhere more obviously.

We find a clearer manifestation of this influence in *Lazarus Laughed*. The negation of death is not interpreted from a Catholic perspective, wherein the belief in the existence of the soul partially refutes this notion. The title seems to indicate that following the example of what happened when O'Neill wrote *Days Without End*, he was once more taking up Christian themes, but this is not really the case. The context may also lead us to this conclusion, but Lazarus' words betray a strong Buddhist strain:

> LAZARUS. What if you are a man and men are despicable? Men are also unimportant! Men pass! Like rain into the sea! The sea remains! Man remains! Man slowly arises from the past of the race of men that was his tomb of death! For Man death is not! Man, Son of God's Laughter, is! [*LL* 361].

Behind the oft repeated affirmation that death no longer exists lies the belief in a vital continuity of humanity. These words contain the fundamental idea of transience,[10] coupled with the concept of *karma*, its fruits, which will last longer than the life of any individual and which comes into play after death although it cannot be assimilated with the soul.[11] His message is aimed at making them aware that the way they are living their lives is not good. He exhorts his followers to make abstractions of themselves, to forget their egos, to break away from an overcautious individualism in such a way that they will no longer be afraid of dying.

> The play's devaluation of the self, in fact, constitutes its sharpest break from the Nietzschean sources, which either affirm the ego or advise only a temporary retreat from it. Viewing egolessness as a desirable permanent state, Lazarus urges mankind "to let a laughing away of self be your new right to live forever."[12]

In this passage, James Robinson stresses the detachment from the self advocated by Lazarus, and one can only agree with him on this point. According to what he declares, those who give up their attachments will find wholeness. On the other hand, contrary to what is affirmed by the critic, it seems to me that Lazarus does not question the reality of the self but rather simply invites his followers to take their distance from themselves, for from this attitude will spring a freedom that will bring happiness.[13] In fact, in the previous quotation, by declaring, "Men are unimportant," he does not deny the specific existence of those around him[14]; he is showing them the extent to which it is fortuitous, by using the plural, and by devaluing the individual in relation to the human race as a whole. This for him is a sign of permanence, as if the end of one life marked the beginning of another.

13. Revelation of an Existential Condition.   159

Until his final moments, Lazarus continually declares that death has no importance, and that after death, the vital cycle of humanity will continue. Having advocated detachment from the self, he comes close to the third Noble Truth,[15] but does not attain the higher level of *Nirvâna*. In only two plays, *Marco Milllions* and *The Fountain*, do we see characters who accede to this level. Kukachin, for example, may claim it, for in *Marco Millions* she declares that she does not exist:

> KUKACHIN. (*Her face now a fatalistic mask of acceptance*)
> I am not.
> Life is.
> A cloud hides the sun.
> A life is lived.
> The sun shines again.
> Nothing has changed.
> Centuries wither into tired dust.
> A new dew freshens the grass.
> Somewhere this dream is being dreamed [*MM* 417].

Her renunciation of life, which seems to mark the apogee of her suicidal attitudes, does not result from an awareness of her blindness regarding her own existence. It is due to the perception of the impossibility of any communion with Marco, whence the lethargic nature of her words. Access to knowledge, which is a prelude to supreme happiness, gives way to a much more exalted description in *The Fountain*, when Don Juan, at death's door, senses both the transience of his condition and his union with the whole and shows that the usual notion of the self has been surpassed:

> JUAN. I am that song! One must accept, absorb, give back, become oneself a symbol! Juan Ponce de Leon is past! He is resolved into the thousand moods of beauty that make up happiness—color of the sunset, of tomorrow's dawn, breath of the great Trade wind—sunlight on grass, an insect's song, the rustle of leaves, an ant's ambitions [*Fou* 448].

Finally, however, what do the protagonists' feelings matter; in reaching *Nirvâna*, they surpass futile preoccupations, and their emotions, if they are not imaginary, cannot be measured in accordance with a system of thought that has lost all relevance.

> When one becomes aware of the transience of life, one develops the perception of the non-self, and it is the perception of the non-self which manages to eliminate the idea: I am, I exist. This elimination is *Nirvâna* in the here and now.[16]

We could ask ourselves about the value of this here and now: There is no longer a self for whom they can have meaning, but these are not the real stakes indicated by Joseph Masson. Indeed, adhesion to Buddhist principles[17] is not merely a phase or a whim of the writer. What comes across in the works where this influence is uncontestable, is the refutation of the *cogito*, the denial of the relevance of concepts, categories and systems of interpretation around which Western thought is articulated, where the existence of an "I" within the universe is replaced by a great Whole, a monistic vision, in which the concept of the phenomenal world is an hallucination. By shelving Descartes, O'Neill places his characters in a new perspective which, at first glance, seems irreconcilable with the subject I have chosen to deal with.

Insofar as the self is the product of an illusion, it is difficult to study the relations it has, through individuals, with the universe, the reality of which is barely more assured. However in spite of this difference in perspective, we will see that the plays under consideration do have a place in this study. The theme of this book, humanity confronted with the world, presupposes the presence of an "I" and therefore of a rupture between the person and what is outside of him. We have noted that this distinction no longer applies in a Buddhist reading, for it refutes any real distinction between the individual being and the space within which he evolves. In a simplified way, one could say that the world is Man, that the fusion of an apparent fragmentation of the latter (in an individual) gives rise to an illusory differentiation from the world. However, we cannot stop there, for this Truth, if it allows access to *Nirvâna*, is not discovered by everyone, whence the description of the process, of the path which leads to the liberation of the self, in the few works where an Oriental interpretation seems to be justified.

In fact, the absence of the self is not immediately imposed on the protagonists, for they imagine themselves to have a unified and permanent personality. For this reason, it is possible to suggest that even if the universe is a whole within which the presence of an ego is illusory, the false perception of the ego engenders suffering, and it is from this suffering experienced by the characters that the action of the plays develops. By affirming their difference, claiming to have, as individuals, a will to act, they exclude themselves from a whole to which they can only belong if they accept their nonexistence (*Anattâ*). Those who believe they have a life of their own try to become masters of the world in which they live; this generates an existential malaise from which they can free themselves only when they have detached themselves from their desire, whatever it may be.[18] From this renunciation there flows a lethargic attitude which is a prelude to the acceptance of death. For this reason, death does not appear as a fissure; it marks the end of suffering, and presents itself as a supreme stage, the final step to make before attaining a liberation of the self, to which the presence of a physical body had been an obstacle. The absence of any metaphysical anxiety is explained by the way in which the end of life is perceived; it is seen here as being only a passage, the consequences of which are in no way negative, for the dissolution of the *ego*, if it is complete, marks the symbiosis with the Whole. In order to make my thesis more explicit, I refer

13. Revelation of an Existential Condition. 161

to the description of the memorable experience undergone by Edmund when he was at sea, a kind of *Nirvâna* but one which cannot be reduced to an Oriental interpretation:

> EDMUND. I was set free! I dissolved in the sea, became white sails and flying spray, became beauty and rhythm, became moonlight and the ship and the high dim starred sky! I belonged, without past or future, within peace and unity and a wild joy, within something greater than my own life, or the life of Man, to Life itself! To God, if you want to put it that way [*LDJN* 153].

From separation to union, this rough summary of the journey undertaken by each character indicates that the development is a very particular one. It nonetheless has its place in this study, for at the beginning we are faced with a rupture. Individuals think they have their own substance, and when their quest is over, opposing terms join together, indicating that beyond appearances there is a unity between elements which had seemed to be antagonistic. The path taken is surprising. In fact, the process is contrary to that involved in a search for identity. During this journey of initiation, in the course of which Oriental principles are revealed, we are no longer dealing with self-discovery but rather the realization of how futile a belief in the self is at all. The protagonists cast aside the veil of ignorance, which makes those who have not drawn it aside believe that there is an intangible schism between what they perceive themselves to be and the world. The moral development of each character consists in becoming conscious of his own insignificance. In this way, each person will be in a position to integrate satisfactorily in a universe from which he can be excluded, by his own fault, or in which he can be accepted, by denying himself.

14. The Acknowledgment of the Individual.

From the monologue to the confession.

We have observed how through a sentence or an unexpected remark the characters suddenly find that they come face to face with themselves, a situation which is all the more difficult to deal with given that it arises when they are least prepared for it. The dialogue is not the only means of breaking down individual defenses; regardless of the way in which a character finds himself under analysis, in the long term, though taken up to fend off disconcerting glances, the masks prove ineffectual. Their inadequacy is a result of the very strategy they are a part of. In fact, by definition, they constitute a ready-made answer which nevertheless leaves unanswered the ever-present, multifaceted questions intrinsic to the characters' essential human nature but suppressed until the moment a weakness appears. It would be misguided to seek to establish a direct correlation, following precise rules, between a dissimulation and the process which leads to its revelation, but throughout O'Neill's works we note that no truth can ever be concealed. Emerging in different guises, it sometimes takes the form of a monologue during which a character will assess his emotional state, or it puts his existentialist journey into perspective in order to establish his position in relation to an environment in which he no longer has a clearly defined role.[1]

This particular aspect of the discourse is the sign of a sense of isolation, however fleeting; the speaker expresses a feeling he cannot share at that moment, all the more so as the utterance sometimes takes on a revelatory aspect. (This introspection does not exclude the possibility that other protagonists, who may intervene at the end of the tirade, are present on stage; the important thing in this process is that the discourse be addressed above all to oneself.) In a theatrical perspective, recourse to this technique allows us insight into the state of mind of the characters at a precise moment, and permits us to identify the evolution of the self-portrait each individual is in the process of creating. Here we have a classic technique. That which is said is "the truth"; a sense of security is attained by a dislocation from the rest of the world; that which was hitherto hidden may be exposed, there no longer being any reason for dissimulation. The following passage is illustrative:

> (...Then this stops and DION comes in. He walks quickly to the bench at center and throws himself on it, hiding his masked face in his hands. After a moment, he lifts his head, peers about, listens huntedly, then slowly takes off his mask. His real face is revealed in the bright moonlight, shrinking, shy and gentle, full of a deep sadness.)
> DION. (With a suffering bewilderment) Why am I afraid to dance, I who love music and rhythm and grace and song and laughter? [GGB 264].

We have seen this many times before. The mask plays a significant role; that is why this liberation is so important, and for Dion, it resembles a metamorphosis, but this gesture is not an end in itself; it indicates that Dion is about to embark upon a road which will lead to the discovery of his true self, for in his present state he proves as yet incapable of even beginning to formulate answers to his questions. His words transmit a sincere desire to define his identity and he tries to elucidate his mysterious behavior. Beyond his questioning of the motives for his actions, the essential question of the self looms large, an uncertainty which he shares with many other characters.

In the works under consideration, suffering remains one of life's inherent constants; contrary to what we observed in the section devoted to Eastern influences, however, in terms of the quest it is no longer a question of the relevance of the reality of the self, but of the necessity to question its nature and to define it. Having taken off his mask, Dion seeks to discover who he really is in all honesty, the understanding being that faced with oneself, one must show absolute sincerity.[2] However it must be noted that if the uncertainty, the doubt as to one's own situation is difficult to reconcile, the confrontation with one's true self is shown to be equally arduous.

Incessantly seeking more effective ways of interpreting human experiences, O'Neill has used the internal monologue in *Strange Interlude* and in other plays. In relation to the classic form mentioned above, this monologue is less structured, less centered on the *ego* of the speaker; in fact, the character develops his train of thought, and expresses his feelings, the discovery of the self not being the sole purpose of his utterance. In *Strange Interlude*, the playwright has used the innovative technique of bestowing a central role on the protagonist's thoughts and, if the "stream of consciousness" also bears the stamp here of existential interrogation, this is no longer of overriding importance, for no character remains within the confines of an analysis of his own personality. This internal monologue at times resembles a commentary, it even takes the form of a dialogue, and the environment is subject to a judgment which is all the more cruel and severe since the declarations of the individual no longer suffer social censure,[3] the only remaining censorship being that of the individual and of the image he has of himself. However even if this soliloquy is not exclusively egocentric, it nevertheless plays a significant role in self discovery, for, in analyzing his relationships with others, his reflections will naturally lead him to analyze himself.

> LIGHT. (*Remorsefully now*) He's right ... I had no right ... no right even to read them ... how I wish I'd never read them! ... (*Lifting his head*) I destroyed them in a fit of anger [*Dy* 465].

In this extract, we notice the to-ing and fro-ing that arise from verbal exchanges, and the repercussions, which take the form of a self condemnation formulated by one of the characters; the dialogue develops on two levels: Here one witnesses exchanges that include all present, and there the speakers draw their own conclusions from the conversation. Whether one considers *Dynamo* or *Strange Interlude*, the results are very similar in that reflection, in spite of its often somewhat erratic nature, leads to an introspection which ends initially in discovery and finally in a judgment of each character vis-à-vis himself. Following lengthy monologues, which often develop tangentially in order to escape reality, some find themselves once again faced with their own image, and their reaction varies according to what they see there.

The revelation of each character's intimate truth proceeds slowly, and the soliloquies, or thoughts, play an undeniable role in the revelatory process of the *ego*. As we have seen throughout the present study, other elements are linked with this; the quantification of one influence in comparison to another is difficult and may be futile, to the extent that there is interaction between the alien and the intimate, between the external accusation and the uncompromising way in which one views oneself. In the course of the play, the secrets hidden to others but also to oneself are divulged. They are, for instance, constituent factors of each personality, forgotten acts voluntarily laid aside in memory, or unconscious elements from which no one can free himself with ease, even by averting his gaze or by retreating behind a mask in an attempt temporarily to escape from self-criticism.

Before considering the relationships which are established between a fault committed by a character and the emotions generated thereby, it appears necessary to see the criteria by which this fault is judged a crime. In fact, if many of them are quick to repent openly, because they believe that their actions are reprehensible, we cannot deduce from this that every attitude running counter to the rules set down by society should be considered a failure of duty. Thus in *Mourning Becomes Electra*, when Christine Mannon confesses to her husband the whole story of her adulterous affair, she professes to feel no regret; she scorns conventional morality and sweeps aside in one sentence the rebukes of Lavinia, whose Puritan principles seem to have no relevance for her:

> CHRISTINE. Yes, I dared! And all my trips to New York weren't to visit Father but to be with Adam! He's gentle and tender, he's everything

14. The Acknowledgment of the Individual. 165

you've never been. He's what I've longed for all these years with you—
a lover! I love him! So now you know the truth!
MANNON. (*In a frenzy—struggling to get out of bed*) You—you whore—I'll
kill you! [*MBE, Homecoming* 61].[4]

According to her, love, or the lack of it, justifies all; she feels no sense of guilt, and in her eyes the lack of affection she feels for her daughter is explained by her unhappy marriage. The terms in which she is described by others have little meaning for her—moreover, knowing full well that her behavior defies the norms of society, she makes no attempt to conceal her true nature; as for the opinions of those around her, or of society in general, she lends them no credence.[5]

Those who find themselves in an identical situation are united by the power of their declarations; each reveals a truth which until then they had made every effort to conceal. Once laid bare, they are not overcome with the disapproval of the community or of those close to them. They allow themselves to be judged for what they are, without trying this time to retreat behind masks which would allow them to avoid facing up to the situation. However, it must be noted that this process is not the result of a desire to question community rules; it is peculiar to each woman in the play, and their virulent words are in fact a manifestation of their existence. Through what they feel, or what they have been, the individuals have acquired a personality the affirmation of which matters more to them than the opprobrium they risk bringing upon themselves. The demand for such deviations from the traditional mores is therefore not a sign of amorality or the expression of a desire to destabilize the established order; each decides for himself whether his actions are reprehensible or not.[6] We may consider the risks of moral decline inherent in such a system, especially when one thinks of the innate weakness of human beings, manifested among other ways in their propensity to hide their faces. Nonetheless, we must point out that when those concerned appoint themselves as judge and find themselves in the dock, acquittals are rare.

The protagonists carry with them the weight of their misdeeds, and the knowledge of having acted inadvisably, or of having behaved in a way unworthy of their self-image, engenders suffering, a feeling of guilt, which does not allow for an untroubled existence. They are sometimes forced to admit to their wrongdoings but more often they set out in search of someone in whom they can confide, so that by listening to them, this person will share a burden which has become too much to bear.[7] Diverse reasons compel them to list to one of their own the actions which they deem blameworthy, and which they believe have rendered them pariahs. In fact, in spite of their denials, which take the form of prevarication designed to escape judgment of any kind, their conduct seems to adhere to a strange logic. On the one hand, they try to flee leaving no trace with the potential to compromise them, and on the other, they strive to communicate with someone in whom to confide, in the hope of hearing that their faults do not condemn them forever more.

> CALEB. You got a right to your own way—even if—(*hopefully*) And maybe if I show you what I done wasn't natural to me—by never doin' it again— maybe the time'll come when you'll be willing to forget—
> EMMA. (*Shaking her head—slowly*) It ain't a question of time, Caleb. It's a question of something being dead. And when a thing's died, time can't make no difference [*Dif* 517].

Not all judges are as intransigent as Emma; she offers no hope of redemption to her fiancé, for in her eyes his infidelity is irreparable and will make him guilty to the end of his days. Contrary to his companions in misfortune, Caleb remains optimistic; he wants to believe that time is on his side, and refuses to be held captive by the past, for he believes that his salvation lies in his future behavior. (This particular temporal perspective forms a connection with Richard Miller in *Ah, Wilderness!* who lives in the hope of an idyllic future.)

Rallying sign of the excluded ones, the key phrase of the dialogue, emblematic of their state of mind, is "what I done wasn't natural to me." This idea can be found formulated in different ways, sometimes implicitly, in the words of those who blame themselves for having committed what they consider to be a crime. In fact, they admit their guilt, but in their defense, they cite the breach between what they have done and their true personality. Their potential for rehabilitation is dependent on the extent to which they separate what they claim to be from their guilty actions, which, they hope to demonstrate, run contrary to their nature; their entire defense is aimed at presenting what has happened as a twist of fate, in the face of which they had been powerless. They must speak; the protagonists show themselves incapable of keeping a secret the revelation of which they think will be beneficial to them.

> But another theme that clearly obsessed him in the last stages of his life was the idea of guilt—this idea so Tolstoyan, so Dostoïevskian—that shows its pale and hideous face in the painful pages of confession in the *Iceman Cometh*, and also in *A Moon for the Misbegotten*, and in *Long Day's Journey into Night*.[9]

Leon Mirlas emphasizes the importance of the fault and of the consequent feeling of guilt, the whole giving rise to confession scenes (this is characteristic of all those who reveal their secrets); one can only agree, bearing in mind nonetheless that it would be imprecise to limit this theme to the latter part of the playwright's work.[10] We have presented several instances where characters who have transgressed society's rules, and who recognize this without any feelings of regret or remorse, take the stage; in other plays, the situation is different. The individuals do not accept their exclusion; quite to the contrary. They do however know they have acted badly, and they admit it to

14. The Acknowledgment of the Individual. 167

outsiders. Hence we can no longer speak of an avowal which is not voluntary but rather the product of circumstance; we now turn our attention to a voluntary act on the part of some who wish to reveal the culpable aspects of their behavior, for they believe they deserve to be punished.

> COLUMBUS. My soul is overburdened, Father.
> MENENDEZ. (*Dryly*) You wish to confess?
> COLUMBUS. (*Surprised*) Confess? (*Then in a loud, ringing tone*) Yes, to all men! Their mouths are full of lies against me [*Fou* 393-4].

This dialogue takes the form of a confession, but in fact, the process followed runs contrary to the principles which govern it, for we find no sign of contrition on the part of Columbus; his speech is motivated by the unease resulting from the confusion of which he is victim and which causes him to suffer. In his self-defense speech, he explains that his fellow travelers are in error if they read into his actions a desire for material gain, when his goal is to strive for the glory of God. In making a favorable reading of his motives, he seeks to exonerate himself; on the other hand, many are those who, overwhelmed by the weight of remorse,[11] repent and completely open themselves to those closest to them.

In the course of lengthy monologues, they draw up a list of their crimes in fine detail, and describe the circumstances in which they went astray. They conceal nothing of their actions, no matter how despicable, because they are seeking an external judgment which will allow them to put an end to a devastating moral self-flagellation. In fact, once they have reached this point of suffering, they are incapable of withholding any longer the secret of a sin which haunts them. They therefore set out in search of a sympathetic person, if not to forgive their transgressions, then at least to listen, and to show them a certain degree of empathy:

> MARSDEN. You've wanted me, Nina?
> NINA. Yes,—awfully! I've been so homesick. I've wanted to run home and 'fess up, tell how bad I've been, and be punished! Oh, I've got to be punished, Charlie, out of mercy for me, so I can forgive myself! And now Father is dead, there's only you. You will, won't you—or tell me how to punish myself? You've simply got to, if you love me! [*SI* 44].

Nina's tirade describes the state of mind of those who wish to pay for their errors. She at no time considers pleading not guilty; she has need of a judge whose verdict will mark, in part, the end of her disarray, to the extent that the condemnation she expects will allow her to recapture a little of her lost innocence. This is a coherent process, because a reprehensible action, whatever it may be, signals the end of the usual existence of the perpetrator; latently, in these voluntary indictments, can be found the hope of being given a last chance, which would perhaps consist in revealing that the faces which the guilty persons disclose to their interlocutors are far from corresponding to their true personality. In spite of the inherent difficulty in this recognition of weakness, they accept being considered malefactors; their repentance is sincere, and the painful confession, during which the individual arrives at a revelation of his whole being, is a final attempt at redemption. By establishing contact with the other person, they express a desire to reunite, and thereby they hope to be able to attain reconciliation not only with the world but also with themselves.[12]

The final point with which I would like to take issue, concerning the idea of guilt as quoted above from Leon Mirlas, has to do with the way in which he presents the unease of those who are aware of having gone astray; he maintains that one sees "its pale and hideous face in the painful pages of confession..."[13] in various plays. In fact, far from being tainted with turpitude, it is the sign of the grandeur of these characters. Their desire for expiation conveys an acceptance of themselves, but also their refusal to consider that the abject state they have experienced is definitive and corresponds to their destiny. They recognize their guilt and bear the burden of their infamy, but their quest aims to renew the connection with an image of themselves which is more positive than the one they still have in mind and which is uniquely representative of the abject facets of their nature.[14]

The monologue evolves into confession, which itself is the culmination of a voyage of self discovery through which each becomes aware of his weaknesses and gives to those around him the means to judge him, without seeking to hide behind masks or to flee from the world so as not to be confronted with the self.

The Oriental point of view, chosen by some, aimed to deny the existence of the ego; in the scenes I have quoted, the path followed is inverted. The revelation of the personality of each is not conceived of solely in terms of exposure of the self; the feeling of guilt stems from their shocking behavior, and their suffering is profound. That which they consider to be a crime provokes in them an intrinsic schism, in that one part of them cannot accept what the other part has done. Hence, telling another the extent to which one is suffering for having behaved badly is the first step towards personal cohesion, and the repentance seals this reconciliation which will allow some to find peace. Leaving behind the ghosts of the past, some turn toward the future, and this redeeming action will perhaps be the source of a new beginning.

Death.

It would appear that the way in which death is perceived varies according to the play and the situations in which the principal characters find themselves; but the first thing that comes to mind, when one broaches this subject, has to do with the importance that is bestowed on it in the works in their entirety.[15] An exhaustive examination of the various instances where death takes a major role would go beyond the scope of the present study. I shall therefore limit my comments to the way in which individuals react in the face of this ineluctable fate.

> MANNON. It was seeing death all the time in this war got me to thinking these things. Death was so common, it didn't mean anything. That freed me to think of life. Queer, isn't it? Death made me think of life. Before that life had only made me think of death! [*MBE, Homecoming* 53].

Ezra Mannon shows how the surrendering of the soul puts one's existence into a particular perspective; in fact, it was by accepting that his life may end on a battlefield that he realized that his life had little meaning, indeed he could call it mere survival. As for his possible death, he perceives it as an annihilation; as such it has the same revelatory function as soliloquies, or confrontations with other characters, because it is at the root of introspection, which leads to a self-evaluation. Seeing his comrades fall on the field of honor, Ezra, lucid and detached, effects a psychological transference; from what he observes, he reflects on his own future demise, and its implications, questioning the meaning his life would have were he to die in battle. His analysis sets him apart from the attitudes of others, for on the one hand he does not fear death, but neither does he seek it, and on the other, his detachment is not based on the Oriental principles to which we shall briefly allude. He envisages his death as a resolution, without bestowing on it a position of cardinal importance. What really matters is the way in which people formulate their personal history and give it meaning. Behind the military insensibility of Mannon lies the affirmation of an ego. He proclaims the import of existential choices for, according to him, success is measured by the capacity each person possesses to attain the goals they have set for themselves. In his case, this signifies achieving a harmony which takes the form of the search for a shared love.

If the individual arrives at self-definition, then acceptance, and finally fulfillment, the rest is fortuitous[16]; everyone must endeavor to attain this union with himself, without which death would be reduced to its mere biological dimension, signifying the end of a state unworthy to be called a life.

At the point where one is able to go beyond what would normally be considered a final step, one finds, opposed to this vision in which the personality prevails, Taoist and Buddhist tendencies that, in effacing the ego, produce an identical result. Ezra Mannon, through a reflection on antitheses, identifies the presence of a link between life and death[17]; as for the Oriental visions,[18] they take a different line, because they deny the notion of the finite, in that successive generations form a permanent lifestream.

> KUBLAI. Know in your heart that the living of life can be noble! Know that the dying of death can be noble! Be exalted by life! Be inspired by death! Be humbly proud! Be proudly grateful! Be immortal because life is immortal [*MM* 435].

The idea of the self fades slowly and then is eclipsed by the vital, interminable cycle; as such, there is no place for individual fears, since the important thing is continuity, which necessarily occupies a superior position within the human perspective. The moral journey of the protagonists will consist in realizing the futility of any belief in the existence of an ego. This realization culminates in a feeling of distress the source of which is the fear of one's own disappearance.

We have seen that this philosophical perspective is by no means applied to all, for the majority of the characters are influenced by Cartesianism, and the notion of no longer being often generates angst. Paradoxically, Larry Slade is emblematic of this tendency, although he claims to have adopted the Taoist principle of self-denial, where inaction is established as a principle and where death, were it to become the subject of reflection, would be regarded with complete detachment.

> LARRY. What's before me is the comforting fact that death is a fine long sleep, and I'm damned tired, and it can't come too soon for me [*IC* 578].

After Hickey's confessions, his desire for death persists, but he also knows that a part of him will cling to life no matter what happens.[19] Do his fears spring from the fact that his days are nothing but a long wait, which renders even more formidable the inevitable day of reckoning? No one knows, and to question his motives is a little paradoxical, for what can be more natural, more human, than the feeling of emptiness one experiences when thinking of one's own death?[20] What is surprising is not Larry's behavior, but rather its atypical nature. In fact, if we take his work as a whole, the fear of death seems almost alien to the O'Neillian universe.

Another example is given in *Bound East for Cardiff*, where Yank, at death's door, illustrates this phenomenon of angst, which diminishes in the course of his confession. One is reminded that, through listing his culpable actions, he is in part freeing himself from the burden weighing upon him, and manages not only to reconcile himself with himself but also with God, whose judgment he fears.[21] Hence, Driscoll plays a central role, that of confessor, his task being to destroy the terror paralyzing his friend; he does not quite achieve this by assuring him that the reproaches which he delivers cannot damn him, and that God will be merciful. Opposed to this anguish of a human being faced with his annihilation, we discover a tendency, this time with no counterpart, which had already been manifested in the character of Larry.

… for the phenomenon of the death wish already was present in his plays preceding the appearance of the English translation of Freud's book, *Beyond the Pleasure Principle*, in which the psychoanalyst introduced his concept of the death instinct. The death wish can be detected in characters like Smitty in *The Moon of the Caribbees* and Robert Mayo of *Beyond the Horizon* (two of the playwright's early achievements).[22]

The longing for death is characteristic of O'Neill's writing, and Robert Feldman underlines this fact; this attribute, present before the author discovered Freud, is a theme that comes from within the dramatist, rather than an idea gleaned from his reading. It must be noted that this death wish is manifested in different forms; first, not all patterns of conduct stem from the same "*état d'âme*," and second, they do not have the same meaning. This composite, of which we have noted the idiosyncratic nature, could not be interpreted individually, even if there are points of convergence in terms of theme or meaning.

In the case of Robert Mayo, we see one of those characters who thinks that life is a long period of suffering, and that in surrendering the soul, human beings fall into an eternal sleep which allows them to find peace. Intellectually, his thought process is opposed to that of Larry, because he sincerely believes that death is a deliverance and could never be in any circumstances a cause for dread. For him and those like him, to live is so difficult that they aspire only to have done with an existence which is no more than a succession of torments.

> ROBERT. (*In a voice which is suddenly ringing with the happiness of hope*) You mustn't feel sorry for me. Don't you see I'm happy at last—free—free!— freed from the farm—free to wander on and on—eternally! [*BH* 167].

Such words may appear surprising coming from a dying man, but he does not see his death as an ending, for his body will certainly turn to dust, but his soul guarantees eternal life. Robert's faith is not clearly defined[23] but his belief in a vital continuity is essential, for it goes beyond the physiological, and challenges the idea that death signifies total annihilation. If dying means finding peace, and the cessation of doubt or of a recurrent nightmare, one can understand why some are seduced by this prospect and some may even think of bringing forward the fatal day (as in, for instance, *Ah, Wilderness!*, *Now I Ask You*, or *Fog*). An end to suffering is an alluring possibility to those for whom existence is little more than a flight from themselves; when they can no longer escape from their own scrutiny, they seek rest, which will mark the end of a passage on earth bearing the stamp of failure.

The world is hell, and men either tormented souls or tormenting devils.[24]

O'Neill seems to have remembered what Schopenhauer said, and his theater is effectively peopled with these two types. There are more tormented souls than there are tormentors; one understands why, after a long struggle, often in vain, some wish to bow out, and why these components play a central role in many works.[25]

Suicide.

Up to now, we have concentrated upon the way in which the characters have reacted when they become aware of their own mortality and their last hours are nearing. We now turn our attention to the motives which made the protagonists alter their behavior, forcing them out of the passive role to which they hitherto had confined themselves in order irrevocably to intervene in their own destiny by putting an end to their life.

If we consider once more *The Iceman Cometh*, for example, we note that the idea of ending one's life is in keeping with the general ethos. When the characters have made their confessions, they are partially reconciled with themselves, but reconciliation is only possible once a punishment has been decided. Thus the prospect of dying, for Hickey in an electric chair, or for Parritt having thrown himself from a roof, is not shadowed with regret. On the contrary, they wait impatiently for the sentence to be delivered; their punishment is like a gift, for it means that they will finally be able to exorcise their pain and their guilt, which have rendered their passage on earth a hell.

Hickey and Parritt are a distinctive pair, for they give themselves over to the judgment of others. As soon as they begin to speak, they sense that when the verdict comes they will be sentenced to death, but this seems easy compared with the torments they have endured. Paradoxically, their condemnation by other men allows them to break with their solitude, and to reintegrate themselves into a world from which they had been excluded, by becoming lost to themselves. Thus the guilty men move towards the final test with ambiguous hope, expecting deliverance.

> PARRITT. (*Stares at Larry. His face begins to crumble as if he were going to break down and sob. He turns his head away, but reaches out fumblingly and pats Larry's arm and stammers*) Jesus, Larry, thanks. That's kind. I knew you were the only one who could understand my side of it. (*He gets to his feet and turns towards the door.*) [*IC* 721].

Unlike Larry, who is the victim of a paralyzing anguish and cannot go through with it, Parritt is ready to surrender his life in order to put an end to the unremitting torment of guilt. In this case an external agent intervenes, a mediator between the crime and the perpetrator; the sentence the agent delivers represents both a return to the social order and also access to an individual inner peace.

In not dissimilar circumstances, some can be found alone, faced with themselves; they give themselves the dual role of judge and judged. When they realize that the crime committed is irreparable, they are ready to accept the full consequences, and their suicide strikingly illustrates their desire for atonement.

> ORIN. (*Guilty and resentful*) You folks at home take death so solemnly! You would have soon learned at the front that it's only a joke! You don't understand, Vinnie. You have to learn to mock or go crazy, can't you see! [*MBE* 94].

It is tempting to see an incoherence, which may be due to madness, between Orin's words and his suicide, which comes later. In fact, such an interpretation would be misleading; for him, dying is nothing in itself but is likely to take on a particular meaning according to the circumstances involved. When he decides to commit suicide, he does not seek to illustrate the theory expounded in the passage quoted above, to prove that he has a sense of humor. Far from it; in choosing to end his life, he confirms his wish to expiate his crimes, the first being that he caused his mother's despair by telling her that he had killed her lover. Orin acts in accordance with a moral code shared by other characters (as in *Abortion, Before Breakfast, Diff'rent, Dynamo, The Iceman Cometh,* and *Warnings*) who decide to end their lives, for they judge that their misdeeds are unforgivable and, in their eyes, an act of expiation becomes an inescapable necessity.

Such an act sometimes originates from one of two elements we have not yet discussed. In the cases of Christine Mannon and Mrs. Baldwin (in *Mourning Becomes Electra,* and *Recklessness*), the source is the despair following the death of their respective lovers; by a mimetic phenomenon, their existence ceases when they learn of the demise of the person with whom they were hoping to begin a new life. By their suicides, they clarify their position in respect to themselves and to the idea of partnership around which they had hoped to build their future union; their presence among the living has lost all meaning, for it was only ever justified with the other person at their side.

The second way in which it is possible to interpret the supreme act of expiation is in terms of reaction. In *Bread and Butter,* John reckons that a bullet in his head will satisfactorily answer his existential failure, which he attributes to various causes, including his marriage, alcohol, and his own weakness, elements which lead him ineluctably to a moral degeneration against which he rebels. While keeping things in proportion, we can still compare his case with that of Yank in *The Hairy Ape* who, in risking his life, attempts to make himself belong and thus prove the reality of his existence.

Throughout this study of the motives and meanings of the personal breakdowns in O'Neill's plays, it transpires that suicide, encompassing all the cases previously cited, must be interpreted as a refusal of insignificance. By ending his life, the character announces to the rest of the world, but also and above all to himself, that he has risen above the embryonic state into which he was assimilated, which he would no longer be able to deny were he to continue to live. Gloriously refusing to be a nonentity, he confirms his own personality, which re-emerges victorious at the moment of his death. In fact, his death is a way of giving his life a completely different meaning; his desire for expiation is a means of returning to a state of innocence.

Time.

We are sometimes present at the dying moments of the protagonists, some of whom commit suicide, but in general, O'Neill's characters appear in less paroxysmal situations, those which highlight a multifaceted existential unease. Sometimes the unease is due to the fear of one day having to die, but more often it results from the anxiety borne of the fact that they are condemned to live. It is impossible to ignore death completely for it is always lurking in the background, and, when it comes, it marks the end of conflicts, which are an ontological part of life. However, having considered the way in which some view their own death, we will now turn our attention to the relationship between individuals and time. These relationships are reflected in everyday life, whence begins each personal history, and the way in which the characters integrate with time plays a fundamental role in their approach to existence.

> LAZARUS. (*Gently*) I know that age and time are but timidities of the thought [*LL* 354].

In an earlier section we studied the links between an Oriental reading of the world and the perception that the individual had of himself. The line quoted above indirectly takes up the principles evoked; here, human time is implicitly refuted, as is death, which Lazarus claims is nothing more than an illusion, wisdom consisting in no longer lending credence to deceptive appearances.

Lazarus Laughed is a play with numerous sources; it has among others certain Nietzschean aspects. The temporal perspective adopted by Lazarus, and which he thinks should be assimilated by his disciples, that they may have access to a more precise representation of reality, is similar to the eternal return theme expounded by Nietzsche. This concept, which introduces the notion of temporality by associating it with a cyclic vision, leaves its mark on numerous works.

> "Now do I die and disappear," wouldst thou say, and in a moment I am nothing. Souls are as mortal as bodies.

14. The Acknowledgment of the Individual. 175

But the plexus of causes returneth in which I am intertwined,—it will again create me! I myself pertain to the causes of the eternal return."[26]

We can see the difference in opinion between this quotation and the disavowal of Lazarus; the opposition has to do with the way in which individuality is eventually envisaged. From the Oriental perspective, we have seen that this was denied; on the other hand, the extract from *Thus Spake Zarathustra* shows very clearly that there is an undeniable link between the ego and the eternal return theory. This inseparable union between the individual and the causal network which surpasses him is presented in some plays without our being able to confirm that the cyclic notion prevails in the work as a whole. We remember that in *The Great God Brown*, for example, there is a perpetual renewal associated with spring and implicitly with nature ("CYBEL. Always spring comes again bearing life!" [*GGB* 322]); we have also noted that the author took account of this in the construction of the play: the illustration of this circular movement was found in the last scene, echoing the first. The aim of these repetitive structures was to reveal the undeniable continuity of the vital process, which one may have thought illusory and which was destroyed by the incessant metamorphoses which appear to be characteristic of life.

In the example just cited, the time scale used by the author was fairly limited; generally, it appeared that the sons unconsciously followed in their fathers' footsteps, and the young girls modeled themselves on the older ones. At first glance, *Abortion* seems to conform to this scheme and to go back to an image of youth which adopts traditional family values; in fact, there is a considerable distance, as Jack, the young student, refuses to accept the idea that human beings have become civilized over the centuries, and declares that deep within him he has retained many of the apparently typical attributes of primitive man.[27] It would perhaps be advisable to refine this, and to speak rather of "eternal human nature," to which a cyclic aspect will be markedly added in other works. Moreover, continuity has even more precise aspects; so it is no longer a question of demonstrating the concept of human immutability, but of revealing that certain characteristics particular to each person have already existed in the past, often unbeknownst to the individual, and that they have an influence on the present.

Welded gives an optimistic illustration of such causal links, for the meeting of two characters is a direct consequence of a determinism of which the two principle actors see only the positive aspects ("CAPE. Life guides me back through the hundred million years to you. It reveals a beginning in unity that I may have faith in the unity of the end!" [*Wel* 488]). Cape and Eleanor have every reason to be happy, since their love was predestined, and their idyll is blessed by Saturn. Hence they seem to be privileged in comparison with other heroes, but as John Henry Raleigh points out, the recurrent phenomena are not necessarily associated with happiness.

A second historical assumption of O'Neill's was that history was a kind of on-going continuum into which he thrust his characters in order that they might reenact once more primordial human situations and eventualities, usually of a tragic nature, as *Desire Under the Elms* reflects the myths and the Greek dramas concerned with Oedipus, Phaedra, and Medea....[28]

Another illustration of this phenomenon is given in *Mourning Becomes Electra*, when Orin, in an episode already mentioned, decides to study his ancestral history so as to be better able to predict his future. His research is justified; in the section devoted to the study of the family, we noted that the descendants reproduced the ways of thinking and the life-styles of their parents—if not exactly, then broadly speaking. The study of the past allows us to anticipate future situations: such is the implicit theory in Orin's actions, the meaning of which we must now consider by comparing it with the attitudes of the other protagonists.

From these examples it becomes clear that one can no longer claim that there is a single model used in all the plays; the general bias is the same, but we notice that the cyclic notion, implicit in Nietzschean theory, must be applied with caution. As such, *Welded* could serve an a counter-example, for the author establishes a link between two periods distant from each other in time, which could definitively validate this theory of recurrence. This he does without alluding to any intermediate stage. It seems more accurate to speak of permanence—the cyclic aspect possibly transplants itself, having a short-term actualizing function—or of continuity, as does Raleigh, or of a discreet immobilizing which calls into question the very idea of progress. From this point of view, the works which confirm the immutable character of the baseness of human nature, while presenting themselves as ontological reflections, deliver a message to the spectator such that he cannot deceive himself as to his status as a civilized person.

On another level, we must draw inferences from this particular relationship to time, for it goes beyond the canon according to which human beings have preserved prehistoric attitudes. The second element, essential to the subject, is the nature of the causal relationships, and the interweavings of the ego, which are mentioned in the passage quoted above from Nietzsche. Apart from the differences in detail, all these extracts converge to highlight an essential element; these confirm that human beings are not born untainted, and that even before birth they have an immemorial genetic inheritance which will have a bearing on their destiny as soon as they enter the world. ("Genetic" is used in a general sense, and not purely in the scientific context sometimes chosen by O'Neill.) When the characters are born, they are caught up in a current, some aspects of which we have already studied, and the fundamental question arising for them is whether, in relation to this "intertwining of causes," they are able to assert themselves as individuals, or if they are condemned to remain objects for which the notion of freedom would have no meaning.

The answer can be found in several works, and we will return to this theme at the end of this book, but for the moment we will content ourselves with an example. We need only to turn our attention to *Mourning Becomes Electra*, and in particular Orin and Lavinia, to see if they are free or merely puppets. Each one embodies simultaneously the notion of cyclic return in the short term, in the bosom of the family (father, mother, grandparents), and permanence in the long term, as is shown by the re-enactment of the story of Agamemnon (Mannon). We have shown in the previous section how suicide was to be seen in terms of refusal, and the suicide of Orin corresponds very well to this definition (though the idea of expiation is not meant to be excluded). By taking his own life, he confirms his freedom and demonstrates not that the "intertwining of causes" is a chimera but that when an individual realizes his condemnation is inevitable, he is in a position to prove that he exists by putting an end to this tragic sequence.[29] Lavinia's progress is even more convincing; when she understands that she possesses within her a destructive force she will be unable to control, she decides to destroy it, by depriving it of any outlet. Her sacrifice is a free choice; it testifies to her existence, to her freedom in the face of a destiny which she momentarily masters, by refusing both to be its plaything and to pass on the curse of the Mannons to future generations.

By tracing the relations that humans have with the past back to very distant origins, we risk overlooking an aspect that has gone unmentioned until now, namely duration. In some plays, the protagonists are placed in an anticipatory situation, and become aware of the indefinable nature of time, when they think about the time which must pass between two events. They conclude from their analysis that objective reality, which can be scientifically measured, has little to do with individual evaluations. (We can see here a dual source, that of the Romantics and also a trace of some of the writings of Kant.)

> JACK. (*His voice thrilling with emotion*) In three months! (*Jokingly*) Do you know those three months are going to seem like three years?
> EVELYN. (*Gaily*) Three centuries... [*Ab* 149].

As is often the case, the quip has hints of dramatic irony, since Jack commits suicide some minutes after this exchange. However, the childish impatience of these young fiancés shows that the way in which they view the delay confirms what is said in other works regarding the subjectivity associated with the perception of the passage of time (see *Ile* 547, *Beyond the Horizon* 132 or *Servitude* 277). One may conclude that this particular form of temporality does not constitute a central theme, for O'Neill's theater is not constructed around anticipation.[30]

On the other hand, the threads woven among the three temporal spheres are the object of a permanent reflection, which may seem paradoxical given the genre of drama: When the actors play a role, the action unfolds at that moment and the spectator is confronted with what seems to be an eternal present.

Whether it be a question of projection into the future, or of retrospection, these shifts in time imply the establishment of a liaison with what is happening on stage. At the moment of utterance, the actor symbolizes a fixed point in an unfolding story within an intrinsically fleeting present. One could compare the present to a vessel adrift on a river. The forces seeking to moor it to one of the two banks are not completely benevolent; they are forces which will find their meaning only in relation to this fixed point so difficult to grasp.

I am, I was... In the course of their interventions the characters sometimes hesitate between these two tenses. The confusion may be the result of heavy drinking, or a wish to cover their tracks, but may also be a reflection of their nostalgia. For the other characters on stage, these are the words of people buried in the past, but they console those who speak them, realizing that over the years they have unconsciously left behind the source of their happiness.

> PADDY. Oh, to be back in the fine days of my youth, ochone! Oh, there was fine beautiful ships them days—clippers wid tall masts touching the sky—fine strong men in them—men that was sons of the sea as if 'twas the mother that bore them. Oh, the clean skins of them! Brave men they was, and bold men surely! [*HA* 213].

The evocation of this paradise lost is not just voiced internally. Paddy's words are a direct critique of a world fallen from grace, where dust of coal is a symbol of long lost harmony. By establishing a comparison between two epochs, he distances them one from the other, and the expression of his regrets is thus an indication that the two can never be confused. The affirmation of this division implies the establishment of individual agenda, but contrary to certain members of the community, Paddy does not delude himself. He recognizes his own degeneration and sees it mirrored in his companions, who are also victims of a corrupt system. This nostalgic lament (found elsewhere with similar connotations: *The Fountain* 402, *The Great God Brown* 324, *Welded* 447) reveals a disjunction between what is happening now and what men did in the past; in this respect, we note that each person's selective memories suffuse their past actions with an implausible golden glow. Regardless of the relevance of the characters' interventions, the crucial thing in the human-time relationship, when they are evoking a long gone era, is the way in which they place themselves in relation to time.

Concerning retrospective speech, it can give rise to two opposing perspectives. Some, following the example of Paddy, establish a link between two eras in order to show how they differ, and therein examine their evolution, which frequently can be summed up in one word: "decadence." Others try to recapture a supposedly glorious past, obtaining a result different from that which follows Paddy's outburst, namely, that the distance separating two events is not acknowledged so that those who have fallen from grace may bask in the light of an ancient glory.

Not everyone has the Irish courage of the ancient mariner who, undaunted, contemplates the extent of the disaster which afflicts the world around him, and from which the only escape is his whiskey-induced oblivion. Some, as we have just seen, are terrified by this uncontrolled degeneration and attempt to conquer it by burying themselves in the past; a similar solution is open to their fellows who also adopt this voluntarily blinkered outlook, though they may find their hope in the future.

> LARRY. They've all a touching credulity concerning tomorrows. (*A half-drunken mockery in his eyes*) It'll be a great day for them, tomorrow—the Feast of All Fools, with brass bands playing! Their ships will come in, loaded to the gunwales with canceled regrets and promises fulfilled and clean slates and new leases! [*IC* 578].

Larry's gaze is pitiless, for he exposes the false hopes which aid his companions' survival.[31] As the action moves forward, we realize that the characters' behavior in many respects parallels that which was described at the beginning of this chapter: By a collapsing of time, they manage to create such an elusive, almost unreal image of their present life, by placing it within the ephemeral sphere, that their future seems to have much more substance.

In the minds of the characters in *The Iceman Cometh*, the reference to a happier future implies a spatial disjunction, and they all announce their intention to leave Harry Hope's bar. In *Mourning Becomes Electra*, Mannon, Orin and Brant evoke a more distant future associated with both exile and an abandonment of New England. This time the final destination is a paradise symbolized here by the Pacific archipelagoes and by going there all hope to find a new life. The embarkation for the islands is seen in a liberating perspective; according to Adam Brant, for example, leaving will solve everything, for in this other world life is not subject to the rules that govern American society, rules which imprison individuals within an excessively strict moral framework.[32] The departure is not envisaged only as a liberation (of the person and in this case the couple), but also as the refusal to accept the impossibility of living, which would stem from an examination of their respective lives, carried out in the light of emasculating community values. Whatever the planned strategies may be, the will to push back the limits, though understandable, is illusory. If space and time are closely associated, it is due to the fact that the evocation of a new universe gives weight to the fiction in the form of a foothold in reality, and the places where they will live in the future, which are mentioned implicitly, refute the vagueness of a speech already marked by uncertainty.

> DEBORAH.—It is a repulsive humiliation to feel yourself a condemned slave to revengeful Time, to cringe while he lashes your face with wrin-

kles, or stamps your body into shapelessness, or smears it with tallow-fat with his malicious fingers! [*MSM* 61].

Once the dream is over, it will hardly make any difference whether one is here or there, and Deborah is under no illusions as to the toll the years will take on her; regardless of the escape route chosen, no one can avoid their decay. They may sometimes accelerate it, but it remains inescapable. Time plays with the characters, while many believe the reverse is true; all lose their game of hide-and-seek, for at the end of a desperate struggle, they always end up betraying themselves. By their rebellious nature, Deborah's interventions show that she is clear as regards her relationship with temporality. A large majority of the protagonists adopt a different attitude; they tend to hide behind words, so as to deny a reality which incessantly points out how far they are straying. Sooner or later, they become aware of their mortality. The third path, followed by Nat Miller in *Ah, Wilderness!*, is chosen by few. The wisdom he displays is rarely duplicated by other individuals, in spite of its importance; this is indicated by its position in the play, stealing the last lines: "MILLER. Well, Spring isn't everything, is it, Essie? There's a lot to be said for Autumn. That's got beauty too. And Winter—if you're together" (*AhW* 298).

Almost all are prisoners of a passing of time which is beyond their control (the only exceptions are those who adopt a timeless Oriental perspective). Sometimes they realize that they are incapable of mastering it, because they are caught up in a moving current, and the intrusions into the present serve to expose a decadence from which they can only free themselves at the time of death. Characters' relations with temporality vary considerably but, paradoxically, rare are those who see the passage of time positively. In fact, knowing how much suffering is brought about by the memory of a misdemeanor, one might imagine that they would rally to a common ethos whereby forgetting would abolish pain, thus breaking down the equation apparently innate to the theater of O'Neill in which living equals suffering.

LUCY. Time heals everything—you will forget [*NLAY* 131].

Can this declaration, atypical by virtue of its optimistic aspect, respond to the insults of time, which accompany without fail the degeneration of each of us? In the previous pages, we have seen how the attempts to distance oneself from reality, through spurious words, end in failure. If these words fail to mask reality, what hope is there for time itself? Is it a balm which soothes the wounds of life, passing from enemy to ally? We are not convinced by Lucy's attempt to answer these questions, for although it is taken from a comedy, the quotation is surprising. The surprising thing is not so much its redeeming aspect—for some try to find comfort by escaping into imaginary worlds, rejecting any factual and honest relationship with the temporal domain—as it is the wager according to which oblivion is available to an individual. (We remember that Emma took an opposite view: "EMMA. It ain't a question of time, Caleb. It's a question of something being dead. And when a thing's died, time can make no diff'rence" [*Dif* 517].)

We pointed out previously the very close relationships between some characters and their origins, which had a definite influence on their existence. A determining factor, but not the only one, this ancestral aspect in the broad sense only partially illuminated the relationships that some had with the world in its contemporary dimension. By examining O'Neill's œuvre as a whole, we see that a return to the past, characteristic of a number of the plays, is often due to a particular relationship each person has with his own history. Hence, it is no longer a question of seeking in the distant past the source of a mode of behavior which the spectator associates with what is present, symbolized by both the words and the actions of the character, but rather to see what in the biography of that character is the reason for this continual intrusion of previous actions which cannot be laid to rest. The lines spoken by Lucy in *Now I Ask You* that were quoted above appeared to proclaim a universal truth—in fact, conveying a hope rarely realized in the plays.

> TYRONE. Mary! For God's sake, forget the past!
> MARY. *With strange objective calm.* Why? How can I? The past is the present, isn't it? It's the future, too. We all try to lie out of that but life won't let us [*LDJN* 87].

Formulated differently but in an equally pessimistic way, the following remarks come from the lips of James Tyrone:

> TYRONE. It was long ago. But it seems like tonight. There is no present or future—only the past happening over and over again [*MMis* 82].

The remark of Mary Tyrone is a little brusque, for she takes the opposite view of a vision whereby the passing of the years dulls the memory; moreover, through her reference to the future, she implies that the individual has no way of escaping his punishment, which takes the form of being condemned to live. In spite of their apparently extreme nature, these words reflect a reality from which few manage to shield themselves. Within this context, we must note that the characters' rewriting of their individual histories is not explained solely by a desire to flee, for other themes would undoubtedly prove more efficient as distractions. The speaker does not quite comprehend the reformulation of these memories, and the case of Erie Smith (in *Hughie*) demonstrates this revealingly; in general, we realize that it is more a case of trying to control rebellious thoughts which no one manages to keep hidden in the recesses of his memory.

Continuously—and my proposition is not limited to *Long Day's Journey into Night*—an unpleasant episode or a past mistake that has produced a feeling of guilt surfaces in the exchanges between the characters, who seem powerless, prisoners of the consequences of events seemingly distant but in fact unceasingly invading their lives.

One may have the impression of a static time because of this collapsing of three temporal spheres. In reality, the present exists: It evolves continuously and seems all the more inaccessible, as a moment does not find its place until the past has re-emerged and been completely exorcized.

> As both calendar and memory fail the characters, who see no hope in the future and cannot recover the past, they labor under the tyranny of history; try as they might, they cannot escape. Almost instinctively, as their search for peace reaches its climax, they turn to the ritual of confession, baring their souls to priests of their own making in an attempt to transcend the limitations of time and space.[33]

Laurin Porter notes that retrospectivity takes on a liberating role as a result of the confession; I agree with this analysis, and we have already seen how the characters relieve themselves of their burdens by confessing to people close to them. What has this do with the Tyrone family? They go through the motions but nevertheless remain bound to their memories; this failure to achieve freedom is doubtless caused by the ever-present denial in their words. In fact, their speeches have undertones of recanting, since after they have made them, they return time and again, in part at least, to their admissions of weakness. Following the example of Mary Tyrone, Porter declares that the protagonists are captives of their own histories and that deliverance is impossible; if the behavior of the members of the Tyrone family tend to prove this theory, still a few counter-examples prevent it from being established as a universal principle.

Let us consider for a moment the case of Eben, who, in *Desire Under the Elms*, is haunted by a maternal image he associates with continual suffering. (We could also mention Simon in *More Stately Mansions*, who, from that point of view, is not very different from Eben.) Eben believes that it is his filial duty to bring her peace, for despite her death, she has not yet found it.[34] As such, he is one of those who do not succeed in living fully, because they have not broken the ties with their former life. However, contrary to Mary Tyrone, and all those who are crushed by the weight of their memories, he is emancipated when he comes into contact with the ghost of his mother, bringing into the present, in that moment, what belongs in a bygone age. This is how he can bring peace to her. The following lines stress the link between the past and the present:

> EBEN. What's come over me? (*Queerly*) Didn't ye feel her passin'—goin' back t' her grave?

CABOT. (*Dully*) Who?
EBEN. Maw. She kin rest now an' sleep content. She's quits with ye [*DE* 246].

From this moment on everything fits back into place; he is able to make the most of the present, and finds himself liberated from a binding which prevented him from being himself.

Beyond the case of Eben, the important thing is the affirmation of a potential for freedom, which was denied by Mary Tyrone and others. Following the example of what we saw regarding the relationship of the individual with temporal cycles, it appears here that human beings are not completely powerless when faced with their own history. To free themselves from this burden, they must confront it.[35] They must have the strength to assimilate it, so as to satisfy a rite of passage at the end of which those who have had the courage to fight against a force keeping them in subjection will regain their freedom. There are few who attain the goal, and many surrender their arms in the face of an exercise which seems to be beyond them. Those who emerge victorious show that in spite of the shackles which have often held them prisoner, it is possible, if they set out with enough moral courage, to overcome all the obstacles: The personal history of each individual is thus not definitively determined by some event in their past.

The weight of destiny.

Ought the relations a character has with destiny be described in the active or the passive voice? This was an underlying question in several works, and we are going to turn our attention to this point, for if none claims to be the master of his fate, many say they are its slaves. If these conclusions are not examined in depth, one risks ending up with an interpretation which apparently contradicts reality or at least what many critics advocate as the truth. In the realm of relationships between human beings and time, we have already established a connection between the individual and his destiny. We have not, however, stressed what the characters have to say on the subject.

Indeed, while recognizing that there is a place where freedom can be found, I do not claim that everyone seizes the opportunity for freedom that is offered to him. In fact, we frequently witness the contrary, and accordingly an opposition emerges in the plays between those who accept servitude, and all its consequences, and those who, having suffered defeat at its hands, recognize the might of destiny.

> BARTLETT. (*Chokingly*) So—that be it—(*Shaking his clenched fist at the sky as if visualizing the fate he feels in all of this*) Curse ye! Curse ye! [*Gold* 673].

This is a common attitude throughout O'Neill's work—two examples, written many years apart, serve to convey this continuity: *The Web* 53 and *A Moon for the Misbegotten* 114—and it corresponds to a recognition of defeat, for by cursing a fatal destiny the characters admit they have lost the battle. In other cases, such as that of Mary Tyrone, some adopt a defeatist attitude: They believe it is futile to swim against the currents that are sweeping them along. Their reasoning is based on a presupposition which justifies their inaction. Indeed they believe that nothing can alter the course of a predetermined existence. This is the opinion of Mary, who symbolizes this resigned attitude shared by many characters.

> MARY. But I suppose life has made him like that, and he can't help it. None of us can help the things life has done to us. They're done before you realize it, and once they're done they make you do other things until at last everything comes between you and what you'd like to be, and you've lost your true self forever [*LDJN* 61].

The protagonists fall into two categories: those who resign themselves beforehand and thus refuse to fight, and the others, who are sometimes conscious of being dominated by supernatural forces but do not mention it until they have recognized their defeat.

What use is it to fight if the end is inevitable, if at the conclusion of this complex game which is life, all wind up surrendering their arms? ("SIMON. Life is a gamble and Fate a master sharper where stacked cards and loaded dice can cheat the cleverest swindler" [*MSM* 241].) While it is true that the fall seems to be the same for everyone and they continually lose the fight, we have nevertheless noted that the way in which they lose it is not without importance. We will not return to the question of suicide, and the consequent interpretation of each character's existence. I shall limit my remarks to emphasizing that, while appearing to be the same (because all are invariably victims of insurmountable forces), the situations vary and sometimes give opposing meaning to the existence of people who share the same fate—

> the classic twofold justification of the ways of God or fate to man: first, that suffering and the very need to explain and symbolize it are the fountainhead of human action and creativity; and second that fated though he may be, man is ultimately a free and responsible agent who brings most of his grief upon himself through pride.[36]

It goes without saying that the idea by which the individual is free in spite of all the forces employed by destiny supports my proposition; on the other hand, to say that pride is the source of all evil seems unjustified. In a general way, it seems more accurate to look for the root cause of the fall of a character in desire, which spawns an opposition between the individual and his life, and then leads to his downfall. (Following the example of suicide, which was not necessarily to be considered a failure, the notion of downfall will have to be put into context and it will be studied later.) A single interpretation of all fifty plays in the O'Neill œuvre is in essence limiting; the notion of desire, of sheer willpower, certainly has a part to play, but will have to be refined according to the individual situation. If we go back to the case of Eben, mentioned above, we note that he is effectively responsible for the misfortunes that beset him. These cannot be attributed to pride, but rather to his desire for possession, and his determination to become the owner of the farm which he claims belonged to his mother. There is certainly nothing glorious about the end of his idyll with Abbie, for they are both headed for the hangman's noose; however, even if their fate is tragic, because they did not choose the road that would have led to happiness, they managed nonetheless to find fulfillment in their relationship. The dramatic irony rests in the fact that at the end of all these tests allowing Eben to know who he really is, and to realize his love for Abbie, he also realizes that he has been the author of his own misfortune.

Destiny must not be understood solely in terms of the influence of the past on the life of an individual, but rather as a culmination of forces acting on his present existence. Edward Shaughnessy gives the example of a meeting between an individual and the indefinable hostility against which he must fight and which no longer belongs to the strictly temporal domain.

> For *Hughie* offers a variation on the problem of modern man's existential fate, the impossibility of belonging and the attendant problem of loneliness. Isolated spiritually and psychologically he can never entirely bridge the gap.[37]

We have already introduced the notion of belonging, in the relationship which human beings have with the world, and it is effectively a question of an essential difficulty with which each individual is confronted. It comes under the category of sources of opposition which stand in the way of human happiness, as the characters have to struggle to be themselves while at the same time trying to be accepted by the community. This attempt to reconcile two antagonistic realities often takes the form of a battle which is lost before it has even begun. Edward Shaughnessy's words are not without underlying meaning, when he presents the image of a void that serves to separate the individual from the rest of the universe. What is wanted is a total commitment by the person, who puts his whole personality on the line and even his existence in his search to overcome, leading to a fusion of two separate elements to form a whole.

> The subject here is the same ancient one that always was and always will be the one subject for drama, and that is man and his struggle with his own fate. The struggle used to be with the gods, but is now with himself, his own past, his attempt to "belong."[38]

O'Neill's remarks clearly indicate that the relationships must be perceived in terms of conflict, with the three panels of a triptych corresponding to the elements previously analyzed (the self, the past, and belonging). As regards the individual and his own interaction it would seem that the struggle alluded to here is in the realm of self-discovery. We have seen how painful it was for each person, and most of them strive to invent escape mechanisms allowing them to avoid any confrontation with themselves. This division into three distinct elements does not imply that the three aspects are approached independently from each other, and that diehards must attack the three fronts simultaneously. If they die in the throes of battle, the reward for their offense will be to leave the larval state to which are confined the deserters, who admit defeat from the start, and to rise to a higher level which will testify to their greatness.

The divine.

We will now turn our attention to a theme the importance of which has been indicated by O'Neill himself, even though, in the tradition of contradictory declarations, he has said on other occasions that this must be considered only relatively. As regards the plays, the characters' relationships with the divine are variable; the first aspect we will consider is that of the place of God in the life of the individual, more precisely in the course of his existence. In fact, if the notion of chance does not figure among the categories in the reference systems of the protagonists, among the forces influencing individual destinies, some are nonetheless of divine origin or are presented as such.

> MRS. BRENNAN. (*Indifferently*) It's God's will, what'll happen [*Straw* 395].

Mrs. Brennan's declaration is emblematic of the reaction of a great many characters. Faced with an uncertain future beyond their control, they relinquish responsibility to what they perceive to be the will of God. Hence, regardless of the nature of events, or the misfortunes which befall them, these things are never perceived as absurd; on the contrary, they are believed to be part of God's great plan, which leaves little scope for those who are the object of his wrath. Whether it be the group or the individual targets of heavenly ire, the victims often endorse what might appear to be a punishment, through rational arguments that aim to explain the reasons for a punishment. This holds true for all creeds: Catholic, for Mrs. Brennan, who declares:

> And I'm thinkin' it's His punishment she's under now for having no heart
> in her and never writin' home a word to you or the children [*Straw* 395].

or Protestant for Cabot, who represents puritanism. When he realizes that his money is gone, he justifies the theft by attributing it to divine intervention:

> I calc'late God give it to 'em—not yew! [*DE* 268].

14. The Acknowledgment of the Individual. 187

In these examples it is clear that the person's destiny is controlled by a God corresponding to the image projected by each denomination. This is not always the case, and some associate the direction their life is taking with an almost pantheistic vision.

> CHRIS. Only God know dat, Anna.
> ANNA. (*Half mockingly*) Then it'll be Gawd's will, like the preachers say—what does happen.
> CHRIS. (*Starts to his feet with fierce protest*) No! Dat ole davil, sea, she ain't God! [*AC* 29].

In spite of his denials, Chris, in *Anna Christie*, implicitly attributes to the sea an ability to decide his fate, to such an extent that at the end of the play he announces that it knows what is in store for them. His words presuppose the existence of a hierarchy between the different forces acting on an individual, but actually if we compare his attitude with that of Mat Burke, who has an unshakable faith, and always wears a crucifix given to him by his mother, we realize that Chris believes primarily in nature; moreover, when he expounds his religious belief, he associates it with a world he has abandoned:

> BURKE. Is it any religion at all you have, you and your Anna?
> CHRIS. (*Surprised*) Vhy, yes. Ve vas Lutheran in ole country [*AC* 77].

Whether it be a question of a Calvinist perspective, in which the idea of predestination is coupled with that of destiny, or whether the protagonists be Catholic, they agree on a coherent interpretation of what has happened to them, by placing these events under the aegis of God. In this view of the world, the individual perceives himself as one whose existence is watched over by a master who sometimes intervenes at critical moments. This master frequently has the attributes of a God of retribution, who punishes those who have failed in their duty. Even if the victims of his anger are aware of the cause, they sometimes revolt against the injustice of the sentence meted out to them. It also happens that the martyrs' lamentations become pleas for forgiveness:

> ELLA. (*After a pause—like a child*) Will God forgive me, Jim?
> JIM. Maybe He can forgive what you've done to me; and maybe He can forgive what I've done to you; but I don't see how He's going to forgive—Himself [*AGCGW* 341].

Those who are subjected to divine wrath attempt to answer back, by cursing Him who is responsible for it, or even by questioning His existence, this being the only means open to them for some kind of revenge on the ills which beset them (note for instance the attitude of Robert following the death of his daughter: "ROBERT. I could curse God from the bottom of my soul—if there was a God!" [*BH* 148]). The plaints of those who have suffered celestial ire are a sign of their impotence, in that they will in no way be able to change their future, crushingly supervised by a merciless divinity. This feeling is not shared by all who sense that a superior force is intervening in their lives. The example of Ephraim Cabot, who turned back after setting out westwards, is significant, because he felt that by taking the easy way out, he was not facing up to the task assigned to him by God; in this example, as in the case of Robert immediately above, He (or She) who wields superior power does not really seem to be an omnipotent dictator, but is more like a guide who points out to those in his charge the risks they are running when they go astray. The task which falls to the character consists in interpreting the message sent to him, and drawing his own conclusions, this leeway being proof of his individual liberty.

The influence of religion can also be seen on another level. We note for example that even those who reject their former beliefs remain subconsciously influenced by them. Frederick Wilkins points this out for the case of Reuben, which will be examined later in greater detail.

> Of course, Reuben, like Eben Cabot, cannot really slough off all the Puritan conditioning he has lived through in the Light home. ... He is "held" in much the same way that the Mannons are "bound"; his prayer to the Dynamo, even when addressed to a feminine deity, sounds distinctly Calvinistic.[39]

He distances himself from his faith, which is from then on obsolete, but as is often the case, in spite of an inner revolution which compels our attention, there is a certain continuity in his attitude. This convergence is not immediately perceptible, for the emphasis is essentially placed on the idea of a separation which masks phenomena of continuity. On the other hand, if we consider the way in which Lavinia, in *Mourning Becomes Electra*, seeks to cast off the weight of her Puritan upbringing, we notice that the process is totally different; in the first part of the trilogy, she tries to deny her desire for freedom, which manifests itself after her mother commits suicide. The spectator witnesses this difference, which is expressed by the altered colors of her costume. In the opening scene, she is dressed in black; her change is conveyed by a green dress, the new color symbolically marking the inner transformation which has taken place. The fight to free herself from repressive Puritan morals leads her from the discovery to the acceptance of physical desire. This reality, denied at the beginning of the play, is granted a place of primary importance as the action progresses. The climax is reached when Orin evokes the Pacific islands where the natives danced naked, an image which captivated his sister; the acceptance of the physical dimension of human nature goes against the smothering moral vestments of the people of New England. Lavinia will not be an exception for long, for soon she will return to her original state. So doing, she will re-embrace the tradition of her people, this time taken to the extreme, and the realm of the body will be completely suppressed by the rejection of procreation. Longevity, which is alluded to in her last tirade, is then seen in terms of a moral punishment.

The relationship between an individual and a divinity, whatever it may be, when the individual is a believer, is dependent on a faith which forms a kind of contract between the human and that which surpasseth understanding. We have seen that some tried to interpret what they saw as the actions of God, and reacted in different ways. For others, the divine Presence is never doubted. It brings them an undeniable sense of well-being manifested by the inner peace they enjoy. Nowhere is it said that all is for the best in the best of all possible worlds, but the impression given by *Ah, Wilderness!* might cause even the most hypochondriacal spectator to draw this conclusion. When Nat Miller has fulfilled his role as paterfamilias, with all the unpleasant aspects that this involves, he finds himself once more in harmony with the world and with his own. The values he embodies have certainly been called into question by his son, but for a short time only, and everything eventually falls back into place—a place characterized by adhesion to the fundamental principles on which society rests. Leaving for a few moments his earthly occupations, Nat mentions humorously in the last scene the One whom he knows to be his creator, but in a way that is very revealing of his own convictions.

> MILLER. (*Then getting to his feet—with a grin*) Mind if I don't say my prayers tonight, Essie? I'm certain God knows I'm too darned tired.
> MRS. MILLER. Don't talk that way. It's real sinful [*AhW* 298].

Through this somewhat childish request to be excused, Nat Miller indirectly confirms his faith in a God whose existence cannot be questioned. In spite of his image as an ideal father, he is not really a hero figure, for his weak points are presented humorously, and he thus preserves his status as an ordinary man. Unlike a number of protagonists who evolve in O'Neill's plays, he is not tormented by doubt. He has a solid grounding on three levels considered essential in the O'Neillian perspective: the familial, social and spiritual. Nat's assurance is echoed in other speeches in which various characters set out their convictions. Unlike him, they are not individuals who are aware of their limits, whose faith would be intact, but people who refute religious dogmas, believing themselves to be strong enough to fight alone against the forces they must confront on their way.

The first example which springs to mind is that of *The Emperor Jones*. Brutus Jones is openly contemptuous of the occult, but turns to it for help when he finds himself alone and in a precarious situation in the depths of the forest (156). In *A Touch of the Poet*, Cornelius Melody is proud of his atheism but this distancing from the dogma instilled in him as a child is not complete. In fact, we learn that he repented on his deathbed, and settled what he called a debt of honor to the Supreme Being (in the next play of the cycle, *More Stately*

Mansions 37). We may also question the sincerity of Hogan's atheism (*A Moon for the Misbegotten* 12), when we think of the curses he utters at the end of the play (114).

In the long run, whether the characters try to move away from God or call themselves atheists is of little importance. In the tradition of paradox, we realize that they draw near to divine reality, even as they think they have nothing more in common with beliefs to which they no longer subscribe. Thus it is necessary to go beyond appearances before making a judgment of the protagonists' attitudes. As we have seen on several occasions, they themselves have a strong propensity to blind themselves from reality, and they do not necessarily take into account the implications of sometimes staggering declarations. In challenging the position of a celestial power to which they would be subjected, they grant themselves a central place and construct the world around it. The vanity of their egocentricity is revealed when they have to fight adversaries who strip away their masks. Amongst the discoveries which follow their defeat, one finds a faith hitherto denied.

We move a step further in the complex relationship between humanity and the Supreme Being in *The Great God Brown*, a work in which the idea of Dion's being a disciple of Pan (he also alludes to Dionysus) is added to the inherent duality of the human condition; his architecture bears this out.

> DION. It's one vivid blasphemy from sidewalk to the tips of its spires!— but so concealed that the fools will never know. They'll kneel and worship the ironic Silenus who tells them the best good is never to be born! [*GGB* 297].

Whether it be he or his fraternal foe, Billy Brown, they both have a diabolic dimension that seems to confirm their schism with orthodox divinities.

> BROWN. Man is born broken. He lives by mending. The grace of God is glue! [*GGB* 318].

The concept of rupture highlighted in these lines is essential to the play, since both suffer from their separation and unconsciously aspire to a reconciliation. This notion is more substantially developed on another level, for individual reconciliation is not just on the social plane. When Dion and Billy are approaching death, they renew their relationship with the divine by reciting the Lord's Prayer. This prayer is a sign of rediscovery. A forgotten belief which had been denied by Dion suddenly emerges when he had all the while apparently sworn allegiance to a figure antagonistic to God.

In fact, this episode is very revealing in that it brings to life two phenomena. The first, already underlined in other episodes, is that the characters are blind; they think or act with an explanatory system at the back of their minds which gives coherence to their actions, but the justifications given are not always the right ones. The second is based on the fact that we cannot claim that one explanation prevails and that each person is heading in the wrong direction if they follow a course contrary to what they believe it to be. In fact the reality is more complex, for in moving away from God, the individual actually draws nearer to him. This is not just due to a human blindness, the effects of which we have seen many times; the devil or manifestations of him are in their way disciples of God,[40] and the venerations end up converging, for the object is the same.

If denying your Creator is the shortest path to meeting Him, and if quasidivine figures (albeit unlike the usual conceptions) are nothing more than masks behind which He hides, what place is left for those who claim to distance themselves from this panoply of heavenly images? The examples which we have just quoted show that it is impossible to find one's path alone. Sooner or later one will hear the still small voice, reminding that the quest is not so solitary as it seems, and that every step of the way one is accompanied by Him who guides many others.

> In *Pierre* as in *Mourning Becomes Electra*, then, one witnesses a movement towards agnosticism. In his trilogy, with the aid of Melville's novel, O'Neill presents us with a portrait of a torn apart family, bereft of the help of God, thus prefiguring the agnostic universe of *Long Day's Journey into Night*.[41]

This critical analysis of Marc Maufort indicates that, in some plays, we find characters who are atheists or, according to him, agnostics. The reference to *Long Day's Journey into Night* might surprise, if we remember the declarations of James Tyrone and of Mary, who proclaim their faith and their allegiance to the Catholic Church. In fact, the remark has to do with the two sons who have broken with the religion of their childhood. This is not the only example in the work, and we note that this rupture is accompanied by a struggle between those who embody the past and their heirs, as if the questioning followed by the refutation of ancestral beliefs would rekindle the opposition between fathers and sons. This stance cannot however, be reduced to a simple antagonism between the generations. The gulf is wider than it appears to be at the start, for by calling into question parental convictions, the sons and daughters show that the religious system which served as a moral guide to their elders is alien to them.

> CABOT. (*Oblivious to him—summoningly*) God o' the old! God o' the lonesome!
> EBEN. (*Mockingly*) Naggin' His sheep t' sin! T' hell with yewr God! [*DE* 227].

The hatred is already present but there is not a complete splitting of the old belief into two, for if Eben distances himself from paternal dogma, he does not deny the reality of a divine presence. The separation will manifest itself more completely elsewhere (in *Days Without End, A Touch of the Poet* and *Long Day's Journey into Night*); in this case, the proclaimed atheism goes beyond dissent between two generations, which will never completely disappear and which will have different effects when the protagonists have totally broken with their previous beliefs.

Such an attitude has innumerable consequences. *Days Without End,* an ambiguous but significant title, illustrates the repercussions of loss of faith. We find a resurgence of familial conflict in that the uncle is a priest and John, by rejecting the vision of a world distorted by the Catholicism of his uncle, begins a long fight against a relation who is loved but subconsciously perceived as an obstacle to John's personal development. The denial of his faith is seen in relation to his ancestors, but it is because he does not accept the idea of a God of retribution, who took his parents from him, that he decides to break away from his Christian universe, which seemed now to him to be devoid of meaning. I have already mentioned this play in the course of this study to illustrate why its analysis should be approached with particular caution. In spite of the reservations the playwright had for a work whose ending had been suggested to him by a Jesuit, it is worthy of consideration—if not for a producer then at least for a critic. In fact, if we lay aside for a moment the controversial ending (O'Neill had hesitated between suicide for his hero and a return to his Catholic roots), we see the importance that the abandonment of religion has in the life of an individual. As such, the comparison with Nat Miller is revealing, for we have seen that religion constituted one of the mainstays allowing an individual to fulfill his potential. It followed from this analysis that a feeling of belonging is born of personal adhesion to a system greater than the individual, a divine mechanism within which human beings find their place. Inversely, one may foresee the disarray which engulfs those who have no firm belief to hold on to.

> FATHER BAIRD. First it was Atheism unadorned. Then it was Atheism wedded to Socialism. But Socialism proved too weak-kneed a mate, and the next I heard Atheism was living in free love with Anarchism, with a curse by Nietzsche to bless the union. And then came the Bolshevik dawn.... [...] First it was China and Lao Tze that fascinated him, but afterwards he ran on to Buddha, and his letters for a time extolled passionless contemplation so passionately that I had a mental view of him regarding his navel frenziedly by the hour and making nothing of it! [*DWE* 502-3].

Father Baird sums up John's spiritual Grand Tour in a humorous manner, but beyond the general survey of intellectual choices made by his nephew, he stresses the idea of a progress, of a quest for the truth upon which the latter has embarked. In his opinion, the answers to the questions he poses are to be found in Catholicism, the power of which is vainly denied by John, whose beliefs remain intact withal. It is immaterial whether he or his uncle is right; the important thing is to recognize that in terms of the systems of reference, "the characters cannot bear nothingness." The long list Father Baird has drawn up bears out this theory in the play.

The second element meriting our attention is suicide. Although this option was not taken up by the author, it did provide an alternative, and this fact is very revealing in itself. In fact, the choice of death proves that human beings cannot live without belief in a divinity, or in a system which elucidates the world of which they are an integral part.[42]

> REUBEN. And that center must be the Great Mother of Eternal Life, Electricity, and Dynamo is her Divine Image on earth! [*Dy* 477].

The anguish generated by the uncertainty of this "must be" is unbearable, and it explains why Reuben is counting in some way on the existence of a mother deity (an idea that can also be found in *Strange Interlude*: "NINA. God is a Mother" [*SI* 110]). He is not the only one: he is alike others who feel the need to create a reference structure which encompasses their own universe and in which they have a place. It is also noteworthy that this transferal of convictions is accompanied by two changes. First, the supreme figure associated with the image of the father disappears and is replaced by a maternal image, which plays an essential role in O'Neill's theater. The second change affects the way in which the encounter plays out: The feminine image allows for more direct contact, and there is a benevolence which permits the individual to feel welcome and no longer repulsed by a cold, repressive God. The reference to electricity and thereby to the scientific, or indeed scientistic, viewpoint places the divine quest in a modern context. The individual does not seek the image of a modernist God, but this emphasizes the gulf between a dogma judged to be obsolete and a celestial presence which is contemporary to the characters, and which must be discovered elsewhere. The opposition between them is marked both by the difference in gender and by the contrast between vengeance and compassion.

Days Without End and *Dynamo* accentuate the search of an individual for a relationship with a divine being. Whether we are speaking of John or Reuben, they both have to face up to an identical phenomenon: The abandonment of their beliefs causes a spiritual void that generates angst, which only a new faith, regardless of its form, could dispel. Far from being an isolated case, the experiences of the two principal actors illustrate a characteristic common to all men. We could sum it up by stressing the need for a firmly established faith, providing a starting point from which the individual would be able to make his own decisions and to take responsibility for himself as a person. Despair and fear, born of uncertainty, are described very well in *Lazarus Laughed*. The eponymous hero takes on the role of prophet, for his passage in the other world has caused him to reach a new maturity; he no longer fears death, and his laugh symbolizes his acceptance of life. Faced with this assurance, some are unnerved, but others want to become his disciples. Their desire to follow him originates from what they imagine to be his knowledge of the beyond; moreover his relationship with a Superior Being, whose nature they do not comprehend, is something to which they aspire.

> LAZARUS. Oh, if men would but interpret that first cry of man fresh from the womb as the laughter of one who even then says to his heart, "It is my pride as God to become Man. Then let it be my pride as Man to recreate the God in me!" [*LL* 352].

Moving from enigmatic phrases to paradoxes, Lazarus illuminates the lives of those around him during his progression towards Rome; from his words, it transpires that he is capable of interpreting for them the messages from a God whom they do not really understand. His words reassure his listeners in that they establish the possibility of a rapport between humanity and the Supreme Being. He may well advocate the recreation of God in oneself, but he subsequently claims that the self does not exist. It is all less obscure than it appears to be, for we have already noticed in other works that opposites end up being the same. Thus, Caligula, who is the incarnation of evil, shows how much he wants to be good, as his diabolical aspect is no more than a product of his fear of life. The potential confusion comes from the term "God" used by Lazarus, for he tells his disciples of the possibility of an encounter with the Divine, without necessarily referring to the New Testament. His proselytes have first of all relinquished their worldly possessions; the second stage is reached when they are ready to lose their own life. To do this they must first accept the idea that the self is nothing more than an illusion; it is only by releasing themselves from their attachment to the human person that they will reach this state of grace where their fears, even that of death, are vanquished.

Not everyone has found a guide who will allow them to discover a path to salvation. How can those still searching live in the face of this doubt, which has already proved so destructive to others who have set out in search of definitive answers? The refusal to understand the divine in the same way as previous generations creates an emptiness, and makes one wish to establish a new relationship with divinity. During his search, the individual will have to face many tests, not the least of which is the lack of assurance concerning one's relationship with the Supreme Being.

> The duty of the modern playwright, he thought, was to "dig at the roots of the sickness of today," the cause of which was "the death of the old God," and the failure to find a new One. Without God, life has no meaning, and the fear of death cannot be comforted.[43]

We must reflect carefully on this kind of affirmation; it would certainly be a little strange to go against the words of the playwright himself. Although O'Neill sometimes strays slightly from what he affirms, the conclusions drawn by Edward Engel seem nevertheless to be dangerous. In fact, we have noted that the fear of death was not a determining factor—a number of suicides testify to this—and what the characters fear above all is a direct confrontation with life. In addition, and this argument seems much more important, this critical discourse leads to confusion; starting from a postulate whereby life no longer has any meaning if God does not exist, we deduce that the refutation of divine images, or doubt, which sometimes leads to despair, implies that the protagonists evolve in a world where everything has become insignificant. Thus, one tends to categorize O'Neill's plays in the theater of the absurd, with nothing whatsoever to substantiate this critical theory but presuppositions whose relevance is debatable.

Throughout this study, we have seen that the means employed by people to enter into contact with God vary with each individual. Catholicism sometimes supplants a Protestant vision, which retreats in the face of an Oriental point of view, which in turn refuses to take into account the Western perception, which rests on an illusion. If we sense a dissatisfaction among some when they speak of the way in which their ancestors perceived their relationship with a divine essence, we cannot deduce from this that they are evolving in a universe devoid of meaning, or that they are agnostic.

The end of egocentric blindness and the discovery of the self.

Faced with this very pessimistic approach to the writings of O'Neill, it seems to me that we must take into account several aspects that have apparently been neglected by certain critics, who see in these works only elements leading to despair. It is not a question of claiming that these plays are boundlessly optimistic but of seeing them rather as a not necessarily negative illustration of life. Often the plays associate existence with the idea of a test in which the individual has the opportunity to reveal his greatness.

The first task of the protagonists, in the brief moments when they are freed from the familial circles or from the society which surrounds them, consists in getting to know themselves. Time and again, we have seen just how great the temptation was to resort to lies that allowed the characters to mask an unbearable reality. However, such self-deception is a prelude to personal ruin, for the first duty of each individual, in the O'Neillian perspective, consists of knowing who he is. One should not read into this any kind of value judgment; my remark on the "personal ruin" is a simple observation, based not on my own ethic, but rather on the one I believe to have discerned in the course of this study.[44] Those who choose escape routes such as alcohol or daydreaming do not meet the criteria for personal fulfillment; it is for this reason that they are associated with the idea of failure in the works, and not for reasons of predefined moral criteria, which did not necessarily correspond to those of the playwright.[45]

> SARA. If I'm humbled, it's by myself and my love, not by you... and I'm proud of that. For, if I'll never rise to owing a grand estate now, I've risen in life now in the only way that counts, above myself, which is more than you'll ever do [*MSM* 293].

The conclusion is unambiguous: Deborah will end her life in an imaginary kingdom, having denied reality as much as was possible; Sara, for her part, refuses these escapes into another world and shows that she has no illusions about herself. *More Stately Mansions* formed part of a cycle whose aim was to show, through the history of one family, how much the country had gone astray in choosing the path of material prosperity. By abandoning what was far more important, an individual ethic on which a great nation could have founded itself, all have forgotten the essential thing, and have ended up losing themselves by paying homage to false idols. The lines are interesting, for they show a parallel between two contradictory visions of the world; in one case, success is measured in dollars, and in the other, it is directly related to the person. Only rising above oneself is important and this attainment, whatever form it may take, gives meaning to existence. The force within human beings that pushes them to rise above their status as simple mortals and attain a spiritual dimension is the very sign of their greatness.

Before beginning a study of the plays from the perspective currently adopted, I hypothesized an O'Neillian moral code according to which we should evaluate the actions of the characters in order to see if they are exceptional beings or losers. Whether they are the one or the other is determined by the way in which they respond to the opposing forces. Sometimes they triumph for a few moments and sometimes they give up and enter the category of the defeated, without being blamed in any way for their failure which is seen simply as a testament to the difficulty of existence.

Sara (above) allows us to verify one aspect of the initial hypothesis, namely that society's usual criteria for recognizing success are not those of O'Neill. This supports a statement I made in the study of the individual and the community in which he evolves. A second point, not without importance, has to do with the continuity of this position as regards notions of success or failure. In fact, we remember *The Hairy Ape* and the vain efforts of Yank, who tries by every means possible to discover a sphere in which he might find his place; time and again, he refuses to give in to the easy option of illusion whereby he would be a part of something he did not really believe in. On stage, we see a wounded character who, going from refusal to rejection, begins the long descent into Hell; he ends up by seeking a companion in the lowest circle, at the risk of losing his repeatedly challenged human dimension.

Apparently, for the spectator, the despair is there right until the end; the reader, however, has another point of view, for O'Neill allows a glimmer of hope that renders the play potentially more optimistic, when he declares in the last sentence, which does not form part of the dialogue, "And perhaps the Hairy Ape at last belongs" (254). In reality, the dénouement emphasizes the strength of Yank, who refuses to give in, although he knows that everything is lost; in the Western style he decides to die with his boots on:

> YANK. (*Then, with sudden passionate despair*) Christ, where do I get off at? Where do I fit in? (*Checking himself as suddenly*) Aw, what de hell! No squawkin', see! No quittin', get me! Croak wit your boots on! [*HA* 254].

Conflict with the world doubles as a struggle with oneself; throughout the final scene, before his last agony, we see him ready to give up, not so much his search (for he knows that his hour is approaching) as what he has been up until this point. The important thing here is not the lost battle, but Yank's lack of renunciation. By his attitude he proves that he could not be confined to the losers' camp. The essential thing in this course of action is not the result, the success of which is measured by a society whose criteria are irrelevant; in the long run, what matters is the moral strength he demonstrates. Faced with adversity, even gnawed by despair, he does not surrender, thus proving his human grandeur.

Yank's courage has manifested itself in rejecting all compromise and in struggling unceasingly to reach a definition of himself, which could have been given by a group in which he hoped to be integrated.

> Man is a rope stretched between the animal and the Superman—a rope over an abyss.
> A dangerous crossing, a dangerous wayfaring, a dangerous looking-back, a dangerous trembling and halting.
> What is great in man is that he is a bridge and not a goal: what is lovable in man is that he is an *over-going* and a *down-going*.
> I love those that know not how to live except as down-goers, for they are the over-goers.[46]

We have noted how fond the playwright is of paradox. Although it is hardly possible to affirm that he had this Nietzschean vision in mind when he wrote *The Hairy Ape*, it remains very probable. The paradoxical nature stems from the fact that for Yank, the road that leads to the status of higher mortal goes via a descent towards the animal state, symbolized here by a great ape. The choice of this descent signifies entrance to a superior level, and access to this higher mortal state is dependent upon the person's putting their life on the line. It is in taking this risk that a life acquires value; in fact, in the other cases, living often means running away or hiding, more a latent state than a real existence.

Death is not an end; certainly for Yank it marks an end point, but it also conveys the triumph of an individual who has not wanted to be trapped in a context preventing him from really existing. His action has consisted in pushing back the limits of what was possible to the point where he could no longer fight forces too strong for him.

> LAZARUS. (*With a smile*) But all death is men's invention! So laugh! [*LL* 294].

Yank's struggle echoes the words of Lazarus in that he refuses to consider death an unbreachable barrier and he is ready to overcome all obstacles to be himself.

If people set out in search of a supreme truth, they will manage to decode Lazarus' message, which is disturbing to those who founded their beliefs solely on the perception of the here and now. Lazarus invites his disciples to surpass themselves; he asks them to dominate the fear which prevents them from living and then to agree to sacrifice themselves in order to be able to attain another dimension. His invitation also includes the idea of rising above oneself, for he does not want his companions to see themselves as mere mortals. This negation of boundaries is a sign of the kind of inner transformation that will refute human impossibilities by equating them with cowardly thought from which the protagonists do not manage to free themselves.

Two examples illustrate Lazarus' words; one will not be surprised, if one bears in mind the studies we have made of family relations, to notice that the revelation of a divine essence is linked to the maternal figure. In fact, in two plays, She suggests that there is a possibility of life after death; She proves, indirectly, that this event does not occasion the disappearance of the former being. Reuben and Eben (in *Dynamo* and *Desire Under the Elms*) enter into a relationship with the deceased; they need this encounter, for they lack a guide who will show them the road to emancipation. Beyond the spectacular nature of this spiritual communion, the implication must be noted of the existence of a reality hitherto unknown to people, which is revealed to them when they seek it. By entering into contact with something "beyond" himself—that is, beyond the immediate but in the depths of one's being; something not toward the exterior but immanent—the individual rediscovers a lost coherence, and by going beyond the sphere of that which is immediately perceptible, takes a narrow road that leads back to a lost inner peace.

15. Nature.

Fog.

Even though fog is only mentioned in seven plays,* one tends to give prominence to this element in thinking of O'Neill's works. More than any other reason, this probably results from the characters' repeated allusions to their blurry surroundings in *Long Day's Journey into Night*. One should perhaps also note that in *Anna Christie* and *Bound East for Cardiff* this white shroud is granted so much importance it becomes one of the main features of the play.

Since O'Neill wrote for the theater, one needs to take into account the potential difficulties resulting from the presence of fog on stage. Indeed, its actual appearance might be contrived when the play is being performed, but if the audience's vision and lungs are to be preserved, it is no doubt better to consider fog as a sign materializing in the spectator's minds through the actors' speech. Its real significance does not lie in its physical presence, but what matters is that it should be part of, or represent, a mental environment. When one knows how important vision is in O'Neill's works, there can be no doubt that the material presence—for the protagonists, not the audience—of an element which impairs people's sight deserves to be studied.

> CATHLEEN. Bad cess to it. I was scared out of my wits riding back from town...
> MARY. (*Dreamily.*) It wasn't the fog I minded, Cathleen. I really love the fog.
> CATHLEEN. They say it's good for the complexion.
> MARY. It hides you from the world and the world from you. You feel that everything has changed, and nothing is what it seemed to be. No one can find or touch you anymore [*LDJN* 98].

Both of them are intoxicated, Cathleen with whiskey and Mary with morphine, but their views differ concerning the merits of fog. One of the reasons for their divergence is rooted in the way they relate to their environment.

---

*Chronologically: *Bound East for Cardiff, Fog, The Long Voyage Home, Anna Christie, The Hairy Ape, Mourning Becomes Electra,* and *Long Day's Journey into Night.*

It would not be quite accurate to state that in this instance one finds an opposition between the characters who have a touch of the poet about them and those who are down-to-earth—still, there is a contrast between the materialistic vision and a wider perspective concerning people who are "diff'rent." Cathleen and Mary react differently, and one should note that this is not the only instance, as one meets with a similar kind of opposition between Anna Christie and Chris. To Chris, as a sailor, fog is an impediment, but also a sign that his inability to control his destiny is even greater than usual, while Anna perceives that, for her, it might be a means of being reborn.

In fact, for the characters who are not aware of their disharmony with the universe, blindness resulting from natural phenomena is felt almost as a curse. Even though she may not be fully aware of it, Cathleen's fright could be due to the fog's reminder of her frailty as an individual confronted with nature. Sailors share this viewpoint and resent the presence of fog because it hinders the progress of their ship. The protagonists' blindness can reach an even greater extent, and Yank's claim to have surmounted this natural element ("YANK. We move, don't we? Speed, ain't it? Fog, dat's all you stand for. But we drive trou dat, don't we, We split dat up and smash trou—twenty five knots an hour!" [*HA* 217]) is yet another proof of delusion concerning his harmony with the ship and with the world at large. As opposed to this materialistic viewpoint by people who vent their anger at a come-to-a-standstill fog, one finds characters who react differently, those who are already conscious of their lack of adequacy in the world, and who are thus not further moved by this natural form of separation. They tend to welcome being shut away by the weather because it is almost a relief compared to what they generally have to endure. They do not belong in the world in general, having left it for morphine, prostitution, or guilt (e.g., for being the cause of their mother's addiction). Consequently, when the elements come to disturb the course of their lives, they understand the positive aspect of this protective wall and do not object. They even welcome fog as an ephemeral paradise which will enable them to escape the multifaceted mirrors reflecting unbearable images of themselves.

The two visions embodied by Cathleen and Mary might almost be reduced to a matter of body versus mind. Fog may be good for people's complexions, but for some characters, it has hidden virtues as well. It serves as a healing mental balm almost comparable to alcohol in that it enables them to escape from the real world, even if only for a short while. Stephen Bloom underlines this connection between drink and fog, referring to Edmund's words when he alludes to his existential condition ("EDMUND. Then the hand lets the veil fall and you are alone, lost in the fog again, and you stumble on towards nowhere, for no good reason" [*LDJN* 53]):

> His analogy of life as "stumbling" though the "fog" implies awareness that the chemically induced intoxication that he and others experience is a

different kind of fog from the one he dreamt of previously; this fog does not allow transcendance.[1]

Fog does play a part in people's transformation, but one could argue about the notion of transcendence. In fact, one might feel that the sea episode which Edmund remembered had more to do with a pantheistic vision, where what prevailed was a sort of immanence—when the individual becomes part of a whole, without there being a transcendent God ruling over the universe—but this passage also sheds light on another aspect. Bloom picks out the verb "stumble," and rightly so; it provides a deeper insight into previously defined categories, and shows that an essential element in the character's liking or disliking fog is linked to an opposition between movement and immobility.

Fog is a catalyst. It reveals people, indirectly exposing the extent of their disharmony with the world or, conversely, it portends their potential salvation. In fact, some may be redeemed, and therefore when Edmund mentions stumbling towards nowhere, one should not infer that he lives in an absurd world; he is merely complaining about his own misunderstanding of the way of the world. Basically, "stumbling" underlines the futility of man's vain attempt at moving ahead, equating movement with progress—and this echoes people's craving for possession which leads them to their destruction.

Some characters are already heading the right way. Mary and Edmund for instance do find peace, even if it is only for a moment. Redemption might be found—indeed, as opposed to the protagonists who reject fog, Mary—and also Edmund (at the point in the play in which the above-quoted lines occur)—are now on a different plane, which could be the prelude to a rebirth that would make them be one again and part of the universe at last.

> CHRIS. Vell, fog lift in morning, ay tank.
> ANNA. (*The exultation again in her voice*) I love it! I don't give a rap if it never lifts! (*Chris fidgets from one foot to the other worriedly. Anna continues slowly, after a pause*) It makes me feel clean—out here—'s if I'd taken a bath [*AC* 26].

Anna has reached another stage. For her, rebirth is at hand, the difference between her and Edmund and Mary being that for Anna the healing process is working, she is to be transformed, allowed to be her true self again. Mat Burke's final display of trust in Anna shows that he thinks she *has* been redeemed, but this recognition on the social level could not come first. It had to be preceded by Anna's own reconciliation with herself. Her immersion in fog, at sea, was the prime condition for her return to innocence.

One notes in her conversation with her father that she claims she does not wish the fog to lift. This might be explained by her reveling in her newly acquired feeling of unity, which she might fear to lose once the fog has lifted. Unlike Edmund, however, she no longer stumbles towards nowhere, but is able to be reborn.

From the study of these characters, one can classify people into three categories, depending on their relationship with fog: those who resent it, their anger revealing how alienated they are from the natural world; those who appreciate it but who do not manage to reach the final stage consisting in regaining harmony with the natural world through acceptance of it; and Anna and Yank (in *Bound East for Cardiff*), who undergo a radical change, their immersion in fog (a prelude to a wider harmony) having led to their purification.

In *Bound East for Cardiff*, Yank goes through three stages. First, he says how unpleasant it is to die on such a foggy night. Later on, his vision becomes so impaired that he comes to believe he is surrounded by fog, even in the forecastle. Then, after remembering some dark episodes of his life, he reveals how much he suffered from his loss of harmony with the universe during the last year on board the ship. The presence of fog during his confession seems to indicate that he is in the process of regaining unity, even if this form of rebirth is paradoxical (but not uncommon in O'Neill) since it is to be found in death. Contrary to his forebodings—"DRISCOLL. (*With forced gaiety*) Is it wishful for heaven ye are? YANK. (*Gloomily*) Hell, I guess" (*BEC* 483)—heaven is his destination and, surrounded by fog, he is in a sort of limbo where he can regain total purity. He will then gain access to "heaven" which should not be understood in a Christian way, but almost literally, and be read in pantheistic terms, that is to say, regarded as harmony with the whole. His longing is explicitly stated a few pages later:

> YANK. I wish the stars was out, and the moon too; I c'd lie out on deck and look at them, and it'd make it easier to go—somehow [*BEC* 489].

His death is all the more moving as his craving for harmony with the whole will only be satisfied after he has died. Cocky's last words to Driscoll—"The fog's lifted" (*BEC* 490)—indicate that a change has taken place, not only within the forecastle with Yank's death, of which Cocky is not aware at that stage, but also in the world, with the lifting of the fog. In this respect, what happens at the end of *Bound East for Cardiff* can be seen as a foreshadowing of the last line of *The Hairy Ape*, where O'Neill indicated to his readers that Yank's tragedy did not necessarily imply a pessimistic conclusion. Living, Yank could not be one with the universe, but in death he achieves the longed-for harmony.

This reading of the role and meaning of fog, together with the other interpretations made of the plays in this book, could be deemed the result of a certain fogginess which would have invaded the critic's mind. This may well be true. Still, if one looks at *Children of the Sea*, which is a first version of *Bound East for Cardiff*, one finds reasons to believe that what I suggest here is not totally groundless. In *Children of the Sea*, Cocky's last words to Driscoll are: "Oh, Driscoll! The bosun says to come aft and give me a 'and for a minute" (105). Basically, the reason for Cocky's return to the forecastle is the same—he wants to ask Driscoll to help him—but the general meaning is different because in *Bound East for Cardiff* the playwright lays stress on the fog's having disappeared, and the change is significant in that it emphasizes a different aspect of the play, namely the link between Yank and the universe.

Fog, rejected at first, then accepted, has acted as a purifying agent. There is no doubt that its presence or absence does not explain everything—it must be included in a wider view of the relationship between human beings and the universe in which other elements, the moon, the sun and the sea also play a part. Still, the disappearance of fog in *Bound East for Cardiff* is the last step in Yank's quest for belonging. Through the presence or disappearance of fog in the plays, one meets with one of the components of man's attempt to relate to the world of which he is a part. Therefore, Yank's desire to die in a universe in which, even if he were a mere fragment of the whole, he would still belong, should be viewed as representative of people's attempts at being reborn through unity regained.

The moon.

Unlike fog, to which one tends to devote a great deal of thought despite its rather restricted presence in the plays, the moon can justly claim our attention since it is present or referred to in a large number of works.* In the study of fog, I mentioned that in spite of the specificity of each natural element, they—fog, the moon, the sun and the sea—had to be viewed in a global perspective. Each of them is both unique and representative of the universe, illustrating the characters' relationships with the world as a whole. Even though each element does shed a specific light on the protagonists' lives, I am well aware of the dangers of fragmentation inherent to a study that focuses on one theme after another. However, for practical, and not interpretative motives, I shall resume the study of the moon without linking it systematically to other natural elements.

When one tries to define the confines of the moon's influence, one notes that almost to the extent of becoming a cliché it is very often associated with love.[2] If, for a moment, we focus our attention on this aspect, we can classify the "love" plays into two categories, depending on the presence or the absence of the beloved.

*Chronologically: *In the Zone, The Moon of the Caribbees, Where the Cross Is Made, The Straw, Anna Christie, Diff'rent, The Emperor Jones, Gold, The Hairy Ape, The Fountain, The Great God Brown, Marco Millions, Lazarus Laughed, Strange Interlude, Dynamo, Mourning Becomes Electra; Ah, Wilderness!, More Stately Mansions, Long Day's Journey into Night* and *A Moon for the Misbegotten.*

Part III. Humans Faced with Themselves and Inner Worlds.

Loneliness.

In the Glencairn cycle for instance, even though very little is said about the whys and hows, Smitty's loneliness is stressed. It follows that in two plays, the sailor looking at the moon becomes a set image intended to reveal emotional disarray. O'Neill's personal preference for *The Moon of the Caribbees* is well-known, possibly because it revealed Smitty's state of mind without naturalistically recording the painful episodes which had led to his unhappiness. Paradoxically, even if less attention is devoted to Smitty's brooding spirit in *In the Zone*, Scotty's short remark about him—"out on the hatch starin' at the moon like a mon half-daft" (*IZo* 518)—is more interesting than what is said in *The Moon of the Caribbees* because it underlines two essential features of the sailor's state.

The first is the sailor's isolation. He sets himself apart from the rest of the crew, as if he could not belong with them. Unlike other protagonists who are excluded from society but can still be united by a common bond—one may think of the derelicts who haunt Harry Hope's bar—the discarded lover is unable to take up his place once again as a full member of the community, despite the help and understanding provided by another character.[3] In this respect, and even though there is no moonlight in *The Iceman Cometh*, Larry Slade could be considered a distant double of the sailors who remained at a distance from their companions. No one will come to heal his wounds, and in the last scene, his stare is akin to Smitty's contemplation of the moon, which makes him realize how lost he is.

The sailors' lost loves are haunting memories, and they suffer so much that the next step in their downfall—to which Cocky alluded—might be madness. Bartlett is punished in this way for making the wrong choice, losing himself trying to become rich. Indeed, in *Where the Cross Is Made*, madness seems to be but another stage of the disease affecting Dion or James Tyrone, in which alcohol leads to destruction.[4]

Lonely men gazing at the moon hold private conversations with themselves, in which they keep track of the folly which began when they yielded to their weakest instincts and abandoned their wives or mistresses, giving up what could have given a meaning to their lives. Self-pity is not the key word, and more often than not, moongazing merely reflects the weight of their guilt.[5] Love stands at the core of their troubles, and their loneliness exemplifies their failure to establish a fulfilling relationship with another person. Consequently, the moon becomes a reminder of a lost harmony, not only with their beloved but also with the universe.

Many fight in order to discover unity within themselves, knowing that, in their struggle, loneliness is a heavy burden to bear. The moon is a cruel mirror revealing how wasted their existence is, but at the same time—when the character is not on his own—it becomes a sign indicating that deliverance could be at hand, provided their companion helps them see the way towards salvation.

Lovers.

> HOGAN. If you got him alone tonight—there'll be a beautiful moon to fill him with poetry and loneliness, and—[*MMis* 18].

Hogan is not simply trying to invent a scheme to make James marry his daughter for money's sake. Basically, he is reflecting on the potential change which could take place in James' attitude towards life, Josie's love being equated with salvation. He deems it possible for her to save him because the farm is far away from the evils of the city in which he cannot regain his poise and is bound to lose himself. To him, the moon in the sky is more than part of the scenery. It is endowed with hidden powers.

In *Ah, Wilderness!*, the new moon symbolizes the beginning of Richard's real love relationship with Muriel. He wishes to moonbathe, while she is still shy and would rather remain in the shade for some time, thus indicating that their shared love has reached only a first stage. It might be tempting to link the presence of the moon in the background to a sort of compulsory "love scenery" proper to immature human beings, the playwright having purposely chosen to paint an expected if hackneyed picture of a love scene. However, the recurrence of such episodes can also be seen as tending to prove the contrary, to show the scenes to be fresh and meaningful. O'Neill certainly does not underestimate the influence of the moon. It has a deeper effect than merely giving a romantic touch to ready-made tableaux of lovers. If one comes back to Hogan's speech about James Tyrone, one can see that his belief does not result from a naive understanding of the links connecting human beings to the natural world but from some instinct which can be trusted. Also, Hogan is not the sole believer in the power of the moon. When James kisses her hand, Josie too mentions the witness in the sky. At that stage however, James is still alienated, unable to be himself, and therefore rejects the moon in favor of Broadway lights (*Moon* 84). However, even though he may not be aware of nature's uncanny powers, after his confession he manages to reach a kind of peace, thanks to Josie's unselfish love. Later on, his sleep seems to indicate that he has momentarily been saved by the united forces of Josie and the moon.

The moon is more than a witness—it almost deserves the title of actor. Combined with love, it helps people find their true nature, even if this discovery may have contradictory consequences, depending on the characters' situations. In *Strange Interlude*, Mrs. Evans explains that the breach of the contract she and her husband had agreed to respect was not simply due to their having drunk too much. It is also to be explained by a cosmic force (60). It made them act, if not in spite of themselves, at least in reaction to an inhuman plight, and made them bring to life a cursed aspect of their fate. In their case, the stifling puritanism which supposedly helped Mrs. Evans fight against her husband's madness—by not giving him a child—is swept away when their true feelings eventually come to light. For James Tyrone, it has positive effects. He loses his mask and is allowed to be purified, which corresponds to the true image of what he is, in spite of his claims to the contrary. One may also remember Lavinia in *Mourning Becomes Electra*, who is allowed to be herself once she reaches the islands, and discovers with pleasure that she has a body. She too is willing to get rid of the Puritan armor in which she has long been clad. Still, she does not reach that stage, even if Orin muses on the possibility of her transformation had they remained on the island. What is striking is his equating her discovery of what she is with lust, associating it—as if the two aspects could not be dissociated—with nakedness and the moonlight (145).

As far as love is concerned, one notes that whatever the consequences, the moon helps make people reach an understanding with themselves. They are sometimes reminded of love affairs they had tried to forget, but what is even more important is the revealing aspect their encounter with the moon has. The eerie light prevents them from shunning what they really are. Consequently, whatever their plight may be—lust or purity—what matters is that they should be forced to be themselves. As a result, some wounds are reopened, but others may be healed, at least for a time, if the protagonists find the support they need and break away from their lonesomeness.

Belonging and oneness.

> YANK. Say, youse up dere, Man in de Moon, yuh look wise, gimme de answer, huh? Ship me de inside dope, de information right from de stable—where do I get off at, huh? [*HA* 254].

A woman has broken Yank's fragile world of illusions. However, as opposed to the characters previously mentioned, when he looks at the sky, it is more to seek an answer regarding his own belonging in the universe than to be reconciled to a former sweetheart. Even if we did not have the last line of the play, which discloses the positive meaning of the work, Yank's speech could give us a hint about what O'Neill may have wished to convey. The stoker has not yet become one with the world, and whether he is ever to find unity is still a question. However, in spite of his tenuous grasp on what is happening, he has found the right "person" to ask. Till this moment, he has been one of the numerous puppets acting like living people but with no real existence of their own. He is trying to regain his lost harmony, and the first step consists in putting himself at a distance from a society which rejects him. In this scene, all impediments have vanished and he can finally come back into existence. He looks at the sky, knowing that if any answers are to be given, they will come thence.[6] His attitude portends that of Orin when he comes back from the war and wishes to see the moonlight invade the house, linking this change to the death of his father (*MBE* 122). He realizes that he can now be himself, having so far had to remain in the shade.

Both Yank and Orin welcome this enlightening presence, while Jones is baffled by his encounter with himself. He understands too late that a part of his personal and racial history which he had hoped to eradicate is still there. Consequently, instead of finding his way through the forest, he gets lost. As was the case for the lovers, the moonlight reveals to him who he really is. In Jones' case, as in Mrs. Evans', the consequences may not be deemed positive by the characters themselves, yet this unmasking even if it results in suffering or death, shows them where their own truth lies concerning their existence in the universe.

> RICHARD. Gee, I love tonight... I love the sand, and the trees, and the grass, and the water and the sky, and the moon... it's all in me and I'm in it... [*AhW* 277].

Oneness, or the rebirth sought by many, is not bestowed directly by the moon, but its light may help the characters in their quest. Masks are cast aside, personalities are laid bare, and in more general terms, one could say that human beings are shown for what they are—frail individuals whose salvation is possible provided they are able to catch sight of what really matters. As opposed to fog, which could heal wounds, the moon has no such healing virtues. It contributes to the bringing to light of the essence of people, making any escape difficult, except into insanity.

Few characters are in a position comparable to that of Richard. To some, lovers and others, the moon may serve as a guiding light. It permits them to proceed towards a first stage, which consists in being oneself, finding unity, and overcoming the numerous divisions which are obstacles to people's fulfillment. Once they have achieved this regained unity—which is a prelude to a complete rebirth—they may hope to join a greater harmony with the whole world, similar to that described by Richard, and be totally reborn.

The sun.

The third heavenly component which deserves our attention is the sun, even if one might feel that it is given less prominence than the natural phenomena previously mentioned. First, one should note that, as was the case for the other natural elements, its presence, through light, is not simply realistic—giving a concrete feel to the scenery—but is intended to impart deeper meanings. Obviously, O'Neill's employment of the sun should neither be neglected nor, in spite of its being very often mentioned in the plays,* be overestimated in importance. Its significance varies according to the works, and putting the same emphasis on its role for every single play might lead to misinterpretations. This being said, there is little doubt that its presence or absence is telling. As opposed to what has been said about the moon, sunlight often gives clues concerning the general atmosphere, and the link between one individual and the universe is not always the focal point.

In the opening stage directions, where its radiance is frequently described, it can be endowed with positive connotations, showing how pleasant it must be to live in such an environment. In the course of the play, its initial characteristics may be transformed, and the "cheerfulness" and "soothing light" (in *Ah, Wilderness!* and *Strange Interlude*, respectively) with which it is associated in these opening scenes may be altered or even disappear. More than anything else, the sun's streaming its light into houses is a propitious sign, symbolizing an initial state of harmony. The sole exception is to be found in *Thirst*. The words used then, are "glare" instead of light, which makes a definite difference for the reader, the more so as further explanations are given to illustrate this particular point: "The sun glares down from straight overhead like a great angry eye of God" (*Thi* 3). (In *Marco Millions* and in *Gold*, the sun's glare could also be seen as nature's condemnation of men's corrupt aims.) It is worth noting that the same expression is used again at the end of *Thirst*, after the three characters have been eaten by sharks, showing that even in death they did not atone for their sins, whatever these may have been. Their death is ignored by the world as a whole, being only acknowledged by the sharks, since the elements representing the universe—except for the color of the sea—remain unchanged by the characters' plight. They are punished, and the angry glare—probably symbolizing Nature's discontent—retains the mystery of its origin.

In other plays—two of which, *Long Day's Journey into Night* and *Strange Interlude*, belong to the aforementioned group where the opening lines depict a supposedly friendly atmosphere—one meets with an opposite situation. The sun cannot penetrate into houses, and the lack of light metaphorically exposes the dark unnatural world in which the characters live. It follows therefore that if the angry glare is presented as negative, sunlight, on the other hand, is deemed positive, since in *Long Day's Journey into Night* its disappearance in the household corresponds to the gradual decay of relationships between the four Tyrones. In the same way as laughter gives way to verbal clashes and sorrowful episodes, the sun is gradually replaced by darkness within the house itself, even though the fog has not yet moved in (*LDJN* 51).

---

*Chronologically: *Thirst*, *The Movie Man*, *The Sniper*, *Beyond the Horizon*, *The Rope*, *Diff'rent*, *The Emperor Jones*, *Gold*, *The Hairy Ape*, *The Fountain*, *Desire Under the Elms*, *The Great God Brown*, *Marco Millions*, *Lazarus Laughed*, *Strange Interlude*, *Dynamo*, *Mourning Becomes Electra*, *Ah, Wilderness!*, *Days Without End*, *Long Day's Journey into Night*, *A Touch of the Poet*, and *A Moon for the Misbegotten*.

15. Nature.

Shady or bright houses give clues concerning the atmosphere one can expect, but these indications—mainly to be found in the stage directions—only give second-hand information about people's relationships with the universe. In two instances, one meets with protagonists who establish a link between themselves and the sun. From what is said, it would seem that enjoying the sun is a sort of primal pleasure—if not a privilege, at least an indication that people belong in the world and that there is no division between themselves and nature. Not surprisingly, Mrs. Fife is one of those who belong (*Dy* 454) and one must not forget Josie, who believes it has healing virtues (*MMis* 23).

> MEDICINE MAN. Pretend to worship their gold devil but pray to our Great Father, the Sun [*Fou* 431].

Josie and Mrs. Fife share—if not a belief—at least an attitude with the Indians who are portrayed in *The Fountain*. Their common bond is harmony with nature, a feeling of unity, alien to many characters but sought by a number of them. When, for instance, they—willfully or not—prevent the sun from sending its rays into their houses, it reveals how lost they are and how unable to relate to the universe. In *The Hairy Ape*, Yank's place is in between the blind and the happy few. He watches the sun, acknowledges its beauty, but is aware that he does not quite belong in this world. From what has been said, one should not infer that the situation of every individual is immutable. On the contrary, for all these truth seekers, the sun can be a help in that it shows them a possible way towards final peace and total harmony with the Whole.

This potential enlightenment comes into being at two specific moments: sunrises and sunsets. These two instants are linked by vision, but differences remain. Whether it be in *The Fountain, Desire Under the Elms*, or *Strange Interlude*, sunset is connected to peace. It corresponds to an attitude which characters develop when they are able to see that they belong in the world. They become sensitive to a particular sort of beauty from which any desire for possession is eradicated, and this seals their union with the universe.

Sunrise is not to be neglected either, because even if in some plays it is associated with the coming of death, one should not limit oneself to appearances. In fact, whether we take *Beyond the Horizon* or *Desire Under the Elms*, sunrise is the moment when after having lost their way, after having failed, the characters can finally be redeemed. (In *The Hairy Ape*, it is only a prelude to Yank's redemption, while in *Days Without End* it corresponds to John's enlightenment.) The characters are granted what they had striven for, a vision of harmony with another person or with the world at large. Then, in spite of their erring, at the last stage of their lives, they are given the opportunity of being reborn through unity regained.

Paradoxically, the sun as such is the only important element in these situations. It does connect people with nature, showing that they are ultimately given the opportunity of being one with nature, but the way in which this revelation takes place is important too. Therefore, we must take into account the *light* of the sun which symbolizes their enlightenment. Indeed, after groping for their way in a dark world, they are provided with the greatest gift of all, that of the vision of their unity with the universe, announcing to them that rebirth cometh, at last.

The sea.

> But the most important and most natural symbol in this sea play is the Sea itself. The sea, so important a part of O'Neill's life, will be felt in many of O'Neill's plays, even those that are landlocked. O'Neill's closeness to the sea seems to have been a necessity, both a physical and spiritual need.[7]

Norman Berlin is one of many who justly underline the importance of the sea in O'Neill's works, and even if a study of the relationship between people and the sea is limited to a few pages and cannot be exhaustive, this natural element deserves as much attention as the moon, the sun, or fog. The sea plays present us with a male universe, and one notes that in the whole O'Neill corpus, women are hardly ever in a position to relate to the sea.

Apart from Anna Christie, women have no direct link with the ocean. In *Ile* for example, Mrs. Keeney remains in the cabin, and when she asks her husband's permission to go on deck, he refuses. The general situation on board may account for his attitude, nevertheless one may infer from her coming madness, and from Keeney's own discourse, that the ocean is totally alien to her. In other words, she does not belong there. Anna is an exception in that she finds healing in fog and the benevolent presence of the sea. For her, the trip on the barge corresponds to a return to innocence. She is temporarily accepted by the sea which, together with fog, plays a motherly role and provides her with the protection that her unreliable father cannot give her. It is worth noting, however, that after this episode she agrees with Mat and Chris, and is of the opinion that she should live in a house. Motherhood will be the final stage of her reconciliation with herself, but it will also bring her back to shore. She will then become one of the sailor's wives pitied by Chris, who spend their lives waiting for their husbands—lives regulated by the melancholy chime of tears responding to the deadly toll of the sea. In *Diff'rent*, O'Neill alludes to the long wait of women, hoping for the uncertain return of their loved ones. To them, the ocean is a rival, a dangerous mistress able to lure their husbands to her bluegreen bed. The lost-at-sea phrases echoed by some characters indicate that they are all too aware of the danger of losing their husbands forever. In *Mourning Becomes Electra*, Christine knows that Adam loves her, and yet she guesses that when she gets older she might be abandoned by her lover. This is the reason she decides to involve him in the murder of Ezra, so that neither young women, ships or the sea can ever take him (42). There may be good grounds for her fear about younger women attracting Adam, but what is striking is the extent of her fear regarding the ocean and ships. The reasons for such a rivalry may appear surprising, as life on board ship, in spite of what Mrs. Knapp says (in *Warnings*), is far from comparable to a luxury cruise. The answer to this mysterious attraction could be given by Paddy, an old sailor who regrets the lost harmony of yesterday:

> PADDY. Oh, there was fine beautiful ships them days—clippers wid tall masts touching the sky—fine strong men in them—men that was sons of the sea as if 'twas the mother that bore them [*HA* 213].[8]

What is put forward here is the presentation of an almost natural link between men and the sea, with Paddy regretting that this happy, golden time is no more. If we bear in mind what had been said in the study of family relationships, we may remember that blood links were shown to be so strong that they made it impossible for individuals to free themselves from the hold of their families. In *Mourning Becomes Electra* and *Strange Interlude*, the characters discovered that such genetic considerations had to be taken into account, even though heredity affected them in mysterious ways. No matter how sailors react to their spiritual bond with the sea, the connection cannot be ignored. It follows that men's relationships with the sea will have points in common with their relationships with families; what prevails is a complex male-female interrelation.

That the sea should be considered feminine is undeniable[9]; and thus the jealousy of women is all the more easily explained, as they feel they will be unable to resist an overwhelming force should they try to wage a battle for influence.

Paddy tries to explain what leads men to choose a life at sea. Despite the indifference of his companions, he reveals to them the truth they ought to be seeking, and which they are probably trying to discover without being aware of it. In the passage quoted above, he alludes to the sky, men and the sea. At the end of his long monologue, he declares that natural elements and men must not be considered alien to each other but part of a whole—words which strike a familiar note when one thinks of the recurring theme of oneness. Despite the pessimistic undertones of his speech, the impression is given that blissful unity, reminiscent of a golden age in the maternal relationship, could probably be regained. Yank goes ashore in search of an answer to his own questions while most of the crew, remaining on board, will have to seek Paddy's truth on the ocean. If they are fortunate, in the course of their journeys they might discover that they are not simply isolated members of that cramped space the stokehold but are part of a whole, and belong in the world.

One should not conclude that universal salvation is to be found on ships. Not all men are fit to become sailors, and they are unlikely to succeed in their quest for harmony if they do not feel the call of the sea. Still, being ill-suited to the sea does not necessarily lead men to their destruction. In *Beyond the Horizon*, Andrew Mayo unexpectedly tries his luck far from his father's farm, and almost "sails before the wind." However, he is dissatisfied with his lot, and is conscious that a sailor's life does not correspond to his real nature, which had formerly been described by Jim Mayo. Andrew's case is not unique. In *The Moon of the Caribbees*, Smitty's alienation from the group is emphasized. Although he is accepted by the other crew members, they are aware that he does not belong. The prostitute hints at his separateness, but his being different is not what really matters. More essential perhaps is the reason why he chose to become a sailor. To him, and this is his common point with Andrew Mayo, sailing was a means of escape and not the meeting of a man with his vocation; hence it was a predictable failure.[10]

SUE. You know he'd die if he hadn't the sea to live with [*WCIM* 563].

Outsiders can find their way on board ships, but they come to realize that despite its strong attraction, the ocean is not where they should be, and sooner or later they are washed back ashore. As opposed to the indifference reserved for the men who cannot be called its sons, the sea mesmerizes its true sailors, who are never released from its clutches. Therefore, Sue merely states a fact when she predicts that away from the sea her father would be unable to survive. Not surprisingly, this echoes our study of mother-son relationships: We noted that except when they were willingly released by their own mother, sons were never in a position to set themselves free. Even in madness, Bartlett is still connected to the sea, and his last interlocutor is his daughter, who, as we have previously seen, is a substitute for the mother figure in the plays.

The attachment of men to the ocean could be found in numerous works but *Where The Cross Is Made* is interesting in that it illustrates two contradictory but coexisting tendencies regarding men's feelings for the sea. In *Anna Christie*, even though Chris keeps cursing "her," he proves unable to leave and accept a job on shore as a janitor, as he had led his daughter to believe he had. This tension between love — or more precisely a basic need — and hate, a common feature among sailors, is exemplified in the two principal male characters portrayed in *Where the Cross Is Made*. Bartlett's need is close to addiction since it proves vital for him, while his son proclaims his hatred for what he perceives as a destructive force. Nat has been maimed and can neither forgive nor forget. At the same time, his hatred follows the same line as that of Parritt (in *The Iceman Cometh*), revealing an extreme tension between opposed feelings. For instance, he blames his father for what happened to him, but in spite of everything, the ocean is also held responsible for his misfortune. Moreover, he seems to resent the loss of his arm as a symbolic castration. Consequently, his physical rejection by the sea proves as unacceptable as Rosa Parritt's attitude toward her son, hence his bitterness and desire for vengeance. In this respect, his decision to take his father away from the sea to "whom" he belongs may not simply be due to financial reasons. He may also be trying to retaliate, depriving the sea of one of her sons, thus avenging himself like a rejected lover. To conclude on this permanent love-hate tension, one should perhaps note that wounds are so deep that relationships follow unexpected lines, and feelings prevail over reason. For instance, many characters are puzzled by Chris's vision of the sea, but his apparently raving speeches testify to the strength of an attachment unwillingly acknowledged, but vital.

Another feature in the bond between two generations is that of the power of mothers over their sons. They frequently rule over their sons' destinies and the ocean seems to be endowed with an identical power over men. It is true that circumstances may force them to release their sons (for instance Nina in *Strange Interlude*), while in other cases they are willing to do so but it is impossible for the young men—Edmund and James testify to that—to free themselves. In *The Long Voyage Home*, Olson remembers that it is high time for him to visit his old mother, and his return journey—planned as a passenger—indicates that he wishes to sever the links with the sea. However, his liberation will probably not correspond to what he had hoped for, since the gloomy predictions made after hearing the name of the ship might well come true. His fate is similar to Chris's, who had attempted to liberate himself from the evil attraction of the ocean, and whose next crossing with Mat may be his last one. Escape is impossible, and unlike many characters who yield to flight impulses and lose themselves, sailors are never given similar permission. Any attempt to leave the ship is severely punished. An instance of this tendency to make sailors pay for their betrayal is given in *Bound East for Cardiff*. Even though Yank's desire to settle in Argentina had not been voiced, and is only expressed on his death bed, it looks as if the "ole davil, she knew." Consequently, he is claimed by an omniscient and relentless ocean.

Death is the price to pay. One could deem it a dramatic irony. Indeed, if oneness cannot be reached while the sailors are still alive, they will find it when their bodies are thrown overboard.

> A third aspect of the two writers' [Melville and O'Neill] sea imagery resides in their common equation of the symbol of the ocean with death. In some of their works, the sea leads the character from a symbolic death to rebirth and regeneration through a ritual of initiation.[11]

Marc Maufort accurately points out that the sea and death are closely interrelated, but their connection is not devoid of ambiguity. Predictability might be a key word in this relationship. In *Thirst*, for example, the gentleman's vision of the ocean forebodes the tragic events which will soon take place, namely the sharks' grand meal ("GENTLEMAN. The very sea itself seems changed to blood" [*Thi* 5]). Here again, he believes that what he sees does not correspond to what is, while in fact he is merely foreseeing his fate. Sailors never give up the fight, and a shipwreck is not synonymous with immediate destruction, as is shown in *Anna Christie* and *Gold*. Still, in *Gold*, the sailors who sail away on Bartlett's new ship are lost at sea, and Chris's last words make one think that the same end awaits him.

Paddy, however, he who longs for his lost unity with the elements, does not view death in a tragic way. He equates it with a reunion, and this is another example of the paradoxical rebirth in death syndrome frequently found in the plays. Men seek peace and can meet it in death, at the bottom of the sea. This vision of abysses as a harbor of peace is not restricted to the sea plays. It is also used metaphorically in other works (one could expect it in *Marco Millions* [409], but similar imagery can also be found in *The Iceman Cometh* [e.g., 625–646]). Should one cry over the fate of sailors? Outsiders would, but those who belong react differently. In *Anna Christie*, after his ship sank, Mat struggled in order not to be drowned like his companions; still he admits that death at sea—the ultimate chapter of a sailor's life—can be "a good end" (36).

The promise of unity seems to be kept when men join the sea for their last journey. The goddess-like ocean, as powerful as mothers over their sons, is triumphant and one more time rules over the sailors' lives. However, this dark vision of the sea as a killer which brings peace to the characters—once it has made sure of owning them—is not representative of all its aspects. A second kind of unity is accessible to the children of the sea (described by Edmund in *Long Day's Journey into Night*), provided they know how to interpret their mother's language. What is sent is a message of hope which marks the reconciliation of men with the feeling of oneness, the loss of which had caused Paddy to grieve. In spite of their harsh lot, one might think that sailors are chosen men, in that they are eligible for a higher vision, knowing that many fail to descry the path towards salvation. To them, the sea offers the supreme gift, that of an intimate knowledge of belonging, harmony within oneself and with the world. The ocean finally becomes a mother in the positive sense, and not in the somber one often encountered in the plays. In the same way as a mother gives birth to her children, the sea is able to bring them back to life.

The natural world.

> MARTHA. Do you remember two years ago when we were camped in Yunnan, among the aboriginal tribes? It was one night there when we were lying out in our sleeping-bags up in the mountain along the Tibetan frontier. I couldn't sleep. Suddenly, I felt oh, so tired—utterly alone—out of harmony with you—with the earth under me. I became horribly despondent—like an outcast who suddenly realizes the whole world is alien [*FM* 585].

Martha's description of her feeling of alienation is specific. At the same time, and we shall come to this point afterwards, it is representative of the impression many characters have of not belonging in the world. Her loss of harmony is explained by her frustration at not having children, but her need cannot be satisfied because she and her husband had pledged they would remain childless after the death of their two little daughters. In the circumstances, the word "need" is more adequate than that of desire, because of the strength of her urge. Indeed, from an O'Neillian perspective, there is little doubt that what she craves is vital. Suffice it to recall Dr. Darrell's speech about Nina's recovery being dependent on her having a child. Martha's case is very similar to Nina's.

As has been seen in the first part of this book, women are basically considered mothers-to-be, and one meets here with a classical pattern, often encountered in O'Neill's works. Motherhood is presented as a natural and almost necessary condition to reach a state of happiness. Here, her craving for a child permeates Martha's speech, but it is put in a wider perspective, and the pursuit of happiness is perceived in existential terms.

What is worth noticing, and will in fact prove essential, is that the lack of harmony should be felt when the character is in a position to meet nature—outside, in the mountain—where no alien elements are likely to pervert her relationship with the natural world. At that stage, she becomes aware of her alienation, and her suffering causes her to discover the source of her unhappiness. In her attempt not to hurt her husband's feelings, she had unconsciously agreed to wear a mask, and as a result, had fled from her true self.

The second important aspect of her monologue is directly connected with the title of this tragedy: "The First Man" implies that what she and Curtis are looking for is clues concerning the origins of humanity. They have not reached the end of their research, but in their quest, the mention of aboriginal tribes is no coincidence. With these people, they are confronted with a primal state of humanity, primal being laudative in this precise O'Neillian perspective. These people stand for humanity in its earliest stage, when human beings had not yet been totally corrupted by the evils of civilization as is later shown in the play. Thanks to their closeness to nature—which she has lost—they will be able to guide her.

What is at stake is her own belonging, and the natural world proves almost divine since it provides a guiding light. Despite the tragic ending, the answer given by nature—through the eyes of an ugly woman—is that motherhood is the path to follow. The conclusion of the play might be felt to weaken the strength of such a vision, but this is not so. In this respect, there is a similarity between Yank's and Martha's death in that if victory should not be viewed in terms of blatant success, conversely, failures should not be equated with defeat, namely death. The tragic ending is not the sole link between the two plays. Yank speaks to the Hairy Ape and states that even behind bars, it cannot lose its deep harmony with nature, as if its beastly aspect guaranteed it (253). No matter how tragic their lost fights may be, what should be taken into account is that both of them have been true to themselves and have gone to the end of their quest.

Nature serves as a catalyst because it enables Martha to understand why she is lost and how far she has run from her true self. In this respect, the natural world is very important since through contact with it the characters themselves are shown where they stand. Not in all the works, but very often, the connection between the protagonists and the universe is most revealing. If we take for instance *The Iceman Cometh*, what is striking is the absence of nature, which becomes a sign of alienation. (When one of the men leaves the bar and is confronted with this particular catalyst, he can measure the extent of his personal failure—see Rocky's description of Jimmy Tomorrow's suicide attempt [*IC* 699].) Nevertheless, one should not infer from these examples that the relationship between people and nature should be perceived in negative terms only. Mrs. Fife, for instance, in *Dynamo*, is on the way to fulfillment—she is one who belongs, in a primal way, a way to that of the aboriginal woman. Therefore, her wish to become a cloud (444) should not be read as an indication of simple-mindedness. On the contrary, it shows her harmony with the outside world. She has almost discovered the truth most characters are in quest of, and which eventually some will come to see, like Edmund, who melts into the universe when he is at sea.

For the audience or the reader, the natural world has a slightly different status. We have seen that part of the protagonists' quest for unity—a prelude to rebirth—consisted in accepting the different facets of themselves, or forming a whole with someone else in order to reach harmony—characterized by an impression of oneness. The individual is never in a position to communicate with the universe until he has accepted the conflicting sides of himself or has found a soulmate. It follows that the distance of a character from the outside world sheds light on his personal situation. This means that one could almost establish a scale of harmony, in which the relationship of the individual with the universe would serve as a revealing feature, reflecting their personal situation, indicating how far they are from a rebirth to which they seem to aspire.

Such an analysis implies that the universe should be considered neutral, insofar as it would not on its own initiative affect the lives of human beings. One may have doubts about this, since in *Thirst* the sun was compared to the angry eye of God, and another natural element, the moon, had changed the course of Mrs. Evans' life. Fate cannot be ignored either, and it would probably be going too far to say that everything rests on the shoulders of individuals. Natural elements or the strong forces which act upon human beings, can do so, however, only because the characters have to bridge a gap between two parts of themselves—one of which is rejected—or between themselves and someone else. It follows that the universe is a mirror more than anything else, and if negative forces come into action, they mainly reflect those emanating from within the characters.

Shakespeare, whose shadow looms over O'Neill's work—particularly perhaps on this specific approach to the natural world—gives an answer to the question of ascribing responsibilities regarding man's feeling of disharmony with the universe:

> The fault dear Brutus is not in our stars but in ourselves that we are underlings.[12]

James Tyrone's quotation from *Julius Caesar* is interesting, not only because it promotes the responsibility of every human being for his own life, but also because it introduces a cosmic dimension to the lives of the protagonists. The conclusion of Tyrone's speech is that the plight of mankind cannot be blamed on external forces alone. Another aspect, which might otherwise be disregarded if one focused only on the question of mastery over life, is that the cosmic dimension is inherent to the characters' lives and their connection with the universe is essential. Stars are also mentioned in other plays, *Now I Ask You, Bound East for Cardiff,* and *Lazarus Laughed,* but even in a casual or comic way ("GABRIEL. I must go out under the stars—to think!" [*NIAY* 176]) they are linked with man's desire to know where he stands.

The protagonists may gaze at the stars or at the sky, but few will find the answers they are looking for. The sky is part of the natural world, and its action is similar to that of other elements. It acts like a mirror, reflecting the characters' harmony or disharmony. James Tyrone's bit of Shakespeare downplayed the potential influence of the universe on people's lives, but it also suggested their delusion concerning their place in the world.

In the introduction to this chapter, when the role of the natural world was addressed, the following hypothesis was made: The relationship of the O'Neillian individual to the universe is a telling feature revealing his personal situation, indicating how far he is from a rebirth or a reunion to which he seems to aspire.

This point could be put to the test in various works. I shall now, however, restrict my analysis to one play, *Desire Under the Elms,* and limit the study to the sky, which is very often described by the members of this New England family. The premise to be examined would be that in *Desire Under the Elms,* the sky is not an active agent, working on people's fates, but serves as an indicator of their feeling of oneness with the universe. It would follow that the acknowledgment of beauty would become a sign of belonging while the blindness of the other protagonists would prove the contrary. To start with, one may remember Eben's conversation with his father, at the end of Part Two, when he mocked Cabot's genuine admiration of nature's beauty. Eben's sarcastic remarks were founded on his father's age—he felt that as an old man he was unable to see. Such an opinion is partly accurate if one bears in mind Eben and Abbie's affair. However, what matters is that Cabot is able to see beauty and praise it as such, and this is but one of the numerous ways in which his harmony with the natural world is underlined. Even though he does not detect what is happening between the two lovers, he is not completely blind, and perceives that something is not right. Eben, on the other hand, is unable to recognize beauty as such, because he is obsessed by his wish to own the farm: "EBEN. (*Looking around him possessively*)" (*DE* 245). He is not blind—he admits that the farm is "purty"—but his father has to show him what he should be looking at—the sky—in order to understand or feel where he belongs:

>   CABOT. Purty, hain't it?
>   ABBIE. I don't see nothin' purty.
>   CABOT. The sky. Feels like a warm field up thar [*DE* 231].

This exchange portends the conversation between Eben and Cabot. The contrast is striking. Cabot is the one who sees, while Abbie remains oblivious to the beauty of the sky. It follows that unlike Eben and Abbie, Cabot is at one with the outside world. Even his harshness is not a sign of alienation, but is in keeping with his God's commands, whom he locates in the stones. He *belongs*, as is proved by his need to go and sleep with the cows, as he cannot live in corrupt surroundings and has to stay in tune with the motherly presence of nature. Even in death, he tells his wife that he will linger on the farm, which is also a sign of his harmony with the natural world. Despite their contrasting personalities, he is very close to *Dynamo*'s Mrs. Fife, who is at one with the universe and knows it without feeling the need to understand.

After his nightly meeting with Abbie, Eben is freed by his mother. Then, thanks to love, he is able to bridge the gap that had prevented him from finding unity with the world. This is why, at the end of the play, and in spite of the murder of their child, the two lovers, united at last, are in a position to recognize the beauty of the sky. They have found in each other a soulmate and got rid of their desire for possession. At that moment they reach oneness and are reborn—even if only for a short while, since death awaits them. Then they belong in the world, and this seems to prove that the hypothesis is correct because they finally perceive what is essential, the beauty of the sky symbolizing their intimate harmony with the universe. On the other hand, and this serves as a contrasting feature, the sheriff is as blind as Eben was since his admiration is restricted to the financial appeal of the farm.[13]

Nature is prominent in O'Neill's theater, and even though for practical reasons it has been studied thematically, one should not forget that it forms a whole, and that from the sky to the earth or the sea, there is a common bond, that of an almost motherly force which can make human beings feel at one with the universe. The evocation of the natural world brings to mind some episodes from the characters' lives—Edmund's experience at sea is one of them, but one can also find it mentioned in more unexpected contexts, where it is always linked with positive aspects, as in the following lines from two different plays:

> EBEN. She's like t'night, she's soft 'n wa'm, her eyes kin wink like a star, her mouth's wa'm, her arms're wa'm, she smells like a wa'm plowed field... [*DE* 211].
> CHRIS. Yust water all round, and sun, and fresh air, and good grub for make you strong, healthy gel [*AC* 23].

A proof of this is given in *Marco Millions* when Kukachin attempts to defend Marco against his critics who view him as a boor. Her mistake concerning the existence of his soul is explained by her love, taking root in her belief that he is endowed with a wider vision of the world ("KUKACHIN. ... once when he looked at sunrise, another time at sunset, another at the stars, another at the moon, and each time he said that Nature was wonderful" [*MM* 397]). In fact, she mistook small talk for a philosophical outlook on life and was deceived about his greatness. In the circumstances, what is striking is the importance which this type of argument takes in her own eyes. It means that people can be judged according to their closeness with the natural world, or at least according to their intimate relationship with the universe. Her bitterness, at the end of her long journey, is easily understood, for at that stage she knows for sure that he belongs to the species of the blind. His total lack of vision is ironically reinforced by the task he had been assigned by Chu-Yin. Unlike Eben, who had first misunderstood his father's acknowledgment of beauty but had finally discovered his way of truth, Marco is unable to find his salvation in the love of Kukachin, in spite of his daily contemplation of the Princess's eyes. Kukachin will obtain an ultimate answer in death. After getting rid of her base attachments to an earthly life, it will enable her to find a way of being one with the universe, to which—to her deep regret—she will have understood that Marco did not belong.

The relationship between human beings and the natural world has proved to be very complex. The much sought sense of belonging is hard to attain. On the other hand, the lack of desire for unity with nature testifies to the characters' blindness concerning what is essential. What then is the place of human beings in the universe, and how should this world be defined?

> All that O'Neill and Beckett have in common is Schopenhauer, with whom they share a Gnostic sense that our world is a great emptiness, the keroma, as the Gnostics of the second century of the common era called it.[14]

The "great emptiness" used to qualify the world is not a very flattering definition. It is true that except for plays like *Days Without End*, the characters do not tend to look for the word of God. On the other hand, it would be hard to deny that there is something divine in the perception they have of the natural world. Very often, it has much to do with a pantheistic vision. The protagonists find themselves included in the universe and then reach a deep harmony, knowing that belonging is the supreme gift they have been looking for.

It follows that their reunion with the world is a rebirth characterized by the feeling of unity they had been in quest of, as for a lost paradise.[15] When they reach their aim, their *ego* is given its proper place—it is not the prominent place they had desired but it is not denied either. Therefore, despite the harsh lot of many individuals, I would find it hard to share Harold Bloom's pessimistic outlook. In fact, in the study of the natural world, we have seen that the universe was far from empty, and that the sea, fog, sun or earth could not be considered as mere scenery.

One could, for instance, refer to the ending of *Strange Interlude*, when Nina mentions electricity. This physical phenomenon is the epitome of the natural elements studied so far.[16] Therefore Nina's last speech is not an acknowledgment of defeat. On the contrary, she implies that to understand that one is part of "the electrical display of God the Father" is what really matters. Paradoxically, in spite of its potentially nihilistic connotations, such a vision is not pessimistic, and Lazarus explains that accepting one's small place in the universe is what makes the grandeur of mankind.

> LAZARUS. As Man, Petty Tyrant of Earth, you are a bubble pricked by death into a void and a mocking silence! But as dust, you are eternal change, and everlasting growth, and a high note of laughter soaring through chaos from the deep heart of God! Be proud, O Dust! Then you may love the stars as equals! [*LL* 309].

Pride is a deadly disease. One may think of Simon Harford in *More Stately Mansions* who had tried to become a financial god and had lost his soul in his meaningless battle. As for Lazarus, he draws a conclusion which many a character has reached following a variety of ways. What matters is not being what one imagines oneself to be, but being part of a whole, belonging in the universe. Thus, human beings are able to get rid of their feelings of alienation, and change them into feelings of harmony which will symbolize their unity with the natural world—the very sign of their rebirth.

16. Conclusion.

Rebirth, and union with the whole.

Whether it be Yank, Reuben or Eben, each tries to discover a higher truth. They seek to attain total unity, which will only exist if they are at peace with themselves; this All-in-One will only be recognized by a chosen few, in one fleeting moment of their lives before it readopts its fragmentary aspect. Yank perceives what this could mean when he refers to Paddy, who had talked of the profound harmony between man, his ship and the universe ("PADDY. 'Twas them days men belonged to ships, not now. 'Twas them days a ship was part of the sea, and a man was part of a ship, and the sea joined all together and made it one" [*HA* 214]), but his intellectual honesty stops him from subscribing to this vision, for he knows that it does not correspond to what he needs.

Beyond the obvious differences, perceptible in the situations and in the very personality of each individual, we glimpse a thematic continuity the stages of which are marked out by the three aforementioned characters. Yank's fight is a prelude to his entry into the world, since above all he wants to define himself and obtain an image of himself which will be the key to his integration. Thereupon he would be able to attain what he desires, namely harmony with a universe that until then had treated him as an outsider. Paddy's words become a kind of model of happiness; Yank's intellectual work, so derided by his companions, consists in defining the form of this model by adapting it to the person in question, that is to say himself.

We also mentioned two other protagonists, whose aspirations to inner peace encompassed an attempt at reconciliation with their mothers, who could, they hoped, give them what they were lacking. Reuben does not fully achieves this; he finds an answer only in the call of the mother-dynamo, who urges him to commit suicide so as to join her once more on the road to a lost paradise. The individual needs to break free from the maternal figure; however when he does not instigate the rupture, it is destructive, creating a void which is very difficult to fill. Reuben manages to do this by sacrificing himself, but if one adheres to the O'Neillian criteria, this is only a partial success, for he does not taste his happiness, since he loses his life. (Fundamentally, the important thing is not the loss of life, but the fact of not having been able to experience a supreme joy by tasting the incomparable pleasure gained by integration with a Whole.)

The case of Eben could seem identical, in that he will end his days hanging from a noose. He did find fulfillment, however, and was able to reach another level which places death in the order of contingent realities. In fact, the conversation with his mother liberated him. It marked his entrance into the adult world and allowed him to enjoy his carnal relationship with Abbie without feeling any sense of guilt. From this moment onwards he became a complete being; his inner harmony allowed him to ascend to a higher level, conveyed this time by his love for his son and for Abbie, even though he only realizes it when it is too late. Eben illustrates the journey each individual must take in order to gain access to a dimension which is not limited to the contingent. The first task of each one is to define himself, then to free himself from the bonds that prevent him from being his true self. Subsequently, once the character has found personal unity, he must also seek it in a wider context, which presupposes a rising above oneself: This union with a Whole implies a preliminary stage of effacing egocentricity, which more often than not exposes a superficial duality heretofore preventing the subject from perceiving the latent harmony. This revelation thus has crucial consequences for the characters' relationships with their environment; literally as well as figuratively, passing this test opened their eyes. We may remember the final scene of *Desire Under the Elms*, and the remark made by Eben, who becomes aware of the beauty of nature while watching the sun rise.

The sheriff contents himself with a down to earth interpretation of the situation, recalling the previous state of Eben, who, at the beginning of the play, desired above all to possess the farm.

> Robert's last words suggest a new beginning, a fulfillment, transcendence in death: "Don't you see I'm happy at last—free—free!—freed from the farm—free to wander on and on—... It isn't the end. It's a free beginning—"[1]

Undoubtedly, a study of vision in O'Neill's theater would be necessary in order fully to appreciate its significance; the opposition which appears in Robert's words substantiates what we have already noted in the final exchange between Eben and Abbie. On one side, we find the majority of men prisoners of their blindness; on the other, those who at the end of a long quest, during which they often lost their way, manage to glimpse a reality that surpasses initial interpretations. A greater degree of perception is often given to those who are at the point of death; they are thus freed from that which, throughout their existence, led them astray and blocked the path of their true development.

16. Conclusion. 223

Robert proclaims his joy, for he is free at last, released of the burden which he has had to carry throughout his whole life. Reaching the end is a liberation, because death does not mark a final stage. It constitutes rather a sort of divine gift, a prelude to a new beginning. In his speech, he tries to comfort those near to him who are suffering through seeing him ready to breathe his last. His sudden lucidity, the reconciliation with a world he aspires to leave in its present form, is not described, but one can imagine what is going on in his mind. We must note here, and this element is not without significance for the interpretation of the whole, that when revelation takes place, it always takes place outside.

The characters finally integrate into a universe within which they are evolving, and this communion, the access to a much sought-after complete unity, gives life its meaning. We shall see why this aspect is so important for our thesis, in that what appears in the passage below marks the end of the spiritual journey of an individual, who understands that he is part of a Whole, and that he is this Whole. This sudden comprehension, emblematic of the winning of a struggle for some, an unexpected discovery for others, gives significance to existence. This pantheistic perspective is described by Edmund, who has been fortunate enough to have had access to a superior reality in the form of a symbiosis with Nature, before the Parcae take hold of him.

> EDMUND. Dreaming, not keeping lookout, feeling alone, and above, and apart, watching the dawn creep like a painted dream over the sky and sea which slept together. Then the moment of ecstatic freedom came. The peace, the end of the quest, the last harbor, the joy of belonging to a fulfillment beyond men's lousy, pitiful, greedy fears and hopes and dreams! And several other times in my life, when I was swimming far out, or lying alone on a beach, I have had the same experience. Became the sun, the hot sand, green seaweed anchored to a rock, swaying in the tide. Like a saint's vision of beatitude. Like the veil of things as they seem drawn back by an unseen hand. For a second you see—and seeing the secret, are the secret. For a second there is meaning! [*LDJN* 153].

These words refute the pessimistic arguments which say that life has no meaning because human beings evolve in a place where God is unknown. In fact, the description quoted above shows that there is unity between human beings and nature, for they are both part of a whole. The discovery of immanence allows Edmund to confirm that, despite an apparent fragmentation, the world is one entity, within which the person has his place since he himself forms this Whole.

We have observed that such a revelation has sometimes occurred in the plays when the protagonists were about to die. Some scholars have deduced from this that the revelation heralded a return to the womb, and constituted in some way the preliminaries of a death ritual. This interpretation is misleading, for if the characters sometimes return to the one who gave them life, it is to gain freedom so that they can be reborn.[2] The immanence perceived by Edmund must not be considered as a contingent experience. It is essential, for the fragmentation—which sometimes takes the form of duality, a division within oneself or for the surrounding universe—is that against which the characters ceaselessly battle.

Edmund's description corresponds to a second birth (which perhaps explains the overly important role some attribute to their mother), of which the principal characteristic is the removal of divisions that have caused so much suffering to the individuals concerned. The effects do not, however, last forever, as could be testified to by Edmund. If need be, we could cite James Tyrone (in *A Moon for the Misbegotten*), who once again finds purity and innocence, for one night, in the company of Josie Hogan. However, his confession one evening—signifying his reconciliation with the world—and the love of Josie—allowing him to find himself again, totally accepting what he is—are not enough to rehabilitate himself in his own eyes. In fact, even if in the first light of day he will still have the memory of a night when he was his true self, stripped of all his wickedness, this balm will be insufficient for him to be reborn and he will condemn himself for a fault which he judges to be irreparable.

This is not the case for Anna Christie, who has a similar experience but for whom the consequences are different; indeed, she does not consider the change in herself to be temporary, but comprehends it as a definitive metamorphosis.

> ANNA. (*Persistently*) But why d'you s'pose I feel so—so—like I'd found something I'd missed and been looking for—'s if this was the right place for me to fit in? And I seem to have forgot—everything that's happened—like it didn't matter no more. And I feel clean, somehow—like you feel yust after you've took a bath. And I feel happy for once—yes, honest!—happier than I ever been anywhere before! [*AC* 28].

Alone on a boat amidst the fog, Anna reunites with her true self, which had never had a chance to blossom but was present nevertheless, awaiting only the right circumstances to reveal itself. This episode echoes all those we have previously quoted, during which the protagonists discovered the existence of a profound unity. Their belonging, which they had sought for so long, was now rightfully theirs since they necessarily formed a part of the Whole and, in a way, were this Whole.

We remember that O'Neill had declared that the human relationship with God occupied a central place in his work. We must therefore pause to consider this aspect, bearing in mind what has just been described. The first observation which arises has to do with the notion of immanence. This implies that, if a Supreme Being exists, it is not an external phenomenon but must rather be recognized in nature, which encompasses the individual. This monistic perspective excludes the idea of a transcendent God which we have seen elsewhere. Each individual must therefore search the depths of his soul so that he might attain a revelation that is undoubtedly of an almost divine nature but that will reveal his fundamental unity with a whole of which he had until this point been unaware even if at times he had sensed it.

This interpretation implies that people are free, since their destiny is not ruled by a Supreme Being, who would decide in advance the way in which their lives would unfold. In the plays, the destiny of each character varies considerably, for access to this discovery takes different forms. Some find the way to happiness, whereas others set out in search of a truth which they may sometimes discover but which more often is merely hypothetical. Human beings emerge the greater from this battle they have waged against themselves. True, they sometimes succumb to the temptations of the easy option; their journey more often, however, takes them in search of a reality higher than their simple mortal state of isolation, and thereby they move into another dimension by finding deep within themselves the key to this longed-for union.

From this analysis, we may question the degree of optimism to be found in the plays. The subjective is of prime importance; I consider that optimism predominates, even if it is reduced to its minimal level, in that we can say that despair does not prevail. The proportions are open to individual interpretation but I maintain that it is not possible to speak of a total pessimism which would take the form of nihilism. In fact, O'Neill always backs life even if he is disenchanted with it and even if a brighter future is indefinitely postponed.[3] The pessimism that does appear is due to the playwright's uncompromising view of the surrounding universe; the path, of which O'Neill shows us many steps, has many pitfalls, and those who travel by it risk dropping into them and thereby losing the most precious part of themselves—but the message contained in the plays is not one of despair.[4] Certain episodes are very black, but they are the reflection of an almost Sisyphean learning process. From this somber observation, the few glimpses of hope in this picture give a positive slant to life, even if what is shown is not idyllic, for the world is composed of human beings who are intrinsically fallible. Despite all these difficulties, the plays powerfully affirm that existence has a meaning, and that each individual must strive to discover it,[5] for it is in the depths of oneself that the foundations will be laid upon which a relationship with the world can be established.[6] When the individual is defined, he must remain faithful to himself, and to do this, he must have the courage to free himself from his chains, which take the most diverse forms.

Beyond the failures, we must see the greatness of a difficult task, which takes the form of an aspiration towards rebirth or a reunion with or redefinition of one's own identity. This fight is often destructive for human beings, but it is essential for it gives meaning to life.

17. Beyond the Conclusions.

MARY. I fell in love with James Tyrone and was so happy for a time [*LDJN* 176].

If I were to extract from the whole of O'Neill's work a single quotation to sum up its essence, I would choose these few words of Mary Tyrone's, which form the conclusion to *Long Day's Journey into Night*. The term "conclusion" is, however, inappropriate and thus I have chosen the above title for this last chapter, remembering that the author once declared that a play, as life itself, never ends.[1] I am in mind of those moments when, just as everything seems to be collapsing, against all expectations the storm abates, and the protagonists come back to life, putting off the final drop of the curtain. In a perspective such as this, the scene which holds our attention stands as a prelude. One perceives that this halt is only temporary, for once the characters have recovered their breath, the dialogue will start afresh, and the slow agony of existence will resume its course. This brief evocation of happy events will then give way to the darkness of a journey, which turns human beings into cripples, where each word wounds, and in which each person's attempt to shake off his chains triggers hostile reactions that thwart the characters' progress, if not towards their development as individuals at least in their quest for peace.

The terseness which characterizes Mary's utterance is also a reflection of O'Neill's writing, for the language is relatively simple. This remark is to be taken as neutral, and in no way detracts from the playwright's greatness as a writer; indeed, a small number of sentences—stark but forceful—form the hub around which he constructs dramas that are never to be forgotten.

One might believe that O'Neill's dramatic expression reaches its highest degree of simplicity in this brief line, and yet, if one looks at it from the dramatist's philosophical perspective, the closing speech is almost redundant. If one provisionally makes an abstraction of the dimension of time contained in these words, and also of the cause of her happiness, one notes that Mary's line is an assertion of her existence. The "I ... was so happy" means that the speaker, at some point in her life, had been in a position to say that she existed or experienced some sensation of existing and therefore, as was demonstrated earlier, regardless of all the discord in her life, had become aware that she formed an entity.

This formulation refers us to the expression of happiness, such as it was revealed with the assessment of what meant the most to the characters; the moment of elation does not find its expression in any single form, for it varies according to the inner truth of each individual. What unites the entire group of O'Neill protagonists is the fact that each has been able, at one time or another, however briefly, to consider himself as a whole, having broken off from an unhappy past in which he was divided against himself, proved to be incapable of reconciling his conflicting impulses, and therefore never savored the joys of completeness. This almost ineffable condition, which Edmund tried to describe in *Long Day's Journey into Night*, is what constitutes the height of elation, and provides access to a state of beatitude—one could also call it a rebirth—which few attain.

Indeed, in spite of what Lazarus says—"I know that age and time are but timidities of the thought" (*LL* 354)—existence is inscribed within the limits of time, the power of which is revealed just when the characters imagine they have conquered it. Bliss is not granted for any length of time, and hardly has a sense of well-being reached the characters' consciousness than it disappears. This revelation is regulated to an unchanging rhythm: the chosen few enjoy a short instant of supreme harmony, then inevitably become once more entangled in the sinister and unending realities of daily life.

"...[F]or a time"—and all is said: Both the optimism of the potential moment, and the inflexibility of Time which, whatever happens, will stand in the protagonists' way to happiness. When some do attain the goal, they know in advance that they have not reached the final stage, but that the oneness of the single moment is bound to shatter, leaving them to return to the tradition of suffering caused by the conflict or conflicts arising within themselves.

Edmund bears witness to this: At the end of the speech during which he tries to explain to his father the state of ecstasy he has enjoyed on several occasions, he shows clearly that although this sensation is very strong, it is short-lived.

> EDMUND. For a second there is meaning! Then the hand lets the veil fall and you are alone, lost in the fog again, and you stumble on toward nowhere, for no good reason! [*LDJN* 153].

A man lost in the fog; this vision is characteristic of the image the playwright gives of life. The protagonists "stumble on," without knowing where the path will lead, or whether their progress has any real meaning. In fact, although some of them have been vouchsafed a revelation of the meaning of life in the form of an understanding of the profound unity between the human being and the universe—a revelation which entails its corollary, that once this notion has been acquired one must remain faithful to oneself—other characters, meanwhile, merely sense this or try to discover it.

Up to this point, we have made an abstraction of the aspect of time in Mary Tyrone's line. The "was" clearly shows that the notion of happiness is related to the past. If the spectator had any doubts, the preceding utterance, "Yes, I remember," emphasizes the necessity of deliberate recollection and therefore focuses on the division between the moment when Mary declares she was happy, and a present which is anything but paradisical. During the play, James Tyrone announces that by the end of the night, following an unchanging ritual, after having taken morphine, she will be taken into the past, to the time before her children were conceived. Unable to face up to the difficulty of living, Mary finds an escape in drugs, and creates a fleeting, artificial paradise for herself. This enables her to relive, for a short while, the blessed period of her life when she had experienced real happiness. But on the other hand, while this disconnection from reality brings her temporary relief, it does not have only positive effects for it inflicts deep wounds upon those around her.

As they start out in quest of their bygone happiness, the characters take various routes. Some steep their memories in whiskey in an attempt to bring them back to life, and thereby forget the darkness of their insignificance. Others enter into the kingdom of illusion, built upon half-truths, and hide behind masks, yet they are aware that these side-stepping strategies turn out to be just as harmful for themselves as whiskey or drugs. We have already examined these various deadly escape impulses in the course of this study; if I take up this subject once more, it is to place them in the updated frame of this final stage of my thesis. I here allude to the desire for rebirth that each character experiences, which in the example above leads Mary to take drugs so as to be able to spend a few moments in the time and space where once she had experienced an impression of well-being, grown out of her love for James Tyrone.

One cannot but note that when the characters resort to make-believe strategies, this is a sign of the desperation of their quest as they strive at all costs to retrieve their bygone happiness. The methods they use are doomed to fail, because they tend to conjure up artificial unity, but this attempt is easily explained, for it proves to be vital to those who would otherwise sink into despair.

> EDMUND. (*He grins wryly.*) It was a great mistake, my being born a man, I would have been much more successful as a sea gull or a fish [*LDJN* 153].

Few of the characters would be likely to echo Edmund's words on their own account. However, if reincarnations were to reflect the inner nature of each of them, we might suggest that more than one would wish to make a fresh start with a different choice. Thus in *Long Day's Journey into Night*, Mary and Edmund are not the only ones who would like to experience rebirth: James Tyrone, in his own way, is affected by this desire. Conscious that his success as an actor is a form of failure, he admits to his son that if he could, he would change course and head a different way, a way which seems to him to be the one leading to truth (*LDJN* 149). Too late, he has become aware of the corrupting nature of money, against which he was too weak to fight. In his heart of hearts, he knows that what matters is to be in harmony with oneself. It is therefore not without some regret that he admits not having felt this way since he stopped playing difficult stage roles and became imprisoned in a routine which, although financially profitable, has led him to his undoing, for he has broken off with himself.

The family, the subject of the first part of this study, is not extraneous to this theme. We noted that the characters, by using various strategies, sometimes including a journey into the past, longed to shake themselves free of the hold exerted over them by the clan. These two aspects in fact coincide, although they may seem contradictory. In each case, the character tries to find unity by detaching himself from a situation which prevents him from developing as a person. In order to do this, he sometimes has to revert to an earlier state so as to undergo a form of birth that is this time more decisive, by symbolically severing an umbilical cord which thwarts his development. In a more general way, when the characters break off the links which, far from favoring their harmonious development instead give rise to internal divisions, since they are a hindrance to self-assertion, the characters are in fact conquering freedom in order to define their identity outside of the family frame.

Internal cohesion does not imply solitude. We have seen that rebirth could arise out of communion with another character. This rebirth is then the result of a love relationship or simply of empathy, when the person's double, whose complementary aspect is reminiscent of the androgyne, at last provides him with the means of being at one with the world. The union between two people can be likened to the application of a magic balm, which heals their deep wounds and helps them to break free from a duality that has generated unbearable sufferings.

Unity is discovered as one sees oneself as a whole and necessarily in harmony with the rest of the world; suddenly, the individual becomes aware of the convergency of a reality which had seemed fragmentary and the similarity of what had seemed antagonistic. This discovery comes as a supreme gift to those who can seize the existential implications. This moment is common to a number of protagonists who strive for harmony by finding where they belong or by reconciling the conflicting aspects of their personalities.

Homo O'Neillius is a strange specimen insofar as he wishes to be born at least twice—not through a desire for immortality but in order to find himself in a situation comparable to that following his birth, when he was undivided, undefiled, and in symbiosis with the world and those who compose it. As his existence unfolds, others gradually become strangers to him. This distancing causes a moral suffering which he tries to remedy by all possible means throughout his life by searching for supreme harmony.

The journey undertaken sometimes takes the form of a return. Each character almost ceaselessly strives to reconcile the conflicting parts of himself and to reconcile himself with the world or a part of it, thus finally to attain to superior truth. This is why Mary Tyrone's line, which may seem contrapuntal but upon which I have chosen to conclude, reveals the essential: not that happiness is conjugated in the past tense—for it has existed at some actual present—but that it can be found, even if the grace it imparts is ephemeral.

Through writing, O'Neill may have been striving to attain a degree of plenitude he failed to reach otherwise. The freedom he achieved enabled him to live with his ghosts, and gave birth to works which, at times, produce effects identical to those described by Mary. In the rapture of an evening, the author and the audience enter into communion, through the medium of a text interpreted by actors. This feeling, which comes as a godsend, echoes that which the characters feel in the plays: The spectator uncovers the urge that had originally drawn him to the theater. He includes himself in the drama and receives the gift he had come in search of, the revelation of a barely perceptible, impalpable unity, to which he belongs.

Notes and References.

Introduction.

1. *The Calms of Capricorn*. Developed from O'Neill's Scenario by Donald Gallup. With a Transcription of the Scenario (New Haven and New York: Ticknor & Fields, 1982). Ulrich Halfmann, ed., *Eugene O'Neill: Comments on the Drama and the Theatre: A Source Book* (Tübingen: Narr, 1987), 222.
2. I shall sometimes use letters when they shed light on the point at hand.
3. Travis Bogard, *Contour in Time: The Plays of Eugene O'Neill*, rev. ed. (New York: Oxford University Press, 1988), 17–8.
4. Wole Soyinka, *Death and the King's Horseman* (London: Methuen, 1982), 51.

1. The Family and Its Environment.

1. Knowing that the works form a whole and that, in the face of this coherence, any division (family, society, inner world) is necessarily artificial.
2. Louis Sheaffer, *O'Neill: Son and Artist* (Boston: Little, Brown, 1990), 405.
3. In *The Rope*, the relations between grandfather and granddaughter lack cordiality, but he is recognized as such:

> SWEENEY. Here's your cane. (*He gives it to the old man as they come to the doorway and quickly steps back out of reach*) An' mind you don't touch the child with it or I'll beat you to a jelly [*Rope* 584].

4. NINA. I have already! I mean—I am, didn't you understand me?
   MRS. EVANS. (*Gently*) I know it's hard. (*Then inexorably*) But you can't go on! [*SI* 58].
5. See *Mourning Becomes Electra*: "(*Her eyes unconsciously seeking the Mannon portraits on the right wall, as if they were the visible symbol of her God*)."
6. *Ah, Wilderness!* and *The First Man* in which O'Neill lays particular emphasis on presenting the family, in the wider sense of the term, will be dealt with under a separate heading.
7. ELIOT. Said he'd just got in from the West.
   JOHN. I haven't seen him since I was a boy [*DWE* 499].
   LUKE. ... it's Luke—back after five years of bummin' round the rotten old earth in ships and things [*Rope* 588].
8. The important role that Luke plays in *The Rope* is due not to his status as an uncle but to that as a son, coming back to fetch gold.
9. Too much importance cannot be given to this point; Edwin Engel, quite justifiably to my mind, uses the idea of "obsession." "Obsessed with the relationship between himself and his family, O'Neill repeatedly returned to the scene of any known

crimes, his family's and his own. Few writers have wrung so much agony and material for so many plays out of their adolescent years." Edwin Engel, "Ideas in the Plays of Eugene O'Neill," 21–36 in Ernest G. Griffin, ed., *Eugene O'Neill: A Collection of Criticism* (New York: McGraw-Hill, 1976), 23.

    10. The couple will be studied in Part II of this book. The characters will be analyzed here as fathers, mothers, sons or daughters.

    11. "...[I]n the sacrifice of the girl to a maternal deity in the end." Eugene O'Neill, in Judith E. Barlow, *Final Acts: The Creation of Three Late O'Neill Plays* (Athens: University of Georgia Press, 1985), 136.

    12. Cf. *Gold, A Moon for the Misbegotten, The Straw,* and *Where the Cross Is Made.*

    13. "[U]n processus intrapsychique, consécutif à la perte d'un objet d'attachement, et par lequel le sujet réussit progressivement à se détacher de celui-ci." Jean Laplanche, Jean-Baptiste Pontalis, *Vocabulaire de la psychanalyse* (Paris: Presses Universitaires de France, 1967), 504 (my translation into English).

    14. O'Neill, in a letter to Eugene O'Neill, Jr. (7 May 1945). In Travis Bogard and Jackson R. Bryer, eds., *Selected Letters of Eugene O'Neill* (New Haven: Yale University Press, 1988), 569.

    15. "[I]it has the greater possibilities of revealing all the deep hidden relationships in the family than any other of the classic tragedies." Sheaffer, *O'Neill*, 372.

    16. Sheaffer, *O'Neill*, 44.

    17.   EDMUND. It may have been all his fault in the beginning, but you know that later on, even if he'd wanted to, we couldn't have had people here-...
          MARY. Don't. I can't bear having you remind me [*LDJN* 45].

    18. Roger Asselineau, "*Desire Under the Elms:* A Phase of O'Neill's Philosophy," 59–66 in Griffin, ed., *Eugene O'Neill: A Collection*, 61.

    19. In *Anna Christie*, Chris refers to the umbilical cord joining men to the sea:
        ANNA. Was the men in our family always sailors—as far back as you know about?
        CHRIS. All men in our village on coast, Sveden, go to sea [*AC* 27].
In his speech, he always associates the sea with the feminine gender:
        Only dat ole davil, sea—she knows! [*AC* 78].

2. The Imprisoned Person.

    1. We note that in 17 out of the 31 "family" plays constituting this corpus, characters refer explicitly to hereditary factors.

    2. O'Neill, in a letter to Harry Weinberger (24 September 1937). In Bogard and Bryer, eds., *Selected Letters*, 469. (Agnes Boulton was his second wife.)

    3.   LAVINIA. You'd be so handsome if you'd only shave off that silly beard and not carry yourself like a tin-soldier!
        ORIN. Not look so much like Father, eh? [*MBE, The Haunted* 115].

    4.   FATHER. Billy a first-rate, number one architect! That's my proposition! What I've wished I could have been myself! [*GGB* 258].

    5. "If I had wanted to, I could have laid the whole play in the farm interior and made it tight as a drum à la Pinero." O'Neill, in a letter to Barrett H. Clark (13 March 1920). In Bogard and Bryer, eds., *Selected Letters*, 119. If he lacked Thornton Wilder's qualities as a theoretician, he was nevertheless far from being the ignoramus certain critics claimed. As in *Anna Christie*, the outdoors symbolizes here the possiblity of liberation and a desire to flee; at present, we shall examine the reverse component.

    6. In this connection we may recall C. Rollyston's apt remarks: "O'Neill's plays are dominated by rooms and other places with low ceilings, cramped spaces, and other

cages for human inhibition. Each of these constricted environments also typify their characters' lack of refuge. Carl E. Rollyson, Jr., "Eugene O'Neill: The Drama of Self-Transcendence," 123–137 in James J. Martine, ed., *Critical Essays on Eugene O'Neill* (Boston: G.K. Hall, 1984), 125.

    7. CHRISTINE. Oh, why can't we go away, Adam? Once we're out of her reach, she can't do anything [*MBE, The Hunted* 111].

    8. The same journey with the same result occurs in *All God's Chillun Got Wings*.

    9. This theme recurs in *The First Man*, where flight characterizes the couple's inability to face their children's death.

    10. Robert Feldman, "The Longing for Death in O'Neill's *Strange Interlude* and *Mourning Becomes Electra*," *Literature and Psychology* 31, 1 (1981): 46.

    11. "Le tragique est produit par un conflit inévitable et insoluble, non pas par une série de catastrophes ou de phénomènes naturels horribles, mais à cause d'une fatalité qui s'acharne sur l'existence humaine. Le mal tragique est irrémédiable." Patrice Pavis, *Dictionnaire du théâtre* (Paris: Éditions Sociales, 1980), 427 (my translation into English).

    12. The stones with which they break a window echo their words about the walls; throwing stones symbolizes their liberation:

        PETER. —stones atop o' stones—makin' stone walls—year atop o' year—him 'n' yew 'n' me 'n' then Eben—makin' stone walls fur him to fence us in! [*DE* 204].

    13. Reuben, in *Dynamo*, comes back with the hope of finding his mother.

    14. This point is expounded in Thierry Dubost, "Renaissance dans *Strange Interlude*," *Americana* 12 (1995): 69–81.

    15. MELODY. The gintleman's sneers he put on is buried with him. I'll be a real husband to you, and help ye run this shebeen, instead of being a sponge [*TP* 174].

3. Relations Between the Characters.

    1. This may seem surprising as O'Neill himself, up to his very deathbed, keenly felt the lack of home life: "[He] raised himself slightly and gasped: 'Born in a hotel room—and God damn it—died in a hotel room!'" Arthur Gelb and Barbara Gelb, *O'Neill*, rev. ed. (New York: Harper and Row, 1987), 939.

    2. "Perhaps I could do with less progeny about for I was never cut out, seemingly, for a pater familias and children in squads, even when indubitably my own, tend to 'get my goat.'" O'Neill, in a letter to Kenneth Macgowan (7 August 1926). In Bogard and Bryer, eds., *Selected Letters*, 210.

    3. It would be difficult to provide an exhaustive list, as some secondary characters may correspond to this criterion, but they appear in the following plays: *Bread and Butter, Desire Under the Elms, Dynamo, Gold, Mourning Becomes Electra, Where the Cross Is Made*, and *Long Day's Journey into Night*.

    4. This has been brought to light by Patrick Bowles, and this aspect is not limited to *Desire Under the Elms*. "And finally, there is Ephraim, whose name suggests the progenitor of the tribes of Israël. These four names are not only appropriate to the rural New England setting of 1850, but resonate well with the legalistic Old Testament ethos of the play as a whole." Patrick Bowles, "Another Biblical Parallel in *Desire Under the Elms*," *Eugene O'Neill Newsletter* 2 (1979): 11.

    5. During the first scene, he wishes to reveal his affliction to his employers, but his wife dissuades him and he recoils before the financial consequences, which would be disastrous for his family. The now deaf radio operator is no longer able to carry out his job correctly and leads his boat to disaster.

6. In this rewritten version of the return of the prodigal son, Bentley, whose son has stolen some of his money, has tied the rest of his savings to a rope. Bentley gives his son to understand that he must hang himself for his crime in order to be forgiven; in fact, the gold is to drop just as the hanging begins. Luke believes that his father really wishes him to hang himself, and strikes the old man.

7. One may quote, for example, the compliment paid to his son by Ephraim Cabot, in the last scene:
> CABOT. (*He comes forward—stares at* EBEN *with a trace of grudging admiration*) Purty good—fur yew! [*DE* 269].

8. In *Strange Interlude*, Marsden (35) is presented primarily as his mother's son:
> NINA. Apron strings... still his devotion to her is touching... I hope if mine is a boy he will love me as much [*SI* 51].

9. Cf. *The Rope, Desire Under the Elms*, and *A Moon for the Misbegotten*. This idea is explicitly expressed in *Where the Cross Is Made*:
> SUE. Two thousand! Why, over and above the mortgage, it's worth—
> NAT. It's not what it's worth. It's what one can get, cash—for my book—for freedom! [*WCIM* 565].

10. O'Neill, in a letter to Beatrice Ashe (25 July 1916). In Bogard and Bryer, eds., *Selected Letters*, 71.

11. Captain Bartlett believed he had discovered treasure on a desert island, but to avoid disclosure he allowed two men to be assassinated. The survivors catch gold fever and the crew set sail without him. In spite of overwhelming evidence, he refuses to believe his boat has sunk with his crew, and manages to convince his son that the ship will eventually come back with the treasure.

12. In *Gold*, a rewriting of *Where the Cross Is Made*, Bartlett is in possession of what he believes to be a map of the treasure island, but refuses to share his secret with Nat; this time, the father's prohibition can be explained by the fear of seeing the curse falling upon him. He eventually tells him the whole story, then shows him a sample, which turns out to be worthless.

13. This theme of honesty towards oneself is to my mind what differentiates this play from the earlier one, for this time Bartlett tells his son the whole truth, and the conclusion seems to be that whatever the circumstances, one must say everything. This difference seems to me to justify this interpretation; another theory could be the reply made by O'Neill to a journalist. He was asked if he didn't agree that he was "full of paradoxes." "What did Walt Whitman say?" O'Neill replied. "He said, 'Do I contradict myself? Well, I contradict myself.'" In Crosswell Bowen, *The Curse of the Misbegotten: A Tale of the House of O'Neill* (New York: McGraw-Hill, 1959), 311.

14. *The Straw* stages a variation of this confrontation.

15. Cf. *A Touch of the Poet*: The welfare of his mare is more important to Con Melody than that of his family.

16. This is not a unique occurrence; cf. *Desire Under the Elms* and *The Rope*. *The Rope* proves that the roles may be reversed, and that the elder generation can opt for clemency.

17. This emerges clearly in *Desire Under the Elms* and *A Moon for the Misbegotten* and somewhat less obviously in *Gold, Where the Cross Is Made, Mourning Becomes Electra* and *Long Day's Journey into Night*.

18. See for instance:
> MANNON. When I came back you had turned to your new baby, Orin. I was hardly alive for you anymore. I saw that. I tried not to hate Orin [*MBE*, Homecoming 55].

The rivalry is heightened by the fact that the type of love the men hope to arouse in their wives is very close to maternal love.

19. Cf. *The Rope*, and also Eben's satisfaction in *Desire Under the Elms*, when he thinks that Abbie has killed Cabot.

20. The only two instances in which son-father relationships are good, are in *Abortion*, but here we noted a blurring of the parent-child relationship, and in *Warnings*, in which dramatic irony brings about the enslavement (kidnapping?) of Knapp by the sincere and mutual affection between himself and his children, and leads him, in spite of himself, to a tragic end.

21. "C'est le cri expressionniste, le cri de la révolte contre l'autorité paternelle— contre toute autorité, c'est la manifestation de la volonté de libération, du désir d'être soi-même." Gabriela Szigeti, "L'Expressionnisme européen et un de ses reflets outre-atlantique: l'œuvre de Eugene O'Neill," dissertation, University of Paris–Sorbonne, 1985, 232 (my translation into English).

22. In the second part of this book we shall come back to the criticism of society, such as it appears in the works. *The Personal Equation*, which is a rewriting of *The Second Engineer*, is the only play in which there is a total opposition between the father, Perkins, who symbolizes American values, and his son, Tom, a member of "International Workers of the Earth," who tries to sabotage the engines of the boat that is his father's reponsibility. Tom is a dominating character, as opposed to Perkins, an insignificant creature, who suffers from his inability to establish a satisfactory relationship with his son.

23. *He carries himself woodenly erect now, like a soldier. His movements and attitudes have the same statue-like quality that was so marked in his father. He now wears a close-cropped beard in addition to his mustache, and this accentuates his resemblance to his father* [*MBE, The Haunted* 137].

24. Gordon's attitude towards his real father is revealing:
   GORDON. I hope he never comes back! ... Why did I like him then?... it was only for a second... [*SI* 152].
He does not manage to achieve perfect hate, and tries to find the reason for this; for the spectator, his attitude can be explained by a sort of instinctive love. This seems to be the theory upheld by O'Neill.

25. See for instance:
   ORIN. I had a queer feeling that war meant murdering the same man over and over, and that in the end I would discover the man was myself! Their faces keep coming back in dreams—and they change to Father's face—or to mine [*MBE, Homecoming* 95].

26. O'Neill, in a letter to his son, aged eight at the time, asking him to take care of his mother and sister, shows the regard he had for women: "You're the only O'Neill man down there now, and I'm relying on you to see that none of these fool women get into trouble! However, they can't help being that way because it isn't their fault they were born girls." O'Neill, in a letter to Shane O'Neill (September 1927). In Bogard and Bryer, eds., *Selected Letters*, 256.

27. *Now I Ask You*, O'Neill's first comedy, deals with this conflict between two generations in a comic mode. Lucy advocates free love, and challenges the traditional values embodied in her father, who is completely disconcerted by her attitude.

28. CHRIS. (*In agony*) Don't talk dat vay, Anna! Ay von't listen! (*Puts his hands over his ears.*) [*AC* 58].
   PROFESSOR LEEDS. (*Thinking worriedly*) I hope she won't make a scene... she's seemed on the verge all day [*SI* 12].

29. PROFESSOR LEEDS. I wanted to live comforted by your love until the end. In short, I am a man who happens to be your father... Forgive that man! [*SI* 20].
This possessive love, close to jealousy, also comes out in *Dynamo*, when Fife is unpleasant to Reuben. Nevertheless, Mrs. Fife lays down its limits when she implies that her

daughter's happiness is more important to her husband than the jealousy which prompts him to attack Reuben:
>MRS. FIFE. He'd be mean at first to any man he thought you cared for [*Dy* 456].

30. Judith Barlow, "O'Neill's Many Mothers: Mary Tyrone, Josie Hogan and Their Antecedents," in Shyamal Bagchee, *Perspectives on O'Neill: New Essays* (Victoria, B.C.: University of Victoria, 1988), 7.

31. Josie Hogan, the heroine of *A Moon for the Misbegotten*, embodies, both literally and figuratively, the force of nature which dominates the men, and is able to bring them the happiness they long for.

32. Lavinia's final slip provides clear evidence of this, and some critics have laid great stress on this legacy:
>LAVINIA. Want me! Take me, Adam! (*She is brought back to herself with a start by this name escaping her—bewilderedly, laughing idiotically*) Adam? Why did I call you Adam? [*MBE, The Haunted* 177].

33. "Il commence à désirer la mère elle-même, au sens qui vient de s'ouvrir pour lui et à haïr de nouveau le père, comme un rival qui se met en travers de son désir." "He begins to desire the mother herself, in the sense which has just opened for him, and to hate the father once again as a rival who thwarts his desire." Sigmund Freud, *La Vie sexuelle* (Paris: Presses Universitaires de France, 1969), 52 (my translation). Freud was conscious of the differences between the Oedipus and the Electra complexes, but the author simply applies to Lavinia a reversed Oedipus complex.

34. LAVINIA. I'm going to stay with you.
>MANNON. (*Patting her hair—with gruff tenderness*) I hope so. I want you to remain my little girl—for a while longer at least [*MBE, Homecoming* 51].

35. SARA. It brings back the past. It makes Father live again. Ah, why can't he be dead—and not have his ghost walk in my heart with the sneer on his lips! [*MSM* 43].

36. Nina is the only character who refuses this task, although this does not imply total rejection of her father.

37. *The Straw* is an exception since Eileen is never staged in this role, for the very first scene shows her to be ailing. However certain indications allow one to suppose that she enjoyed an autonomy similar to that granted the other daughters.

38. One recalls an episode from *The First Man*, which sums up what the family and society expect from a woman, once she is married:
>MRS. DAVIDSON. I never liked that woman. I never understood her. But now—now I love her and beg her forgiveness. She died like a true woman in the performance of her duty. She died gloriously—and I will always respect her memory [*FM* 616].

39. See for instance:
>HOGAN. (*With admiring appreciation*) Yes, she could do it, God bless her. I only raised my hand to her once—just a slap because she told me to stop singing, it was after daylight. The next moment I was on the floor thinking a mule had kicked me [*MMis* 12].

40. This image of the mother as an ideal, protective figure occurs in quite a large number of plays: *Abortion, Ah, Wilderness!, All God's Chillun Got Wings, Beyond the Horizon, Before Breakfast, Desire Under the Elms* (Eben's mother), *Fog, The Great God Brown, A Moon for the Misbegotten, Now I Ask You, The Rope, Servitude, A Touch of the Poet,* and *Where the Cross Is Made*.

41. TIBERIUS. We were happy. Then that proud woman, my mother, saw my happiness. Was she jealous of my love? [*LL* 356].

42. Cf. Christine in *Mourning Becomes Electra*, Nina in *Strange Interlude*, Deborah in *More Stately Mansions* and Mrs. Light in *Dynamo*. This feeling is not shared by everybody:
>DEBORAH. I have forgotten him several times before in my life. Completely as if he had never been born. That is what he has never forgiven [*MSM* 222].

43. One recalls the attempted dialogue between Edmund and Mary (*LDJN*), and the reproach made by Orin to Christine:
ORIN. So lonely you've written me exactly two letters in the last six months! [*MBE, The Hunted* 84].
44. Barlow, *Final Acts*, 138.
45. Suicide is a means of ending their suffering; cf. *Abortion, Dynamo, A Moon for the Misbegotten,* and *Mourning Becomes Electra*.
46. TIBERIUS. My mother—her blood is in that blot, for I revenged myself on her. I did not kill her, it is true, but I deprived her of her power and she died, as I knew she must, that powerful woman who bore me as a weapon! [*LL* 355].
47. See for instance:
REUBEN. Mother! ... where are you? ... I did it for your sake! [*Dy* 488].
48. We shall come back to this complex aspect in the course of Part III of this work. For the present, I shall limit my remarks to the following observation: the only one who successfully manages the relationship with his mother is Eben, who, after having obtained what he feels is her consent, is in a position to define himself as an individual.
49. In *A Moon for the Misbegotten*, Josie Hogan is also presented as a reincarnation of her mother:
HOGAN. Since you've grown up, I've had the same trouble. There's no liberty in my own home [*MMis* 12].
After Christine's death, Lavinia is presented as her double:
She now bears a striking resemblance to her mother in every respect, even to being dressed in the green her mother had affected [*MBE, The Haunted* 137].
50. The interest of the melancholy Mrs. Atkins, who sets the couple at loggerheads and who embodies the other possible facet of the mother figure (her double in the play being Mrs. Mayo), is somewhat limited.
51. Christine admits her abhorrence for her daughter, and entertains no illusions as to Lavinia's feelings:
CHRISTINE. After all, Vinnie, I am your mother. I brought you to the world. You ought to have some feeling for me [*MBE, The Hunted* 76].
52. LAVINIA. I've felt it ever since I can remember—your disgust! (*Then with a flare-up of bitter hatred*) Oh, I hate you! It's only right I should hate you! [*MBE, Homecoming* 31].
53. CHRISTINE. You've tried to become the wife of your father and the mother of Orin! [*MBE, Homecoming* 33].
54. Only Lavinia puts forward her own desires:
LAVINIA. I want a moment of joy—of love—to make up for what's coming! [*MBE, The Haunted* 177]
before her individuality disappears, crushed under Mannon's weight.
55. *All are dressed in the height of correct Prep-school elegance. They are all tall, athletic, strong and handsome looking* [*GGB* 324].
56. *He is a tall, slender young man of twenty three. There is a touch of the poet about him expressed in his high forehead and wide dark eyes* [*BH* 81].
57. This Manicheism is also found in *More Stately Mansions*, when Joel is despised by Simon, the poet who has become a triumphant industrialist; the primary contrast, between the genius and the office drudge, detracts from the characters' interest.
58. One recalls Jamie's advice:
JAMIE. Make up your mind you've got to tie a can to me—get me out of your life— think of me as dead—tell people, "I had a brother, but he's dead" [*LDJN* 166].
59. TOWNSEND. Come, Jack, that is pure evasion. You are responsible for the Mr. Hyde in you as well as for the Dr. Jekyll [*Ab* 155].
60. ORIN. Perhaps I love you too much, Vinnie!
LAVINIA. You don't know what you're saying!

ORIN. *There are times now when you don't seem to be my sister, nor Mother, but some stranger with the same beautiful hair*—(*He touches her hair caressingly*) [*MBE, The Haunted* 165].

61. This is not the case for Hattie in *All God's Chillun Got Wings*, a play which stages the clash between Hattie and Jim, Hattie trying to persuade her brother to break up with his white wife. The fraternal link is severed when Hattie can no longer bear seeing her race insulted, but Jim prefers this estrangement to the prospect of losing Ella.

4. From the Microcosm to the Macrocosm.

1. The cycle remained unfinished, but with time it had grown: "The following day, he takes up *More Stately Mansions*, working on it continuously until January 20, 1939. The next two days he writes general notes 'on all 9 plays, interrelationship.'" Virginia Floyd, ed., *Eugene O'Neill: A World View* (New York: Frederick Ungar, 1979), 221.
2. Gelb and Gelb, *O'Neill*, 804.
3. LILY. (*Stops at the door in rear and catching Martha's eye, looks meaningly at the others*) Phew! I need fresh air! [*FM* 571].
4. MARY. Big frogs in a small puddle. It is stupid of Jamie. *She pauses, looking out of the window*—*then with an undercurrent of lonely yearning.* Still, the Chatfields and people like them stand for something [*LDJN* 43–4].
5. The stakes had been laid down by Lily in Act One.
   LILY. The trouble with Bigelow, Martha, is that he was too careless to conceal his sins—and that won't go down in this Philistine small town. You have to hide and be a fellow hypocrite or they revenge themselves on you [*FM* 559].
6. This reminds one of what was said in one of the author's first plays:
   TOWNSEND. We've retained a large proportion of the original mud in our make-up [*Ab* 154].
7. In this connection, Kublai's judgment of Marco is edifying:
   KUBLAI. He has not even a mortal soul, he has only an acquisitive instinct. We have given him every opportunity to learn. He has memorized everything and learned nothing. He has looked at everything and seen nothing. He has lusted for everything and loved nothing. He is only a shrewd and crafty greed. I shall send him home to his native wallow [*MM* 387].
8. Marco shows himself to be incapable of understanding the person concealed within Kukachin, while she sketches a realistic portrait of her chaperon:
   KUKACHIN. I implored an ox to see my soul! [*MM* 415].
9. One remembers the pride of John Jayson, the advocate of this philosophy, and O'Neill's irony towards him:
   JOHN. It's one of the most prosperous and wealthy towns in the U.S.—and that means in the world, nowadays [*FM* 571].

5. The Image of the Family.

1. In *Mourning Becomes Electra*, the Mannons' house, which symbolizes this dynasty, was erected in hatred, the ferments of which have an effect on the following generations:
   CHRISTINE. It was just like old Abe Mannon to build such a monstrosity—as a temple for his hatred [*MBE, Homecoming* 17].
2. One notes a similarity in the exchanges in *Ah, Wilderness!* and *The First Man*. The reaction of the unmarried women show how sore this point is:

MARTHA. You're lonely, that's what, Lily.
LILY. (*Dryly*) Don't pity me, Martha—or I'll join the enemy [*FM* 561].
MRS. MILLER. You that would have made such a wonderful wife for any man—that ought to have your own home and children!
LILY. (*Winces but puts her arm around her affectionately—gently*) Now don't you go feeling sorry for me. I won't have that [*AhW* 214].

3. Cf. Olga in *The Personal Equation*; she is pregnant at the end of the play but had previously declared:
OLGA. (*Passionately*) We'll never have children. No, no, anything but that! I would go through anything, kill myself rather than have that happen! [*PE* 11].
Before changing her mind, in *Now I Ask You*, another of the earlier works, Lucy declares:
LUCY. It is mutually agreed there shall be no children by our union. (*Directing a searching look at Tom*) I know you're far too intelligent not to believe in birth control [*NIAY* 133].

4. "And, of course, Dalmatians are not only superior to other dogs, they are like all dogs, infinitely less stupid than men." O'Neill, in a letter to Sophus Keith Winther (26 December 1942). In Bogard and Bryer, eds., *Selected Letters*, 539.

5. This point of view can be explained by O'Neill's optimism—albeit a moderate one—in the future of humanity: "I am sorry if I have said something to affront your faith in an upward spiral of mankind. Because I myself believe that perhaps a million years from now it may begin to dawn on Man (only when he has a crying jag, I fear) that he has been a damned fool." O'Neill, in the letter to Winther, Bogard and Bryer, eds., *Selected Letters*, 539.

6. Keeping in mind the line quoted in note 7 (immediately below), one could say that *Long Day's Journey into Night* is the same play, showing, this time, "what his adolescence had been."

7. *Ah, Wilderness!*, said O'Neill, was a nostalgic dream of what he would have liked his adolescence to have been: "The Truth is I *had* no youth." Gelb and Gelb, *O'Neill*, 81.

8. MILLER. But this looks—I wonder if he is hanging around her to see what he can get? (*Angrily*) By God, if that's true, he deserves that licking McComber says it's my duty to give him! I've got to draw the line somewhere! [*AhW* 205].

7. *Worlds and the Representation of Them.*

1. This does not imply fixity: In *Anna Christie*, we go from a scene in a bar to a scene outside, which is followed by a scene on a ship. We see that even in the exterior scenes presented in *Beyond the Horizon* or *A Moon for the Misbegotten*, the space in which the characters find themselves is open to nature, but remains turned in on itself, enclosed by imaginary walls. The exterior scenes do not therefore mark the unification of the characters and society.

2. Thus, *A Wife for a Life* takes place in the desert, outside, but the interior-exterior opposition matters very little to our present study. What we are concerned with is the idea of a universe which is limited, or isolated from the rest of the world.

3. For the symbol of fog, see also *Bound East for Cardiff* and *Fog*; for the symbol of sounds, see also *Abortion*, *The Emperor Jones*, *Long Day's Journey into Night*, *The Moon of the Caribbees*, and *Strange Interlude*.

4. The meeting of people from different milieux can take place in street scenes, but these are rare. We remember Yank (*The Hairy Ape*) in the streets of New York and the impossibility of contact with the city dwellers, not to mention Jim and Ella (*All*

God's Chillun Got Wings) playing in the street, and the few crowd scenes in *Lazarus Laughed* and *Marco Millions*.

5. We remember the difficulties associated with the production of a play such as *Lazarus Laughed*. "In *Lazarus Laughed*, O'Neill's experimentation with masks reached its peak (at least quantitatively). All characters except Lazarus wore masks, resulting in a total of three hundred masks for staging the play at Pasadena." Ronald H. Wainscott, *Staging O'Neill* (New Haven: Yale University Press, 1988), 221.

6. Jean Chothia quotes another revealing example: "More typically, perhaps, the zoo scene still has 61 lines of directions to 86 of speech." Jean Chothia, "Theatre Language: Word and Image in *The Hairy Ape*," 31–46 in Marc Maufort, ed., *Eugene O'Neill and the Emergence of American Drama* (Amsterdam: Rodopi, 1989), 32.

7. Two very useful works edited by Virginia Floyd, *The Unfinished Plays* and *Eugene O'Neill at Work*, show how necessary it was for him to develop his ideas in written form and through drawings, before beginning the writing of the dialogues.

8. "...[S]ome of the playwright's intentions are impossible to render. Many of the stage directions, even if carried out, could only work for the first eight rows of a narrow theater's stalls." Ann Massa, "Intention and Effect in *The Hairy Ape*," *Modern Drama* 31, 1 (1988): 49.

9. Nancy Roberts and Arthur Roberts, eds., *As Ever, Gene: The Letters of Eugene O'Neill to George Jean Nathan* (Rutherford, N.J.: Fairleigh Dickinson University Press, 1987), 50.

10. Jones' throne is obviously a counter-example, and will have to be placed in a second category, namely that of a sign which is symbolic of power.

> *The room is bare of furniture with the exception of one huge chair made of uncut wood which stands at center, its back to rear. This is very apparently the Emperor's throne* [*EJ* 173].

11. This limited reading has not entirely disappeared: "...the Provincetown group created ... a vivid tragedy of labor, *The Hairy Ape*." Malcom Goldstein, *The Political Stage* (New York: Oxford University Press, 1974), 6.

12. "I somehow feel there's enough in it to get over to unsophisticated audiences. In one sense, *Brown* is a mystery play, only instead of dealing with crooks and police it's about the mystery of personality and life. I shouldn't be surprised if it interested people who won't bother too much over every shade of meaning, but follow it as they follow any story. They needn't understand with their minds, they can just watch and feel." Eugene O'Neill in Barrett H. Clark, *Eugene O'Neill: The Man and His Plays* (New York: Dover Publications, 1967), 162.

13. We think of the production of *The Rime of the Ancient Mariner* and the comments of George Jean Nathan: "O'Neill's theory of dramatizing the Coleridge ululation reposed in the typical cinema notion of leaving nothing to the imagination. While an actor declaimed the lines ... a group of sailors engaged in retailing a pantomimic accompaniment." George J. Nathan, *"The Rime of the Ancient Mariner,"* in Oscar Cargill, N. Bryllion Fagin, and William J. Fisher, eds., *O'Neill and His Plays: Four Decades of Criticism* (New York: New York University Press, 1961), 166.

14. "The hell of it seems to be, when an artist starts saving the world, he starts losing himself. I know, I have been bitten by the salvationist bug myself at times." O'Neill, in a letter to George Jean Nathan (13 May 1939). In Bogard and Bryer, eds., *Selected Letters*, 486.

15. His change in attitude motivated by the Second World War is evidence of this: "The author was deeply disturbed during this period by the threat fascism posed to the free world; he was annoyed by "Hitler's war speech against Poland" (work diary 8/31/39) and his subsequent invasion of that defenseless country. A few months later

on January 4, 1940, he records his first idea for a political propaganda play, *The Visit of Malatesta*." Virginia Floyd, ed., *The Unfinished Plays: Notes for The Visit of Malatesta, The Last Conquest, Blind Alley Guy* (New York: Ungar, 1988), xv.

16. "Time was when I was an active socialist, and, after that, a philosophical anarchist. But today, I can't feel that anything like that really matters." O'Neill, "What the Theatre Means to Me," in Cargill, Fagin, and Fisher, eds., *O'Neill and His Plays*, 107.

17. We may also remember this caustic vision: "LARRY. (*Sardonically*) It's a great game, the pursuit of happiness" (*IC* 19).

18. Jane Torrey, "O'Neill's Psychology of Oppression in Men and Women," in Richard F. Moorton, Jr., ed., *Eugene O'Neill's Century: Centennial Views on America's Foremost Tragic Dramatist* (Westport, Conn.: Greenwood, 1991), 165.

19. MRS. HARRIS. (*Solemnly*) De white and de black shouldn't mix dat close [*AGCGW* 323].

To my mind, we must consider Mrs. Harris more as the spokesperson for a community (cf. Seth's friends in *Mourning Becomes Electra*) than as a minor character.

20. SECOND VOICE. The child was diseased at birth, stricken with a hereditary ill that only the most vital men are able to shake off.
FIRST VOICE. You mean?
SECOND VOICE. I mean poverty—the most deadly and prevalent of all diseases [*Fog* 89].

21. There is no shortage of examples, *Abortion*, *The First Man* or *The Straw*, among others. I quote the following because it is revealing of a state of mind represented many times:
PROFESSOR LEEDS. I think, the boy, for all his good looks and prowess in sport and his courses, really came of common people and had no money of his own except as he made a career for himself [*SI* 9].

22. Edward, for example, wishes to wipe out from people's memory that which could be a hindrance to his political success.
EDWARD. (*Shocked—considering his father's acknowledgment of his humble origin a grave social error*) You have risen beyond all such comparisons [*B&B* 9].

23. His point of view is close to that which we find in *Thus Spake Zarathustra*, on the subject of the crowd: "Where solitude endeth, there beginneth the market-place; and where the market-place beginneth there beginneth also the noise of the great actors, and the buzzing of the poison flies." Friedrich Nietzsche, *Thus Spake Zarathustra* (London: T. N. Foulis, 1911), 57.

24. SARA. ...and write a book about how the world can be changed so people won't be so greedy to own money and land and get the best of each other but will be content with little and live in peace and freedom together, and it will be like heaven on earth. (*She laughs fondly—and a bit derisively.*) I can't remember all of it. It seems crazy to me, when I think of what people are like [*TP* 29].

25. Frederick I. Carpenter, *Eugene O'Neill* (Boston: Twayne, 1979), 135.

26. We can see how far they have come by the following exchange:
SIMON. As you know there's been some discontent about our lowering wages and the hands are sending a deputation to ask me to reconsider.
SARA.(*Her face hardening—commandingly*) You put your foot down on that! Fire them! There's plenty to take their place, and starving will teach them a lesson. [*MSM* 236].

27. Cf. *Servitude* 238-9 and this:
TYRONE. But land is land, and it's safer than the stocks and bonds of Wall Street swindlers [*LDJN* 15].

28. Another example of self-destruction, this time on a larger scale, is war, the motives for which are never given (*In the Zone, Mourning Becomes Electra, Shell Shock,*

The Sniper, Marco Millions, Strange Interlude), and of which the devastating effects are reinforced by its absurd and suicidal aspects; cf. Orin, *MBE*.

29. We can only agree with Michael Basile's comments: "Although O'Neill insisted throughout his career that "the Negro question ... it must be remembered, is not an issue in the play" [quoted in Gelb 536], his public felt otherwise." Michael Basile, "Semiotic Transformability in *All God's Chillun Got Wings*," *Eugene O'Neill Review* 16, 1 (spring 1992): 26. Without exaggerating the point, the repeated refusal, aimed at denying the importance of this theme, recalls what he said about Freud's having no influence on his writing, and we have seen the limits of this.

30. Speech of Alfred Jarry, at the première of *Ubu Roi*, in Alfred Jarry, *Tout Ubu* (Paris: Le livre de Poche, Librairie Générale Française, 1962), 21.

31. Clark, *Eugene O'Neill*, 152–3.

32. In Pittsburgh it was damned by the secretary of the local Chamber of Commerce, and in Detroit it was closed on the night of its second performance by a police censor who considered it an obscene slander on American motherhood, and demanded that the work be rewritten. He adds in a footnote: "Miss Marshall's account is quoted in *The Magic Curtain*, 408. The charges of obscenity arose from such sensitivity as the discovery that the words 'mother' and 'prostitute' were used in the same sentence." Bogard, *Contour in Time*, 452.

33. When *Desire Under the Elms* premiered at the Greenwich Village Theatre, on November 11, 1924, most reviewers were shocked. "A tale of almost unrelieved sordidness," the *Post* declared, and *Time* concurred, calling it "the kind of thing the spectator will object to on the score that existence cannot possibly be so brutal." Susan H. Tuck, "Reviews of O'Neill Plays in Performance," *Eugene O'Neill Newsletter* 7, 1 (spring 1983): 15.

34. Franck Tetauer, "Tragic Wandering" in Horst Frenz and Susan Tuck, eds., *Eugene O'Neill's Critics: Voices from Abroad* (Carbondale: Southern Illinois University Press, 1984), 21.

35. "I loathe also this great city, and not only this fool. Here and there—there is nothing to better, nothing to worsen. Woe to this great city! And I would that I already saw the pillar of fire in which it will be consumed. For such pillars of fire must precede the great noontide." Nietzsche, *Thus Spake Zarathustra*, 217.

36. But it is difficult to go along with Lionel Trilling when he declares: "It is the ultimate of individual arrogance, the final statement of a universe in which society has no part. For O'Neill, since as far back as *The Hairy Ape*, there has been only the individual and the universe. The social organization has meant nothing." Lionel Trilling, "Eugene O'Neill," in Harold Bloom, ed., *Eugene O'Neill* (New York: Chelsea, 1987), 19. The social component cannot be reduced to nothing, even if the relationship of humanity to the universe is undoubtedly important.

8. *The Place of the Human Being in the World.*

1. O'Neill, "On Man and God," in Cargill, Fagin, and Fisher, eds., *O'Neill and His Plays*, 115.

2. A variant of Erie's speech can be found in *A Moon for the Misbegotten*, where Hogan suggests to his daughter that he should come to her room the following morning with witnesses in order to force James Tyrone to marry her. O'Neill had envisaged using the same strategy in *The Visit of Malatesta*.

3. ERIE. Hughie and her seemed happy enough the time he had me out to dinner in their flat. Well, not happy. Maybe contented. No, that's boosting it, too. Resigned comes nearer, as if each was givin' the other a break by thinking, "Well, what more could I expect?" [*Hu* 24].
4. "For the most part, O'Neill's female characters are perceived from outside, from a masculine perspective that wishfully invests them with powerful maternal desires or condemns them for the lack of such feelings." Barlow, "O' Neill's Many Mothers," in Bagchee, *Perspectives*, 7.
5. NINA. Yes, you're here, Charlie—always! And you, Sam—and Ned! (*With strange gaiety*) Sit down, all of you! Make yourselves at home! You are my three men! This is your home with me! (*Then in a strange half whisper*) Ssshh! I thought I heard the baby. You must all sit down and be very quiet. You must not wake our baby [*SI* 133].

Father, husband, lover, the trilogy surfaces again, this time in the opposite sense, demonstrating the necessity of finding someone capable of fulfilling the specific needs for each role. Another illustration of this:

ELSA. Oh, much more so, for he's become my child and father now, as well as being husband and—
LUCY. Lover. Say it [*DWE* 518].
6. THE DONKEYMAN. (*Spitting placidly*) Queer things, mem'ries. I ain't ever been bothered much by 'em. ...
SMITTY. But suppose you couldn't put them out of your mind? Suppose they haunted you when you were awake and when you were asleep—what then?
THE DONKEYMAN. (*Quietly*) I'd get drunk, same's you're doin' [*MCa* 467].

The hope of an alcoholic amnesia proves to be illusory. At the end of the play, Smitty is still haunted by his memories, in spite of all the rum he has consumed.

7. ORIN. Do you know his nickname in the army? Old Stick—short for Stick in the Mud. Grant himself started it—said Father was no good on an offensive but he'd trust him to stick in the mud and hold a position until hell froze over!
LAVINIA. Orin! Don't you realize he was your father and he is dead?
ORIN. (*Irritably*) What Grant said was a big compliment in a way [*MBE, The Hunted* 94].
8. It does not seem possible to me to subscribe to John Alvis' vision—
As with Ezra Mannon, the pretense of public service actually serves passions of vanity and greed and thus is a parcel of Edmund's despised world of "lousy, pitiful, greedy fears and hopes."

John Alvis, "On the American Line: O'Neill's *Mourning Becomes Electra* and the Principles of the Founding," *Southern Review* 22, 1 (winter 1986): 83—when we consider his critique in the light of what Mannon says:

MANNON. That's why the shipping wasn't enough—why I became a judge and a mayor and such vain truck, and why folks in town look on me as so able! Ha! Able for what? Not for what I wanted most in life! Not for your love! No! Able only to keep my mind from thinking of what I'd lost! [*MBE, Homecoming* 55].
9. The veil is torn aside with a violence that Mary does not hesitate to point out:
MARY. But I must confess, James, although I couldn't help loving you, I would never have married you if I'd known that you drank so much. I remember the first night your barroom friends had to help you up to the door of our hotel room, and knocked and then ran away before I came to the door. We were still on our honeymoon, do you remember? [*LDJN* 113].

We find similar realizations in *Before Breakfast*, *Bread and Butter*, *The Iceman Cometh*, *Mourning Becomes Electra*, *Recklessness*, and *A Wife for a Life*.

10. We note that in couples, a triangular relationship is set up with the world or its representatives. Jealousy can be provoked by a third party, by children, or simply by the existence of a universe outside of the individuals, whence the frequent evocation

of desert islands, which symbolize not only a return to childhood but also a desire for total communion with the other person.

   11. O'Neill presents an opposition of archetypes which contaminate the characters and dominate them (the id expresses itself without their being able to react to it), and this brings about incessant confrontations.
   12. EBEN. I was waiting. I got to thinkin' o' yew. I got to thinkin' how I'd loved ye. It hurt like somethin' was burstin' in my chest an' head. I got t' cryin'. I knowed sudden I loved ye yet, an' allus would love ye! [*DE* 266].
   13. LEDA. Aren't we animals? Can you go to bed with a soul? Poetic drivel aside, love may start in heaven, but it goes on or dies in bed [*The Calms of Capricorn*].
In Bogard, *Contour in Time*, 387.
   14. The androgyne, *symbol of totality*, thus appears at both the end and the beginning of time. In the eschatological vision of salvation, the human being restores a wholeness where the separation of the sexes is repealed. This is what the *mystery of marriage* evokes in numerous traditional texts, by joining in this way the image of Siva and his Shakti. "...L'union de la *semence* et du *souffle* pour la production de l'Embryon d'immortalité se fait dans le corps même du *yogi*. Le retour à l'état primordial, la libération des contingences cosmiques se font par la *coincidentia oppositorum* et la réalisation de l'unité première: fondre *ming* et *sing*, disent les alchimistes chinois, les deux polarités de l'être." "...The union of *seed* and *breath* for the production of the Embryon of immortality is accomplished within the actual body of *yogi*. The return to the original state, the liberation of the cosmic contingencies is brought about by the *coincidentia oppositorum* and the realization of the first unity: merging *ming* and *sing*, as the Chinese alchemists say, the two polarities of the human entity." Jean Chevalier and Alain Gheerbrant, eds., *Dictionnaire des symboles* (Paris: Robert Laffont, 1982), 40 (my translation). We know of the interest the author had in Oriental philosophies; the figure of the androgyne, described above, is compatible with the Platonic legend, and seems to have found its place in the plays.
   15. The idea of union, of wholeness found at last, is taken up again in *Welded*, where Cape gives it a more scientific tone.
   CAPE. Then let's be proud of our fight! It began with the splitting of a cell a hundred million years ago into you and me, leaving an eternal yearning to become one life again [*Wel* 448].
   16. On learning of the death of his lawyer, Harry Weinberger, O'Neill talks of how important his friendship had been for him, and is eager to show that this was of crucial importance in his life. "My great hope, now that he is gone, is that he realized the depth of my friendship for him, that he knew if things ever got tough and down to cases with him, and every other friend in the world had failed, I would never have failed him, no matter what, any more than, if the reverse were true, he would have failed me. I think he knew this, I hope to God he did! Because more than anything else, friendships like this give life value, and recompense for all its double-crossing opportunism and meannesses." O'Neill, in a letter to Harold Wayne (5 March 1944). In Bogard and Bryer, eds., *Selected Letters*, 551.
   17. YANK. Sea-farin' is all right when you're young and don't care, but we ain't chickens no more, and somehow, I dunno, this last year has seemed rotten, and I've had a hunch I'd quit—with you, of course—and we'd save our coin, and go to Canada or Argentine or some place and get a farm, just a small one, just enough to live on. I never told you this, 'cause I thought you'd laugh at me.
   DRISCOLL. (*Enthusiastically*) Laugh at you, is ut? When I'm havin' the same thoughts myself, toime after toime [*BEC* 486].
   18. In one of his very early writings, O'Neill takes the love of sharing quite far.
   OLDER MAN. Greater love hath no man than this, that he giveth his wife for his friend [*WJL* 223].

9. Belonging.

1. Krutch writes in his overview of O'Neill's œuvre, that the playwright's characters are divided into two categories: "Those who feel that they do and those who feel that they do not 'belong'" (285). The Glencairn sailors easily fall into the latter class as homeless men who sail an endless sea, stopping briefly at ports to drink, brawl, and fornicate. Kelli A. Larson, "O'Neill's Tragic Quest for Belonging: Psychological Determinism in the SS *Glencairn* Plays," *Eugene O'Neill Review* 13, 2 (fall 1989): 15.
2. The proof of the existence of a community, which implies codes, is that its members know how to identify those who are not part of it.
   DAVIS. An' look here, ain't you noticed he don't talk natural? He talks it too damn good, that's what I mean. He don't talk exactly like a toff, does he, Cocky?
   COCKY. Not like any toff as I ever met up wiv [*IZo* 521-2].
In a slightly different context we could make the same remark about *The Iceman Cometh*.
   ROCKY. Yeah, I figgered he don't belong, but he said he was a friend of yours [*IC* 583].
3. A counterexample is given by Robert Mayo, who stays on his father's farm, and does not make his own way. Conversely, traveling can also bring about the downfall of characters. Immobility or movement do not have a unique and predefined relation to belonging. The meaning depends on the context.
4. To find unity, they must redefine their place on the ship, which will allow them to be in harmony with their environment.
   YANK. I was lookin' at de sky-scrapers—steel—and all de ships comin' in, sailin' out, all over de oith—and dey was steel, too. De sun was warm, dey wasn't no clouds, and dere was a breeze blowin'. Sure, it was great stuff. I got it aw right—What Paddy said about dat bein' de right dope—onl'y I couldn't get *in* it, see? I couldn't belong in dat [*HA* 252].
5. Michael Manheim, *Eugene O'Neill's New Language of Kinship* (Syracuse, N.Y.: Syracuse University Press, 1982), 22.
6. There are certainly counterexamples—Smitty in *The Moon of the Caribbees*—but in the sea plays, the protagonists can recount their stories, made up of half-lies. To speak, to express oneself and to be understood, even if the audience is not of the same quality as the lovers' partners, allows them to exist.
7. *The Hairy Ape* is not the only play which deals with the mental prison of conformism. We have already noted it in *The First Man*, and the latent or manifest social criticism exposes the lack of intellectual courage of the communities and their members. O'Neill does not attack only the bourgeoisie. An example of caustic satire of those who consider themselves to be out of the ordinary is given when Gabriel speaks of his marriage.
   GABRIEL. The only reason we concealed it was because we were taking a studio in Greenwich Village together when we moved to New York and we were afraid they'd consider us provincial down there if they knew [*NLAY* 175].
8. Edwin Engel, *The Haunted Heroes of Eugene O'Neill* (Cambridge, Mass.: Harvard University Press, 1953), 55.

10. Non-Belonging.

1. *The Emperor Jones, The Hairy Ape, The Fountain, All God's Chillun Got Wings, The Great God Brown, Marco Millions, Lazarus Laughed, Mourning Becomes Electra*, and *Days Without End*.

2. "Lavinia tout entière n'est qu'un masque, le masque hideux du 'puritanisme' dont elle est sans le savoir la première victime." Anne-Marie Soulier, "Le Héros et son double dans les pièces masquées d'Eugene O'Neill: *The Great God Brown* et *Mourning Becomes Electra*," dissertation, University of Strasbourg, 1984, 231 (my translation into English).

3. In *A Touch of the Poet,* Con Melody's uniform has an actualizing function, similar to what Roland Barthes qualified as an *effet de réél* for the narrative. The truth of his exploits, cast into doubt by his barman, is corroborated by the words of Jimmy Cregan, but when he appears in uniform, memory and illusion become more authentic than the immediate reality.

4. Some characters, marked by their Irish roots, give the impression of having "kissed the Blarney Stone" (as *A Touch of the Poet* puts it), not forgetting the Hogans, Hickey and other patter merchants of the same calibre as James Tyrone.

5. When this last veil disappears, the characters discover their soul, but the lucky ones are few and far between. We remember what O'Neill said on this subject: "It will take man" he says "a million years to grow up and obtain a soul" (Halfmann, *Eugene O'Neill: Comments,* 144). As such, Josie appears as an exceptional character:

> TYRONE: You're real and healthy and clean and warm and strong and kind—
> JOSIE: I have a beautiful soul, you mean? [*MMis* 77].

6. TYRONE. (*He quotes, using his fine voice.*) We are such stuff as dreams are made on, and our little life is rounded with a sleep [*LDJN* 131].

7. The part played by this kind of dream is fairly limited in the works. It can have a prophetic value.

> ORIN. Their faces keep coming back in dreams—and they change to Father's face—or to mine—What does that mean, Vinnie? [*MBE, The Hunted* 95].

8. The fanciful nature of the American dream, to which I shall now allude, was declared by the author, who had no illusions on this subject. "This American Dream stuff gives me a pain," he went on. "Telling the world about our American Dream! I don't know what they mean. If it exists, as we tell the whole world, why don't we make it work in one small hamlet in the United States?" O'Neill, in Bowen, *The Curse of the Misbegotten,* 315.

9. The voice of Mrs. Frazer is full of sarcasm for her past innocence, but she conveys one of the two ways ("MRS. FRAZER. He ... said there were two ways of looking at everything" [*Ser* 238]), in which the world is viewed by Americans.

> MRS. FRAZER. The house he was connected with is one of the largest on the Exchange and some of the so-called Napoleons of finance, whose names were forever in newspaper headlines, did their business through it. I thought of him doing his part in their gigantic enterprises, laboring to effect ever larger combinations in order that this glorious country might thrive and become ever greater and more productive [*Ser* 235].

10. In *Servitude,* it is the wife who becomes aware of the illusion. In the later plays, the revelation will directly concern those engaged in speculation.

> MRS. FRAZER. Of course, in the light of what you have taught me, I can see it was merely a stupid happiness, the content of the born blind who have never seen the light [*Ser* 235].

11. Roberts and Roberts, eds., *As Ever, Gene,* 84.

12. "Le théâtre me demande un acte de foi qui m'engage comme spectateur devant la scène et non comme un homme devant le monde." "The theater demands of me an act of faith which commits me as a spectator before the stage and not as a person before the world." Henri Gouhier, *Le Théâtre et l'existence* (Paris: Librairie Philosophique J.Vrin, 1991), 175 (my translation).

13. He stated this only too clearly in the course of an interview: "Yes, I care only

for humanity. I wish to arouse compassion. For the unfortunate. The suffering. The oppressed."... "I do not write with a premeditated purpose. I write of life as I see it. As it exists for many of us. If people leave the theater after one of my plays with a feeling of compassion for those less fortunate than they, I am satisfied—I have not written in vain." Carol Bird, "Eugene O'Neill—The Inner Man," in Mark W. Estrin, ed., *Conversations with Eugene O'Neill* (Jackson: University Press of Mississippi, 1990), 52.

    14. BRANT.(*Brought back to earth—gloomily*) I know it's only a dream.
        CHRISTINE.(*Turning to stare at him—slowly*) You can have your dream—and I can have mine. There is a way [*MBE, Homecoming* 39].

    15. Another example of dramatic irony, the words of Mannon, who hopes to be able to put the past behind him, and begin a new life with Christine.
        MANNON. (*Finally blurts out*) I've dreamed of coming home to you, Christine! [*MBE, Homecoming* 52].

    16. For instance, Robert Mayo. In other cases, the confrontation with reality is nightmarish, and the impossibility of escaping the world as it really is, leads to madness; see the end of *Ile*. Before she loses contact with reality for good, she explains why she went wrong:
        MRS. KEENEY. Oh, I know it isn't your fault, David. You see, I didn't believe you. I guess I was dreaming about the old Vikings in the story-books and I thought you were one of them [*Ile* 546].

    17. *Gold* (1920) is a rewriting of *Where the Cross Is Made* (1918).
    18. With the exception of the few moments when he is totally absorbed in his past, the rest of the time, the consequences of his dreaming are comparable with those of Don Juan.
        JUAN. If I could be once more the man who fought before Granada! But the fire smolders. It merely warms my will to dream of the past [*Fou* 402].

    19. Carpenter, *Eugene O'Neill*, 76.
    20. Cf. The pregnant Nina, for whom life suddenly takes on an unreal and blissful aspect.
        NINA. ... the world is whole and perfect... all things are each other's... life is... and this is beyond reason... questions die in the silence of this peace... I am living a dream within the great dream of the tide... [*SI* 91].

    21. We know how difficult it is for the characters to leave. Tiusanen, who is concerned with the scenic dimension of the plays, underlines the importance of the places represented, at the moments when important decisions are taken in the plays. "*Welded* is the first play in which stairways have specific functions; ... it is followed by *Mourning Becomes Electra, More Stately Mansions*, and *A Moon for the Misbegotten*. ... [And] we add to this list of symbolic areas the gate in *Desire Under the Elms*, the doors in *The Iceman Cometh*, and *A Touch of the Poet*. In each of theses cases the specific area is a meeting place of private and public worlds. This is where the characters act out decisive crises of their lives." Timo Tiusanen, *O'Neill's Scenic Images* (Princeton, N.J.: Princeton University Press, 1968), 335.

    22. This aspect has been rightly underlined by Linda Ben-Zvi, and is confirmed by the number of plays, which will be listed later on, where we find the departure/return cycle. "Other characters in later plays leave their homes and families only to find that in adulthood they still yearn for their original fixity and for those from whom they have never psychically separated, most often the mother." Linda Ben-Zvi, "Freedom and Fixity in the Plays of Eugene O'Neill," *Modern Drama* 31, 1 (March 1988): 21.

    23. Cf. *All God's Chillun Got Wings, Anna Christie, Beyond the Horizon, Bread and Butter, Days Without End, Desire Under the Elms* (Cabot), *Diff'rent, Dynamo, The Great God Brown, The Iceman Cometh, Long Day's Journey into Night, Marco Millions, More

Stately Mansions, Mourning Becomes Electra, The Rope, Servitude, Strange Interlude, and *Welded.*

    24. BESSIE. You're sure you're not letting your troubles drive you to drink, or anything like that? [*B&B* 53].

We find almost identical terms in *Anna Christie.*

        ANNA. So I'm driving you to drink, too, eh? I s'pose you want to get drunk so's you can forget—like him? [*AC* 61].

However Chris does not blame her. His resentment is against destiny, symbolized here by "dat ole davil, sea."

    25. They often carry on living as if it were proof of cowardice, as this extract from *Ah, Wilderness!* shows:

        SID. If I had any guts, I'd kill myself, and good riddance!—but I haven't—I'm yellow, too! a yellow drunken bum! [*AhW* 258].

Other examples are in *Mourning Becomes Electra* 166 and *The Iceman Cometh* 170.

    26. Emil Roy, "The Archetypal Unity of Eugene O'Neill's Drama," 1–15 in John H. Stroupe, *Critical Approaches to O'Neill* (New York: AMS, 1988), 14.

    27. This ought to be seen in the Nietzschean perspective. "My death, praise I unto you, the voluntary death, which cometh unto me because *I* want it." Nietzsche, *Thus Spake Zarathustra,* 82.

    28. The perspective is different, and Schopenhauer states what can be behind such an act: "L'homme n'est point exposé aux douleurs *physiques* seulement, à ces douleurs tout enfermées dans le présent: il est encore livré en proie à des douleurs incomparables, dont la nature est de déborder sur l'avenir et sur le passé, aux douleurs *morales*; aussi, en compensation la Nature lui a accordé ce privilège, de pouvoir, alors qu'elle-même n'impose pas encore un terme à sa vie, la terminer à son gré." "Man is not exposed to merely physical pain, pain which is confined to the present: he also falls prey to the kind of incomparable pain which runs into the past and future, that is *moral* pain; to compensate for this, Nature grants him the privilege of being able, when she herself has not yet chosen to end his life, to terminate it of his own free will." Arthur Schopenhauer, *Le Fondement de la morale* (Paris: Livre de Poche, 1991), 54 (my translation).

12. *The Discovery of Human Beings.*

    1. Jackson R. Bryer and Ruth M. Alvarez, eds., *"The Theatre We Worked For": The Letters of Eugene O'Neill to Kenneth Macgowan* (New Haven: Yale University Press, 1982), 256.

    2. "Both the mask of the house and the character's masked faces symbolize the opposition between the conscious lives of the Mannon and their subconscious conflicts and motives." Alvis, "On the American Line," 72.

    3. Cf. the pertinent remark of Linda Stanich: "The conflict is not simply between individuals, but rather between the individual and his/her own story." Linda Stanich, "*The Iceman Cometh* as Ethnographic Text," *Eugene O'Neill Review* 13, 2 (fall 1989): 59.

    4. Maurice Le Breton, "O'Neill and American Theatre" in Frenz and Tuck, eds., *Eugene O'Neill's Critics,* 67.

    5. Cf. the attitude of Con Melody, and his insistence on the ephemeral nature of his destitution, when the lawyer proposes an amicable settlement.

        MELODY. I will be frank with you, sir. The devil of it is, this comes at a difficult time for me. Temporary, of course, but I cannot deny I am pinched at the moment—devilishly pinched [*TP* 120].

In this case, another person is involved, but the process is the same in cases of self evaluation.
6. Respect disappears before the need for expression.
JAMIE. Where's the hophead? Gone to sleep?... Thanks; Kid. I certainly had that coming. Don't know what made me—booze talking—You know me Kid [*LDJN* 161-2].
7. Self awareness is destructive, but seems inescapable:
TYRONE. I found that everyday I was glad when the last race was over, and I could go back to the hotel—and the bottle in my room [*MMis* 93].
and also this:
SID. I'm a no-good drunken bum!—you shouldn't even wipe your feet on me!—I'm a dirty, rotten drunk!—no good to myself or anybody else!—if I had any guts I'd kill myself, and good riddance!—but I haven't! [*AhW* 258].

13. Revelation of an Existential Condition.

1. "Si elle n'a pas pour but immédiat la douleur, on peut dire que notre existence n'a aucune raison d'être dans le monde. Car il est absurde d'admettre que la douleur sans fin qui naît de la misère inhérente à la vie et qui remplit le monde, ne soit qu'un pur accident et non le but même." Arthur Schopenhauer, *Douleurs du monde* (Paris: Éditions Rivages, 1990), 27 (my translation into English).
2. 1. *Dukkka*; 2. *Samudaya*, the appearance or the origin (of *dukkka*); 3. *Nirodha*, the end (of *dukkka*); 4. *Magga* the path (which leads to the end of *dukkka*)—in Walpola Rahula, *L'Enseignement du Bouddha* (Paris: Points-Seuil, 1978), 35. He explains what the notion of *dukkka* entails a little later, for unlike other interpreters, he refuses to associate it solely with the idea of suffering, of pain. "La première Noble Vérité est Dukkka, la nature de la vie, sa souffrance, ses chagrins et ses joies, son imperfection, et son insatisfaction, son impermanence et son insubstantialité," 74. "The first Noble Truth is Dukkka, the nature of life, its suffering, its pain and its joy, its imperfection and its dissatisfaction, its transitoriness and its insubstantiality" (my translation).
3. (This influence was felt even in his everyday life; thus the house he had built in California was called "Tao House," and some critics, referring to plays written in this house, apply this term to them). In the following pages, I shall try to identify what allows me to make a Buddhist reading, and what results from this. At the same time, I shall make some observations on Taoism, for we will see that in spite of obvious differences, the two approaches intersect at the main point which concerns us.
4. James A. Robinson, *Eugene O'Neill and Oriental Thought: A Divided Vision* (Carbondale: Southern Illinois University Press, 1982).
5. "La seconde Noble Vérité est l'origine de *dukkka*, qui est désir, 'soif' accompagné de toutes les autres passions, souillures et impuretés. La simple compréhension de ce fait n'est pas suffisante. Ici notre fonction est d'écarter ce désir, de l'éliminer, le détruire et le déraciner. La troisième Noble Vérité est la cessation de *dukkka*, le *Nirvâna*, la Vérité absolue, la Réalité ultime. Ici notre fonction est de l'atteindre, de la comprendre." "The second Noble Truth is the origin of *dukkka*, which is desire, 'thirst,' with all the other passions, blemishes and impurities that go with it. Merely understanding this is not enough. Here our purpose is to push aside this desire, to eliminate, destroy and eradicate it. The third Noble Truth is the end of *dukkka*, *Nirvâna*, absolute Truth, the ultimate reality. Here our purpose is to attain it and to understand it." Rahula, *L'Enseignement du Bouddha*, 74 (my translation).
6. We noted that there was a reference to Thoreau when the existential choice

of Simon was evoked, but in the background one can also see an allusion to the life of the Buddha.

7. Which ties in with the words of Lao-tzu: "Does anyone want to take the world and do what he wants with it?/ I do not see how he can succeed./ The world is a sacred vessel, which must not be tampered with or grabbed after./ To tamper with it is to spoil it, and to grasp it is to lose it." Lao-tzu, *Tao-Teh-Ching*, transl. John C.H. Wu (Jamaica, N.Y.: St. John's University Press, 1961), p. 61.

8. Note the interesting reading made by Robinson in James A. Robinson, "O'Neill's Indian *Elms*," *Eugene O'Neill Review* 13, 1 (spring 1989): 40–46.

9. Which is also Larry's attitude:

> LARRY. So I said to the world, God bless all here, and may the best man win and die of gluttony! And I took a seat in the grandstand of philosophical detachment to fall asleep observing the cannibals do their death dance [*IC* 579].

His behavior is very similar to that of *wou-wei*, often translated as "principle of non-action."

10. Developed previously:

> LAZARUS. As Man, Petty Tyrant of Earth, you are a bubble pricked by death into a void and a mocking silence! But as dust, you are eternal change, and everlasting growth,... [*LL* 309].

11. The Taoist point of view is somewhat different: "L'idée de mutation ôte tout intérêt philosophique à un inventaire de la nature où l'on se proposerait de constituer des séries de faits en distinguant des antécédents et des conséquents." "The idea of mutation removes any philosophical interest from the idea of constructing an inventory consisting of series of facts, the antecedents being differenciated from the consequences." Marcel Granet, *La Pensée chinoise* (Paris: Editions Albin Michel, 1990), 272 (my translation).We could add to this remark the note quoted by Jean Grenier: "Transformisme taoïste. Pas de mort et pas de vie. Des germes indestructibles, qui constituent les individus; mais transformation continuelle des formes, du revêtement sensible de ces individus. (Note du P. Wieger.)" "Taoist transformism. No death and no life. Indestructible seeds which make up individuals; but continual transformation of the form, of the outer layer of these individuals." Jean Grenier, *L'Esprit du Tao* (Paris: Champs-Flammarion, 1992), 67 (my translation).

12. Robinson, *Eugene O'Neill and Oriental Thought*, 136.

13. The terms used by Carpenter indicate that the *ego* is not denied by Lazarus: "O'Neill's Lazarus was no Occidental superman, performing victorious acts of will. Rather, he became an Oriental superman, whose triumph was that he refused to act in opposition to evil." Frederic I. Carpenter, "Eugene O'Neill, the Orient, and American Transcendentalism," 37–44 in Griffin, ed., *Eugene O'Neill: A Collection*, 41.

14. If we remove the adjective, we are left with "Men are," which indicates the limits of the Buddhist nature of his message.

15. "'Tous les problèmes sont sans soi.' Voilà la troisième racine de la loi sur laquelle il vous faut méditer." "'All problems are without the self.' This is the third principle of the law on which we must meditate." Jean Eracle, *Paroles de Bouddha* (Paris: Points-Seuil 1990), 23 (my translation).

16. "En celui qui perçoit l'impermanence, s'établit la perception du non moi, c'est la perception du non moi qui arrive à éliminer l'idée: Je suis, j'existe; cette élimination, c'est le *Nirvâna*, ici et maintenant." Joseph Masson, *Le Bouddhisme* (Paris: Desclée De Brouwer, 1975), 63 (my translation into English).

17. Or Taoist, for the important thing for us in the parallel consideration of the two systems is the remark made by J. Robinson on their convergence regarding the ego: "The major false distinction created by rationalism is that of the separate ego. This concept—vital to Western thought—is repudiated by all three systems [Hinduism,

Buddhism, and Taoïsm] which agree that the individual personality possesses at best a provisional reality." Robinson, *Eugene O'Neill and Oriental Thought*, 5.

18. Definitively, the principles extricated from the individual experiences shown on stage are in line with the four Noble Truths enunciated by the Buddha, and the lives of the characters retrace the steps which allow one to reach the awakening, the awareness of the non-self.

14. The Acknowledgment of the Individual.

1. We find this style of discourse in the following plays: *Ah, Wilderness!*, *All God's Chillun Got Wings*, *Before Breakfast*, *Days Without End*, *Dynamo*, *The Emperor Jones*, *The Fountain*, *Gold*, *The Great God Brown*, *The Hairy Ape*, *Hughie*, *The Iceman Cometh*, *Long Day's Journey into Night*, *A Moon for the Misbegotten*, *More Stately Mansions*, *Mourning Becomes Electra*, *Strange Interlude*, *A Touch of the Poet*, *Warnings*, *The Web*, *A Wife for a Life*. For a typology of this form of expression, see Lisa Dahl, *Linguistic Features of the Stream of Consciousness Techniques of James Joyce, Virginia Woolf and Eugene O'Neill* (Turku, Finland: Turun Yliopisto, 1970), 78, and Egil Törnqvist, "To Speak the Unspoken: Audible Thinking in O'Neill's Plays," *Eugene O'Neill Review* 16, 1 (spring 1992): 55–70.

2. It is sometimes extremely difficult for characters to adhere to this rule:
   MARY. *The front screen door is heard closing after them... She stares about the room with frightened, forsaken eyes and whispers to herself.*
   It's so lonely here.
   Then her face hardens into bitter self-contempt.
   You're lying to yourself again. You wanted to get rid of them [*LDJN* 95].

3. See for instance:
   NINA. These men make me sick!... I hate all three of them!...they disgust me!...the wife and mistress in me has been killed by them [*SI* 149].

4. This is almost a typical scene. Similar exchanges can be found elsewhere (*Beyond the Horizon*, *Desire Under the Elms*, *Recklessness*): During an altercation the wives confess to their husands the love they feel for other men, the strength of their emotions crushing the fears that they might hitherto have felt.

5. Initially Anna behaves in the same way. She reminds everyone that she was once a prostitute, for she refuses to be considered any longer as someone who knows nothing of the realities of life, whose opinion cannot be taken into account when discussing a hypothetical marriage. Subsequently, when she has revealed her past, she distances herself from Mat's preconceived notions of how she feels:
   ANNA. (*Savagely*) I hated 'em, I tell you! Hated 'em, hated 'em, hated 'em! And may Gawd strike me dead this minute and my mother, too, if she was alive, if I ain't telling you the honest truth! [*AC* 73].

6. One could draw a parallel with the attitudes of the prostitutes in *The Iceman Cometh* and *The Long Voyage Home*; in one case the fact of having profited from a sailor's drunken state is considered an excellent joke, in the other, one senses the first prickings of remorse, for the stakes are not the same.
   OLSON. ...my mother get very old, and I want see her. She might die and I would never—
   FREDA. (*Moved a lot in spite of herself*) Ow, don't talk like that! [*LVH* 506].

7. The mere fact of being there, receptive to the outpourings of the sufferer, makes them worthy of the title of "saint," which F. Wilkins defines: "O'Neill's 'saints' know they can't change the world; but they add considerable light and warmth to the little clearing (the little human 'center') within the menacing 'margin' out there." Fred-

erick C. Wilkins, "O'Neill's Secular Saints," *Eugene O'Neill Review* 14, 1-2 (spring-fall 1990): 78.

8. Caleb was forced to admit the truth, because it had been partly uncovered by his entourage; had he been able, he would have kept his adventure to himself.
> CALEB. But that ain't no good reason for tellin' it. Them sort o' things ought to be kept among men [*Dif* 515].

9. Leon Mirlas, "Scope of O'Neill's Drama," in Frenz and Tuck, eds., *Eugene O'Neill's Critics*, 103.

10. In fact, such scenes can be found (as distinct from avowals), in the following plays (listed chronologically): *Warnings* (1913), *Bound East for Cardiff*, *Bread and Butter*, *Servitude* (all 1914), *The Long Voyage Home* (1917), *Beyond the Horizon*, *Shell Shock*, *The Straw*, *Anna Christie* (1920), *Gold*, *The First Man*, *The Fountain*, *The Great God Brown* (1925), *Strange Interlude*, *Dynamo*, *Mourning Becomes Electra* (1931), *Ah, Wilderness!*, *Days Without End*, *The Iceman Cometh*, *Hughie*, *Long Day's Journey into Night* (1941), *A Moon for the Misbegotten*.

11. Barlow has identified this in four cases, but her comments remain relevant for other examples: "The four major confessions in these works—Hickey's and Parrit's in *Iceman*, Jamie's in *Journey*, and Jim's in *Moon*—are remarkably similar. In each instance the one confessing is compelled to do so by the pressure of his guilt." Barlow, *Final Acts*, 142.

12. The alternative open to them is summed up clearly by C. Mihelich: "In each case, certain characters either find peace after confessing or face psychological ruin when they refuse to confess." Christine Mihelich, "The Rite of Confession in Five Plays by Eugene O'Neill," *Dissertation Abstracts International* 38 (1976): 265A (University of Pittsburgh).

13. Mirlas, "Scope," in Frenz and Tuck, eds., *Eugene O'Neill's Critics*, 103.

14. Cf. the opinion Jamie has of himself:
> TYRONE. Thanks, Josie. I mean, for not believing I'm a rotten louse. Everyone else believes it—including myself— [*MMis* 86].

15. For information only, one can bear in mind what Arthur and Barbara Gelb had to say on the subject: "...other evidence of the death wish may be found in twenty-five of his forty-five published plays in which a total of forty characters suffer violent or unnatural deaths. Of these, nine are suicides. Twenty-one of the poisoned, diseased, mangled, strangled, sliced, drowned, electrocuted, cremated or bullet-riddled men, women and children meet their ends in full view of the audience." Gelb and Gelb, *O'Neill*, 189.

16. This point of view is developed in the last scene of *Desire Under the Elms*, when Abbie and Eben, united in their love, are ready to accept their chatisement, whatever form it may take:
> EBEN. I want t' share with ye, Abbie—prison 'r death 'r hell 'r anythin'! [*DE* 267].

17. In another play, O'Neill illustrates directly the immediate nature of the continuity which exists between the living and the dead:
> SAILOR. It is lucky for us she is dead.
> GENTLEMAN. What do you mean? What good can her death do us?
> SAILOR. We will live now. (*He takes his SAILOR's knife from its sheath and sharpens it on the sole of his shoe.*) [*Thi* 30].

18. The starting points are different, as the remarks of Haiping Liu illustrate, but there are points of convergence between the two approaches: "In Taoist perspective, however, life and death are not in opposition but are merely two aspects of the same reality. They are arrested moments of never ceasing transformations, like day and night, or summer and winter. Death is seen as the natural result, and also a new beginning, of life." Haiping Liu, "Taoism in O'Neill's Tao House Plays," *Eugene O'Neill Newsletter* 12, 2 (summer-fall 1988): 31.

19. We can see how far he has come by comparing the dialogue quoted in the text (*IC* 578), and that quoted below, in which the truth is finally heard:
   LARRY. You think when I say I'm finished with life, and tired of watching the stupid greed of the human circus, and I'll welcome closing my eyes in the long sleep of death—you think that's a coward's lie?
   HICKEY. (*Chuckling*) Well, what do you think, Larry? [*IC* 689].
   LARRY. Be God, I'm the only real convert to death Hickey made here. From the bottom of my coward's heart I mean that now! [*IC* 727].
His realization, which is accomplished in the final scene, has consisted of a recognition of the fear he felt in the face of death, whence we find the repetition of the word "coward" which he feels corresponds to what he really is.
   20. "Et de même ma mort pour moi est la fin de tout, la fin totale et définitive de mon existence personnelle et la fin de l'univers tout entier, la fin du monde et la fin de l'histoire; la fin de mon temps vital est bien pour moi la fin des temps, la tragédie métaphysique par excellence, l'inconcevable tragédie de ma nihilisation." "And likewise my death for me is the end of everything, the complete and definitive end of my personal existence and the end of the whole universe, the end of the world and the end of history; the end of my vital time is for me the end of all time, the metaphysical tragedy par excellence, the inconceivable tragedy of my nihility." Vladimir Jankelevitch, *La Mort* (Paris: Champs-Flammarion, 1977), 24 (my translation). Faced with this communal vision, one understands why Lazarus must increase his efforts to convince his disciples that to die is nothing.
   21. Finding herein the fundamental vocation of confession, the definition of which we should perhaps remind ourselves: "La confession est un des éléments du sacrement de pénitence, qui désigne souvent dans la langue courante le sacrement lui même. La confession des péchés est la reconnaissance devant Dieu et son Eglise de son état de pécheur." "Confession is one of the elements of the sacrament of penance, which in current usage often denotes the sacrament itself. The confession of sins is the acknowledgment before God and the Church of one's state of sin." Guy-Marie Oury, ed., *Dictionnaire de la foi catholique* (Chambray: Éditions CLD, 1986), 51 (my translation). Regarding the consequences of this action, they are defined as follows: "Le sacrement de pénitence apporte au pécheur la grâce dont il a besoin pour cela, en même temps qu'il ratifie sa rentrée en grâce à la fois avec l'Eglise et avec Dieu." "The sacrament of penance gives the sinner the grace he needs, at the same time as it ratifies his return to grace with the church and with God." Louis Bouyer, *Dictionnaire théologique* (Paris: Desclée De Brouwer, 1990), 267 (my translation).
   22. Robert Feldman, "The Longing for Death in O'Neill's *Strange Interlude* and *Mourning Becomes Electra*," *Literature and Psychology* 31, 1 (1981): 40.
   23. The two passages which follow show how his faith in God fluctuates.
   ROBERT. I could curse God from the bottom of my soul—if there was a God! [*BH* 148].
   ROBERT. I'm a failure, and Ruth's another—but we can both justly lay some of the blame for our stumbling on God [*BH* 161].
   24. "Le monde, mais c'est l'enfer, et les hommes se partagent en âmes tourmentées et en diables tourmenteurs." Schopenhauer, *Douleurs du monde*, 33 (my translation into English).
   25. Formulated in a different way, one finds this aspiration in *Fog*, *The Fountain*, *The Great God Brown*, *Bound East for Cardiff*, and *Strange Interlude*.
   26. Nietzsche, *Thus Spake Zarathustra*, 270.
   27. JACK. Do you suppose it was the same man who loves Evelyn who did this other thing? No, a thousands time [*sic*] no, such an idea is abhorrent. It was the male beast who ran gibbering through the forest after its female thousands of years ago [*Ab* 154].

28. John Henry Raleigh, "Strindberg and O'Neill as Historical Dramatists," 59–75, in Maufort, *Eugene O'Neill and the Emergence*, 67.

29. Nietzsche closely associates the notions of death and freedom, his theory illustrating what is implicit in Orin's gesture: "My death, praise I unto you, the voluntary death, which cometh unto me because *I* want it." Nietzsche, *Thus Spake Zarathustra*, 93.

30. As opposed to Beckett's theater—to which O'Neill's writing has often been compared—the despair Simeon feels here is not a feeling of disarray arising from his confrontation with an impenetrable universe, but the despair of leaving the land which has given meaning to his life up until now.

> SIMEON. (*Stamps his foot on the earth and addresses it desperately*) Waal—ye've thirty year o' me buried in ye—spread out over ye—blood an' bone an' sweat— [*DE* 218].

31. In this case, Larry guides the spectator and suggests how the words of his acolytes should be interpreted. In *The Straw*, the future is also an illusion marker. It conveys the unreasonable hope of a sick woman who does not know that according to the doctors her chances of survival are slim.

> EILEEN. I'll surprise you, Stephen, the way I'll pick up and grow fat and healthy. You won't know me in a month [*Straw* 411].

32. His optimism as to the future is barely shared by Christine, who does not place spatial limits on a potential liberation:

> CHRISTINE. But I'll grow old so soon! And I'm afraid of time! [*MBE*, Homecoming 39].

33. Laurin Porter, *The Banished Prince: Time, Memory and Ritual in the Late Plays of Eugene O'Neill* (Ann Arbor: UMI Research Press, 1988), 10.

34. The son is a liberator for his mother. This is opposed to what happens in *Dynamo*, but when Eben brings her what she needs, he becomes free in his turn.

35. This going back to the past is very painful, and many characters back away from it; we may for example think of Simon Harford in *More Stately Mansions* and his difficult journey before he could be truly himself.

36. Doris Falk, *Eugene O'Neill and the Tragic Tension* (New Brunswick, N.J.: Rutgers University Press, 1958), 4.

37. Edward Shaughnessy, "Question and Answer in *Hughie*," *Eugene O'Neill Newsletter* 3, 2 (September 1978): 3.

38. O'Neill, "O'Neill Talks about His Plays," in Cargill, Fagin, and Fisher, eds., *O'Neill and His Plays*, 111.

39. Frederick Wilkins, "The Pressure of Puritanism in Eugene O'Neill's New England Plays," in Floyd, *Eugene O'Neill*, 242.

40. We are reminded of the words of Virginia Floyd regarding the relationship between the divine and the diabolic: the Devil becomes literally, by the time O'Neill finished his notes for it, "The 13th Apostle," cursing the fate that condemns him throughout time to murder repeatedly the God-Man he secretly loves and worships. Virginia Floyd, ed., *Eugene O'Neill at Work: Newly Released Ideas for Plays* (New York: Ungar, 1981), 320.

41. Marc Maufort, "The Legacy of Melville's *Pierre*: Family Relationships in *Mourning Becomes Electra*," *Eugene O'Neill Newsletter* 11, 2 (summer-fall 1987): 28.

42. Faith represents at least a double adhesion: in the religious sphere of course, but also implying automatic membership to a community. "Il en résulte que la foi, en tant que réponse à la Parole de Dieu, fonde la communauté des croyants, de ceux que la parole appelle dans le monde à n'être plus du monde.... Qui veut venir à la foi doit s'agréger à cette communauté des croyants, s'y insérer, s'y adjoindre, être accepté en son sein et se trouver en accord avec elle." "Consequently, faith, as a response to the word of God, founds the community of believers, of those whom the word calls in the world

to be no longer of the world.... Those wishing to come to the faith must incorporate themselves into this community of believers, fit into it, attach themselves to it, be accepted within it and in agreement with it." Pierre Eicher, ed., *Dictionnaire de théologie* (Paris: Editions du Cerf, 1988), 72 (my translation).

43. Engel, "Ideas," 21-36 in Griffin, *Eugene O'Neill: A Collection*, 23.

44. I am aware of the inherent difficulty in defining a person's philosophy, especially when, following the example of O'Neill, it has come up against numerous different thought systems. However, despite risking an analysis lacking comprehensiveness, I have chosen this perspective so as to present what seems to me to stem from the writings of O'Neill.

45. Two examples, one taken from his correspondence, the other an extract from a play, show that, as regards alcohol, O'Neill does not attempt to be a paragon of virtue: "You forget there were men in those days, and when they decided it was fitting they should go on a drunk, *they went on a drunk*. Not like the weaklings of today, who after two days of much mixed drinks have to have an animal trainer bed them down in Bellevue and gently subdue their menagerie visions! In the old days when I was born, a man—especially one from Kilkenny—went on a five year drunk and finished by licking four cops, and then went home to raise hell because dinner was late." Gelb and Gelb, *O'Neill*, 57.

CATHLEEN. *Philosophically*. It's a good man's failing. I wouldn't give a trauneen for a teetotaler. They've no high spirits [*LDJN* 101].

46. Nietzsche, *Thus Spake Zarathustra*, 9.

15. Nature.

1. Steven F. Bloom, "Empty Bottles, Empty Dreams: O'Neill's Use of Drinks and Alcoholism in *Long Day's Journey into Night*," 172 in Martine, *Critical Essays*.

2. *Beyond the Horizon* is an exception since it is a star, and not the moon, that is alluded to.

3. One thinks for example of Dion in *The Great God Brown* and James in *A Moon for the Misbegotten* (neither of whom is quite redeemed from a social point of view). In the case of James, his filial love makes the word lover inappropriate, but one feels he belongs to the clan of sufferers.

4. Bartlett's case is an exception however. As was the case with fog, delusion becomes the undeniable proof of the characters' lack of belonging in the world. Unlike Smitty, he cannot accept the reality of his loss, and claims to see his ship, which was lost at sea. The moonlight helps him build a new world corresponding to what he wishes to see (*WCIM* 569) but the golden light of the moon ironically reveals the extent of his own destruction.

5. Since they are fully aware of the responsibility they carry for these wasted lives, their ruined loves produce a feeling of guilt. They haunt them, and remind one of the murder mentioned by Silva.

SILVA. A man got knifed and pushed overboard. After that, on moonlight nights, they'd see him a-settin' on the yards and hear him moanin' to himself [*MBE* 132].

6. A connection could be made with Mrs. Fife (*Dy*). Beyond her simplistic love for dynamos, she embodies an ability to communicate with essential natural elements. She prefers watching the moon to reading the newspaper, showing she perceives that what really matters is not the daily activities and social events summarized in newspaper columns, but nature.

7. Normand Berlin, *O'Neill's Shakespeare* (Ann Arbor: University of Michigan Press, 1993), 16.

8. This filiation of men to the sea reminds us that the first version of *Bound East for Cardiff* was entitled *Children of the Sea*.

9. In addition to the previous remarks regarding the mother-son connection, one should bear in mind that Paddy's speech is not the sole instance of such a vision. We have already pointed out that Chris (in *Anna Christie*), when he does not call it "ole davil," always uses "her" or "she" to refer to the sea.

10. One meets here with a theme which goes beyond the limited frame of the sea plays: Regarding Smitty and his being a sailor, the verdict is sharp and his affinity for the sea bluntly denied.

> THE DONKEYMAN. What ever set you goin' to sea? You ain't made for it [*MCa* 467].

11. Marc Maufort, *Songs of American Experience: The Vision of O'Neill and Melville* (New York: Peter Lang, 1990), 77.

12. *Julius Caesar*, Act 1, Scene 2; quoted in *Long Day's Journey into Night*, 152.

13. Being able to see is not, however, enough. Dion is like Yank in that he is aware of his lack of belonging in the world, even though he knows that he should find his place in it.

> DION. Why am I afraid to live, I who love life and the beauty of flesh and the living colors of earth, sky and sea? [*GGB* 264].

He is in between those who have reached the final stage of harmony and those who are unable to perceive how lost they are. Cf. Nietzsche's idea according to which man is a bridge.

14. Harold Bloom, "Introduction," in Bloom, *Eugene O'Neill*, iv.

15. See for instance the death of Lazarus:

> (*his voice... followed by a faint dying note of laughter that rises and is lost in the sky like the flight of his soul back into the womb of infinity*) [*LL* 371].

16. One should not forget that some characters have shown its links with the origin of mankind; cf. Reuben, in *Dynamo* (452).

16. Conclusion

1. Albert Kalson and Lisa Schwedt, "Eternal Recurrence and the Shaping of O'Neill's Dramatic Structures," *Contemporary Drama* 24, 2 (1990): 142.

2. The process recalls what we observed in an episode from *A Moon for the Misbegotten* where Josie Hogan takes on the role of the mother and tells her brother to leave, for if he stays on the farm he will never be himself.

3. See again note 5 of Chapter 5, above (page 239).

4. The remarks made by O'Neill retain their relevance today: "But happiness is a word. What does it mean? Exaltation, an intensified feeling of the significant worth of man's being and becoming? Well, if it means that—and not a mere smirking contentment with one's lot—I know that there is more of it in one real tragedy than in all the happy ending plays ever written. It is a present-day judgment to think of tragedy as unhappy. The Greeks and the Elisabethans knew better. They felt the tremendous lift to it. It roused them spiritually to a deeper understanding of life. Through it they found release from the petty considerations of everyday existence. They saw their lives ennobled by it. ¶ But it might be easier to sum the whole matter up in a few words and say: A work of art is always happy; all else is unhappy." O'Neill, in a letter to Malcom Mollan (December 1921). In Bogard and Bryer, eds., *Selected Letters of Eugene O'Neill*, 159.

5. This last lesson is not given by Spinoza, but by Nietzsche: "That is why the image of the *dying Socrates*, man freed by insight and reason from the fear of death, became the emblem over the portals of science, reminding all who entered of their mission: to make existence appear intelligible and consequently justified." Friedrich Nietzsche, *The Birth of Tragedy*, transl. Shaun Whiteside (London: Penguin, 1993), 73.

6. This must not be interpreted as an invitation to a cult of the self. On the contrary, by numerous examples of characters broken by the consequences of their egotistical or materialistic choices, the playwright indicates to the spectator that it must not be understood in this way.

17. Beyond the Conclusions.

1. "The final curtain falls just as a new play is beginning. At least, that is what I meant by it. A naturalistic play is life. Life doesn't end. One experience is but the death of another. And even death—" O'Neill, in the letter to Mollan, Bogard and Bryer, eds., *Selected Letters of Eugene O'Neill*, 159.

Chronological List of the Plays.

1913
Recklessness. Thirst. Warnings. The Web. A Wife for a Life.

1914
Abortion. Bound East for Cardiff. Bread and Butter. Fog. The Movie Man. Servitude.

1915
The Personal Equation. The Sniper.

1916
Before Breakfast.

1917
Ile. In the Zone. The Long Voyage Home. Now I Ask You.

1918
Beyond the Horizon. The Dreamy Kid. The Moon of the Caribbees. The Rope. Shell Shock. Where the Cross Is Made.

1919
The Straw.

1920
Anna Christie. Diff'rent. The Emperor Jones. Gold.

1921
The First Man. The Hairy Ape.

1922
The Fountain.

The intent of this chronology is to give a general idea of the dates of the writing of the plays. For more accurate information, it would be wise to consult Margaret Loftus Ranald, The Eugene O'Neill Companion *(Westport, Conn.: Greenwood Press, 1984),* 731–3.

1923
All God's Chillun Got Wings.   *Welded.*

1924
Desire Under the Elms.

1925
The Great God Brown.   *Marco Millions.*

1926
Lazarus Laughed.

1927
Strange Interlude.

1928
Dynamo.

1931
Mourning Becomes Electra.

1933
Ah, Wilderness!   *Days Without End.*

1938
More Stately Mansions.

1939
The Iceman Cometh.

1941
Hughie.   *Long Day's Journey into Night.*

1942
A Touch of the Poet.

1943
A Moon for the Misbegotten.

List of "Family Plays."

Abortion
Ah, Wilderness!
All God's Chillun Got Wings
Anna Christie
Beyond the Horizon
Bread and Butter
Days Without End
Desire Under the Elms
Diff'rent
The Dreamy Kid
Dynamo
The First Man
Gold
The Great God Brown
The Hairy Ape
The Iceman Cometh

Lazarus Laughed
Long Day's Journey into Night
Marco Millions
A Moon for the Misbegotten
More Stately Mansions
Mourning Becomes Electra
Now I Ask You
The Personal Equation
The Rope
Servitude
Strange Interlude
The Straw
A Touch of the Poet
Warnings
The Web
Where the Cross Is Made

Bibliography.

O'Neill's writings.

O'Neill, Eugene. *"Children of the Sea" and Three Other Unpublished Plays by Eugene O'Neill.* [*Bread and Butter; "Children of the Sea,"* an early draft of *Bound East for Cardiff; Now I Ask You; Shell Shock.*] Jennifer McCabe Atkinson, ed. Washington, D.C.: NCR Microcard Editions, 1972. 214 p.
_____. *Eugene O'Neill: Work Diary, 1924-1943.* Preliminary Edition. Donald Gallup, ed. New Haven: Yale University Press, 1981. (2 vols.)
_____. *Eugene O'Neill at Work: Newly Released Ideas for Plays.* Virginia Floyd, ed. New York: Ungar, 1981. xxxix, 407 p.
_____. *Hughie.* New Haven: Yale University Press, 1959. 38 p.
_____. *Long Day's Journey into Night.* New Haven: Yale University Press, 1989. 176 p.
_____. *A Moon for the Misbegotten.* New York: Random House (Vintage Books), 1974. 115 p.
_____. *More Stately Mansions.* Martha Gilman Bower, ed. New York: Oxford University Press, 1988. 313 p.
_____. *The Personal Equation; The Reckoning and The Guilty One; The Ole Davil: Act Four; The Ancient Mariner: A Dramatic Arrangement of Coleridge's Poem; Marco's Millions.* In Travis Bogard, ed., *The Unknown O'Neill.* New Haven: Yale University Press, 1989. 434 p.
_____. *The Plays of Eugene O'Neill.* [*Anna Christie, Beyond the Horizon, The Emperor Jones, The Hairy Ape, The Great God Brown, The Straw, Dynamo, Days Without End, The Iceman Cometh.*] Vol. 1. (The Modern Library.) New York: Random House, 1982. 728 p.
_____. *The Plays of Eugene O'Neill.* [*Mourning Becomes Electra, Ah, Wilderness!, All God's Chillun Got Wings, Marco Millions, Welded, Diff'rent, The First Man, Gold.*] Vol. 2. (The Modern Library.) New York: Random House, 1982. 692 p.
_____. *The Plays of Eugene O'Neill.* [*Strange Interlude, Desire Under the Elms, Lazarus Laughed, The Fountain, The Moon of the Caribbees, Bound East for Cardiff, The Long Voyage Home, In the Zone, Ile, Where the Cross Is Made, The Rope, The Dreamy Kid, Before Breakfast.*] Vol. 3. (The Modern Library.) New York: Random House, 1982. 633 p.
_____. *Ten "Lost" Plays of Eugene O'Neill.* [*Thirst, The Web, Warnings, Fog, Recklessness, Abortion, The Movie Man, The Sniper, A Wife for a Life, Servitude.*] New York: Random House, 1964. 303 p.
_____. *A Touch of the Poet.* New Haven: Yale University Press, 1957. 182 p.
_____. *The Unfinished Plays: Notes for The Visit of Malatesta, The Last Conquest, Blind Alley Guy.* New York: Ungar, 1988. xxviii, 213 p.

Reference sources.

Alexander, Doris. *Eugene O'Neill's Creative Struggle*. University Park: Pennsylvania State University Press, 1992.
____. *The Tempering of Eugene O'Neill*. New York: Harcourt, Brace, 1962. 300 p.
Alvis, John. "On the American Line: O'Neill's *Mourning Becomes Electra* and the Principles of the Founding." *Southern Review* 22, 1 (winter 1986): 69–85.
Asselineau, Roger. "*Desire Under the Elms*: A Phase of O'Neill's Philosophy," 59–66 in Ernest Griffin, ed., *Eugene O'Neill: A Collection of Criticism*. New York: McGraw-Hill, 1976. 151 p.
Atkinson, Jennifer M. *Eugene O'Neill: A Descriptive Bibliography*. Pittsburgh: University of Pittsburgh Press, 1974. 410 p.
Bagchee, Shyamal, ed. *Perspectives on O'Neill: New Essays*. Victoria, B.C.: University of Victoria, 1988. 112 p.
Barlow, Judith E. *Final Acts: The Creation of Three Late O'Neill Plays*. Athens: University of Georgia Press, 1985. 215 p.
____. "O'Neill's Many Mothers: Mary Tyrone, Josie Hogan and Their Antecedents," 7–16 in Shyamal Bagchee, ed., *Perspectives on O'Neill: New Essays*. Victoria: University of Victoria, 1988. 112 p.
Basile, Michael. "Semiotic Transformability in *All God's Chillun Got Wings*." *Eugene O'Neill Review* 16, 1 (spring 1992) 25–37.
Ben-Zvi, Linda. "Freedom and Fixity in the Plays of Eugene O'Neill." *Modern Drama* 31, 1 (March 1988): 16–27.
Berlin, Normand. *Eugene O'Neill*. London: Macmillan; 1982. 178 p.
____. *O'Neill's Shakespeare*. Ann Arbor: University of Michigan Press, 1993. 268 p.
Bird, Carol. "Eugene O'Neill—The Inner Man," 50–55 in Mark W. Estrin, ed., *Conversations with Eugene O'Neill*. Jackson: University Press of Mississippi, 1990. xxxv, 242 p.
Black, Stephen A. "Reality and Its Vicissitudes: The Problem of Understanding in *Long Day's Journey into Night*." *Eugene O'Neill Review* 16, 2 (fall 1992): 57–72.
____. "The War Among the Tyrones." *Eugene O'Neill Newsletter* 11, 2 (summer-fall 1987): 29–31.
Bloom, Harold, ed. *Eugene O'Neill*. New York: Chelsea, 1987. viii, 183 p.
Bloom, Steven F. "Empty Bottles, Empty Dreams: O'Neill's Use of Drinks and Alcoholism in *Long Day's Journey into Night*," 159–177 in James J. Martine, ed., *Critical Essays on Eugene O'Neill*. Boston: G.K. Hall, 1984.
Bogard, Travis. *Contour in Time: The Plays of Eugene O'Neill*, rev. ed. New York: Oxford University Press, 1988. xx, 507 p.
____, and Bryer, Jackson R., eds. *Selected Letters of Eugene O'Neill*. New Haven: Yale University Press, 1988. xi, 602 p.
Bowen, Crosswell, with the assistance of Shane O'Neill. *The Curse of the Misbegotten: A Tale of the House of O'Neill*. New York: McGraw-Hill, 1959. 384 p.
Bowles, Patrick. "Another Biblical Parallel in *Desire Under the Elms*." *Eugene O'Neill Newsletter* 2,3 (January 1979): 10–12.
Bryer, Jackson R., and Alvarez, Ruth M., eds. *"The Theatre We Worked For": The Letters of Eugene O'Neill to Kenneth Macgowan*. New Haven: Yale University Press, 1982. xi, 274 p.
Cargill, Oscar; Fagin, N. Bryllion; and Fisher, William J., eds. *O'Neill and His Plays: Four Decades of Criticism*. New York: New York University Press, 1961. 528 p.
Carpenter, Frederic I. *Eugene O'Neill*, rev. ed. Boston: Twayne, 1979. 192 p.
____. "Eugene O'Neill, the Orient, and American Transcendentalism," 37–44 in Ernest

Griffin, ed., *Eugene O'Neill: A Collection of Criticism*. New York: McGraw-Hill, 1976. 151 p.
Chabrowe, Leonard. *Ritual and Pathos: The Theatre of Eugene O'Neill*. Lewisburg, Pa.: Bucknell University Press, 1976. 192 p.
Chothia, Jean. "Theatre Language: Word and Image in *The Hairy Ape*," 31–46 in Marc Maufort, ed., *Eugene O'Neill and the Emergence of American Drama*. Amsterdam: Rodopi, 1989. v, 205 p.
Chothia, Jean. *Forging a Language: A Study of the Plays of Eugene O'Neill*. Cambridge, England: Cambridge University Press, 1979. 243 p.
Clark, Barrett H. *Eugene O'Neill: The Man and His Plays*. New York: Dover, 1967. xi, 214 p.
Commins, Dorothy, ed. *"Love and Admiration and Respect": The O'Neill-Commins Correspondance*. Durham, N.C.: Duke University Press, 1986. xxi, 248 p.
Cunningham, Frank R. "Romantic Elements in Early O'Neill," 65–72 in James J. Martine, ed., *Critical Essays on Eugene O'Neill*. Boston: G.K. Hall, 1984.
Dahl, Lisa. *Linguistic Features of the Stream of Consciousness Techniques of James Joyce, Virginia Woolf and Eugene O'Neill*. Turku, Finland: Turun Yliopisto, 1970, 78 p.
Driver, Tom. "On the late Plays of Eugene O'Neill," in Nathan A. Scott, Jr., ed., *Man in the Modern Theatre*. Richmond, Va.: John Knox Press, 1965. 100 p.
Dubost, Thierry. "Masques et miroirs dans *A Touch of the Poet* de Eugene O'Neill," 151–62 in Josette Leray, ed., *Masques et miroirs dans le monde anglo-saxon*. Caen: Presses Universitaires de Caen, 1996. 200 p.
———. "Renaissance dans *Strange Interlude*." *Americana* 12 (1995): 69–81.
Engel, Edwin. *The Haunted Heroes of Eugene O'Neill*. Cambridge, Mass.: Harvard University Press, 1953. x, 310 p.
———. "Ideas in the Plays of Eugene O'Neill," 21–36 in Ernest Griffin, ed., *Eugene O'Neill: A Collection of Criticism*. New York: McGraw-Hill, 1976. 151 p.
Estrin, Mark W., ed. *Conversations with Eugene O'Neill*. Jackson: University Press of Mississipi, 1990. xxxv, 242 p.
Falk, Doris. *Eugene O'Neill and the Tragic Tension*. New Brunswick, N.J.: Rutgers University Press, 1958. vii, 211 p.
Feldman, Robert. "The Longing for Death in O'Neill's *Strange Interlude* and *Mourning Becomes Electra*." *Literature and Psychology* 31, 1 (1981): 39–48.
Floyd, Virginia, ed. *Eugene O'Neill: A World View*. New York: Frederick Ungar, 1979. 309 p.
Frenz, Hortz, and Tuck, Susan, eds. *Eugene O'Neill's Critics: Voices from Abroad*. Carbondale: Southern Illinois University Press, 1984. xx, 225 p.
Gassner, John, ed. *O'Neill: A Collection of Critical Essays*. Englewood Cliffs, N.J.: Prentice-Hall, 1964. viii, 181 p.
Gelb, Arthur, and Gelb, Barbara. *O'Neill*, rev. ed. New York: Harper and Row, 1987. xx, 969 p.
Goldstein, Malcom. *The Political Stage*. New York: Oxford University Press, 1974. 482 p.
Griffin, Ernest, ed. *Eugene O'Neill: A Collection of Criticism*. New York: McGraw-Hill, 1976. 151 p.
Halfmann, Ulrich, ed. *Eugene O'Neill: Comments on the Drama and the Theatre: A Source Book*. Tübingen: Narr, 1987. xxxv, 225 p.
———. "Eugene O'Neill: Eine Bibliographie." 251–262 in Ulrich Halfmann, ed., *Eugene O'Neill 1988: Deutsche Beiträge zum 100. Geburstag des amerikanischen Dramatikers*. Tübingen: Narr, 1990. 273 p.
Hirsch, Foster. *Eugene O'Neill: Life, Work and Criticism*. Fredericton, N.B.: York Press, 1986. 48 p.

Josephson, Lennart. *A Role: O'Neill's Cornelius Melody.* (Stockholm Studies in the History of Literature, 19.) Stockholm: Almqvist & Wiskell, 1977. 166 p.

Kalson, Albert, and Schwedt, Lisa. "Eternal Recurrence and the Shaping of O'Neill's Dramatic Structures." *Comparative Drama* 24, 2 (1990): 133–150.

Kobernick, Mark. *Semiotics of the Drama and the Style of Eugene O'Neill.* Philadelphia: John Benjamins Pub. Co., 1989. xiv, 161 p.

Larson, Kelli A. "O'Neill's Tragic Quest for Belonging: Psychological Determinism in the SS Glencairn Plays." *Eugene O'Neill Review* 13, 2 (fall 1989): 12–22.

Le Breton, Maurice. "O'Neill and American Theatre," in Horst Frenz and Susan Tuck, eds., *Eugene O'Neill's Critics: Voices from Abroad.* Carbondale: Southern Illinois University Press, 1984. xx, 225 p.

Leech, Clifford. *Eugene O'Neill.* New York: Grove Press, 1963. 120 p.

Liu, Haiping. "Taoism in O'Neill's Tao House Plays." *Eugene O'Neill Newsletter* 12, 2 (summer-fall 1988): 28–33.

____, and Lowell Swortzell, eds. *Eugene O'Neill in China.* New York: Greenwood Press, 1992. xix, 308 p.

Manheim, Michael. *Eugene O'Neill's New Language of Kinship.* Syracuse: Syracuse University Press, 1982. xii, 240 p.

Martine, James, ed. *Critical Essays on Eugene O'Neill.* Boston: G.K. Hall, 1984. vii, 214 p.

Massa, Ann. "Intention and Effect in *The Hairy Ape.*" *Modern Drama* 31, 1 (March 1988): 41–51.

Maufort, Marc, ed. *Eugene O'Neill and the Emergence of American Drama.* Amsterdam: Rodopi, 1989. v, 205 p.

____. "The Legacy of Melville's *Pierre*: Family Relationships in *Mourning Becomes Electra.*" *Eugene O'Neill Newsletter* 11, 2 (summer-fall 1987): 23–28.

____. *Songs of American Experience: The Vision of O'Neill and Melville.* (American University Studies.) New York: Peter Lang, 1990. 224 p.

Mihelich, Christine, I.H.M. "The Rite of Confession in Five Plays by Eugene O'Neill." *Dissertations Abstract International* 38 (1976): 265A (University of Pittsburgh).

Miller, Jordan Y. *Eugene O'Neill and the American Critic: A Bibliographical Checklist,* 2d. ed. rev. Hamden, Conn.: Archon, 1973. 553 p.

Mirlas, Leon. "Scope of O'Neill's Drama," in Horst Frenz and Susan Tuck, eds., *Eugene O'Neill's Critics: Voices from Abroad.* Carbondale: Southern Illinois University Press, 1984. xx, 225 p.

Moorton, Richard F., Jr., ed. *Eugene O'Neill's Century: Centennial Views on America's Foremost Tragic Dramatist.* Westport, Conn.: Greenwood, 1991. xxiv, 231 p.

Mounier, Catherine. "L'Expressionnisme dans l'œuvre d'Eugene O'Neill," 329–340 in Denis Bablet and Jean Jacquot, eds., *L'Expressionnisme dans le théâtre européen.* Paris: Centre National de la Recherche Scientifique, 1984. 406 p.

Nathan, George J. *"The Rime of the Ancient Mariner,"* in Oscar Cargill; Fagin, and Fisher, eds., *O'Neill and His Plays: Four Decades of Criticism.* New York: New York University Press, 1961. 528 p.

O'Neill, Eugene. "On Man and God," 115 in Oscar Cargill; Fagin, and Fisher, eds., *O'Neill and His Plays: Four Decades of Criticism.* New York: New York University Press, 1961. 528 p.

____. "O'Neill Talks About His Plays," 110–112 in Oscar Cargill; Fagin, and Fisher, eds., *O'Neill and His Plays: Four Decades of Criticism.* New York: New York University Press, 1961. 528 p.

____. "What the Theatre Means to Me," 107 in Oscar Cargill; Fagin, and Fisher, eds., *O'Neill and His Plays: Four Decades of Criticism.* New York: New York University Press, 1961. 528 p.

Orlandello, John. *O'Neill on Film*. Rutherford, N.J.: Fairleigh Dickinson University Press, 1982. 182 p.
Porter, Laurin. *The Banished Prince: Time, Memory and Ritual in the Late Plays of Eugene O'Neill*. Ann Arbor: UMI Research Press, 1988. 144 p.
Raleigh, John. *The Plays of Eugene O'Neill*. Carbondale: Southern Illinois University Press, 1965. 304 p.
____. "Strindberg and O'Neill as Historical Dramatists," 59–75 in Marc Maufort, ed., *Eugene O'Neill and the Emergence of American Drama*. Amsterdam: Rodopi, 1989. v, 205 p.
Ranald, Margaret Loftus. *The Eugene O'Neill Companion*. Westport, Conn.: Greenwood Press, 1984. 827 p.
Roberts, Nancy, and Roberts, Arthur, eds. *As Ever, Gene: The Letters of Eugene O'Neill to George Jean Nathan*. Rutherford, N.J.: Fairleigh Dickinson University Press, 1987. 248 p.
Robinson, James A. *Eugene O'Neill and Oriental Thought: A Divided Vision*. Carbondale: Southern Illinois University Press, 1982. xi, 201 p.
____. "O'Neill's Indian *Elms*." *Eugene O'Neill Review* 13, 1 (spring 1989): 40–46.
Rollyson, Carl E., Jr. "Eugene O'Neill: The Drama of Self-Transcendance," 123–137 in James J. Martine, ed., *Critical Essays on Eugene O'Neill*. Boston: G.K. Hall, 1984. vii, 214 p.
Roy, Emil. "The Archetypal Unity of Eugene O'Neill's Drama," 1–15 in John H. Stroupe, ed., *Critical Approaches to O'Neill*. New York: AMS, 1988. x, 219 p.
Sarrazac, Jean-Pierre. "Le Roman dramatique familial d'Eugene O'Neill," 47–62 in *Théâtres intimes*. Arles: Actes Sud "Le Temps du théâtre," 1989. 168 p.
Shaughnessy, Edward L. *Eugene O'Neill in Ireland: The Critical Reception*. Westport, Conn.: Greenwood Press, 1988.
____. "Question and Answer in *Hughie*." *Eugene O'Neill Newsletter* 3, 2 (September 1978): 3–7.
Sheaffer, Louis. *O'Neill: Son and Artist*, rev. ed. Boston: Little, Brown, 1990. xviii, 750 p.
____. *O'Neill: Son and Playwright*, rev. ed. Boston: Little, Brown, 1990. xvi, 543 p.
Smith, Madeline, and Richard Eaton. *Eugene O'Neill: An Annotated Bibliography*. New York: Garland, 1988. xii, 320 p.
Soulier, Anne Marie. "Le Héros et son double dans les pièces masquées d'Eugene O'Neill. *The Great God Brown* et *Mourning Becomes Electra*." Dissertation, University of Strasbourg, 1984.
Stanich, Linda. "*The Iceman Cometh* as Ethnographic Text." *Eugene O'Neill Review* 13, 2 (fall 1989): 55–62.
Stroupe, John H., ed. *Critical Approaches to O'Neill*. New York: AMS; 1988. x, 219 p.
Szigeti, Gabriela. "L'Expressionnisme européen et un de ses reflets outre-atlantique: l'œuvre de Eugene O'Neill." Dissertation, Université de Paris–Sorbonne, 1985.
Tetauer, Franck. "Tragic Wandering," in Horst Frenz and Susan Tuck, eds., *Eugene O'Neill's Critics: Voices from Abroad*. Carbondale: Southern Illinois University Press, 1984. xx, 225 p.
Tiusanen, Timo. *O'Neill's Scenic Images*. Princeton, N.J.: Princeton University Press, 1968. xiv, 388 p.
Törnqvist, Egil. *A Drama of Souls: Studies in O'Neill's Super-naturalistic Technique*. New Haven: Yale University Press, 1969. 284 p.
____. "To Speak the Unspoken: Audible Thinking in O'Neill's Plays." *Eugene O'Neill Review* 16, 1 (spring 1992): 55–70.
Torrey, Jane. "O'Neill's Psychology of Oppression in Men and Women," 165–170 in

Richard F. Moorton, Jr., ed., *Eugene O'Neill's Century: Centennial Views on America's Foremost Tragic Dramatist.* Westport, Conn.: Greenwood, 1991. xxiv, 231 p.
Trilling, Lionel. "Eugene O'Neill," in Harold Bloom, ed., *Eugene O'Neill.* New York: Chelsea, 1987. viii, 183 p.
Tuck, Susan H. "Reviews of O'Neill Plays in Performance." *Eugene O'Neill Newsletter* 7, 1 (spring 1983): 15–25.
Vena, Gary. *O'Neill's The Iceman Cometh: Reconstructing the Première.* Ann Arbor: UMI Research Press, 1988.
Wainscott, Ronald H. *Staging O'Neill.* New Haven: Yale University Press, 1988. 384 p.
Wilkins, Frederick C. "A Decade's Riches: Articles in the *Newsletter*, 1977–1986." *Eugene O'Neill Newsletter* 11, 1 (spring 1987): 27–32.
———. "O'Neill's Secular Saints." *Eugene O'Neill Review* 14, 1-2 (spring-fall 1990): 71–78.
———. "The Pressure of Puritanism in Eugene O'Neill's New England Plays," 237–244 in Virginia Floyd, ed., *Eugene O'Neill: A World View.* New York: Frederick Ungar, 1979. 309 p.
———. "Publications by and about O'Neill, 1980-1983." *Eugene O'Neill Newsletter* 8 (summer-fall 1984): 22–28.
Winther, Sophus Keith. *Eugene O'Neill: A Critical Study.* New York: Russell & Russell, 1961. 319 p.

General interest.

Abirached, Robert. *La Crise du personnage dans le théâtre moderne.* Paris: Grasset; 1978. 512 p.
Artaud, Antonin. *Le Théâtre et son double* (1964). Paris: Idées-Gallimard, 1979. 251 p.
Aurigemma, Luigi. *Perspectives jungiennes.* Paris: Albin Michel, 1992. 280 p.
Barthes, Roland. *Sur Racine.* Paris: Points-Éditions du Seuil, 1963. 157 p.
Bouyer, Louis. *Dictionnaire théologique.* Paris: Desclée De Brouwer, 1990. 352 p.
Chevalier, Jean, and Gheerbrant, Alain, eds. *Dictionnaire des symboles.* Paris: Robert Laffont, 1982. xxxii, 1060 p.
Eicher, Pierre, ed. *Dictionnaire de théologie.* Paris: Éditions du Cerf, 1988. ix, 839 p.
Eracle, Jean. *Paroles de Bouddha.* Paris: Points-Éditions du Seuil, 1990. 246 p.
Freud, Sigmund. *La Vie sexuelle,* transl. by Denise Berger, Jean Laplanche, et al. Paris: Presses Universitaires de France, 1982. 161 p.
Genet, Jean. "L'Étrange mot d'...," 9–18 in Jean Genet, *Oeuvres complètes.* Paris: Gallimard; vol 4., 1968.
Gouhier, Henri. *Le Théâtre et l'existence.* Paris: Librairie Philosophique J.Vrin, 1991. 224 p.
Granet, Marcel. *La Pensée chinoise.* Paris: Éditions Albin Michel, 1990. 568 p.
———. *La Religion des Chinois.* Paris: Payot, 1980. 192 p.
Grenier, Jean. *L'Esprit du Tao.* Paris: Champs-Éditions Flammarion, 1992. 218 p.
Jankelevitch, Vladimir. *La Mort.* Paris: Champs-Éditions Flammarion, 1977. 474 p.
Jarry, Alfred. *Tout Ubu.* Paris: Le Livre de Poche, Librairie Générale Française, 1962. 502 p.
Lao-tzu. *Tao-Teh-Ching,* transl. by John C. H. Wu. Jamaica, N.Y.: St. John's University Press, 1961.
Laplanche, Jean, and Pontalis, Jean-Baptiste. *Vocabulaire de la psychanalyse.* Paris: Presses Universitaires de France, 1992. xix, 523 p.

Larthomas, Pierre. *Le Langage dramatique*. Paris: Presses Universitaires de France, 1980. 478 p.

Masson, Joseph. *Le Bouddhisme*. Paris: Desclée De Brouwer, 1975. 293 p.

Nietzsche, Friedrich. *The Birth of Tragedy*, transl. by Shaun Whiteside. London: Penguin, 1993.

———. *Thus Spake Zarathustra*. London: T. N. Foulis, 1911. 458 p.

Oury, Guy-Marie, ed. *Dictionnaire de la foi catholique*. Chambray: Éditions CLD, 1986. 267 p.

Pavis, Patrice. *Dictionnaire du théâtre*. Paris: Éditions Sociales, 1980. 482 p.

Rahula, Walpola. *L'Enseignement du Bouddha*. Paris: Points–Éditions du Seuil, 1978. 191 p.

Schopenhauer, Arthur. *Douleurs du monde*, transl. by Jean Bourdeau. Paris: Éditions Rivages, 1990. 231 p.

———. *Le Fondement de la morale*, transl. by Auguste Burdeau. Paris: Livre de Poche, 1991. 255 p.

Tchouang-tseu. *Oeuvre complète*, transl. by Liou Kia-hway. (Connaissance de l'Orient.) Paris: Gallimard, 1992. 390 p.

Ubersfeld, Anne. *Lire le théâtre*. Paris: Essentiel–Éditions Sociales, 1982. 294 p.

Wilder, Thornton. *American Characteristics and Other Essays*. New York: Harper & Row, 1979. 277 p.

Index.

Abbie 41, 52, 57, 100, 104, 155, 157, 185, 218, 222, 235*n19*, 252*n16*
Abortion 4, 30, 31, 36, 94, 134, 154, 173, 175, 177, 235*n20*, 236*n40*, 237*n45*, 237*n59*, 238*n6*, 239*n3(ch7)*, 241*n21*, 253*n27*
ABSENCE 10, 11, 12, 51, 56, 57, 76, 203, 208
ABSURD 3, 58, 89, 143, 156, 186, 195, 201
Ada 51, 134
Adam *see* Brant
Adams 87
Ah, Wilderness! 7, 32, 73, 74, 75, 78, 92, 94, 114, 156, 171, 180, 189, 203, 205, 208, 231*n6*, 236*n40*, 238*n2(ch5)*, 239*n2*, 239*n7*, 239*n8*, 248*n25*, 249*n7*, 251*n1*, 252*n10*
ALCOHOL 29, 30, 31, 32, 35, 37, 75, 77, 82, 85, 88, 99, 100, 107, 110, 114, 117, 129, 130, 131, 132, 133, 136, 143, 148, 149, 173, 178, 179, 196, 199, 200, 204, 205, 228
All God's Chillun Got Wings 16, 53, 62, 65, 85, 86, 91, 101, 111, 112, 137, 233*n8*, 236*n40*, 238*n61*, 240*n4*, 241*n19*, 242*n29*, 245*n1(ch10)*, 247*n23*, 251*n1*
Alvarez 248*n1*
Alvis 144, 243*n8*, 248*n2*
Amelia 42
Ames 14
Andrew 19, 40, 41, 63, 90, 123, 212
Anna 47, 48, 50, 102, 103, 111, 148, 187, 200, 201, 202, 210, 224, 232*n19*, 235*n28*, 248*n24*, 251*n5*
Anna Christie 27, 46, 48, 49, 50, 83, 102, 103, 111, 148, 149, 187, 199, 201, 203, 212, 214, 219, 232*n5*, 232*n19*, 235*n28*, 239*n1(ch7)*, 247*n23*, 248*n24*, 251*n5*, 252*n10*, 256*n9*
Annie 46, 47, 61
Ashe 234*n10*

Asselineau 17, 232*n18*
Atkins, Mrs. 237*n50*
AUDIENCE 7, 12, 14, 25, 58, 60, 63, 84, 125, 127, 142, 188, 197, 199, 216, 235*n24*

Babbitt 70
Bagchee 236*n30*, 243*n4*
Baldwin, Mrs. 102, 173
Barlow 49, 95, 232*n11*, 236*n30*, 237*n44*, 243*n4*, 252*n11*
Bartlett 39, 43, 127, 128, 183, 212, 214, 234*n11*, 234*n12*, 234*n13*, 255*n4*
Bartlett, Mrs. 69
Basile 242*n29*
Beckett 219, 254*n30*
Before Breakfast 93, 97, 134, 153, 173, 236*n40*, 243*n9*, 251*n1*
BELONGING 3, 13, 30, 35, 40, 46, 52, 54, 67, 76, 82, 101, 110, 111, 112, 113, 114, 115, 116, 117, 118, 120, 121, 132, 133, 135, 136, 140, 153, 160, 161, 173, 185, 186, 192, 200, 203, 206, 209, 210, 211, 212, 213, 214, 215, 217, 218, 219, 220, 223, 224, 230
Ben-Zvi 247*n22*
Benarès 157
Benny 9, 11
Bentley 37, 46, 47, 61, 234*n6*
Berlin 210, 256*n7*
Bessie 28, 149, 248*n24*
Beyond the Horizon 8, 9, 15, 19, 24, 33, 40, 46, 48, 55, 61, 63, 90, 93, 99, 100, 123, 171, 177, 187, 208, 209, 212, 236*n40*, 237*n56*, 239*n1(ch7)*, 247*n23*, 251*n4*, 252*n10*, 253*n23*, 255*n2*
BIBLE 144
Bigelow 87, 107, 238*n5*
Billy *see* Brown
Bird 247*n13*
Blarney Stone 246*n4*,

271

BLINDNESS 26, 37, 58, 96, 100, 125, 129, 142, 143, 144, 148, 155, 157, 159, 190, 195, 200, 218, 219, 222
Bloom 200, 201, 220, 242n36, 255n1, 256n14
Bogard *(Contour)* 3, 4, 91, 231n3(introd), 242n32, 244n13
Bogard & Bryer 232n2, 232n5, 232n14, 233n1, 234n10, 235n26, 239n4(ch6), 239n5, 240n14, 244n16, 256n4, 257n1
Borden, Mrs. 19
Boulton 232n2
Bound East for Cardiff 81, 105, 170, 199, 202, 203, 213, 217, 239n3(ch7), 244n17, 252n10, 253n25, 256n8
Bouyer 253n21
Bowen 234n13, 246n8
Bowles 233n4
Brant 21, 26, 35, 55, 72, 132, 144, 145, 164, 179, 210, 211, 233n7, 236n32, 247n14
Bread and Butter 30, 35, 63, 65, 69, 93, 96, 99, 134, 149, 173, 233n3, 241n22, 243n9, 247n23, 248n24, 252n10
Brennan, Mrs. 186
Brown (Billy) 107, 108, 117, 118, 190
Bryer 232n2, 232n5, 232n14, 233n1, 234n10, 235n26, 239n4, 239n5, 240n14, 244n16, 248n1, 256n4, 257n1
BUDDHISM 3, 4, 156, 157, 158, 159, 160, 161, 169, 192, 249n2, 250n14, 250n15, 250n16, 251n18
Burke *see* Mat
Byron 16, 63, 129, 143

Cabot (Ephraim) 8, 14, 17, 22, 24, 35, 37, 38, 41, 43, 47, 52, 53, 92, 98, 99, 100, 183, 186, 188, 191, 217, 233n4, 234n7, 235n19, 247n23
Calderon 121
Caleb 9, 96, 181, 252n8
Caligula 97, 194
The Calms of Capricorn 1, 103, 231n1(introd), 244n13
Cape 101, 175, 244n15
Cargill 240n13, 241n16, 242n1, 254n38
Carmody 48
Carpenter 130, 241n25, 247n19, 250n13
Cathleen 14, 199, 200, 255n43
CATHOLICISM 3, 4, 158, 186, 187, 191, 192, 193
Charlie *see* Marsden
Chevalier 244n14

Children of the Sea 202, 203, 256n8
Chothia 240n6
Chris 27, 48, 49, 102, 148, 187, 200, 201, 210, 212, 213, 214, 219, 232n19, 235n28, 248n24, 256n9
Christine 21, 26, 55, 61, 62, 65, 100, 103, 126, 134, 144, 164, 173, 210, 233n7, 236n42, 237n43, 237n49, 237n51, 237n53, 238n1(ch5), 247n14, 247n15, 254n32
Chu-Yin 127, 219
CLAN 13, 15, 16, 19, 21, 26, 27, 28, 33, 40, 47, 48, 53, 54, 66, 67, 69, 70, 71, 75, 76, 77, 113, 115, 117, 118, 140, 145, 229
Clark 232n5, 240n12, 242n31
Cocky 202, 203, 204, 245n2
Coleridge 84, 125
Columbus 167
CONFESSION 28, 30, 61, 90, 99, 100, 103, 119, 134, 144, 145, 162, 164, 167, 168, 170, 172, 182, 202, 205, 224
CORRUPTION 54, 71, 91, 111, 122, 124, 136, 178, 218
Cregan 106, 246n3
the Crowd 69
Curtis 12, 15, 34, 35, 68, 94, 107
Cybel 24, 40, 97, 108, 175

Dahl 251n1
Darrell 26, 56, 118, 215, 243n5
David *see* Keeney
Davidson, Mrs. 236n38
Davis 245n2
Days Without End 9, 56, 95, 97, 118, 152, 158, 192, 193, 208, 209, 220, 243n5, 245n1(ch10), 247n23, 251n1, 252n10
DEATH 8, 10, 11, 12, 17, 21, 22, 26, 28, 29, 30, 31, 34, 35, 38, 39, 40, 41, 43, 44, 45, 47, 51, 53, 57, 59, 60, 61, 65, 69, 77, 88, 96, 97, 99, 105, 107, 108, 113, 119, 122, 123, 124, 126, 132, 133, 134, 140, 143, 144, 145, 150, 151, 154, 158, 159, 160, 167, 168, 169, 170, 171, 172, 173, 174, 180, 182, 190, 193, 194, 195, 197, 198, 202, 203, 207, 208, 209, 210, 213, 214, 215, 218, 222, 223
Deborah 22, 29, 57, 62, 63, 70, 71, 120, 122, 126, 128, 132, 146, 150, 179, 180, 196, 236n42
DECLINE 33, 58, 69, 90, 91, 113, 123, 128, 132, 135, 149, 180
Descartes 160, 170
DESIRE 27, 29, 30, 35, 43, 45, 52, 53, 57,

Index. 273

58, 62, 64, 71, 77, 82, 89, 90, 94, 95, 96,
101, 105, 107, 108, 112, 120, 121, 124, 127,
133, 135, 139, 142, 145, 146, 149, 153,
154, 157, 160, 163, 167, 168, 184, 185,
188, 194, 201, 218
Desire Under the Elms 1, 8, 14, 15, 17, 22,
24, 29, 33, 35, 37, 41, 43, 44, 52, 53, 54,
60, 84, 98, 99, 103, 131, 134, 155, 157,
176, 182, 183, 186, 191, 198, 208, 209,
217, 219, 222, 232n18, 233n3, 233n4,
233n12, 234n7, 234n9, 234n16, 234n17,
235n19, 236n40, 242n33, 244n12,
247n21, 247n23, 250n15, 251n4,
252n16, 254n30
DIFFERENCE 15, 16, 17, 49, 76, 82, 100,
101, 104, 113, 117, 119, 133, 135, 142, 146,
150, 155, 160, 200
Diff'rent 9, 11, 16, 53, 65, 96, 98, 134, 152,
173, 181, 203, 208, 210, 247n23, 252n8
Dion 40, 97, 107, 108, 163, 190, 204,
255n3, 256n13
Doctor 127
Don Juan 120, 150, 155, 159, 247n18
Donkeyman 243n6, 256n10
DOUBLE 21, 22, 32, 41, 44, 61, 62, 89, 108,
109, 117, 143, 148, 168, 204, 229
DREAM 22, 29, 31, 32, 35, 38, 69, 71, 77,
88, 94, 100, 102, 105, 121, 122, 123, 124,
125, 126, 127, 128, 129, 130, 131, 132,
133, 136, 143, 146, 147, 159, 180, 196,
223
The Dreamy Kid 8
Driscoll 81, 105, 131, 170, 202, 203, 244n17
DRUGS 11, 17, 39, 64, 89, 90, 132, 133, 136,
142, 148, 200, 228
Du Bellay 131
Dubost 233n14
Dynamo 10, 21, 42, 51, 56, 57, 58, 59, 60,
61, 84, 94, 96, 103, 124, 134, 164, 173,
193, 198, 203, 208, 209, 216, 218, 233n3,
233n13, 235n29, 236n29, 237n45,
237n47, 247n23, 251n1, 252n10,
254n34, 255n6, 256n16

Eben 8, 14, 17, 22, 41, 42, 43, 44, 45, 57,
59, 60, 103, 104, 155, 182, 183, 185, 191,
198, 217, 218, 219, 221, 222, 233n12,
235n19, 236n40, 237n48, 244n12,
252n16, 254n34
Edmund 10, 12, 40, 42, 45, 56, 59, 63, 81,
161, 200, 201, 213, 214, 219, 223, 224,
227, 228, 232n17, 237n43, 243n8
Edward 241n22

Eicher 255n42
Eileen 48, 98, 236n37, 254n31
Eleanor 101, 175
Eliot 231n7
Ella 16, 56, 101, 102, 187, 238n61,
239n4(ch7)
Elsa 56, 86, 243n5
Emma 9, 16, 181
The Emperor Jones 85, 86, 111, 113, 155,
189, 203, 208, 239n3(ch7), 240n10,
245n1(ch10), 251n1
Engel 115, 195, 232n9, 245n7, 255n43
Ephraim *see* Cabot
Eracle 250n15
Erie 94, 105, 106, 119, 120, 151, 181,
242n2, 243n3
ESCAPE 3, 10, 17, 21, 23, 26, 27, 28, 31,
34, 39, 40, 41, 43, 44, 50, 57, 64, 68, 71,
76, 77, 82, 89, 92, 99, 101, 103, 105, 110,
111, 113, 119, 121, 126, 128, 129, 130, 131,
132, 133, 134, 135, 141, 143, 145, 146,
149, 150, 151, 156, 165, 180, 181, 182, 186,
196, 200, 212, 213
Estrin 247n13
Ethan 63
Eugene 12
Evans, Mrs. 8, 20, 73, 205, 206, 207,
231n4(ch1)
Evelyn 94, 96, 145, 154, 177
Ezra *see* Mannon

Fagin 240n13, 241n16, 242n1, 254n38
Falk 254n36
FATE 4, 9, 19, 20, 21, 22, 23, 24, 27, 28,
32, 36, 63, 72, 87, 88, 94, 99, 102, 105,
111, 121, 131, 140, 172, 176, 177, 183, 184,
185, 187, 200, 206, 213, 214, 216, 225
Father (character) 232n1
FATHER 9, 10, 11, 12, 19, 21, 22, 30, 31, 34,
35, 36, 37, 38, 39, 40, 41, 42, 43, 44, 45,
46, 47, 48, 49, 50, 51, 55, 58, 61, 62, 67,
69, 74, 77, 89, 100, 127, 144, 154, 164,
167, 175, 177, 189, 191, 193, 201, 207,
210, 212, 213, 217, 218, 219, 220, 232n3,
235n29, 236n35, 243n5
Father Baird 9, 192, 193
FAULT 134, 145, 153, 161, 164
Feldman 27, 171, 233n10, 253n22
Fife 96, 235n29
Fife, Mrs. 209, 216, 218, 235n29, 236n29,
255n6
The First Man 12, 15, 34, 41, 53, 66, 67,
68, 75, 87, 94, 95, 107, 214, 215, 231n6,

233n9, 236n38, 238n2(ch5), 238n3,
  238n5, 238n9, 239n2(ch6), 241n21,
  245n7, 252n10
Fisher 240n13, 241n16, 242n1, 254n38
Floyd 238n1(ch4), 240n7, 241n15,
  254n40
Fog 54, 82, 87, 171, 199, 236n40,
  239n3(ch7), 241n20, 253n25
The Fountain 120, 150, 159, 159, 178, 203,
  208, 209, 245n1(ch10), 247n18, 251n1,
  252n10, 253n25
Frazer, Mrs. 146, 246n9, 246n10
Fred 102
Freda 251n6
FREEDOM 3, 21, 22, 25, 28, 29, 30, 31, 32,
  43, 55, 59, 65, 68, 70, 74, 77, 78, 91, 97,
  101, 108, 115, 121, 137, 156, 157, 158, 160,
  163, 164, 171, 176, 177, 182, 183, 184, 188,
  211, 213, 222, 223, 224, 225, 229, 230
Frenz 242n34, 248n4, 252n9
Freud 12, 50, 144, 171, 236n33, 242n29
Frost 72,
FUTURE 72, 87, 88, 101, 102, 105, 121, 168,
  178, 179, 181, 182, 186, 188

Gabriel 217, 245n7
Gallup 231n1(introd)
Gelb 2, 233n1, 238n2(ch4), 239n7,
  242n29, 252n15, 255n43
Gentleman 214, 252n17
Gheerbrant 244n14
GOD 10, 35, 36, 41, 42, 53, 55, 57, 58, 60,
  70, 90, 93, 97, 98, 100, 108, 110, 113,
  124, 155, 161, 167, 170, 184, 186, 187,
  188, 189, 190, 191, 192, 193, 194, 195,
  201, 202, 208, 216, 218, 220, 223, 224,
  225, 231n5, 232n11, 253n23
Gold 10, 16, 35, 39, 46, 48, 51, 62, 65, 89,
  127, 183, 203, 208, 214, 232n12, 233n3,
  234n12, 234n17, 247n17, 251n1, 252n10
Goldstein 240n11
Gordon 49, 56, 143, 235n24
Gouhier 125, 246n11
Granet 250n11
The Great God Brown 23, 24, 40, 56, 62,
  69, 97, 107, 117, 163, 175, 178, 190, 203,
  208, 232n4, 236n40, 237n55, 240n12,
  245n1(ch10), 246n2, 247n23, 252n10,
  253n25, 255n3, 256n13
Grenier 250n11
Griffin 232n9, 232n18, 250n13, 255n43
GROUP 3, 110, 114, 116, 117, 120, 124, 132,
  133, 135

The Hairy Ape 9, 22, 83, 84, 86, 92, 110,
  111, 114, 115, 116, 141, 153, 173, 178, 196,
  197, 199, 200, 202, 203, 208, 211, 221,
  239n4(ch7), 240n6, 240n8, 240n11,
  242n36, 245n1(ch10), 245n4, 245n7,
  251n1
Halfmann 231n1(introd), 246n5
HAPPINESS 3, 4, 48, 65, 73, 78, 87, 95, 96,
  98, 100, 116, 126, 130, 135, 136, 143, 145,
  157, 158, 159, 175, 178, 185, 215, 221,
  222, 224, 226, 227, 228, 230
Harder 48, 87
Harford 87
Harris, Mrs. 241n19
HATRED 13, 41, 43, 45, 58, 59, 61, 62, 64,
  77, 93, 97, 101, 108, 109, 144, 191, 212,
  213
Hattie 62, 86, 112, 238n61
Hedda Gabler 30, 69, 97
Hegel 123
HEREDITY 9, 19, 20, 21, 22, 23, 26, 27, 29,
  31, 72, 73, 77, 86, 87, 126, 139, 211,
  232n1
Hickey 96, 107, 134, 145, 151, 155, 170,
  172, 246n4, 252n11, 253n19
Higgins 126
HISTORY 67, 85, 86, 88, 130, 135, 139, 140,
  150, 176, 181, 183, 196, 207
Hitler 240n15
Hogan 15, 48, 51, 87, 205, 236n39,
  237n49, 242n2, 246n4
Honey 62
HOPE 27, 28, 47, 75, 88, 98, 99, 100, 101,
  114, 115, 121, 122, 123, 124, 125, 126, 127,
  130, 136, 140, 144, 151, 167, 168, 171, 173,
  179, 182, 197, 207, 213, 223, 225
Hope (Harry) 82, 147, 179, 180, 181, 204
Hughie 105, 106, 119, 120, 243n3
Hughie 82, 92, 94, 105, 106, 120, 130, 151,
  181, 185, 243n3, 251n1, 252n10, 254n37
Hugo 132

Ibsen 97
The Iceman Cometh 4, 11, 53, 54, 59, 79,
  81, 82, 83, 96, 99, 107, 111, 120, 130, 132,
  134, 145, 147, 148, 149, 151, 155, 172,
  173, 179, 204, 212, 214, 216, 241n17,
  243n9, 245n2, 247n21, 247n23, 248n3,
  248n25, 250n9, 251n1, 251n6, 252n10,
  252n11, 253n19
IDENTITY 29, 30 45, 64, 67, 75, 78, 85,
  86, 102, 108, 111, 117, 153, 154, 155, 161,
  163, 225

Ile 73, 89, 98, 177, 210, 247*n16*
ILLUSION 3, 44, 76, 78, 88, 94, 100, 105, 106, 107, 115, 120, 121, 123, 125, 126, 127, 128, 129, 130, 132, 136, 143, 144, 148, 151, 206, 217
In the Zone 99, 118, 131, 203, 204, 242*n28*, 245*n2*
INDIVIDUAL 68, 72, 74, 75, 76, 86, 88, 89, 90, 92, 93, 101, 102, 110, 114, 115, 117, 118, 121, 136, 141, 144, 149, 156, 160, 161, 168, 169, 196, 198, 208, 209, 216, 222, 223, 224, 227, 229
INSIDE 24, 25, 83, 95
Ireland 13, 15, 30, 179, 232*n14*, 246*n4*

Jack 30, 31, 36, 154, 175, 177, 253*n27*
Jackson 87, 88
James (Tyrone, *MMis*) 30, 44, 48, 59, 104, 116, 119, 134, 181, 205, 206, 224, 242*n2*, 246*n4*, 246*n5*, 249*n7*, 252*n11*, 252*n14*, 255*n3*
James Mayo (*BH*) 17, 19, 40, 41, 63, 212
James Tyrone (*LDJN*) 20, 37, 40, 42, 43, 45, 81, 90, 154, 181, 191, 204, 217, 228, 241*n27*, 246*n4*, 246*n6*
Jamie 20, 39, 40, 42, 56, 59, 63, 64, 213, 237*n58*, 249*n6(ch12)*, 252*n11*
Jankelevitch 253*n20*
Jarry 242*n30*
Jayson 66, 67, 75
Jim 16, 86, 101, 102, 112, 113, 137, 187, 238*n61*, 239*n4(ch7)*
Jimmy 148, 151, 216
Joe 112
Joel 237*n57*
John *see* Loving
John (*B&B*) 28, 30, 35, 63, 96, 97, 99, 143, 145, 149, 173
John (*FM*) 68, 238*n9*
Jonathan 62
Jones 85, 86, 88, 113, 155, 189, 207, 240*n10*
Josie 28, 29, 44, 48, 64, 83, 104, 116, 134, 205, 209, 224, 236*n30*, 236*n31*, 237*n49*, 246*n5*, 252*n14*, 256*n2*
Julius Caesar 217, 256*n12*

Kalson 256*n1*
Kant 177
Keeney (David) 98, 99, 210
Keeney, Mrs. 73, 98, 210, 247*n16*
Knapp 235*n20*

Knapp, Mrs. 211
Krutch 245*n1*
Kublai 170, 238*n7*
Kukachin 70, 141, 156, 159, 219, 238*n8*

Lao-tzu 192, 250*n7*
Laplanche 232*n13*
Larry 11, 79, 81, 82, 99, 130, 170, 171, 179, 204, 241*n17*, 250*n9*, 253*n19*
Larson 111, 245*n1*,
Lavinia 21, 22, 23, 26, 27, 28, 49, 50, 61, 62, 65, 72, 100, 118, 144, 145, 152, 173, 177, 188, 206, 232*n3*, 236*n32*, 236*n33*, 236*n34*, 237*n49*, 237*n51*, 237*n52*, 237*n54*, 237*n60*, 243*n7*, 246*n2*, 246*n7*
Lazarus 88, 158, 159, 174, 175, 194, 198, 220, 227, 250*n10*, 250*n13*, 256*n15*
Lazarus Laughed 88, 97, 158, 174, 193, 194, 198, 203, 208, 217, 220, 236*n41*, 237*n46*, 240*n4*, 240*n5*, 245*n1(ch10)*, 250*n10*, 256*n15*
Le Breton 146, 248*n4*
Leda 244*n13*, 253*n20*
Leeds 25, 48, 143, 144, 145, 235*n28*, 235*n29*, 241*n21*
Lewis 107
Light 36, 42, 164
Light, Mrs. 56, 57, 236*n42*
Lily 67, 68, 74, 238*n3*, 238*n5*, 239*n2(ch6)*
Lily (*FM*) 239*n2*
Lincoln 69
Liu 252*n17*
Long 85, 92
Long Day's Journey into Night 10, 11, 12, 14, 16, 20, 35, 39, 40, 42, 43, 45, 54, 56, 59, 63, 64, 68, 69, 81, 86, 90, 100, 140, 142, 148, 154, 181, 184, 191, 192, 199, 200, 203, 208, 214, 223, 226, 227, 228, 229, 232*n17*, 233*n3*, 234*n17*, 237*n43*, 237*n58*, 238*n4*, 239*n3(ch7)*, 239*n6*, 241*n27*, 243*n9*, 246*n6*, 247*n23*, 249*n6*, 251*n1*, 251*n2*, 252*n10*, 252*n11*, 253*n22*, 255*n43*, 256*n12*
The Long Voyage Home 131, 199, 213, 251*n6*, 252*n10*
Louis XIV 128, 146
LOVE 17, 35, 38, 42, 47, 48, 55, 56, 58, 59, 61, 62, 63, 64, 70, 71, 73, 74, 77, 93, 94, 95, 96, 97, 98, 99, 100, 102, 103, 104, 108, 109, 129, 131, 134, 140, 141, 155, 156, 165, 169, 175, 203, 204, 205, 206, 207, 210, 212, 213, 219, 222, 228, 229, 235*n27*

Loving 9, 97, 192, 193, 209, 231*n7*
Lucy (*DWE*) 118, 243*n5*
Lucy (*NIAY*) 51, 69, 156, 180, 181, 235*n27*, 239*n3(ch6)*
Luis 93
Luke 37, 44, 47, 231*n7*, 231*n8*, 234*n6*

McComber 74, 75, 239*n8*
Macgowan 233*n1*, 248*n1*
MADNESS 10, 16, 17, 20, 38, 39, 98, 102, 113, 119, 127, 128, 129, 145, 149, 173, 204, 206, 207, 210, 212
Maffeo 70
Manheim 114, 245*n5*
Mannon 13, 19, 21, 26, 27, 36, 43, 45, 49, 50, 99, 100, 103, 117, 118, 132, 133, 140, 145, 165, 169, 177, 179, 188, 211, 234*n18*, 236*n34*, 237*n54*, 238*n1(ch5)*, 243*n8*, 247*n15*
Marco 21, 36, 70, 125, 141, 142, 159, 219, 238*n7*, 238*n8*
Marco Millions 21, 36, 66, 70, 125, 127, 141, 156, 159, 170, 203, 208, 214, 219, 238*n8*, 240*n4*, 242*n28*, 245*n1(ch10)*, 247*n23*
Margaret 40, 62, 97
Marsden 26, 27, 29, 45, 59, 144, 167, 234*n8*, 243*n5*
Martha 12, 15, 53, 67, 68, 95, 214, 215, 216, 238*n5*, 239*n2(ch6)*
Martine 233*n6*, 255*n1*
Marx 87
Mary 10, 11, 12, 16, 17, 20, 37, 48, 50, 86, 100, 101, 142, 145, 148, 181, 182, 183, 184, 191, 199, 200, 201, 226, 228, 230, 232*n17*, 236*n30*, 237*n43*, 238*n4*, 243*n9*, 251*n2*
MASK 13, 14, 15, 25, 31, 40, 44, 45, 47, 65, 70, 99, 101, 107, 108, 117, 118, 119, 120, 121, 122, 129, 131, 136, 140, 141, 142, 143, 145, 146, 147, 148, 149, 151, 154, 161, 162, 163, 164, 165, 168, 191, 195, 206, 207, 215, 228
Massa 240*n8*
Masson 159, 250*n15*
Mat (Burke) 102, 103, 148, 187, 201, 210, 213
Maud 96, 149
Maufort 191, 240*n6*, 254*n28*, 254*n41*, 256*n11*
Mayo *see* James Mayo
Mayo, Mrs. 55, 237*n50*
MEANING 3, 12, 40, 56, 59, 61, 69, 71, 85, 89, 99, 102, 104, 105, 110, 114, 116, 124, 151, 169, 192
Medea 176
Medicine Man 209
Melody 16, 30, 47, 51, 87, 88, 106, 128, 129, 132, 133, 143, 148, 189, 233*n15*, 234*n15*, 246*n3*, 248*n5*,
Melville 191, 213
Menendez 167
Mickey 112
A Midsummer-Night's Dream 85
Mihelich 252*n12*
Mike 28, 64
Mildred 9, 22, 111, 152, 153
Miller (Nat) 74, 75, 180, 189, 192, 239*n8*
Miller, Mrs. 74, 75, 180, 189, 239*n2(ch6)*
Mirlas 166, 168, 252*n9*, 252*n13*
Mr. ... (character) *see under* name
Mollan 256*n4*, 257*n1*
MONEY 17, 21, 37, 38, 40, 47, 54, 59, 64, 69, 70, 71, 87, 89, 90, 99, 100, 102, 113, 121, 122, 123, 125, 126, 127, 135, 136, 142, 157, 167, 186, 196, 205, 229
MONOLOGUE 142, 162, 163, 164, 167, 168, 169, 211, 215
A Moon for the Misbegotten 15, 28, 29, 30, 41, 44, 46, 48, 49, 51, 59, 64, 65, 83, 87, 91, 96, 104, 116, 119, 134, 184, 190, 205, 209, 224, 232*n12*, 234*n9*, 234*n17*, 236*n31*, 236*n39*, 236*n40*, 237*n45*, 237*n49*, 239*n1(ch7)*, 242*n2*, 246*n5*, 247*n21*, 249*n7*, 251*n1*, 252*n11*, 252*n14*, 255*n3*, 256*n2*
The Moon of the Caribbees 99, 171, 203, 204, 212, 239*n3(ch7)*, 243*n6*, 245*n6*, 256*n10*
Moorton 241*n18*
More Stately Mansions 1, 8, 21, 22, 29, 57, 58, 62, 63, 66, 70, 71, 89, 90, 95, 96, 106, 120, 122, 123, 128, 129, 146, 150, 157, 180, 182, 196, 203, 208, 220, 236*n35*, 236*n42*, 237*n57*, 238*n1(ch4)*, 238*n7*, 241*n25*, 247*n21*, 247*n23*, 251*n1*, 254*n35*
MOTHER 8, 10, 12, 17, 19, 20, 21, 22, 26, 28, 31, 35, 39, 41, 42, 46, 48, 49, 50, 51, 52, 53, 54, 55, 56, 57, 58, 59, 60, 61, 62, 64, 65, 70, 73, 76, 77, 95, 97, 99, 104, 119, 123, 131, 134, 173, 177, 185, 187, 188, 193, 211, 212, 213, 214, 218, 221, 237*n47*
Mourning Becomes Electra 13, 14, 15, 19, 21, 22, 23, 24, 26, 28, 33, 35, 45, 46, 49, 50, 54, 55, 61, 62, 65, 72, 88, 99, 100, 103, 118, 132, 133, 134, 144, 152, 164,

165, 169, 173, 176, 177, 179, 188, 191, 199, 203, 206, 207, 208, 211, 231*n5*, 232*n3*, 233*n3*, 233*n7*, 233*n10*, 234*n17*, 234*n18*, 235*n23*, 235*n25*, 236*n32*, 236*n34*, 236*n42*, 237*n43*, 237*n45*, 237*n49*, 237*n51*, 237*n52*, 237*n54*, 238*n1(ch5)*, 238*n60*, 241*n19*, 242*n28*, 243*n7*, 243*n8*, 243*n9*, 245*n1(ch10)*, 246*n7*, 247*n14*, 247*n21*, 248*n23*, 248*n25*, 251*n1*, 252*n10*, 253*n22*, 254*n32*, 255*n5*
The Movie Man 208
Mrs. ... (character) *see under* name
Muriel 74, 94, 205
Murray (Stephen) 5, 98, 103, 254*n31*

Nano 150
Nat 38, 39, 43, 126, 127, 128, 234*n9* (for *AhW*, see Miller)
Nathan 240*n9*, 240*n13*, 240*n14*
NATURALISM 140, 204, 207,
Nicolo 36, 70
Nietzsche 3, 92, 98, 123, 158, 174, 176, 192, 197, 241*n23*, 242*n35*, 248*n27*, 253*n26*, 254*n29*, 256*n13*, 257*n5*
Night Clerk 92, 130, 131
Nina 8, 20, 29, 30, 34, 47, 49, 51, 53, 56, 73, 95, 144, 167, 213, 215, 220, 231*n4(ch1)*, 234*n8*, 236*n36*, 236*n42*, 243*n5*, 247*n20*, 251*n3*
Nora 106
Now I Ask You 30, 51, 54, 61, 69, 156, 171, 180, 181, 217, 235*n27*, 236*n40*, 239*n3(ch6)*, 245*n7*

Oedipus 176
Older Man 244*n18*
Olga 239*n3(ch6)*
Olson 131, 213, 251*n6*
Olunde 4
O'Neill, Eugene, Jr. 232*n14*
O'Neill, Shane 235*n26*
Orestes 108
ORIENTAL 141, 160, 161, 168, 169
Orin 21, 22, 23, 26, 28, 43, 45, 65, 100, 118, 126, 140, 173, 176, 177, 179, 206, 207, 232*n3*, 234*n18*, 235*n25*, 237*n43*, 237*n53*, 237*n60*, 238*n60*, 242*n28*, 243*n7*, 246*n7*, 254*n29*
Oury 253*n21*
OUTSIDE 13, 24, 25, 26, 28, 33, 76, 81, 82, 83, 141, 154, 160, 223

Paddy 110, 111, 178, 179, 211, 214, 221, 245*n4*, 256*n9*
Pantheism 4, 201, 220, 223
Parritt 11, 59, 82, 99, 172, 212
PAST 7, 11, 23, 28, 57, 69, 71, 73, 86, 102, 104, 110, 112, 113, 128, 129, 131, 140, 145, 147, 148, 149, 155, 159, 161, 168, 176, 178, 181, 182, 183, 185, 186, 191, 228, 230
Pavis 27, 233*n11*
Perkins 235*n22*
The Personal Equation 69, 152, 235*n22*, 239*n3(ch6)*
Peter 22, 23, 29, 42, 43, 50, 72, 131, 144, 145, 233*n12*
Phaedra 176
Plato 104
Poland 90
Ponce de Leon 120
Pontalis 232*n13*
Porter 182, 254*n33*
PRESENT 147, 148, 149, 150, 178, 179, 181, 182, 183, 230
PURITANISM 26, 35, 36, 41, 97, 103, 118, 164, 186, 188, 206
Pylades 108

RACE 16, 17, 19, 85, 86, 102, 112, 113, 118, 135, 155, 207
Rahula 249*n2*, 249*n5*
Raleigh 175, 176, 254*n28*
Ranald 259
REALITY 3, 66, 82, 83, 84, 90, 94, 118, 119, 121, 123, 126, 127, 128, 129, 142, 146, 147, 149, 150, 151, 155, 160, 163, 164, 174, 179, 180, 181, 183, 190, 195, 198, 222, 228, 229
Recklessness 102, 173, 243*n9*, 251*n4*
RETURN 11, 27, 30, 59, 63, 69, 70, 75, 77, 94, 104, 123, 131, 132, 149, 151, 174, 175, 176, 177, 201, 210, 213, 223, 230
Reuben 10, 11, 21, 56, 57, 59, 94, 103, 134, 188, 193, 198, 221, 233*n13*, 235*n29*, 237*n47*, 256*n16*
Richard 73, 74, 75, 94, 205, 207
The Rime of the Ancient Mariner 111, 240*n13*
Robert 8, 15, 17, 19, 48, 50, 63, 89, 90, 171, 187, 188, 222, 223, 245*n3*, 247*n16*, 253*n23*
Roberts 240*n9*, 246*n11*
Robinson 157, 158, 249*n4*, 250*n8*, 250*n12*, 250*n17*, 251*n17*
Rocky 147, 216, 245*n2*

Rollyston 232*n6*
The Rope 9, 14, 15, 29, 37, 44, 46, 49, 51, 54, 208, 231*n3(ch1)*, 231*n7*, 231*n8*, 234*n9*, 234*n16*, 235*n19*, 236*n40*, 248*n23*
Rosa 11, 99, 213
Rose 28, 87
Rousseau 88
Rowland, Mr. 153
Rowland, Mrs. 153
Roy 134, 248*n26*
Roylston, Mr. 96
Roylston, Mrs. 96
Ruth 15, 90, 253*n23*

SAILORS 9, 82, 84, 85, 88, 98, 105, 110, 111, 114, 115, 118, 131, 200, 204, 210, 211, 212, 213, 214, 252*n17*
Sam 20, 21, 56
Sara 21, 47, 51, 54, 70, 71, 88, 89, 95, 102, 129, 146, 196, 236*n35*, 241*n24*, 241*n25*
Sarah 10, 154
Schopenhauer 156, 172, 219, 248*n28*, 249*n1*, 253*n24*
Schwedt
Scotty 204
The Second Engineer 235*n22*
Secretary 115
SELF 88, 90, 143, 158, 159, 160, 163, 168, 170, 186, 194, 195, 215, 216, 224
Servitude 96, 146, 177, 236*n40*, 241*n27*, 246*n9*, 246*n10*, 248*n23*, 252*n10*,
Seth 13, 14, 241*n19*
Shakespeare 121, 217, 256*n7*
Shaughnessy 185, 254*n37*
Sheaffer 2, 231*n1(ch1)*, 232*n15*, 232*n16*
Shell Shock 119, 242*n28*, 252*n10*
Sheriff 157
Sid 74, 75, 156, 248*n25*, 249*n7*
Silva 255*n5*
Simeon 22, 29, 37, 42, 43, 254*n30*
Simon 21, 54, 57, 58, 70, 71, 87, 88, 89, 90, 102, 122, 123, 126, 128, 131, 150, 152, 157, 182, 184, 220, 237*n57*, 241*n25*, 250*n6*, 254*n35*
Smitty 118, 131, 171, 204, 212, 243*n6*, 245*n6*, 256*n10*,
The Sniper 208, 242*n28*
SOCIETY 14, 16, 17, 21, 22, 26, 28, 31, 40, 44, 51, 53, 58, 59, 63, 66, 68, 70, 71, 75, 76, 78, 81, 82, 85, 86, 87, 88, 89, 90, 91,

92, 101, 107, 109, 111, 112, 115, 117, 118, 119, 120, 121, 124, 125, 126, 132, 134, 135, 136, 139, 141, 147, 149, 150, 152, 154, 163, 165, 172, 179, 189, 196, 197, 201, 204, 206
SOLITUDE 16, 48, 49, 100, 104, 110, 112, 114, 116, 136, 141, 172, 185, 204, 206, 214
SOUL 29, 89, 91, 100, 104, 120, 122, 139, 141, 143, 158, 167, 169, 171, 216, 218, 219, 220, 225, 238*n7*, 238*n8*, 244*n13*, 246*n5*, 256*n15*
Soulier 118, 246*n2*
Soyinka 4, 231*n4(introd)*
SPACE 23, 24, 25, 26, 33, 41, 44, 76, 77, 81, 135, 179
Spinoza 257*n5*
SS Glencairn 111, 114, 204, 245*n1(ch9)*
STAGE DIRECTIONS 13, 24, 25, 45, 83, 118, 208, 209, 240*n8*
Stanich 248*n3*
Stephen *see* Murray
Strange Interlude 8, 20, 25, 26, 27, 29, 30, 33, 34, 45, 46, 48, 49, 51, 53, 55, 56, 73, 95, 119, 144, 163, 164, 193, 203, 205, 208, 209, 211, 213, 220, 231*n4(ch1)*, 233*n10*, 233*n14*, 234*n8*, 235*n24*, 235*n28*, 235*n29*, 236*n42*, 239*n3(ch7)*, 241*n21*, 242*n28*, 243*n5*, 247*n20*, 248*n23*, 251*n1*, 251*n3*, 252*n10*, 253*n25*
The Straw 5, 46, 48, 49, 51, 65, 86, 88, 98, 103, 152, 186, 203, 232*n12*, 234*n14*, 236*n37*, 241*n21*, 252*n10*, 254*n31*
Strindberg 97, 254*n28*
Stroupe 248*n26*
STRUGGLE 3, 13, 16, 20, 21, 23, 27, 28, 30, 32, 34, 38, 42, 43, 44, 45, 47, 50, 51, 53, 55, 61, 62, 65, 69, 70, 71, 73, 75, 76, 77, 78, 85, 94, 99, 106, 113, 123, 129, 132, 136, 140, 141, 143, 144, 147, 150, 172, 180, 183, 184, 185, 186, 191, 196, 204, 206, 211, 216, 220, 221, 223, 224, 225, 229
Sue 127, 212, 234*n9*
SUFFERING 18, 34, 40, 59, 62, 95, 97, 100, 105, 106, 118, 120, 126, 133, 143, 150, 151, 153, 156, 157, 159, 160, 163, 165, 167, 168, 171, 172, 182, 184, 207, 215, 223, 224, 227, 229
SUICIDE 4, 11, 30, 31, 32, 35, 36, 45, 59, 65, 77, 89, 94, 96, 97, 99, 133, 134, 136, 143, 153, 156, 172, 173, 173, 174, 177, 185, 188, 192, 193, 195, 221
Sweeney 231*n3(ch1)*
Szigeti 43, 235*n21*

A Tale of Possessors Self-Dispossessed 1, 66, 90
Taoïsm 157, 169, 170, 249*n2*, 249*n3*, 250*n11*, 250*n16*, 250*n17*
Tetauer 242*n34*
The Thirst 82, 91, 213, 214, 216, 252*n17*
Thoreau 21, 123, 249*n6*
Thus Spake Zarathustra 175, 241*n23*, 242*n35*, 248*n27*, 254*n29*
Tiberius 59, 236*n41*, 237*n46*
Tim 87
TIME 23, 24, 26, 52, 56, 72, 77, 103, 127, 131, 132, 133, 140, 149, 169, 174, 177, 178, 179, 180, 181, 182, 198, 226, 227
Tiusanen 247*n21*
Tom 69, 235*n22*, 239*n3*
Törnqvist 251*n1*
Torrey 86, 241*n18*
A Touch of the Poet 16, 47, 54, 66, 67, 87, 88, 89, 96, 102, 132, 133, 143, 152, 157, 189, 192, 233*n15*, 234*n15*, 236*n40*, 241*n24*, 246*n3*, 246*n4*, 247*n21*, 248*n5*
Townsend 36, 237*n59*, 238*n6*
Trilling 242*n36*
TRUTH 2, 19, 61, 76, 82, 91, 99, 106, 107, 108, 112, 118, 119, 125, 127, 131, 140, 141, 142, 143, 144, 145, 150, 151, 153, 154, 156, 160, 162, 164, 165, 192, 198, 211, 216, 221, 225, 227, 229
Tuck 242*n33*, 242*n34*, 248*n4*, 252*n9*
Tyrone *see* James Tyrone (*LDJN*)

Ubu Roi 242*n30*
UNITY 14, 24, 33, 40, 68, 69, 94, 104, 110, 111, 136, 161, 168, 175, 185, 198, 201, 203, 204, 206, 207, 209, 210, 211, 214, 216, 217, 218, 220, 221, 222, 223, 224, 225, 227, 228, 229, 230

The Visit of Malatesta 241*n15*, 242*n2*

Wainscott 240*n5*
Warnings 36, 65, 87, 134, 173, 211, 235*n20*, 252*n10*
Wayne 244*n16*
The Web 1, 28, 87, 184, 251*n1*
Weinberger 19, 232*n2*, 244*n16*
Welded 101, 175, 176, 178, 244*n15*, 247*n21*, 248*n23*
Werther 125
Wetjoen 107
Where the Cross Is Made 10, 16, 35, 38, 43, 46, 48, 49, 51, 65, 69, 89, 126, 127, 203, 212, 232*n12*, 233*n3*, 234*n9*, 234*n12*, 236*n40*, 247*n17*, 255*n4*
Whitman 234*n13*
A Wife for a Life 54, 239*n2(ch7)*, 243*n9*, 244*n18*, 251*n1* 232*n5*
Wilkins 188, 251*n7*, 252*n7*, 254*n39*
Winther 239*n4(ch6)*, 239*n5*
Wolfe 62

Yank (*BEC*) 105, 170, 202, 203, 213, 244*n17*
Yank (*HA*) 22, 33, 85, 88, 92, 110, 114, 115, 116, 153, 173, 196, 197, 198, 200, 206, 207, 211, 215, 221, 239*n4(ch7)*, 245*n4*, 256*n13*

www.ingramcontent.com/pod-product-compliance
Lightning Source LLC
Chambersburg PA
CBHW051211300426
44116CB00006B/526